# ASSIGNMENTS IN EXPOSITION

# ASSIGNMENTS IN EXPOSITION

## LOUISE E. RORABACHER
*formerly of Purdue University*

## AND GEORGIA DUNBAR
*Hofstra University*

*SEVENTH EDITION*

1817

**HARPER & ROW, PUBLISHERS**, *New York*
*Cambridge, Philadelphia, San Francisco*
*London, Mexico City, São Paulo, Sydney*

*Sponsoring Editor:* Phillip Leininger
*Project Editor:* Brigitte Pelner
*Designer:* Frances Torbert Tilley
*Production Manager:* Marion A. Palen
*Photo Researcher:* Mira Schachne
*Compositor:* University Graphics

*Art Studio:* Danmark & Michaels

**Assignments in Exposition**

**Library of Congress Cataloging in Publication Data**

Rorabacher, Louise Elizabeth, 1906–
    Assignments in Exposition.

    Includes index.
    1. Exposition (Rhetoric)   I.   Dunbar, Georgia
Dolfield Sherwood, 1919–          II.   Title.
PE1429.R5  1982        808'.042        81–17128
ISBN 0–06–045576–4                   AACR2

# Contents

°Selections marked with an asterisk have marginal notes.

**PART THREE   *Aids in Reasoning*   161**

# Supplementary List of Examples

## SUBJECT MATTER AND APPROACH

*Family Influences and Conflicts:*  Unit 3-C and F;  Unit 4-C and D;
Unit 6-A;  Unit 9-E;  Unit 11-C. D, and H;  Unit 12-D, E, and F;
Unit 13-E;  Unit 14-A, C, and D;  Unit 15-G;  Unit 16-E;  Unit 17-D and E

*Facing Contemporary Problems:*  Unit 3-A and B;  Unit 4-C;
Unit 5-D;  Unit 6-A;  Unit 9-C, D, E, and F;  Unit 10-D and G;  Unit 11-
C and D;  Unit 12-B, C, D, E, and H;  Unit 13-G;  Unit 14-A, C, D, F,
and G;  Unit 16-A, B, C, D, E, and F

*Searching for Ideals:*  Unit 2-H;  Unit 3-A and C;  Unit 4-C, E, and G;
Unit 5-D;  Unit 6-A;  Unit 9-D, E, and F;  Unit 10-E;  Unit 11-B and C;
Unit 12-D and G;  Unit 13-C, E, and G;  Unit 14-A, C, D, E, F, and G;
Unit 15-G;  Unit 16-A, B, C, and G;  Unit 17-F

*Making Difficult Decisions:*  Unit 3-A, B, and F;  Unit 5-D;  Unit 9-E;
Unit 11-B, C, and D;  Unit 14-C, D, F, and G;  Unit 15-F and G;
Unit 16-A, B, C, and D

*Changing as We Grow Older:*  Unit 3-B and F;  Unit 4-C and D;
Unit 5-D;  Unit 9-C, E, and G;  Unit 11-D and E;  Unit 12-D, F, and G;
Unit 13-C, D, F, and G;  Unit 14-A, D, and G;  Unit 15-F and G;  Unit 16-
A and E;  Unit 17-D and H

*Examining Values and Behavior:*  Unit 2-G and H;  Unit 3-B, C, D,
and F;  Unit 4—all examples;  Unit 5-B and D;  Unit 6-A;  Unit 8-F;
Unit 9-B, D, E, F and G;  Unit 10-A, B, E, G, and H;  Unit 11-B, C, D,
and E; Unit 12-D, E, F, G, and H;  Unit 13-C, E, and G;  Unit 14-A, B, C,
F, and G;  Unit 15-F and G;  Unit 16-A, E and G;  Unit 17-F, H, and K

*Love, Affection, Admiration, and Pity:*  Unit 1-C;  Unit 2-B, C,
and H;  Unit 3-A and C;  Unit 4-C, D, E, and G;  Unit 5-C;  Unit 9-D;
Unit 11-B and E;  Unit 12-C, F, and G;  Unit 14-A;  Unit 16-A and F

***Special Places and Ways of Living:***   California surfing, Unit 1-A and
Unit 4-F;   Haiti, Unit 1-B;   Japan, Unit 2-G;   the Italian island of
Stromboli, Unit 4-D;   the North Woods, Unit 4-G;   Spain, Unit 5-A;
Yamacraw, South Carolina, Unit 2-F, Unit 8-F, and Unit 12-B;
Antarctica, Unit 9-A;   South Africa, Unit 10-D;   Peru, Unit 12-A;   the
Himalayas, Unit 13-F;   the American suburbs, Unit 11-D, Unit 12-D, Unit
14-F, G, and H, Unit 16-F

***Satire:***   Unit 17-I, J, and K;   also, in varying degrees in Unit 5-C, Unit 6-D,
Unit 8-D, Unit 9-C and G, Unit 10-E and H, Unit 11-H

---

## *PARAGRAPHING*

In some examples in the units, the organization of the paragraphs as
paragraphs or as parts of a logical sequence is especially evident because of
such devices as transitional words and repetitions of topic statements.

The following were composed as independent essays or form self-contained
subdivisions of a longer work:

1. Examples complete in one paragraph:   Unit 2-E;   Unit 13-C;
   Unit 15-B;   Unit 17-K
2. Examples composed of three or more paragraphs: Unit 2-F and H;
   Unit 3-A, C, and D;   Unit 4-B, C, and D;   Unit 6-A and D;   Unit 8-D;
   Unit 9-C, D, E and G;   Unit 10-B, E, G, and H;   Unit 11-B, D, and H;
   Unit 12-B, D, E, F, G, and I;   Unit 13-A, D, and G;   Unit 14-G;   Unit
   15-F and H;   Unit 16-B, C, D, F, and G

The following are clearly tied to the longer works from which they are
taken, but each has a definite beginning, main body, and ending:

Unit 4-E;   Unit 8-E;   Unit 14-H

Several of the examples were composed for newspaper publication, and as a
result many of the paragraphs in them are very short. If the writers of the
following examples had intended them for book publication, what changes
would they probably have made in paragraphing?

Unit 11-E;   Unit 13-E;   Unit 14-A;   Unit 16-E

# Acknowledgments

**UNIT 1**  **A.** "The Surfer's Day"—from William Murray, "Hanging Five," *Holiday*, September 1967. Permission to reprint granted by Travel Magazine, Floral Park, New York 11001.  **C.** "One-Man Show"—from Red Smith, "The Moving Finger Writes." © 1977 by The New York Times Company. Reprinted by permission.

**UNIT 2**  **B.** "The Great Blue"—from Lucian K. Truscott IV, "Two Fishermen," *Saturday Review*, November 25, 1972. Reprinted by permission of *Saturday Review-World*.  **C.** "More Power to You"—courtesy of *Time*. Copyright Time Inc., 1948.  **D.** "The Hellbender"—from the *Encyclopedia Americana*, 1969 edition. Reprinted by permission of the Americana Corporation, Publishers.  **E.** "The House"—from Anne Moody, *Coming of Age in Mississippi*, The Dial Press, Inc., New York, 1968. Copyright © 1968 by Anne Moody.  **F.** "Yamacraw"—from *The Water Is Wide* by Pat Conroy. Copyright © 1972 by Pat Conroy. Reprinted by permission of Houghton Mifflin Company.  **G.** "The Japanese Train"—from Paul Theroux, *The Great Railway Bazaar*. Copyright © 1975 by Paul Theroux. Reprinted by permission of Houghton Mifflin Company.

**UNIT 3**  **A.** "Yumbo"—by Andrew Ward. Copyright © 1978 by Andrew Ward. From the *Atlantic Monthly*, May 1977.  **B.** "A Loaf of Bread and the Stars"—from pp. 201–204 in *Black Boy* by Richard Wright. Copyright 1937, 1942, 1944, 1945 by Richard Wright. Reprinted by permission of Harper & Row, Publishers, Inc.  **D.** "The Logical Cab Driver"—from David Schoenbrun, *As France Goes*. Copyright © 1957 by David Schoenbrun. Reprinted by permission of Harper & Row, Publishers, Inc.  **E.** "On a Commuter Train"—from Willie Morris, *North Towards Home*. Copyright © 1967 by Willie Morris. Reprinted by permission of Houghton Mifflin Company.

**UNIT 4**  **A.** "The Derelict"—from Willie Morris, *North Towards Home*. Copyright © 1967 by Willie Morris. Reprinted by permission of Houghton

Mifflin Company. **C.** "Amid Bounty, Longing"—by Leo Hamalian. © 1976
by The New York Times Company. Reprinted by permission. **E.** "Benjamin
Banneker: Room to Dream and Dare"—from Lerone Bennett, Jr., *Before the
Mayflower: A History of the Negro in America 1619–1964* (revised edition).
Copyright © 1961, 1962, 1964 by Johnson Publishing Company, Inc. **F.**
"The Surfer"—from William Murray, "Hanging Five," *Holiday*, September
1967. Permission to reprint granted by Travel Magazine, Inc., Floral Park,
New York 11001. **G.** "The North Woods Guide"—from J. Donald Adams,
"Farewell to the North Woods Guide." Copyright © 1957 by the *Atlantic
Monthly*. Reprinted by permission of Harold Matson Co., Inc. Untitled
paragraph—from p. 53, *We Took to the Woods* by Louise Dickinson Rich (J.
B. Lippincott Company). Copyright 1942 by Louise Dickinson Rich.
Reprinted by permission of Harper & Row, Publishers, Inc.

**UNIT 5** Dictionary entry for *pleasure*. With permission. From *Webster's
New World Dictionary*, Second College Edition. Copyright © 1980 by Simon
& Schuster, Inc. **A.** "The Flight of Refugees"—from Ernest Hemingway,
*By-Line: Ernest Hemingway*, edited by William White. Copyright 1937,
1938 New York Times and North American Newspaper Alliance Inc.;
copyright renewed. Reprinted by permission of Charles Scribner's Sons. **B.**
"On Societies as Organisms"—from "On Societies as Organisms" in *The Lives
of a Cell* by Lewis Thomas. Copyright © 1971 by Massachusetts Medical
Society. Originally appeared in *The New England Journal of Medicine*.
Reprinted by permission of Viking Penguin Inc. **C.** "Farewell, My
Lovely"—from "Farewell, My Lovely," by Lee Strout White reprinted by
permission; © 1936, 1964 The New Yorker Magazine, Inc. (The essay was the
collaborative effort of Richard Lee Strout and E. B. White.) **D.**
"Challenge"—from Jesse Jackson, "Make a Decision," an address to the
Eighth Annual Convention of Operation PUSH, July 12, 1979, Cleveland,
Ohio. Reprinted by permission. **E.** "A Metaphor Used Twice"—from Jacob
Bronowski, *Science and Human Values*. Copyright J. Bronowski, 1956, 1965.
Reprinted by permission of Julian Messner, a Simon & Schuster division of
Gulf & Western Corporation.

**UNIT 6** **A.** "The Fifth Freedom"—by Seymour St. John," in *Saturday
Review*, October 10, 1955. Reprinted by permission of *Saturday Review-
World*. **D.** "Clutter"—from William Zinsser, *On Writing Well*, ©
copyright 1980 by William Zinsser. Reprinted by permission of the author.

**UNIT 8** **B.** "Baking Beans"—from pp. 113–114 in *We Took to the Woods*
by Louise Dickinson Rich (J. B. Lippincott Company). Copyright 1942 by
Louise Dickinson Rich. Reprinted by permission of Harper & Row,
Publishers, Inc. **E.** "How Dictionaries Are Made"—from *Language in
Thought and Action*, Fourth Edition by S. I. Hayakawa, copyright © 1978
by Harcourt Brace Jovanovich, Inc. Reprinted by permission of the

publisher. **F.** "Death and Burial on Yamacraw"—from *The Water Is Wide* by Pat Conroy. Copyright © 1972 by Pat Conroy. Reprinted by permission of Houghton Mifflin Company.

*UNIT 9* **B.** "Tolstoy's Contradictions"—from Henri Troyat, in the *Literary Guild Magazine*, January 1968. **D.** "No More Moon-June: Love's Out"—by Richard Stengel, © 1980 by The New York Times Company. Reprinted by permission. **F.** "New and Old Stereotypes"—from Addison Gayle, Jr. *The Way of the New World: The Black Novel in America*. Originally published by Anchor Press. Copyright © 1975 by Addison Gayle, Jr. **G.** "The Boy Who Came to Supper"—Russell Baker, © 1980 by The New York Times Company. Reprinted by permission.

*UNIT 10* **A.** "Book Owners"—from Mortimer J. Adler, "How to Mark a Book," first published in *Saturday Review*, July 6, 1940. Reprinted by permission of *Saturday Review-World*. **C.** "Mental Depression: The Recurring Nightmare"—by Jane Brody, © 1977 The New York Times Company. Reprinted by permission. **D.** "The South Africans"—Selection is reprinted from *The Separated People, A Look at Contemporary South Africa*, by E. J. Kahn, Jr., by permission of W. W. Norton & Company, Inc. Copyright © 1968, 1966 by E. J. Kahn, Jr. **F.** "Four Kinds of Talking"— from Desmond Morris, *The Naked Ape*, Copyright © 1967 by Desmond Morris. Used with permission of McGraw-Hill Book Company. **G.** "American Magazines and American Culture"—from Peter McGrath, "A Balkanized Business," *New Society*, 31st July 1980, Copyright © New Society, London. Reprinted by permission. **H.** "Business Status—How Do You Rate"—by Enid Nemy, "New Yorkers, etc." © 1980 by The New York Times Company. Reprinted by permission.

*UNIT 11* **A.** "The Structure of a Comet"—from C. C. Wylie, *Astronomy, Maps, and Weather*, Harper & Row, Publishers, Inc. 1942. **B.** "What Winning and Losing Really Are"—from Michael Novak, *The Joy of Sports; End Zones, Bases, Baskets, Balls, and the Consecration of the American Spirit*, © 1976 by Michael Novak, Basic Books, Inc., Publishers, New York. **C.** "Motherhood in Bondage," Adrienne Rich, © 1976 by The New York Times Company. Reprinted by permission. **E.** "Why They Mourned for Elvis Presley"—by Molly Ivins, © 1977 by The New York Times Company. Reprinted by permission. **F.** "Splitting the Word"—from Anthony Burgess, *Language Made Plain*, The English Universities Press. 1964. Copyright © by Anthony Burgess. **G.** "Three Languages in a Novel"—from Addison Gayle, Jr., *The Way of the New World: The Black Novel in America*. Originally published by Anchor Press. Copyright © 1975 by Addison Gayle, Jr. **H.** "The Bad and Worse Sides of Thanksgiving"— from "Notes and Comments." Reprinted by permission; © 1978. The New Yorker Magazine, Inc.

**UNIT 12   A.** "Living on the Altiplano"—from Georgie Anne Geyer, "Peru's Inca Renaissance," in "Reports: Washington, Hong Kong, Peru," *The Atlantic Monthly,* November 1967. Copyright © 1967 by the Atlantic Monthly Company, Boston, Mass. Reprinted with permission.   **B.** "Death of an Island"—from *The Water Is Wide* by Pat Conroy. Copyright © 1972 by Pat Conroy. Reprinted by permission of Houghton Mifflin Company.   **C.** "The Decisive Arrest"—from pp. 43–44 in *Stride Toward Freedom* by Martin Luther King, Jr. Copyright © 1958 by Martin Luther King, Jr. Reprinted by permission of Harper & Row, Publishers, Inc.   **F.** "On Being a Twin"—from Jeremy Seabrook, "On Being a Twin," *New Society,* 30 June 1977.   **G.** "New-Born Mother"—by Marina Warner, *The Observer,* London, 24 July 1977. Reprinted by permission of A. D. Peters & Co., Ltd.   **H.** "The Role of Race"—from Kenneth B. Clark, "The Role of Race," © 1980 The New York Times Company. Reprinted by permission.   **I.** "The Method of Scientific Investigation"—from Thomas H. Huxley, *On the Origin of Species,* D. Appleton, 1880.

**UNIT 13   A.** "Three Incidents"—from "Talk of the Town." Reprinted by permission; © 1980. The New Yorker Magazine, Inc.   **B.** "The Language of Uncertainty"—from John Cohen, "Subjective Probability," Copyright © 1957 by Scientific American, Inc. All rights reserved.   **E.** "Occasions of Hope"— from Phyllis Theroux, "Hers," © 1977 by The New York Times Company. Reprinted by permission.   **F.** "Epitaph to the Elusive Abominable Snowman"—by Sir Edmund Hillary for *Life.* Copyright © 1961 Time Inc.   **G.** "Your Generation, My Generation"—from Jonathan Steinberg, "Your Generation, My Generation," *New Society,* 10 July 1980. Copyright © New Society, London. Reprinted by permission.

**UNIT 14   A.** "An Open Letter to Black Parents: Send Your Children to the Libraries"—by Arthur Ashe, © 1977 by The New York Times Company. Reprinted by permission.   **B.** "Alexander the Great and Alcoholism"—from John Noble Wilford, "Alcoholism Defeated Alexander the Great," © 1980 by The New York Times Company. Reprinted by permission.   **C.** "Letter from Home"—by William Zinsser, © 1977 by The New York Times Company. Reprinted by permission.   **D.** "After Graduation, What Next?"—from Fred Hiatt, "Valediction to Complacency," first published in the *Boston Globe,* 1977.   **E.** "Education by Books"—by Mark Van Doren, the *Nation,* 6 December 1933.   **F.** "The Hell of Affluence"—by George Will. Copyright 1977 by Newsweek, Inc. All rights reserved. Reprinted by permission.   **H.** "The Light from an Ape's Jaw"—Excerpt from *African Genesis* by Robert Ardrey. Copyright © 1961 by Literat S. A. Reprinted by permission of Atheneum Publishers.

**UNIT 15   A.** "Cyclones"—by Walter Sullivan, © 1977 by The New York Times Company. Reprinted by permission.   **B.** "Parentage and

Parenthood"—from Ashley Montagu, *The American Way of Life*, G. P. Putnam's Sons, © 1952, 1962, 1967 by Ashley Montagu.  **C.** "The Musician's Filibuster"—by Karen Thompson, *The Green Caldron*, the University of Illinois.  **D.** "Lagniappe"—from Mark Twain, *Life on the Mississippi*, Harper Brothers, 1875.  **H.** "The Meaning of Negro"—Editorial, *Negro History Bulletin*, February 1971. Reprinted by permission of the Association for the Study of Afro-American Life and History, Inc.

**UNIT 16**  **A.** "America, the Revolutionary"—by the Honorable Andrew J. Young. Commencement address delivered at Michigan State University, June 1977. First published in *Sepia*, September 1977. Reprinted by permission.  **B.** "Defending Free Speech for Those We Despise Most"—Aryeh Neier, *Civil Liberties*, November 1977. Reprinted by permission.  **C.** "ACLU's Grievous Mistake"—by Abba P. Lerner, letter to the editor, 20 March 1978. © 1978 by The New York Times Company. Reprinted by permission of The New York Times Company and the author.  **D.** "This Land Is Whose Land"—by Meg Greenfield. Copyright 1977 by Newsweek Inc. All rights reserved. Reprinted by permission.  **E.** "Where Is My Child?"—by Dorothy Collier. *The Sunday Times*, London, 13 November 1977.  **G.** "Killing for Sport"—from Joseph Wood Krutch, "If You Don't Mind My Saying So." Reprinted from *The American Scholar*, Vol. 25, No. 3, Summer 1956. Copyright © 1956 by the United Chapters of Phi Beta Kappa. By permission of the publishers.

**UNIT 17**  **A.** "Misadventures in Verona"—from Brendan Gill, "Misadventures in Verona." Reprinted by permission; © 1977 The New Yorker Magazine, Inc.  **B.** "Clues to Meaning"—from John E. Hankins, "Introduction" to William Shakespeare, *Romeo and Juliet*, edited by John E. Hankins, in "The Pelican Shakespeare," General Editor: Alfred Harbage (rev. ed.; New York: Penguin Books, 1970), pp. 20–22. Copyright © Penguin Books, Inc., 1960, 1970. Reprinted by permission of Penguin Books.  **C.** "Puns and Other Wordplay in *Romeo and Juliet*"—from M. M. Mahood, *Shakespeare's Wordplay*. Methuen & Co., Ltd., 1957. Reprinted by permission of the publishers.  **F.** "The Tragic Sense of Love"—Selection is reprinted from *Love and Will* by Rollo May, with permission of W. W. Norton & Company, Inc. Copyright © 1969 by W. W. Norton & Company, Inc.  **G.** "The Holes in Black Holes"—from Martin Gardner, "The Holes in Black Holes." Reprinted with permission from *The New York Review of Books*. Copyright © 1977 Nyrev, Inc.  **H.** "David Bowie Looks Back in Horror"—from Tom Carson, "David Bowie Looks Back in Horror," *The Village Voice*, 8–14 October 1980. Reprinted by permission.  **J.** "How to Write like a Social Scientist"—from Samuel T. Williamson, "How to Write like a Social Scientist," *Saturday Review*, 4 October 1947. Reprinted by permission of Saturday Review-World.  **K.** "Virtuous Sin"—Editorial, © 1977 by The New York Times Company. Reprinted by permission.

# To the Instructor

How best to help students develop writing skills has always been the concern of writing teachers. Now it has become a much wider concern, with new methods and test results often appearing as front-page news.

Central to the problem is the fact that a short paragraph or even a single sentence of effective exposition may be the product of using many methods, such as logical analysis, comparison, criticism, description, and narration, more or less simultaneously. Compounding the problem is another fact—that most students entering college today have had little practice in writing. At one extreme, they may have written only simple book reports and short-answer quizzes, and at the other, free-form expressions of emotion.

If writers must have skills in many methods to compose effective sentences and paragraphs and if students have only a few of these skills, it is no wonder that the bewildered students often sigh, "But what do you *want?*" If the instructor answers, "Clear, effective exposition," they grow even more bewildered.

Where and how should a course in expository writing begin so that students can quickly grasp the principles of effective exposition and develop their skills with a clear knowledge of what they are doing? This edition of *Assignments in Exposition*, like the previous ones, primarily emphasizes those overall structures and patterns of organization most often used by experienced writers to present information and opinions. It is intended, as were the previous editions, for use in composition courses required of average college students—courses designed to develop not necessarily professional writers but men and women who can write. These patterns and structures are essential to enable us to think clearly, to communicate our thoughts to others, and to understand their thoughts, because they indicate the relationships and relative significance of all thoughts. This book does not, however, insist on inflexible formulas for writing. Instead, it shows how patterns can reveal and clarify content and how they can be varied and adjusted to meet particular needs. Structure, used as a support, becomes not a straightjacket but a liberation.

The patterns of organization most easily recognized and understood are spatial and chronological. Part One begins with an introductory discussion at some length of fundamental principles of writing, with many illustrations, and goes on to units on description, narration, and characterization, with detailed analyses emphasizing the various patterns appropriate for each. These types of writing, besides having easily recognized patterns, have several other important advantages. In them, students can draw on their biggest natural resource—their own experiences. Moreover, as is shown in the discussions in each unit, they give the students the greatest opportunity to use the many enriching devices of writing, such as sensory detail, and to increase their awareness of connotative as well as denotative distinctions in word meanings. A new unit on words concludes Part One.

The same principles underlie the rest of the book, with emphasis on basic patterns of perceiving, understanding, and evaluating information and opinions and of communicating information and opinions to others. Each unit consists of two parts:

1. Discussion of pattern or type of writing
   a. definition of the pattern or type and of its variations
   b. occasions for which it is appropriate or required
   c. concise directions on how to use and how not to use it
2. Illustrative material with questions and assignments
   a. several selections on a wide variety of subjects, for the most part fairly short and straightforward, but of varying length and difficulty, to show how the type or pattern has been used by students as well as by professional writers
   b. study questions and exercises emphasizing the type or pattern (rather than the content) of each selection
   c. suggested subjects for writing assignments using the type or pattern

The advice in this book is given in full awareness of how the various skills involved in effective writing overlap and intertwine almost inextricably, but by isolating each of the principal types or patterns, the various units show the students the essential elements involved. Moreover, although each unit concentrates on one particular kind of writing or thinking, it also emphasizes the interdependence of that kind and others, frequently referring the reader to examples elsewhere in the book where the particular type or pattern appears in combination with others.

While the sequence of assignments is designed to show the relation of each pattern to preceding ones, it is not intended to be unchangeable. For example, although the unit on defining terms (Unit 15) uses all the patterns of organization and thought discussed in the preceding fourteen units, a class could begin with this unit for an overview of the patterns and then proceed to the other units for a more detailed examination. The discussion of outlining in Unit 6 could be studied with that of organization in Unit 1, with the second essay in Unit 6 saved for use after Unit 5. Similarly, the discussion of summary writing in Unit 7 could be studied in relation to the basic principles of organization presented in Unit 1.

As indicated before, the cross-referencing throughout the book suggests the use of many reading selections as examples of more than one type or pattern of writing. In addition, several writers are represented by more than one selection so that students may observe how writers use a variety of types and patterns while maintaining a recognizable stylistic consistency: William Murray in Unit 1-A and Unit 4-F; Pat Conroy in Unit 2-F, Unit 8-F, and Unit 12-B; Louise Dickinson Rich in a question following Unit 4-G and in Unit 8-A; Willie Morris in Unit 3-E and Unit 4-A; Addison Gayle, Jr., in Unit 9-F and Unit 11-G; and William Zinsser in Unit 6-D and Unit 14-C.

This edition, like the previous one, particularly emphasizes organization. The changes, described in the paragraphs that follow, are all intended to clarify and strengthen the original purpose and plan of the book.

The sections titled in former editions "To the Student" and "Introduction: The Preliminaries" are now Unit 1, "The Fundamentals of Writing," to make clear their importance to the main body of the book. Also, this unit has been considerably developed, with added practical advice on the composing process. To stimulate discussion and suggest topics for writing, several photographs are also included here.

A new unit, "Words" (Unit 5), ends Part One. Although, of course, students must consider their word choice whenever they write, a detailed discussion will probably be more fruitful after they have experimented with assignments in the first four units. In all subsequent units, with every example for which it would be appropriate, there is a question on word use. "Words" includes the discussion of diction and figures of speech formerly in the unit on description. Instead of forming a separate unit, the uses of analogy are now discussed as a subdivision of "Comparison" (Unit 9).

Satire now appears as a subdivision of "Critical Writing" (Unit 17), with three examples concluding the unit. A satiric approach adds a light touch to several other examples. See the list on page xii.

The unit on the research paper again encourages students to work on topics of genuine research that are within their scope, instead of merely collating quotations and paraphrases. The unit again gives detailed instruction in the MLA system of documentation and now also gives information on the APA system, which is increasingly popular.

Twenty-one new examples of writing appear, and ninety from the 6th edition are retained. In several units the sequence has been changed to place the shorter and less complex examples at or near the beginning, and Krutch's "Killing for Sport" now ends "Argument and Persuasion" (Unit 16).

Also new to this edition are headnotes for most of the examples, identifying the authors and giving some publication data and the context of the excerpts to aid in discussion. A supplementary table of contents lists many of the examples according to subject matter so that students may readily compare and contrast approaches to particular subjects. Another supplementary list groups some examples according to overall structure.

Dr. Rorabacher ended her preface to the 5th edition by thanking her former students at the University of Illinois, Purdue University, and Western Carolina

University. She also thanked *The Green Caldron*, a magazine of freshman writing at Illinois, Professor Janet McNary of South Carolina State College at Orangeburg, Dr. Mildred Martin of Bucknell University, Mrs. John Karling of West Lafayette, Indiana, and Miss Carol Lawrence of Cullowhee, North Carolina. As the reviser of the 6th edition and now of the 7th, both direct descendants of the 5th, I too thank all those named, since I have been their beneficiary.

In addition, I thank all my own students at Hofstra University, Borough of Manhattan Community College (CUNY), and the Hofstra-District 65 Institute of Labor Studies; the many colleagues and friends at Hofstra and Adelphi universities who gave invaluable help in finding appropriate student papers, particularly Professors Donald Wolf, Gloria Beckerman, Robert Sargent, Hyman Enzer, Robert Keane, Ruth Smith, David Moriarity, and Michael Steinman; and last but most important, Dr. Rorabacher herself, who so generously gave me a free hand and a fine book—any flaws in this edition are mine, but the virtues are hers.

G. D.

# PART ONE

# Aids to Exposition

This book concentrates on practical writing, that useful kind of expression most often required of us: informative—or expository—writing.

Whatever your college specialization or later career, you will often be expected to present information on facts and opinions in writing. This book is designed to help you do so. Its purpose is not to produce the professional writers of the future, such as the poets and journalists, but to help future doctors and lawyers, engineers and teachers, farmers and business people of all types to present facts and opinions clearly, efficiently, and effectively in writing.

The kinds of writing that are ordinarily required, in or out of college—such as essay examinations, summaries, explanations of facts, or critical analyses of theories—may vary considerably. The principles underlying them, however, are similar. Once learned, they can guide you in writing all kinds of exposition. These principles are the central concern of this book.

# The Fundamentals of Writing

Three things are necessary for effective writing of all kinds: mechanical correctness (your grammar, spelling, punctuation, and general form), content (what you have to say), and organization (how you present your content). The reasons that these are necessary are discussed in some detail in this unit, and there are many suggestions throughout the book on the mechanics of special kinds of writing and on how to recognize and develop your content. But the main emphasis of this book is on organization because, of the three necessities, organization is the most important.

You can have fascinating material and present it in perfectly grammatical sentences, but if your remarks are disorganized and seem unrelated to each other, your readers will be confused and miss your point. This book presents the patterns of thought commonly used in expository prose and shows how you can adapt these patterns to strengthen what you want to say.

The two papers that follow were written as homework after the first class meeting of the fall term. At that meeting, the students interviewed each other in groups of four or five. Each then wrote a paper about one of the students in his or her group and at the next class meeting read it aloud to introduce that student to the rest of the class.

These papers have the same purpose and use the same kind of material: they present facts on their subjects' choice of major, high school activities, summer holidays, and so on. Moreover, both subjects, Michael and Jane, seem to have supplied a variety of information. The errors in spelling, grammar, and punctuation have all been corrected. Nevertheless, the paper by student Y is much more effective than that by student X. The difference is primarily in organization.

## MY INTERVIEW WITH MICHAEL
### Student X

I would like to introduce Michael. I really enjoyed interviewing him. He is a great guy. He played a lot of basketball in high school and hopes to go out for the team, and he likes dramatics a lot, too. He played the lead in *Death of a*

*Salesman* in his senior year in high school. We read that play in my senior
English class, and it's very sad. Michael comes from Texas and agrees with me ₅
that living in the dorms is great. Last summer he and a friend backpacked in
Colorado. The scenery in the Rockies must be great. I would like to go there
sometime, especially for the skiing. Right now, Michael thinks he will probably
major in accounting because that field offers the best chances for a career these
days, but maybe he will change his mind when he has had more time to look ₁₀
over the possibilities.

He wants to get a job on campus because that would be convenient. He hopes
to save up enough to get a car. A car is practically a necessity when you're living
in the dorms here. At home I can borrow my mother's car a lot, but here I have
to hitch rides with friends, and because I'm only a freshman I don't know a lot ₁₅
of people here yet. Michael is taking the same psych course I am. It's a great
course to take because knowing something about people is always helpful, whatever you do in later life. Michael's family lives in Texas, and Michael grew up
there, but he was born in New Jersey. He has two sisters and a brother.

If he can't get a job on campus, Michael will try to get one at McDonald's ₂₀
because it's nearby. He worked at a McDonald's in Texas for a month last summer. He knows a lot about music and plays a guitar. He also knows a lot about
rocks. While he was in Colorado he collected a lot of different ones. I said I
thought he might major in geology.

Michael's brother graduated from a college in California last year and is now ₂₅
working in Los Angeles. If Michael ever visits him he should go to see Disney-
land. It's a great place for grown-ups as well as children. He likes to read science
fiction and histories and biographies about the Civil War. At the end of the
interview I said I would like to learn the basic fingering for the guitar, and
maybe I'll ask Michael to teach me. ₃₀

JANE
*Student Y*

I would like to introduce Jane, a commuting student, whose biggest interest
is science. In her senior year in high school she organized the Chemistry Club
and was elected president. She also set up a small lab of her own in a corner of
her family's garage. She plans to major in chemistry and become a research
scientist, and so she foresees many years of study ahead of her. ₅

Her other interests include sports, popular music, and travel. In high school
she played on the girls' basketball team, but she does not think that she will
have time to go out for the team here. She has a large collection of albums,
particularly of British rock groups. Last summer she combined her interests in
music and travel and went to England for two weeks where she was able to see ₁₀
some of her favorite groups perform.

Jane, like most students these days, needs money for college expenses, and
she is looking for a part-time job. She has had some experience already, having

worked as a counselor at a day camp last summer and in the post office during the Christmas rush last winter. 15

Jane lives with her family about ten miles from the campus, and she grew up in this part of the state. She has an older sister and a younger brother. Her sister shares Jane's interest in science and is now in medical school, but her twelve-year-old brother, David, has so far shown no interest in anything but baseball and his stamp collection. Jane hopes to convert him before too long. With a 20 sister who is such a dedicated scientist, young David will probably soon be trading his stamp collection for a microscope.

*Organization.* X seems to have had no organization in mind and hops from one topic to another and back again, probably in the way the conversation hopped around. In the first third we are told about Michael's extracurricular activities in high school, his family home, his summer vacation trip, and then his probable choice of major, with no suggestion that these are in any way related to each other. This chaotic jumble continues throughout the paper, and the ending is the author's purely personal wish to learn to play the guitar. Properly organized, with important points emphasized and less important ones subordinated in a logical order, the information on Michael could have made an interesting picture of someone with a variety of experiences and activities. The poor organization has spoiled it.

The paper by Y is only two-thirds as long but says much more because the information is grouped logically. Y begins with Jane's main interest in college, the one that will take the greatest part of her time and effort, and goes on to her other interests, then to her need to find a job, and finally to her family background. At the end of the paper, Y makes information on Jane's brother and sister seem relevant by connecting it to Jane's interest in science. The ending therefore helps to unify the paper by reminding readers of the point established at the beginning.

*Content.* X has plenty of information on Michael but seems almost as much interested in telling about X. For this assignment, to introduce Michael to the class, much of X's paper is irrelevant. Another weakness that suggests carelessness is X's frequent use of vague words, such as "a lot" and "great," which are almost meaningless here. Y, on the other hand, concentrates entirely on Jane, mentioning Jane's brother and sister only in order to relate them to Jane's interest in science.

*Paragraphing.* Paragraph divisions should help the reader to see how the content is organized. Although at first glance X's paper seems to have conventional paragraphs, a closer look shows that the paragraph divisions have no connection with the content. Apparently, X started a new paragraph when enough paper had been covered with writing to *look* like a paragraph. Each of Y's paragraphs, however, is introduced by a remark clearly indicating its general topic, and the rest of the paragraph develops that topic.

To sum up, X and Y had exactly the same assignment and the same kinds of information for their material. By selecting and organizing the information and sticking to the subject, Y produced a satisfactory paper that fulfilled the assignment, but X did not.

With even the most specific assignment, you have many choices for words and for the structures of your sentences and paragraphs. An overall plan will guide you to make the best choices. Moreover, as you jot down notes for a plan with your material at hand, the sight of your notes will suggest new insights into the material. You will see new connections and interpretations that may strengthen and enrich your paper.

Whenever you write, be sure to have something to say, but do not start until you have a plan for saying it.

The other units in this book concentrate on the particular kinds of expository writing that you are most likely to use and on the common, logical patterns—the "brain paths"—that our minds must follow to make what we write understandable. The rest of this unit concentrates on general suggestions for composing a paper—organizing the material, writing and revising rough drafts, and arriving at a final version—suggestions that should help you with all types of writing.

Most of your writing, in college and out, will be to fulfill assignments of some kind. In college you will be limited at least by the subject of the course, probably also by a list of specific topics given to you by your instructor. After college, the field in which you work, your leisure interests, and your community activities will impose similar limitations when you write a report or formulate a suggestion. To do much of that writing, you will have to spend time in gathering facts and opinions on your topic. In this book, however, most of the assignments ask you to draw on information you already have so that you can devote your time and effort to the writing itself.

## Beginning by Not Writing

When you receive a writing assignment, what do you do next? What are the best procedures to follow? For the sake of our discussion, let us imagine that you are a full-time freshman and must write an essay of about 500 words on a typical day in your life as a college student. Let us also imagine that your instructor plans to give copies of the essays written by your class to the guidance counselors in several high schools. Juniors and seniors in those high schools will read them to get up-to-date, firsthand information on what to expect in college.

Whatever the success of your past procedures when you faced an assignment, the best way to begin to write is by *not* writing. First, think of the assignment and the exact nature of the constraints that are part of it—the limitations placed on you not only by the deadline and required length but, more important, by the subject, purpose, and readers. Make sure that you understand precisely what and who these are; if you have any doubts, ask your instructor for clarification.

## Gathering and Grouping Your Material

For many assignments, gathering material may require research in the library, laboratory experiments, interviews, or a survey. For our imaginary assignment, your memories are your material, but whatever the sources, the general methods for using your material in writing are the same. For this assignment, think over what your experience at college has been like so far, and, at the same time, jot down notes. At this stage, do not be selective or critical. Jot down everything that comes to mind—what seems trivial now may seem significant later.

Give yourself ample opportunity for two very different kinds of thinking—logical analysis and free-wheeling association. Because our minds are wonderfully complex, we can switch back and forth between the two many times in a few moments, with each kind contributing to the other. In the first, we concentrate on the subject and systematically examine all its parts and purposes. In the second, we let our minds range freely over and around the subject, even off it, and ideas seem to pop up without our conscious search. Never be in such a hurry that you limit yourself to the logic of the first kind of thinking and do not take advantage of the imaginative insights of the second.

With both kinds of thinking, be sure to take short notes on scratch paper—the shorter the better, perhaps only a word or two for each or a symbol of some kind, just enough to serve as a reminder later. The notes will free you of the burden of remembering, and, even more important, seeing several together may suggest new associations that in turn may suggest new thoughts and interpretations. This is why your notes should be short enough for you to read several at a glance. Sight can give us insight.

If your mind goes blank, as it will sometimes, try to see your subject from your reader's point of view. Jog your imagination with questions:

> What do your readers probably already know about your subject?
> What do they probably not know about it?
> What opinions may they now have about it?
> What do you think will be most valuable or interesting in it for them and why?

Don't stop when you think you have enough material for a paper of the assigned length. The more material you have to choose from, the more you can make your paper a selection of the very best. Continue until you have exhausted the possibilities. Then look over your jottings and consider the same questions again, but this time keep your specific purpose in mind. In our imagined case, your purpose is to inform your readers. Make a fresh list of everything in your notes that could possibly be of any help in accomplishing your purpose, particularly your answers to the fourth question. Then consider these questions:

> What is the exact nature of each item?
> To which items, if any, is each related and how?
> Under what headings can the items be grouped? (For this imagined assignment, some headings might indicate the nature of your activities, such as "recreation"

and "classes"; others might indicate the time of day, the location, the number of people involved, and so on.)

What combinations of headings can you think of, such as "morning classes" or "dorm room late night snacks"?

What subdivisions and sub-subdivisions can you think of? (For example, under "morning classes" you might list their size, academic level, location, and type, such as discussion, laboratory or lecture.)

As you make notes on all these groupings, additional memories and ideas may occur to you. Be sure to jot these down, too, and sort them under headings.

## Choosing a Thesis

When you have thought of all the groupings that you can, begin to narrow your subject by considering these questions in relation to your purpose (in this case, to inform your readers):

What general parts of your material do you want your readers to notice most? what specific parts?

What opinions do you want them to form?

What interests you most in your material? (You are more likely to be able to interest your readers in something that you find interesting.)

Whatever you most want your readers to see in your material will be your main point. (For example, for this imaginary assignment, you might want them to see that college level work is more difficult than work in high school or that your program is more demanding than is suggested by the number of hours you spend in classes.) Your main point will determine what material you use in the paper and how you organize it. When you have chosen a main point, make it definite in your own mind by expressing it in as few words as you can, preferably in a single sentence. This will be the rough draft of the **thesis statement** for your paper.

A thesis is a proposition, the main point that a writer not only presents and explains but defends throughout a particular piece of writing. In the thesis statement the writer is, in effect, saying "I believe that this is true and hope to make my readers agree or at least give it serious consideration."

In most expository writing you will find the thesis directly stated, but sometimes it is only implied. We will look at examples of both methods in the essays in this book. Whichever method you finally choose, you should now compose a rough draft of your thesis. With both a definite thesis and your readers in mind, you will be able to decide fairly easily what information to include and how to organize it. But do not close your mind to change. At every stage, test the validity of your thesis in relation to the particular part of the material you are then working on. You may decide that you should modify it or even reject it entirely and start again.

**Note:** With many writing assignments, particularly essay examinations, you will be given a thesis and expected to find material to support it, but the procedures for gathering and sorting the material are the same, and so are those for organizing it.

## *Organizing the Main Body: Basic Considerations*

With your readers and thesis in mind, consider three more questions:

What general background information will your readers need to understand your thesis?

What specific information will they need to understand it?

What information, general or specific, will they need to become convinced that your thesis is valid or that, at least, it deserves serious consideration?

For our imaginary assignment, for example, you would need to write little or nothing about a typical day in high school because your readers would know all about that, but you would have to explain such things as the long lists of difficult readings that some of your instructors have already given you and the frequency and nature of your writing assignments. Mark in your notes all the material that directly explains or supports your thesis. If you find many items, make a fresh list so that you can see them more easily. These will form the main body of your paper.

When you believe that you have found every usable item, ask yourself what will be the best way of arranging them to make your thesis clear, interesting, and convincing for your readers. On fresh scratch paper, try out as many arrangements as you can imagine. If you see any items that duplicate others, or seem weak, or are not very relevant, cut them out. Such changes are all part of the two kinds of thinking required for writing. Nothing is final until you hand in your paper.

If at this stage you fear that you will not have enough material for a 500-word paper, or whatever length is required for the assignment, examine your earliest notes in close detail, rethink them from every angle, and discuss your thesis with friends, asking for their suggestions. You may think of material you overlooked before or have new insights into what you had already gathered. Whatever you find, add it to your notes. Achieve the required length by going more deeply into material that contributes to your thesis, not merely by adding words.

The simplest pattern of organization is chronological, and you probably will try it first. Your list of points to cover for this imaginary assignment might then look like this:

1. Getting up
2. Washing and dressing
3. Eating breakfast
4. Going to English class
5. Going to economics class
6. Eating lunch
7. Working in chemistry lab
8. Having coffee with friends
9. Working at a part-time job
10. Eating dinner
11. Studying

12. Telephoning a friend
13. Watching TV
14. Undressing and washing
15. Going to bed

To go ahead with the writing of your paper from such a scattering of notes will be unwise, however, even if you decide to keep to the order of time in your presentation. You—and consequently your readers—could be confused by the number of small details, which seem rather aimless when merely set down one after another. Your next step, then, is to group them into larger units of related items that will be more manageable. Your plan may now look like this:

I. Early morning activities
   A. Getting up
   B. Washing and dressing
   C. Eating breakfast
II. Late morning activities
   A. Going to English class
   B. Going to economics class
   C. Eating lunch
III. Afternoon activities
   A. Working in chemistry lab
   B. Having coffee with friends
   C. Working at a part-time job
IV. Evening activities
   A. Eating dinner
   B. Studying
   C. Telephoning a friend
   D. Watching TV
   E. Undressing and washing
   F. Going to bed

You may well ask what has been accomplished by this grouping, since the items and their order have been left unchanged. The answer is that your approach to your material will be changed, for instead of handling fifteen small items, you are now planning in terms of four larger sections made up of varying numbers of subpoints. The effect on your sense of proportion resulting from this new perspective will be as useful to the reader who must follow your train of thought as to you, the writer who must construct it.

## Organizing the Main Body: Other Possibilities

So much for the chronological order, which involves simply a grouping of items in a time relationship. But perhaps, looking again at the same fifteen items, you feel that the time in which these events take place is relatively unimportant—that there is a logical order of another sort which may provide a more satisfactory pattern for your paper. Items such as dressing and eating, which are the mere routine of daily existence anywhere, may well be handled briefly together or even omitted; others, your classes and study periods, are more vital matters peculiar to academic life; still others constitute the social contacts, near and far, which enliven the college routine. If you follow this line of thought, your main headings might be:

I. Routine activities
II. Academic activities
III. Recreation

(You can supply the appropriate subpoints under each from the original list.)

*Arranging main headings.* Now, with the chronological order removed, a second problem appears—how to arrange these main headings. Here, you may choose among many principles of order, depending on your subject and purpose:

1. from the known to the unknown
2. from the simple to the complex
3. from the specific to the general (see pages 202–03)
4. from the general to the specific (see pages 220–24)
5. from the less important to the more important

On the simple subject of how busy your day is, matters of routine might reasonably be handled first, briefly, to get them out of your way. Which of the two remaining topics to place next will depend on what you want to emphasize. If education is more important, stress the fact by writing last and longest about your classes and study periods; if your social contacts with others are more significant to you, discuss these last. However difficult your subject and however many main points you may have, always arrange them in an *ascending* order of difficulty or importance—build up to the most important. Your readers will expect that order and will feel let down if you anticlimactically fire your smaller guns after your larger ones.

*Arranging subpoints.* Good preliminary organization involves not only determining the main points and their logical arrangement but also discriminating carefully among them. What is really of first importance? What is second? and so on. A student writing on the harvest of carnations on a commercial scale first divided the process into four main steps:

I. Picking
II. Wrapping
III. Tying
IV. Putting in water

But on second thought, the student saw that the last three steps were too closely related to be treated as separate divisions. They formed parts of a single phase of the process, a phase comparable to the first division, "Picking." The student then rewrote the outline:

I. Picking
II. Preparing for sale
   A. Wrapping
   B. Tying
   C. Putting in water

Notice that this change did not affect the order of the items because they are controlled by a time pattern; but it did ensure that the writer saw the true relationships among the various divisions of the subject and so gave appropriate space to each in the finished theme.

In the plan for your day's activities suggested earlier, a completed outline of the first division might show these subordinate relationships:

I. Routine
   A. Preparations for the day
      1. Getting up
      2. Washing and dressing
      3. Straightening room and making bed
   B. Eating and drinking
      1. Regular meals
         a. Breakfast
         b. Lunch
         c. Dinner
      2. Snacks
   C. Preparations for the night
      1. Undressing and washing
      2. Setting the alarm
      3. Going to bed

For a short paper you may not need a formal outline, but a list that shows the relative importance of your material will help you keep your sense of proportion as you write so that you will not devote too much space to a minor point or too little to a major one.

## Writing the Rough Draft

When you have chosen what appears to be the best arrangement for your material, you are ready to write a rough draft of the whole paper. Everything that you have listed should lead your readers to see by the end of the paper that your thesis is valid. To make sure of this, you must choose a beginning that will catch their attention and start them on the right track and an ending that will be as convincing to them as you can make it.

The ending is what readers are likely to remember best, simply because it comes at the end—your last words with nothing following to overshadow them or alter their meaning. You will be wise, therefore, to plan now what you want to say at the end of the paper—not the precise words and sentences, but the content, the essence. Some preparation for your ending is essential so that your beginning will start your readers off properly. Of course, when you have written the complete rough draft and can reread it as a whole, you may want to change the ending, perhaps drastically, but until then it can stand as the goal for your readers' journey through your material.

Let us assume, for the sake of discussion, that you decide to end with the comment that the typical day for a college freshman can be long and hectic but that it is worth the struggle. Your beginning should indicate your general subject (the typical day) and what you want your readers to notice most in the main body (the hectic quality of the day). Don't spend time and energy now on composing the perfect beginning. You can do that best when you have finished the rough draft and can see your work as a whole. For this imaginary paper, perhaps the only information essential for readers at the beginning is that on a typical day in college you are very busy.

Now, armed with the essence of the beginning and ending, with all the notes on your material handy to refresh your memory and with your thesis statement and notes on arrangement in an eye-catching position nearby, you can forge ahead and write a rough draft of the main body. Leave until later any questions on small points of spelling, grammar, and punctuation. You can correct these in your final version. Also postpone any questions on choosing a precise word or constructing a forceful sentence, even on where to divide your paragraphs. Remember that this is a *rough* draft. You can polish it more effectively when you have it all in hand.

As you write and see your thoughts take shape in words, other ideas will probably occur to you, other interpretations of your material, even other material that you had overlooked before. Make notes on all these so that you can use them later if you wish, with no strain on your memory. If you think of a better way to arrange your material and decide to start a new draft from the beginning, be sure to keep the old version—later you may decide that your first choice was best after all, or you may merely want to salvage part of it. If you have planned carefully up to this point, you will probably not make big revisions as you go along, but when you see the draft as a whole, you may want to perform major surgery.

When you have finished the rough draft, set it aside for a while, preferably overnight, certainly for at least an hour or two while you do something else quite different. Then, refreshed mentally, read it through quickly, trying to see it through your readers' eyes and considering these questions:

> Does the main line of thought develop clearly?
> Do the examples and details give good support to the thesis?
> Are there parts that are not necessary?
> Are there parts that need strengthening?
> Would any part be more effective in another position?

Keep rethinking and rewriting the rough draft until you can answer all these questions satisfactorily.

When you feel satisfied with the draft as a whole, it is time to polish the writing—to compose an effective beginning and ending, to rethink your word choice and your sentence and paragraph structure, to give your readers clues that something is particularly important or that it has a special relationship with something else.

## Beginnings

When your readers have finished your paper, they may not remember the beginning—the effectiveness of the main body and the force of the ending may put it out of their minds—but it is as essential to your paper as any other part. It creates your readers' first impression, and their ability to understand your general purpose and thesis will at first depend on it. But their ease of understanding is not enough. The beginning must also catch their interest. If it fails in that, you will have no readers.

The length of the beginning will depend on the length and complexity of what you are writing. Most books need a chapter, but shorter works may begin with a few paragraphs, a single paragraph, even a single sentence, or—very rarely—a single word. A fairly brief beginning is usually most effective—roughly one-seventh or less of the whole. For our imaginary paper any of the most frequently used forms could be appropriate.

**1.** An **explicit statement** of your topic and purpose or of your thesis is preferred for more technical types of writing, such as reports, and for anything based on material that will be difficult or unfamiliar for the readers:

> A typical day in the life of a college student is likely to be long and full of varied activities—academic study, a part-time job, extracurricular affairs, social gatherings, and the routine duties of daily living.

Caution: Avoid, however, flatfooted turns of phrase such as:
In this paper I intend to show that a typical day in the life of a college student is. . . .

**2.** The **history** or **background** of a subject is often helpful to give the context and suggest why it is important:

> The number of high school graduates who go on to college has steadily increased over recent years, but many of these students have no idea beforehand what a typical day in the life of a college student is like.

**3.** A **definition** of your subject or of the key terms you used to discuss it can also help readers to follow an argument easily:

> A "typical day" is probably one that never occurs in reality because no two days are ever exactly the same. A typical day for me as a college freshman would be a composite picture, an average, formed from several quite different days.

(Caution: Definitions quoted from dictionaries make boring beginnings because they are of necessity so general. Use one only when you must define something both complicated and unknown to your readers. Even then, you should reword the definition to make it fit smoothly into your own writing.)

**4.** An indication of your **qualifications** to discuss the subject, if it is unusual or specialized, may be needed at the beginning, and, in any case, should appear early in the paper so that the readers will have confidence in your accuracy:

> As an entering freshman in college, I have been on campus only a week, but I have met a great many other freshmen and think that my experiences have been fairly typical.

These forms are very clear and widely used, but, unless the subject is unusual or very timely, they will attract only readers who already have a wish to be informed on it. To attract other readers, consider using a rhetorical device.

**5.** A **rhetorical question** may arouse readers' curiosity:

> With only a few hours a week spent in class, how can a typical college freshman claim to be busy?

**6.** A **startling statement** or exclamation may also arouse curiosity:

> (a)  On a typical day, most college freshmen have had about four hours sleep, missed breakfast, slept through most of their classes, and have been thinking about nothing but drugs and the opposite sex—or so some magazine writers suggest.
> (b)  Work! Work! Work! Nobody warned me that I'd have my nose in a book ten hours a day.

**7.** A bit of **narrative,** especially if humorous or dramatic, that illustrates your main point, appeals to almost anyone:

> My alarm rings—7:15. I leap from my bed and dash to the bathroom in hopes of a vacant shower stall. No luck. Back to my own room and a quick wash in the basin. I pull on underwear, tee shirt, and blue jeans, and by 7:35 I'm in the cafeteria line for breakfast. At 7:59 I slide into my seat in English class, ten seconds before the professor arrives. Another typical day has begun.

**8.** **Quoted remarks** can draw the reader into the situation being described:

> "Read at least the first forty pages before Thursday," the instructor announced at the end of our first class meeting. "Take full, careful notes. It's a vital section of the book." In all my other classes the instructors had made much the same announcement.

**9.** An **appropriate quotation,** preferably from a well-known source, is an old device that works well:

> "Of making many books there is no end, and much study is a weariness of the flesh"—the Book of Ecclesiastes in the Bible was written many centuries ago, but the message is truer than ever, especially for college freshmen.

**10.** A **description of something familiar** that is comparable to your subject in important ways can help your readers picture it:

Ants seem to lead frantically busy lives. Around an ant hill we can watch lines of creatures rush in different directions, intent on reaching their destinations as quickly as possible, but sometimes pausing to greet each other with a wave. Between classes the campus resembles a busy ant hill.

**11.** A **direct appeal** to your readers' concerns or a reminder of a current problem or issue may make readers identify with your subject:

If you are like most high school students who plan to go to college, you are concentrating now on your grades, thinking that once you are accepted by the college of your choice your problems will be over and you will relax.

**Caution:** Do not overdo your use of rhetorical devices. The more natural interest your readers are likely to have in your material, the less you need to make a "hard sell." Like hot spices in food, a little rhetoric can go a long way. Practice composing different beginnings for each assignment to try out their effect. Also, practice composing different beginnings for some of the examples in this book.

## Endings

Endings, like beginnings, should be relatively brief, preferably not more than one-seventh of the whole paper. Most of the devices suggested for beginnings can be appropriate for endings.

**1.** A **brief restatement** of the thesis after a capsule summary of the main body will not be dramatic, but the brevity can give it force; it may be the best ending if your readers are unfamiliar with your subject or likely to be hard to convince.

**2.** Saving the only **complete statement of your thesis** for the end can have great dramatic force if your readers can follow the logic of everything leading up to it. This inductive pattern of organization (see Unit 13) may be difficult to handle but is worth trying.

**3.** A **redefinition** of the meaning of a key term in the light of what you have said in the main body of your paper may pinpoint your meaning for your readers.

**4.** Suggesting a **result** or finding a **significance** that goes beyond the immediate scope of the paper can show your readers the wider importance of your thesis and material.

**5.** A specific **reference to the beginning** or to the title may round off the whole by "framing" it—as Y did at the end of the paper on Jane.

**6, 7, 8.** A **rhetorical question**, an **exclamation**, a **challenging statement**, or a **direct appeal** to your readers for action can make them rethink your thesis and the whole paper.

**9, 10, 11.** An appropriate bit of **narrative**, a **quoted remark**, or a **quotation** from a well-known source that sums up or illustrates your main point may be easily remembered.

## Revising, Polishing, and Correcting

When you have added a full beginning and ending to your rough draft, set it all aside for a while, as you did before—if possible, overnight; certainly for a few hours during which you do something entirely different. Then you will see it from a fresh viewpoint when you make your revisions.

A revision, as the root of the word shows us, is a *reseeing*, not a mere hunt for mistakes. In planning and writing the rough draft, you probably had many moments of reseeing what you wrote and made changes accordingly. Now you can resee everything as parts of the whole. Imagine as strongly as you can that you are seeing the paper through your readers' eyes, and read it quickly to form what you think would be their general impression. Then ask yourself how they would probably answer these questions:

1. Was the thesis clear?
2. Did the main body support and explain the thesis enough to make it convincing or at least worth considering seriously?
3. Did each paragraph of the main body contribute something necessary to support and explain the thesis?
4. Were the points supporting the thesis arranged in an order that made them easily understandable?
5. Did the beginning arouse interest?
6. Did the ending reinforce the thesis?

If you think that your readers would answer "no" to any of these questions, go back to your notes on your material and plans for organizing it and also review the questions you were advised earlier to ask yourself about selecting and organizing your material. Then rethink and rewrite your paper as necessary.

Probably, if you planned carefully and thought through your material thoroughly before you wrote the paper and if you continued to think of the whole paper—of both your plan and thesis—as you wrote each part, you will now feel confident that, by and large, your readers will form the general impression that you intended. You can now devote the rest of your time, before making the final copy, to revising, polishing, and correcting your paragraph and sentence structure and word choice.

## Paragraphs

A paragraph is one or more sentences that develop one main thought. The purpose of a paragraph is to help readers to *see*, in every sense of the word, that it forms a subdivision of the whole, to see it both as a unit in itself and as a part of a larger unit. That is why we indent the beginning and leave the rest of the line blank after the last word.

A paragraph may be any length, from one sentence to hundreds, just as a sentence may have from one word to hundreds, or a book from a few pages to thousands. The length of a paragraph depends on the subject matter, the intended reader, and the form in which the reader will read it. Newspaper paragraphs are usually very short, often only one sentence each, because the narrow columns cause most sentences to occupy several lines and therefore to appear longer than they are.

In most other forms of writing, paragraphs are longer, and the one-sentence paragraph is rare, reserved to emphasize a dramatic or significant remark. A series of short paragraphs will make a piece of writing look choppy, even more than a series of short sentences will. Conversely, a series of paragraphs each more than a page long will discourage readers from even starting. In most writing, paragraphs between 75 and 175 words are average, or from roughly one-third to two-thirds of a double-spaced, typed page.

Whatever its length, a paragraph should contain only one main thought, but it may have many related thoughts to make the main one clear. It may be organized in any of the ways that an essay is organized, and many paragraphs can be read alone as if they were miniature essays. All the patterns of organization discussed in the units that follow apply to paragraphs as well as to whole papers. Choose the structure of each of your paragraphs just as you choose the organization of the whole paper, according to your thesis, content, and readers' needs.

When you are revising, check the structure of each paragraph by considering these questions:

**1.** Does this paragraph have one main point? Could it be given a heading, like the headings for points in an outline, that would cover everything in it? Are all its less important points clearly related to the main one? If you answer "no" to any of these questions, make one or more of these revisions:

**a.** Remove any parts that are not clearly related to the main point and put them elsewhere in the paper or leave them out altogether.

**b.** Rearrange the order of the parts so that they fit together more clearly.

**c.** Add one or more of the transitional devices described in answer to question 5 that follows.

**2.** Is the paragraph roughly between 75 and 175 words long?

**a.** If it is much shorter, ask yourself whether it is more important than the paragraphs before and after it. If it is more important, keep it short. If it is not, combine it with another paragraph, revising both as necessary to fit them together.

**b.** If it is much more than 175 words, ask yourself if everything in it is not only related to your main point but essential to it. If everything is essential, try to find a way to divide the paragraph logically in two (you will then probably need to revise some of your sentences to form the beginnings and endings of the two paragraphs that result from the division).

**3.** Do the paragraph and sentence structures emphasize your important points?

**a.** Is there variety in the length and structure of this paragraph in relation to those near it? Is there variety in the sentences in this paragraph? Avoid the monotony of using the same pattern again and again, especially in paragraphs or sentences of about the same length, unless you want to emphasize similarities in their content (see below 3(d)).

**b.** Does the paragraph build up to the important point? If you lead to that point with sentences of average length and complexity and then present the point in a short, uncomplicated sentence, it will stand out by contrast and catch your readers' eyes. Similarly, a very short paragraph coming after several moderately long ones will be eye-catching.

**c.** Have you taken advantage of "end focus" in your paragraphs and sentences to emphasize important points? We tend to notice the end of something simply because it is the end. If you construct a sentence or a paragraph that presents a particularly important point so that the most signfiicant words are at the end, they will stand out as a climax. Note how Murray ends his third paragraph (page 24) and how Smith ends his narrative (page 27).

**d.** Have you taken advantage of parallelism to emphasize a comparison, contrast, or list of any kind? To compare, contrast, or list two or more opinions or pieces of information, present them in parallel structures—ones that are as nearly the same as possible. The repetition will emphasize what is similar, and the differences will stand out by contrast. Note Murray's use of parallelism in the sentences that start with "If" in his first paragraph (pages 23–24).

**4.** Are pronouns, verb tenses, and terminology clear and logically consistent within the paragraph and between it and the rest of the paper?

**a.** Switch pronouns (*I, you, it, he, she, they,* and so on) only to indicate a different person or thing. If you write "People want peace," don't switch later to "You want peace" or "We want peace," unless you mean to make a distinction between "people" and "you" or "we."

**b.** Make sure that each pronoun's references are clear and that there is no word nearby that a reader could possibly mistake for its reference. In "The students took their coats off because they were wet," does "they" refer to "students" or to "coats"?

**c.** In narrating events, change from one verb tense to another only to indicate a difference in time.

**d.** Stick to the same names whenever possible for what you are discussing. If you have referred to a "residence hall," don't later call the same building a "dormitory"—your readers may think that you mean a different building. If the result is monotonously repetitious, try to recast your sentences so that you can use a pronoun instead of repeating the word. If using a synonym seems essential, be sure that the reference is clear.

**5.** Is the paragraph's relationship to what precedes it clear? Is the relationship directly stated or strongly implied by the content? Are the relationships among the points within the paragraph similarly clear? If not, add transitional words or phrases to indicate relationships. Usually, the best position for a transition is at or very near the beginning of the paragraph or sentence that you wish to link to what has gone before, but sometimes you may want to put it at the end to lead to what follows. Transitional words and phrases are most commonly used to indicate these kinds of relationships:

    **a.** a **sequence** according to space or time or relative importance, as with *next, in the meantime, later, behind, above all, most* or *least of all, first, second, finally*

    **b.** an **addition** to the preceding material, as with *and, also, furthermore, moreover, in addition to, incidentally, similarly*

    **c.** a **contrast,** as with *but, however, on the other hand, yet, nevertheless, in contrast*

    **d. results** or **conclusions** drawn from preceding material, as with *so, therefore, consequently, as a result, thus, hence.*

**Note:** You may have been warned when you were younger never to start a sentence with "and" or "but." In general, this is good advice to follow. Strings of "ands" make all your points seem equal; nothing stands out. Strings of "buts" will make you seem to go round in self-contradicting circles. But an occasional "but" or "and" can make an effective start for a sentence whose connection with what precedes it deserves emphasis. You may also have been told never to start a sentence with "because"; the danger is that you might forget to complete the sentence with a main clause, but a modifying clause such as "Because these actions were dangerous" can make a useful link between the sentence it begins and the information in the preceding sentence.

Not every paragraph, by any means, needs a transitional device, but in the examples in this book you will see how often such devices help to guide the reader and unify the thought. Note, for instance, the way a student writer, William Nilsson, begins the five successive paragraphs of the main body of his essay (pages 187–88): "A good starting point.... Another source.... Still another reason.... Economic factors, too, may.... The question that may follow from this...."

## Word Choice

Now that you are almost ready to make the final copy of your paper, examine your choice of words. This is such an important part of writing that a whole unit (5), on which this checklist of reminders is based, is devoted to it. Rereading your paper slowly, consider these questions:

**1.** Have you used words accurately and in their generally accepted meanings?

    **a.** If you have any doubts about accuracy, look up the word immediately in a good desk-size or unabridged dictionary.

    **b.** If you want your readers to give a special interpretation to a word, make sure that you include an explanation.

**2.** Is the level of word choice appropriate for this assignment—for this subject and these readers?

For most writing assignments, aim for a level somewhere between the very literary or very technical and the very informal. Some of the examples in this book are more formal than others and some less formal, but none goes to an extreme. All are meant for the "general reader," someone who is not a specialist in the subject being discussed but who is educated and intelligent. Probably, most of what you write, now and later, will be for the general reader.

**3.** Do your words express your meaning forcefully?

**a.** Whenever possible, choose words with specific, concrete associations. For example, Murray writes "other surfers *clutter* up the waves" (page 23), a more forceful word than *crowd* or *fill;* Red Smith writes "The crowd was still *bawling* for him" (page 26), not merely *shouting* or *calling.*

Caution: Like many other devices and practices recommended here, this can easily be overdone. If you make every remark colorful, nothing stands out.

**b.** Avoid clichés—expressions used so often that they have become colorless, as in "It rained cats and dogs," or "Their hearts were as big as all outdoors."

**c.** Such words as "really," "very," "terribly," and "awfully" add little or nothing. "They were really terribly happy" would be better as "They were delighted" or "They were overjoyed."

**4.** Do your words express your meaning compactly?

**a.** "Brevity is the soul of wit" is a cliché but also a valuable truth. For example, "The subject that was discussed in Green's essay was that of the next election" would be better as "Green's essay was on the next election."

**b.** Deliberate repetition of an important word or phrase can give it effective emphasis. Note Red Smith's repetition of "again" in "there was a runner on base again, and again he hit the first pitch. Again it reached the seats in right" (page 26). Careless repetition, however, is boring. Don't, for example, repeat "college program" five times in six lines if "program" or, better still, "it" would be clear.

## *Title*

This may seem a rather belated mention of the words that stand first in any paper. You have known your general topic all along, of course, and it has determined your choice of plan and treatment, but only now, with the last rough draft before you, can you decide definitely what to call it.

A title should be brief, a word or phrase, not a complete sentence, and it should indicate not only the specific content of the paper but its purpose. For matter-of-fact, informative writing, such as reports, a descriptive title stating the actual content of the paper as clearly as possible in a few words is best, as in a recent magazine article "Alcohol, Marijuana, and Memory." This kind of title is also good when you are sure that your subject will interest your readers. For less strictly utilitarian writing, you may prefer an imaginative title to catch a reader's attention, such as *Life for Death,* a book on the results of a murder trial. Often, writers add a subtitle to explain such a title, as in another magazine article "Matter over Mind: The Big Issues Raised by Newly Discovered Brain Chemicals."

## Form for the Final Copy

**1.** Use white, standard-size paper ($8\frac{1}{2} \times 11''$). Do not use pages torn from a spiral binder.

**2.** Write or type on only one side of each page.

**3.a.** If you are writing, choose wide-lined paper (about $\frac{3}{8}''$ between lines) or skip a line after each line of writing. Leave a left-hand margin at least $1\frac{1}{2}$ inches wide. Use ink, either blue or black, not any other color. Never use pencil.

**3.b.** If you are typing, double space (skip a line after each typed line). Leave margins at least $1\frac{1}{2}$ inches wide at the left side and the top and bottom of the page; leave at least a 1-inch margin on the right. Skip one space after each comma and semicolon and two after all other forms of punctuation except dashes. Indicate a dash by typing two hyphens with *no* space before, after, or between them. Add in ink any symbols that are not on the typewriter.

**4.** Try to avoid splitting a word to fill up the end of a line. Instead, leave the extra space blank and put the whole word on the next line—your readers will be grateful.

**5.** Indent the beginning of each paragraph the equivalent of a five-letter word.

**6.** Spell out all numbers below ten unless you are using several in a small space (many authorities recommend spelling out all numbers below a hundred). Spell out any number, large or small, that begins a sentence. If the result seems awkward, as it will in a sentence with other numbers that are not spelled out, try to revise the sentence so that you can begin it with a word instead.

**7.** Correct any slips of your pen or typewriter by firmly crossing out the error and writing the correct version neatly above it. Erasures are usually messy. If you find several errors on a page, or if you have a large one, recopy the page.

## Mechanics

Grades on your college written work will result from a combination of the impressions made on your readers by your content, plan, and accuracy in the details called *mechanics:* your spelling, punctuation, grammar, and usage. Accuracy in mechanics will not guarantee you a good grade, but it is essential. The best subjects and plans will not impress readers who are constantly distracted or confused by mechanical errors. If you have difficulties with mechanics, you can overcome them by careful drill with a good handbook. Ask your instructor for a recommendation if one has not been assigned for the course.

Also, beware of the careless mistakes that slip in because your mind travels ahead of your hand. You may know the difference between *to* and *too*, but just "didn't think." You must try to develop the eagle eye of the professional proofreader, who is responsible for the almost flawless pages of the better books and magazines. Careful correction is an essential last step for anything you write outside of class; but remember that it is equally important in letters, in-class themes, and examinations written under pressure. Write less, if necessary, to save time for proofreading. It is a good rule never to give anything you have written to a reader until you have checked it carefully, *letter by letter*, for possible slips.

## EXAMPLES

Since much of this book is devoted to various patterns of logical organization, the examples that follow are limited to the simplest one—the chronological pattern. The first gives the experiences of a single day, as did the outline for a paper discussed earlier in the subsection called "Organizing the Main Body." The other examples cover only a few consecutive hours. All the writers have the same purpose—simply to share enjoyable experiences with their readers. You will notice that their paragraphs have topics but no topic sentences and that the one complete essay, "Sunday Morning in Haiti," does not have a thesis statement, but the thesis is implied throughout.

*1-A*                    THE SURFER'S DAY
*William Murray*

"Hanging Five," the essay from which this example is taken, appeared in a travel magazine, *Holiday*, in 1967. Directed to both surfers and armchair athletes, it describes surfing as a way of life for many young Californians and is illustrated by large color photographs of the magnificent coast.

OUTLINE
I. First time
   division:
   morning

A. Water conditions
   1. First type
   2. Response

The serious surfer arrives at the beach very early, sometimes at dawn. This is partly because he wants to be in the water before too many other surfers clutter up the waves for him, but also because, in Southern California, a sea breeze almost always comes up in the early afternoon, 5 causing a wind chop that ruins the best wave surfaces and can beach everybody until just before dusk, when it dies down again. If the swell is favorable, and the waves have that glassy look that delights surfers everywhere, or stokes them, as they say, the aficionado will persevere for seven 10

B. Water conditions
  1. Second type
  2. Response

C. Water conditions
  1. Third type
  2. Response

D. Water conditions
  1. Fourth type
  2. Response

E. Water conditions
  1. Other types
  2. Responses

II. Second time
  division:
  afternoon
A. Activities
B. Limitations
  1. First type
  2. Second type

III. Third time
  division: evening
  Activities

IV. Conclusion
A. First advantage
B. Second
  advantage

or eight hours, practicing his specialty or whatever the surf dictates. If the waves are huge, fifteen feet or higher, the big-wave rider will concentrate on staying alive, shooting across a wall of heaving ocean only instants ahead of disaster. If the waves run to three or four feet, he will hotdog 15 them, practicing such intricate and delicate maneuvers as hanging first five toes, then ten over the nose; fast turns like left-go-rights and whips and cutbacks; standing islands, reverse kickouts, Quasimodos, head dips, spinners and other technical marvels. If the waves are poor and 20 uneven—real junk surf—he will paddle faster, avoid sliding out onto the shoulders, stay always in the curls, drive hard into the sections, hug the inside rails, and get out to the nose of his board to perfect his trimming. Above all, he will avoid getting locked in when the wave tubes, or get- 25 ting lost in the soup, which is what he calls the unmanageable foam. Miscalculations will inevitably result in a wipeout, which is not a good way to stay stoked—a condition of the spirit indistinguishable from nirvana.

Much of the afternoon will be spent snoozing, grabbing 30 hamburgers and milk shakes and fruit salads, indulging in occasional volleyball games, and socializing. The pecking order will be rigidly adhered to, perhaps even enforced. On no account must a true surfer be seen hobnobbing with a valley cowboy (an inlander), a gremmie (a youthful neo- 35 phyte), a hodad (a pretentious fraud) or a kook (a nut). The conversation will be restricted to surfing, certain other In sports, the more interesting local court cases, gambling, the stock market, movies and—yes—girls.

In the evening, the beach crowd will find its way to a 40 good party, often given in rented quarters, or maybe just take in the flicks or bask in front of the TV set or whoop it up at some favorite shoreside eatery with the requisite bar, jukebox and pinball machines. It doesn't cost much to live the good beach life in Southern California. The climate is 45 mild all year, and the waves roll in ceaselessly. Two or three changes of costume, a couple of pairs of good surfing trunks, a wet suit, a board and a car, preferably an old station wagon of the type called a woody, and the surfer is fully equipped. 50

1. How does the writer indicate the main divisions of the surfer's day?
2. Can you sum up the main point of the first paragraph in a single sentence?
3. Why is the first paragraph three times as long as either of the other two paragraphs?

4. What seems to be the basis for the order in which the writer takes up the five types of water conditions?
5. Does the writer's use of special terms and slang make the description more effective or less so? Check the writer's word choice in another selection drawn from the same essay but illustrating another type of writing (Unit 4-F).

---

*1-B*     SUNDAY MORNING IN HAITI
*Anaica Lodescar (student)*

Three o'clock on Sunday morning. I have been sound asleep. I hear only the end of the carillon for the first call to go to mass. Three-thirty. The sound of steps breaks the silence of the dark street outside my window and tells me that I am already almost late. Dogs are barking everywhere. Alarm clocks are ringing in other houses. People from a distance are arriving, rushing toward the 5 cathedral. Even people in the neighborhood are hurrying because the seats will soon be filled with churchgoers.

At a time like this, so early in a Sunday morning, a stranger would not believe that there are so many people going to mass. He would think that there must be some very unusual event—a fire or some other disaster, perhaps, to bring so 10 many people out into the streets when it is still dark.

By the time I reach the stairs of the big cathedral, the carillon wakes me up. My ears ring with the ringing bells. The churchyard is full of cars and of early vendors of fruit, vegetables, milk, patés, candles. Inside, the cathedral is crowded. There are no more seats. Some people would rather stand up so that 15 they won't fall asleep during the service, and others have brought their own chairs. The priest is wide awake in his white robe. He moves quickly to and fro as he conducts the mass. The attendance of the choir is excellent, and all through the service the singing is loud, clear, very alive. Outside, the streets are calm again and the latecomers move quietly, trying to slip in unobserved.     20

The service is long, but at last it reaches the end. It's five-thirty, still dark, and almost time to go back home. I must choose what to do: go back to bed, or study my many lessons for Monday, or go to the market or to the baker. The streets are full of people now, and there are many more food vendors. From each corner they're calling "Paté, paté." Oh, how I love those patés! Other ven- 25 dors are selling candles to people coming for the next service.

About five or six blocks away from the cathedral are the vendors of "café" and bread. They are not calling anybody. They don't have to. The smell of their merchandise is call enough. They're sitting calmly in front of their big pots, an oil lamp standing behind each vendor on a small table. For some grown-ups a 30 good cup of black coffee is a delight, but the "café au lait" I'll have at home will be even better.

A new carillon in the air is announcing the next service. The roosters everywhere are calling "co-co-ri-co." The dogs sound louder—they are competing

with each other. From the radios in the houses comes soft music or hymns. A  35
new group of churchgoers streams toward the cathedral. I hear many greetings—"Bonjour," "Bonjour!"

The sky in the east has turned a golden pink. Soon a beautiful sun will show
its round face in a beautiful blue sky. In Haiti it seems that the weather is always
lovely on Sunday.

40

1. Why does the writer tell us so much about the sounds?
2. What transitional devices do you find?
3. Why are almost all the verbs in the present tense?
4. How does the writer indicate the passing of time?
5. What seems to be the basis for the paragraph divisions?

---

*1-C*                                   ONE-MAN SHOW
                                          *Red Smith*

The writer has for many years been a columnist for the *New York Times* and is one
of the most popular sportswriters in the country. The selection that follows forms the
second half of a column on Reggie Jackson's remarkable performance on October 18,
1977, when he hit three home runs in a row so that the Yankees won the World Series.
In the first half of the column Smith gave the highlights of the games leading up to
Jackson's special triumph.

The stage was set when he [Reggie Jackson] went to the plate in last night's
second inning with the Dodgers leading, 2–0. Sedately, he led off with a walk.
Serenely, he circled the bases on a home run by Chris Chambliss. The score was
tied.

Los Angeles had moved out front, 3–2, when the man reappeared in the  5
fourth inning with Thurman Munson on base. He hit the first pitch on a line
into the seats beyond right field. Circling the bases for the second time, he went
into his home-run glide—head high, chest out. The Yankees led, 4–3. In the
dugout, Yankees fell upon him. Billy Martin, the manager, who tried to slug
him last June, patted his cheek lovingly. The dugout phone rang and Reggie  10
accepted the call graciously.

His first home run knocked the Dodgers' starting pitcher, Burt Hooton, out
of the game. His second disposed of Elias Sosa, Hooton's successor. Before Sosa's
first pitch in the fifth inning, Reggie had strolled the length of the dugout to
pluck a bat from the rack, even though three men would precede him to the  15
plate. He was confident he would get his turn. When he did, there was a runner
on base again, and again he hit the first pitch. Again it reached the seats in
right.

When the last jubilant playmate had been peeled off his neck, Reggie took
a seat near the first-base end of the bench. The crowd was still bawling for him  20
and comrades urged him to take a curtain call, but he replied with a gesture

that said, "Aw, fellows, cut it out!" He did unbend enough to hold up two fingers for photographers in a V-for-victory sign.

Jackson was the leadoff batter in the eighth. By that time, Martin would have replaced him in an ordinary game, sending Paul Blair to right field to help protect the Yankees' lead. But did they ever bench Edwin Booth in the last act?

For the third time, Reggie hit the first pitch but this one didn't take the shortest distance between two points. Straight out from the plate the ball streaked, not toward the neighborly stands in right but on a soaring arc toward the unoccupied bleachers in dead center, where the seats are blacked out to give batters a background. Up the white speck climbed, dwindling, diminishing, until it settled at last halfway up those empty stands, probably 450 feet away.

This time he could not disappoint his public. He stepped out of the dugout and faced the multitude, two fists and one cap uplifted. Not only the customers applauded.

"I must admit," said Steve Garvey, the Dodgers' first baseman, "when Reggie Jackson hit his third home run and I was sure nobody was listening, I applauded into my glove."

1. Where has the writer used the ends of a paragraph or sentence to emphasize an important or dramatic point?
2. What is the effect of starting the second and third sentences in the same way? of repeating "again" three times at the end of the third paragraph?
3. What specific details help us to picture the event and the emotions of all concerned?

## ASSIGNMENTS

1. For each of the following general subjects, make a list of five or six specific topics on which you feel you could write, *from your own experience,* 250–500 word papers of interest to the nonspecialist reader: chemistry, religion, education, cars, music, agriculture, sports, literature, television programs, nature, social change, art.
   *Example:* General subject—Education
            Specific topics—My First Day of College Classes
                     Taking Examinations
                     My Interview for Admission to College
                     My Worst Teacher
                     My Favorite Extracurricular Activity
                     Graduation Day
2. For any one of the topics you listed in answer to the preceding question, write five different openings, a sentence to a paragraph in length, suitable for different purposes or directed to different types of readers. Discuss what you hope the effects of each will be.
3. Prepare a plan for a paper on several hours spent at a fair, in a city, on a job, at a beach, at a family picnic, or in some other specific environment.
   a. Set down in chronological sequence the dozen or so items you wish to discuss.
   b. Group them under appropriate headings into a few manageable units.

    **c.** Regroup them according to some order other than time sequence.

    **d.** Arrange your groupings in **c** into what you consider the most effective order and explain why you chose it.

4. Look over the photographs on pages 89–92. In what groups can you arrange them, according to subject matter, the number of people involved, the types of people. and so on? List them in as many combinations as you can imagine.

5. Go through a unit of this book (both text and examples), a chapter of another textbook, or a current magazine article, as assigned, pointing out transitional devices, both between paragraphs and within them.

6. **a.** For six of the theme subjects you listed in 1 of these assignments, compose titles that will be appealing as well as informative, for example: Graduation Day— Start or Finish?

    **b.** Choose one of the groups in which you arranged the photographs; compose a title for the group and a separate title for each photograph in it. Compose titles that will catch your readers' attention.

    **c.** For class discussion, bring in a list of ten titles of nonfiction books or magazine articles that have especially caught your attention, listing after each the subject with which it deals.

7. Having noted the divisions of the *chronological* patterns used in the three examples in this section, try your hand at other *logical* arrangements of their material. (See the illustration of the two types under "Organizing the Main Body" on pages 9–12.) What are the advantages and disadvantages of these differing patterns?

8. Using as material some job you have had or some particular kind of life you have lived (at school or camp, for instance), write an essay in which you present your experience chronologically, as a typical "day in the life of—." Limit your material by excluding all irrelevant details, as the authors of the examples have done; include only experiences appropriate to your limited subject and to the particular attitude you decide to take.

# UNIT 2

# *Description*

Our minds must often deal with the **abstract**—concepts such as dishonesty, nature, humanity; but we are much more readily impressed by the **concrete**— a bad check, a tree, a child. Yet even these things are general, and our imaginations respond more to the **specific**—a check for ten dollars signed by George Henderson and stamped "No Funds"; a stately elm towering alone in a pasture against a red-gold sunset; a curly haired eight-year-old trudging dejectedly along a dry creek bottom, fishing pole in hand. Carefully chosen words and specific, concrete details can make a vivid and memorable point of something that readers might otherwise forget or never notice.

## *Description as an Aid to Exposition*

Description is essential in most expository writing because it adds the same vividness that our senses continually add to our daily lives. But a steady bombardment of the senses, even vicariously through the printed page, is soon numbing; the bored reader begins to think "Yes, yes, but go on—what's the point?" In the eighteenth and nineteenth centuries, when the novel was a new literary form, writers introduced characters through long, elaborate descriptions. Most modern writers, however, give only a few significant details to stimulate the reader's imagination, bringing the details out gradually in the course of the story or essay.

In this unit you are asked to write short pieces of almost unadulterated description for practice in careful observation and word choice. But remember that description is best used only to assist you in your larger purpose of informing or persuading your readers. In ordinary exposition, include only the descriptive details that will make your main point clear and memorable. Spread them throughout your essay so that they will clarify and enliven it for your readers without slowing down their reading.

## Diction and the Five Senses

Your description must depend primarily on the power of your diction—your choice of words. Avoid the abstract and general when you can; instead, use the concrete and specific. Saying that a room is clean or a girl beautiful will give your opinion but will create no picture for the reader. A mention of a freshly waxed floor, however, or of large brown eyes with long lashes will stimulate your reader's imagination.

Your description must create sense impressions for your readers. Remember that there are still five senses, even though our civilization may have dulled their keenness. Most of us tend to be visually minded, thinking of description primarily in terms of what we see. But the sensations of sound and scent, touch and flavor, can be essential in descriptions. Imagine trying to tell a foreigner about the fun of an American county fair. If you described only what you saw, you would have to omit much of the experience—the shouts of the barkers at the amusement concessions and the clatter of the machinery for the various rides; the odors from the food stands, the barns, and the crowd; the spicy flavor of the hot dogs and the intense sweetness of the cotton candy; and everywhere the grittiness of the dust stirred up by hundreds of feet.

The English language is rich in words describing size, shape, and color but not in ones describing sound, flavor, odor, or texture. Once you have classified a taste sensation as sweet or sour, bitter or salty, you have almost exhausted our supply of appropriate adjectives, but you haven't done much to re-create that sensation for the reader. A useful descriptive device is a **comparison** or **contrast** with something familiar: "Venison tastes like beef but has a more intense flavor." The comparison does not have to be literal; it may only suggest a point of similarity as in "The bad news was like a slap in the face," or, more forcefully, "The bad news was a slap in the face." Describing animals, inanimate objects, or abstractions as if they have human characteristics can also help the reader to imagine them more vividly, as in "The bad news slapped them in the face," "The engine coughed and sneezed before it died," or "The neighborhood dogs held a committee meeting behind the garage." Of special help are **onomatopoetic** words—words whose sound imitates the sound they describe—such as buzz, sigh, crash, murmur, or whir.

Use a few fresh, strong words in description rather than many weak from overuse. Search first for vivid nouns and verbs—words that name things and actions. One specific word like *shuffle* or *trudge* or *saunter* is not only briefer than *walk slowly* but more precise and therefore more effective. See Unit 5, "Words," for more discussion of word choice.

## Kinds of Description

Description can be **informative** or **evocative,** depending on your purpose. You may wish merely to inform your readers, or you may wish to give them pleasure as well. Either type of description aids exposition—the first is a necessity, the second an enjoyable luxury.

To explain a mechanism or a process, you must use informative description. Give the essential facts in the briefest and clearest terms you can find, unambiguous terms in their simplest denotative meanings. If these are not sufficient, use comparisons with more familiar objects: "The plunger looks like a fountain pen"; "The shovel handle is D-shaped." If you call on senses other than sight in informative description, be practical, not poetic. "Sand the wood until smooth to the touch"; "Allow the mixture to stand until there is an odor of rotten eggs." Drawings may well supplement or replace words in such descriptions. Be brief, as brief as you can without losing clarity and completeness. Your goal is information, only information. Such description is required in technical reports and all writings calling only for facts.

Not all situations, however, limit you to presenting facts. Even those that do are often best presented in words that go beyond mere information and add vividness by evoking emotions. In "Your dollar will help to feed this haggard mother and her crippled child," what might have been bare fact becomes a plea because of the emotional power of specific details that *suggest* as well as *mean*. A general idea—your money is needed—comes alive in the particulars. *Money* is your tangible dollar; *need* is the hunger of a definitely pictured woman and child.

## Organization

Description is usually a matter of details scattered throughout other forms of writing to enliven them, rather than something written for its own sake. We cannot talk of it, therefore, in terms of definite logical patterns. But it is nevertheless governed by certain patterns of design.

Your selection of details must be the right one for your purpose. Your subject will confront you with a mass of sense impressions from which you must select the few that are relevant. In describing a machine in terms of its function, you need not mention its color; in creating a mood of gloom, omit any details that do not contribute to that atmosphere, either directly or by contrast. Your selection will be governed not only by this mental point of view, your purpose, but also by your physical point of view, which limits you to the sensations you would actually have at a given time or place. You cannot see the back jeans pocket of the person who meets you at the door or smell the flowers on a distant hillside. If you are moving around a building or down a river, your description must take into consideration your change of viewpoint.

Usually, you will need only an occasional descriptive detail to illuminate a point in your exposition. But when you must describe something at greater length, the arrangement of your details becomes important.

**1.** The simplest arrangement is **chronological,** the arrangement of detail according to the time sequence in which it was observed. The examples in Unit 1 and the first three in this unit are organized chronologically.

**2.** Next in simplicity is the **spatial** order. In it, details are arranged according to physical shape and position. In describing a room, for instance, you might start at one side and work around it, mentioning the objects you see as you progress; you might describe a person from head to foot, or a landscape from near to far or far to near.

**3.** An arrangement based on the **most noticeable feature** is more selective. In describing the room, you might first mention a piano or a fireplace, for the person perhaps a big nose, and for the landscape a large tree; then you would give the rest of the details in their relationship to the outstanding feature.

**4.** A still more selective arrangement is by **relative importance.** This centers on what you want your readers to notice most—an unmade bed, a shy smile, the honeysuckle on a fence—including only the other details that you have selected to reinforce this impression and omitting the rest.

## EXAMPLES

*2-A*                    COLD ORANGE JUICE
                     *Wayne Smith (student)*

This description was written as an in-class exercise. The students were given fifteen minutes in which to describe in detail the sensations of drinking something very cold.

I was so thirsty that I could already taste the orange and feel the cold go down my throat. My mouth started to water when I picked up the glass. As the cold numbed my fingers I felt the frost melt under them. I took my first gulp. It was so cold that I had to squint my eyes. My teeth tingled. The tiny fruit cells popped against my tongue and filled my mouth with acid sweetness. A piece of 5 ice slid down, leaving my mouth numb and my throat aching. I sucked in air to make my throat warm again and licked my teeth to warm them, too.

How does each of these words chosen by the writer differ from the near synonym paired with it: *gulp* and *swallow*, *squint* and *narrow*, *tingled* and *felt cold*, *popped* and *broke open*, *sucked* and *breathed in?*

*2-B*                    THE GREAT BLUE
                     *Lucian K. Truscott IV*

This excerpt forms the second half of an informal essay published in the *Saturday Review* in 1972. The writer's description, in the first half, of an uneventful afternoon fishing alone in Maine serves as a background to set off the drama of his sudden view of the rare bird.

I had just fished the pool and was rounding a gradual bend upstream, wading slowly so as not to disturb the slow-moving clear water, when up ahead I noticed a gigantic bird atop a tiny, demure beaver dam, a creature almost too large to be real. He had his back to me and seemed to be peering intently into the pool on the other side of the dam. I froze, stood perfectly still as I watched him 5 preside magnificently over the pond. I was only about fifteen or twenty feet away, and he was an elegant sight—a great blue heron.

The beaver pool was twenty or thirty yards in length and pear-shaped; it was shallow at the near end, deep at the far. Over to one side I could see a beaver lodge—still lived in, it appeared; in good repair at any rate—and at the far end 10 a brief falls, where water rushed into the pond with a white giggle, audible even from where I stood. The woods were that quiet.

The heron had the hue of a blue-point Siamese cat, a dusky grayness, bluish only on the edges, the high points in the fading, late-afternoon sun. Maybe three feet tall, he towered greatly over the beaver pond. I wondered: Do the beavers 15 know he is here, and if so, does his great size cause them to slap the water and crash-dive, heading for the womb of their upside-down coffee-cup lodge?

Then, suddenly, he whooossshhhed his wings upward once, then down, stretched to their full four or five feet—it seemed like six—and took off from the dam, glided over the beaver pond for a few yards, and rose slowly, his wings 20 beating the air slowly like a rug strung over a clothes line in the backyard, his great neck doubled back arrogantly against his chest, then thrust forward almost wantonly as he passed above the trees, heading north.

I watched his slow and easy disappearance against the sky until he was as blue as it was. 25

1. Which words and groups of words give you the most precise impressions of what the writer saw and heard?
2. Why does he describe the bird's color twice in one sentence: "the hue of a blue-point Siamese cat" and "a dusky grayness, bluish only on the edges"?
3. What is gained by the spelling "whooossshhhed"?
4. What may have been his reason for comparing the bird's wings to a rug on a clothes line instead of to something graceful?

---

**2-C**                    MORE POWER TO YOU
                              *Time*

This description was written in 1948, when jet engines were new, but the thrill for an observer can be much the same today. Vivid description is as possible in the mechanical world as in the natural.

DESCRIPTIVE DEVICES          Bolted motionless on a test stand, the little monster is not
                             impressive. It has no coolly symmetrical propeller, no phal-
Negatives (3)                anx of cylinderheads, none of the hard geometrical grace
                             of the conventional aircraft engine. Yet the unprepossess-

Contrast

ing turbojet engine has thrown the air designers into 5
ecstatic confusion: nobody yet knows how fast the jet will
enable man to fly, but the old speed ceilings are off. In their
less guarded moments, sober designers talk of speeds so
high that aircraft will glow like meteors.

Comparison
Animation

To watch a jet engine spring into life is to feel that 10
power. (Only when the engine is set up with a pipe to catch
its gases is it safe to watch the fires kindle.) Dimly visible

Comparison

inside is the turbine, like a small windmill with close-set

Sound

vanes. When the starting motor whines, the turbine spins.

Smell

A tainted breeze blows through the exhaust vent in the tail, 15
followed by a thin grey fog of atomized kerosene. Deep in

Onomatopoeia
Sight

the engine a single spark plug buzzes. A spot of fire dances
in a circle behind the turbine. Next moment, with a hollow

Onomatopoeia
Comparison

*whoom,* a great yellow flame leaps out. It cuts back to a
faint blue cone, a cone that roars like a giant blowtorch. 20
The roar increases to thunder as the turbine gathers speed.
Then it diminishes slightly, masked by a strange, high snarl
that is felt rather than heard. This is "ultrasonic" sound (a
frequency too high for the ear to hear). It tickles the deep

Feeling

brain, punches the heart, makes the viscera tremble. Few 25
men like to stay in a test room when a jet is up to speed.

The engine now has the fierce beauty of power. Its massive rotor, the principal moving part, is spinning some

Informative
comparisons

13,000 times per minute (though with only the faintest
vibration). The fire raging in its heart would heat 1,000 30
five-room houses in zero weather (though much of the
engine's exterior is cool). From the air intake in its snout,

Animation

invisible hooks reach out; their suction will clasp a man
who comes too close and break his body. The blast roaring
out the tail will knock a man down at 150 feet. The reac- 35

Informative
comparisons

tion of the speeding jet of gas pushes against the test stand
with a two-ton thrust. If the engine were pointing upward
and left unshackled, it would take off like a rocket, each
pound of its weight overbalanced by more than two
pounds of thrust. 40

1. Point out in this section any effective adjectives and adverbs and concrete verbs.
2. What is the cumulative effect of the words *life, tail, snarl* (¶2), *heart, snout* (¶3)?

---

**2-D**

### THE HELLBENDER
*The Encyclopedia Americana*

This paragraph from an encyclopedia is intended to give facts. It is typically informative description in which essential details are listed in such an objective manner that

only one word, "repulsive," expresses an opinion. Scientists in all fields use objective description as an aid in explaining all kinds of natural phenomena.

**Hellbender,** hĕl-bĕn′dẽr, *Cryptobranchus alleganiensis,* most robust and second largest of North American salamanders. It attains a length of slightly more than two feet. Despite a somewhat repulsive appearance, and the presence of teeth in both upper and lower jaws, the hellbender is quite harmless. The small eyes are set in a massive head. Both head and body are much depressed, 5 and the outlines of the body are disguised by a fleshy fold of wrinkled skin along either side and the posterior aspects of each limb. Though relatively short, the limbs are functional, the front pair being provided with four toes, the hind limbs with five. A crest is present along the upper side of the strongly compressed tail. Hellbenders are entirely aquatic, yet the adults are without gills 10 and have only a single pair of inconspicuous gill slits, which are more or less concealed by skin folds. Their coloration varies considerably, ranging from yellowish brown through dull brick red to near black.

The organization of Examples A, B, and C was determined by the chronology of the experiences. What principle of organization is used here? What reason may the writer have had to use it?

---

*2-E*                                    THE HOUSE
                                      *Anne Moody*

This is the first paragraph of a book, *Coming of Age in Mississippi,* published in 1968. It is the autobiography, starting with her childhood, of a young black woman who was active in the Civil Rights movement of the 1960s when she was a college student.

I'm still haunted by dreams of the time we lived on Mr. Carter's plantation. Lots of Negroes lived on his place. Like Mama and Daddy they were all farmers. We all lived in rotten wood two-room shacks. But ours stood out from the others because it was up on the hill with Mr. Carter's big white house, overlooking the farms and the other shacks below. It looked just like the Carters' 5 barn with a chimney and a porch, but Mama and Daddy did what they could to make it livable. Since we had only one big room and a kitchen, we all slept in the same room. It was like three rooms in one. Mama [and the rest of] them slept in one corner and I had my little bed in another corner next to one of the big wooden windows. Around the fireplace a rocking chair and a couple of 10 straight chairs formed a sitting area. This big room had a plain, dull-colored wallpaper tacked loosely to the walls with large thumbtacks. Under each tack was a piece of cardboard which had been taken from shoeboxes and cut into little squares to hold the paper and keep the tacks from tearing through. Because there were not enough tacks, the paper bulged in places. The kitchen 15 didn't have any wallpaper and the only furniture in it was a wood stove, an old table and a safe.

1. How has the writer used a spatial order to organize details?
2. What details support her point that her parents tried to make the shack livable?
3. Why does she devote one-fifth of the paragraph to the wallpaper?

## 2-F                          YAMACRAW
### *Pat Conroy*

This excerpt comes from *The Water Is Wide* (1972), in which the writer describes a year he spent as a teacher on Yamacraw. The book has been made into a movie, "Conrack."

Yamacraw is an island off the South Carolina mainland not far from Savannah, Georgia. The island is fringed with the green, undulating marshes of the southern coast; shrimp boats ply the waters around her and fishermen cast their lines along her bountiful shores. Deer cut through her forests in small silent herds. The great southern oaks stand broodingly on her banks. The island and 5 the waters around her teem with life. There is something eternal and indestructible about the tide-eroded shores and the dark, threatening silences of the swamps in the heart of the island. Yamacraw is beautiful because man has not yet had time to destroy this beauty.

The twentieth century has basically ignored the presence of Yamacraw. The 10 island is populated with black people who depend on the sea and their small farms for a living. . . . Thus far, no bridge connects Yamacraw with the mainland, and anyone who sets foot on the island comes by water. The roads of the island are unpaved and rutted by the passage of ox carts, still a major form of transportation. The hand pump serves up questionable water to the black resi- 15 dents who live in their small familiar houses. Sears, Roebuck catalogues perform their classic function in the crudely built privies, which sit, half-hidden, in the tall grasses behind the shacks. Electricity came to the island several years ago. There is something unquestionably moving about the line of utility poles coming across the marsh, moving perhaps because electricity is a bringer of miracles 20 and the journey of the faceless utility poles is such a long one—and such a humane one. But there are no telephones (electricity is enough of a miracle for one century). To call the island you must go to the Beaufort Sheriff's Office and talk to the man who works the radio. Otherwise, Yamacraw remains aloof and apart from the world beyond the river. 25

1. What characteristics of the island does Conroy emphasize?
2. What pattern of arrangement does he use for the details?

2-G                           THE JAPANESE TRAIN
                                 *Paul Theroux*

This excerpt comes from *The Great Railway Bazaar*, published in 1975, an account
of the writer's journey on an assortment of trains from England across Europe and Asia
and then back to England.

The bullet-nosed Hatsukari Limited Express (its name, "Early Bird," refers
to its arrival in Aomori, not its departure from Tokyo) leaves Ueno Station every
afternoon on the dot of four. Ueno is crowded with people wearing fur hats,
carrying skis and heavy coats for the snow at the end of the line: these are the
vacationers. But there are returning residents, too, smaller, darker, Eskimo- 5
faced people, on their way back to Hokkaido. The Japanese expression *nobori-
san* ("rustics") describes them: it literally means "the downers"; having taken
the *nobori* "downtrain," these visitors, country-cousins spending a holiday in
Tokyo, are considered yokels. On the train they stay in their seats, kick their
heavy shoes off, and sleep. They look relieved to be going home and carry with 10
them souvenirs from Tokyo: cookies wrapped in cellophane, flowers in paper
cones, dried fruit bound with ribbon, dolls in tissue, stuffed toys in boxes. The
Japanese are marvelous packagers of merchandise. These souvenirs are
crammed in the plastic shopping bags that form the basis of the Japanese trav-
eler's luggage. And there are other parcels, for the *nobori-san*, not trusting the 15
food on Japanese National Railways, brings his own lunch pail. When he wakes,
he rummages at his feet and discovers a sealed tin of rice and fish that, without
stretching or rising from his padded armchair, he eats, blowing and smacking.
The train itself is silent; my memory of Japanese train noises was this sound of
eating, which is also the sound of a grown man inflating a balloon.                    20
    An amplified music box, ten plunking notes, and a recorded message pre-
ceded our stops. A warning is necessary because the stops are so brief: fifteen
seconds at Minami-Urawa, a minute at Utsunomiya, and, two hours later,
another one-minute halt at Fukushima. An unprepared passenger might be
mangled by the door or might miss his stop altogether. Long before the music 25
and the message, the experienced Japanese carry their shopping bags to the exit,
and as soon as the train stops and a crack appears in the door, they begin pushing madly towards the platform. The platform, designed for laden, shopping
people, is level with the threshold. The lights in the carriages are never off,
making it impossible to sleep, but enabling a passenger to gather up his belong- 30
ings at two in the morning when the train pulls in and pauses for fifteen seconds
at his station.
    Such efficiency! Such speed! But I longed for the sprawl of Indian Railways,
the wide berths in the wooden compartments that smelled of curry and cher-
oots; the laundry chits with "camisoles" and "collars" marked on them; over the 35
sink a jug of water; and out in the hall a man with a bottle of beer on his tray:
trains that chugged to the rhythm of "Alabammy Bound" or "Chattanooga
Choo-Choo," embodying what was best in the railway bazaar. On such a slow
train it was almost impossible to get duffilled [be left behind].

The odorless Japanese trains unnerved me and produced in me a sweaty ten- 40
sion I had always associated with plane travel. They brought back the symptoms
of encapsulated terror I had felt in southern Thailand's International Express—
a kind of leaden suspense that had stolen upon me after several months of
travel. Travel—even in ideal conditions—had begun to make me anxious, and
I saw that in various places the constant movement had separated me so com- 45
pletely from my surroundings that I might have been anywhere strange, nagged
by the seamless guilt an unemployed person feels moving from failure to failure. This baffled trance overtook me on the way to Aomori, and I think it had
a great deal to do with the fact that I was traveling in a fast, dry bullet-train,
among silent people who, even if they spoke, would be incomprehensible. I was 50
trapped by the double-glazing. I couldn't even open the window! The train
swished past the bright empty platforms of rural stations at night, and for long
moments, experiencing a heightened form of the alienation I'd felt before,
briefly, in secluded pockets of time, I could not imagine where I was or why I
had come.   55

1. How has the writer organized his details?
2. Which details in the first two paragraphs prepare us for the author's feeling of tension and alienation described in the third and fourth paragraphs?
3. What details appeal to our senses?
4. Where does Theroux use comparisons (metaphors and similes)?
5. What examples can you find of onomatopoetic words?

**2-H**                          TIMSHEL
                         *Pat Vance (student)*

During the summer of my nineteenth year, I began to do some serious thinking about how I would spend the remaining three-score years that God might
see fit to give me. With the idea of seeing as many facets of life as possible, I
applied for summer work at a center for retarded children. What I saw, what
I heard, and what I felt during my first hour at Western Carolina Center have 5
gone into a mental file marked "Learn and Grow." These sixty minutes have a
most important spot in that file.

I first saw the Center on a sunny May morning. It looked the way most
schools would like to look. Its manicured lawns extended north, south, east, and
west, the flawless green expanse broken only by small beds of fragrant roses. A 10
black bracelet of pavement encircled the grounds, drawing attention to the
almost geometrical layout of the buildings. The structures themselves, brick and
glass tributes to the ingenuity of man, were the latest word in modernity. Nine
of them, long, low, and flat-roofed, seemed to be clinging to the landscape as if
to draw strength from the earth. Two others stood on sharp rises, lifting pointed 15
roofs toward the blue heavens as if in supplication for help with the need housed
within their walls.

Contrary to my expectations, there were no bars on the doors or windows, no iron fences, no restraining walls. The patients were not restricted in any way. Hordes of screaming children swarmed everywhere, playing tag, hide-and-go- 20 seek, and other games for which names have not been devised. Up and down, around and around they ran, young vikings with shocks of hair the color of ripe corn and yelling gypsies with dark limpid eyes. These were the Einsteins of the Center; their intelligence measured in the seventies, eighties, nineties—even one hundred and above. 25

Watching them from the shaded nooks of the buildings were the children who, for one reason or another, would not or could not take part in the activity. Here was the boy who had such a severe emotional problem that he could do nothing but talk of religion; here was the boy who was deathly afraid of letting the sunlight touch him; here was the girl who was just learning to walk—at age 30 twenty-five; here was the boy who was so badly deformed that he would not speak or be spoken to.

And these children were far removed from the ones still to be seen. Within the buildings dwelt the pariahs. Some had known neither love nor joy nor family nor friends. Often their entire vocabulary was one word—"Mamma"—and 35 no mother to answer the call because she no longer admitted the existence of this, her child. Others dwelt in private worlds all their own—worlds of no hatred or pain, no strife or envy. They simply sat, day after day, staring vacantly into space, being fed, bathed, and clothed by more intelligent hands. Here also dwelt the hydrocephalics and microcephalics, the birth-injured, the 40 severely deformed. Here were the creatures barred from an outside world that could not face their imperfections. Not for that world the children at Western Carolina Center who had to be tied to their chairs because they could not sit alone; not for it the children here who had to wear gloves constantly in order to keep from swallowing their hands; not for it the bodies here locked in gro- 45 tesque positions—bodies that had to be massaged and straightened and pushed and pulled frequently in order to keep the blood in circulation. No, none of this was its concern.

But someone has to be concerned. Twelve weeks, I meditated, would be a long, long while to work with these mentally retarded. But a lifetime is a long 50 while to be mentally retarded.

1. What part does place have in the order of what is described?
2. Could the writer's expository purpose be fulfilled without the descriptive details here? Check those that you find particularly effective.

## ASSIGNMENTS

1. Make the following bare statements vivid through descriptive details, using concrete nouns, verbs, adjectives and adverbs to evoke a particular situation and mood. Then rewrite each in different words so that you present an entirely different picture.

*Example:* A child was looking out of a window.

> A chubby girl of six with a tangle of brown curls pivoted on her stomach across the window ledge as she surveyed the empty street with a bored stare.

> A skinny, undersized girl of six, her matted brown hair hanging to her shoulders and her smudged cheeks streaked by tears, shivered fearfully in a corner of the window as she peered through the slats in the Venetian blind at the angry, shouting mob in the street below.

    a. A car went by.
    b. The rain fell.
    c. The music began.
    d. The man started to speak.
    e. The woman stood still.
    f. The crowd began to move.

2. Replace the following trite descriptions with fresher ones.
    *Example:* My feet felt as cold as ice.

> My feet felt like gravestones in a lonely cemetery.

    a. You look as fresh as a daisy.
    b. He turned as white as a sheet.
    c. The price of steak has gone sky-high.
    d. We laughed our heads off.
    e. The flowers danced in the breeze.

3. a. Imagine yourself somewhere alone in the dark, obliged to rely on senses other than sight, and write a paragraph describing your sensations.
    b. Then imagine yourself in the same place in daylight with a blind person, and write another paragraph describing it to that person.

4. Choose one of the photographs on pages 89–92. What in it first catches your attention? Why? Compose a paragraph of about 150 words explaining your answers to these questions. Imagine that your readers will be from one of the following groups, and indicate which you have chosen: (a) people living and working in small towns; (b) people living and working in large cities; (c) elderly people; (d) students in your college; (e) tourists from foreign countries who want to learn about American life.

5. Choose one of the photographs on pages 89–92, and compose a detailed description of it in about 250 words. Imagine that you will read your description to another student who is suffering from temporary eye trouble and who wants to be able to follow class discussion of the photograph.

5. a. Using strictly informative words, describe your room at home or at college so factually and accurately that the reader could readily draw a floor plan, complete with furnishings.
    b. Then write an evocative description of the same place, determining before you start exactly how you wish your reader to react and choosing your details carefully to evoke that reaction.

6. Write an exposition of some personal experience, enlivening it by the generous use of whatever descriptive devices you find suitable, particularly those that will evoke for the reader the sensations you yourself experienced. Look through the examples of descriptive writing in this unit for suggestions. Other possible subjects (which may remind you of still better ones) are getting up on a cold morning, attending a football game, participating in a swimming meet, riding on a roller coaster or an

iceboat or in a racing car or a small plane, eating at a quick-lunch counter, visiting a fair or a stockyard, attending a religious service or a wedding reception.

7. Study the use of description as an aid to exposition in other examples, particularly Unit 1-A, B, and C; Unit 3-A and E; Unit 4-D; Unit 5-A and C; Unit 8-B and F; Unit 9-E; Unit 10-D; Unit 11-H. Determine whether the authors are using description informatively or evocatively and how effective it is, making a note of what seem to you to be particularly successful descriptive words, phrases, or figures of speech.

# UNIT 3

# *Narration*

Narration and description strengthen expository writing by involving readers personally, not just informing them. Both particularize rather than generalize, and both deal in the concrete rather than the abstract. Together, not only in art forms such as the novel and the short story but also in more practical forms such as news reports, history, and biography, they contribute to readers' understanding and enjoyment. They can enliven otherwise dull and workaday expository writing as well—the feature article, the letter, the college English theme, the term report, even the examination paper.

The essence of description is its record of the senses; of narration, its report of events. Description adds reality to all sorts of writing by giving readers an illusion of experiencing the sensations described; narration adds reality by giving readers the illusion of experiencing events. By satisfying our ever-present natural curiosity as to what happened, it adds both immediate reading interest and lasting effect to what otherwise might be tedious even though useful.

## *Narration as an Aid to Exposition*

Your uses of narration as an aid in exposition may vary from the insertion of a little narrative incident, an anecdote, to enliven explanatory matter, to constructing a complete narrative framework in which your expository purpose may only be implied.

**1. A brief narrative as introduction.** A serious discussion may start with an anecdote to catch the reader's interest; speakers often begin with a funny story to put the audience in a receptive mood. Such an anecdote may be merely humorous or may also be provocative, but it should be related in thought to your main idea and should lead your readers pleasantly into the main body of your essay. For example, the story of the three blind men who each felt a different part of the elephant and formed a different idea of what the animal was like could appropriately begin a discussion of some serious social problem that you feel is largely the result of misunderstanding.

**2. Brief narratives throughout the main body.** Use them not only to stimulate interest but to illustrate difficult or important points in your thought by making the points more understandable and vivid.

**3. A long narrative as the main body.** Half the essay or even more may be narrative, ending with an expository discussion of the point made. Look, for example, at the parables of Jesus, in which an applicable story is told and then interpreted. The interpretation may not only explain but may also expand the idea that the story presents more memorably. The familiar old *Aesop's Fables* are almost entirely narrative, with only a single final line stating the expository purpose, the "moral."

**4. A narrative as the entire essay.** An account of a process or an activity that lists consecutive actions or events is essentially narration; yet it is intended, of course, to explain, and as such is basically informative rather than entertaining. More obvious forms of narrative, besides the fable, are the allegory, such as Bunyan's *Pilgrim's Progress*, in which what seems at first to be only storytelling is really a symbolic presentation of deeper moral meanings; the satire, such as Swift's *Gulliver's Travels*, in which the adventures in the land of the little and the big peoples afford children sheer narrative delight but give adults a series of thought-provoking commentaries on human failings; and the "social purpose" novel of the present century, which, though fiction, concentrates on some problem of which the story is merely an illustration. The experiences of the Joad family in Steinbeck's *Grapes of Wrath*, for instance, exemplify the economic distress of the dust-bowl farmers generally. In all these forms, the "moral," or expository meaning, is usually only implied, but it is nevertheless clearly present. Completely narrative in substance, such works are thoroughly expository in purpose.

## Narrative Techniques

Whether you plan to use narrative as an overall device or only in anecdotes, you should take full advantage of the effects that narrative can achieve. The strength of narrative lies in its ability to create an illusion of reality, whether or not the story is true. It does this through three devices: **characters** (people, or animals, or personified concepts), **setting** (a place and a time), and **plot** (an ordered series of events involving those characters in that setting).

**1. Creating reader interest.** Contrary to popular opinion, some of the most successful storytelling springs from the commonplaces of existence. Your choice of narrative material will be determined by the purpose of your essay, but neither a plane crash nor a sandlot ball game, a trip around the world nor a backyard picnic, can guarantee that you will write an effective story. Your handling of it is what matters.

    **a.** Choose an event that has **significance** for you—an emotional force or an intellectual meaning that you can pass on to your readers. If your only point about a trip is that "We went to Key West" or about a ball game that "Our side won," your narrative will not interest your readers. The more strongly you care about the event you choose, the more likely you are to make it interesting for your readers, and your point of view, whether humorous, whimsical, or serious, will give it unity.

**b.** All narratives should have **suspense.** They should make readers want to know what happened next, who won, what was the final outcome.

**c.** This interest in the outcome is based primarily on **conflict**—whether mild or intense—between characters, between character and circumstance, between conflicting desires within a single character's mind. Two students striving to win the same honor, a man attempting to recover his lost health, a teenager torn between love for parents and for a sweetheart—all these conflicts and similar ones create suspense.

**d.** Narrative incidents should build up progressively to the **climax,** the highest point of interest. Some narratives stop short at that point, as O. Henry did with his "surprise endings"; others coast more slowly to a close. Any material included after the peak of interest has been reached is likely to seem anticlimactic and dull.

**2. Handling time.** Description deals primarily with objects in space, but narration deals primarily with events in time.

**a.** For short incidents the normal time order of start to finish may be successfully retained; for longer ones it is often more effective to begin in the midst of the action (at an exciting point, of course, for the sake of reader interest), returning later to fill in briefly any necessary background. Compare these two ways of handling the same material:

(1) One fine April afternoon three of us sixth-grade boys decided to skip school. We wandered indecisively for an hour or two through the outskirts of the town and finally landed at the ball park, where we began a game of old cat, doubly delightful because illicitly enjoyed. Bill finally hit the ball over the fence, where it went through the window of the caretaker's cottage.

(2) "Home run!" yelled Bill triumphantly, leaning on his bat while he watched the ball he had just struck sail over the park fence. But his triumph was short—a shattering of glass from the caretaker's cottage struck us all numb. A broken window on top of our earlier sin! For we three sixth-grade boys had skipped school that fine April afternoon, and after an hour or so of indecisive wandering through the outskirts of town had wound up at the ball park for a game of old cat—doubly delightful because illicitly enjoyed.

**b.** You are free, in narration, to compress or expand the time element to suit your purpose, getting rid of ten unimportant years in less than a sentence and spending pages, if need be, to recount the profound events of ten seconds. Such a handling of time, skillfully done, will help you to emphasize incidents important to your purpose and to ignore unimportant ones.

**3. Creating the illusion of reality.** Such violent compression and expansion of time can be justified on the grounds that we sometimes live through moments that seem like years and through years that later may seem like moments. Since the effectiveness of narrative depends on an illusion of reality, you should consider every device that can help to establish that illusion.

**a.** The **present tense** for events in the past can create an impression of immediacy, as in "Then I start to run, and he throws to first, but Mac fumbles the ball." Take care to use tenses consistently in any given part of your narrative.

**b. Concrete** and **specific diction** is as important to narrative as it is to description. Help your readers to see and hear the events you narrate (and to smell, taste, and feel them if they involve other sensations). In dialogue, for instance, if the speakers' emotions are revealed by their tone of voice, choose verbs that suggest the tone, such as *mutter, sigh,* or *yell.* (Caution: Do not over do this. Vigorous words call attention to themselves. If what is said is important but not the manner of speaking, a simple *said* will be better.)

**c. Dialogue,** directly transcribed, is more lifelike and often more compact than indirect reporting of what was said. For example, compare the directly reported dialogue in "Yumbo" (page 47) with this indirectly reported version:

> The eruptive girl at the counter asked what the man wanted. He repeated that he wished to order a ham and cheese sandwich. The girl said that she was sorry but that they did not carry ham and cheese sandwiches. All that they had was what was on the menu board above her.

If you must make up the dialogue, take care that the content and the manner of speaking are both appropriate to the speakers. For the conventional methods of punctuating dialogue, consult a handbook and note the examples in this unit.

**d. Characters, setting,** and **details** should be as real and vivid as the events of the narrative. Action does not occur in a vacuum. Give carefully chosen descriptions to show your readers when, where, and how it takes place. Also show them briefly—through speech, action, and specific details of appearance, rather than through long expository characterizations—the kinds of people to whom it is happening. Readers cannot have much interest in "us" if they are never told who "we" are. Compare these two versions of the same incident:

> (1) We had been working for an hour to get our truck jacked up so that my companion could change a tire that had gone flat on our way to town. Once more the jack slipped, and he started to try yet again.
> (2) The slab of wood on which the jack was resting tilted gently into the roadside ooze and let the rear of the heavy truck down for the third time in that hour of mud and sweat.

> "Dang it! Er—pardon me, miss" was the only reaction of the patient, elderly "hired hand" who was helping me to deliver my load of sheep. Without another word he gave his suspenders a hitch and crawled doggedly under the truck to try again.

**e. Personal experience** is always the best source of narrative material. A student once wrote very dramatically of a parachute jump; but errors in reporting fact revealed what she later confessed—that she had never so much as been up in an airplane. Some professional writers of fiction can produce the illusion of reality even when they have not actually known the people, visited the scenes, or experienced the events they describe. As a beginning writer, however, you will be wise to base your narratives entirely on your own experience in order to have the virtues of firsthand material and sincerity. But you should, of course, select and handle events to give them the unity and concentration that real life rarely has.

## EXAMPLES

3-A

YUMBO
*Andrew Ward*

This short essay appeared in the *Atlantic Monthly* in 1977. The writer narrates two experiences to illustrate his reasons for disliking the practices of some fast-food restaurants.

| | |
|---|---|
| NARRATIVE DEVICES<br>setting, character | I was sitting at an inn with Kelly Susan, my ten-year-old niece, when she was handed the children's menu. It was printed in gay pastels on construction paper and gave her a choice of a Ferdinand Burger, a Freddie the Fish Stick, |
| generalization | or a Porky Pig Sandwich. Like most children's menus, it 5 first anthropomorphized the ingredients and then killed them off. As Kelly read it her eyes grew large, and in them I could see gentle Ferdinand being led away to the stock-yard, Freddie gasping at the end of a hook, Porky stutter-ing his entreaties as the ax descended. Kelly Susan, alone 10 |
| details | in her family, is a resolute vegetarian and has already faced up to the dread that whispers to us as we slice our steaks. She wound up ordering a cheese sandwich, but the chil-dren's menu had ruined her appetite, and she spent the meal picking at her food. 15 |
| generalization | Restaurants have always treated children badly. When I was small, my family used to travel a lot, and waitresses |
| details | were forever calling me "Butch" and pinching my cheeks and making me wear paper bibs with slogans on them. Res- |
| generalization | taurants still treat children badly; the difference is that res- 20 taurants have lately taken to treating us all as if we were children. We are obliged to order an Egg McMuffin when |
| details | we want breakfast, a Fishamajig when we want a fish sand-wich, a Fribble when we want a milkshake, a Whopper |

when we want a hamburger with all the fixings. Some of 25
these names serve a certain purpose. By calling a milkshake
a Fribble, for instance, the management need make no
promise that it contains milk, or even that it was shaken.

generalization

But the primary purpose is to convert an essentially
bleak industry, mass-marketed fast foods, into something 30
festive. The burger used to be a culinary last resort; now
resorts are being built around it. The patrons in the com-

details

mercials for burger franchises are all bug-eyed and goofy,
be they priests or grandmothers or crane operators, and
behave as if it were their patriotic duty, their God-given 35
right, to consume waxy buns, translucent patties, chewy
fries, and industrial strength Coca-Cola.

setting, character

Happily, the patrons who actually slump into these
places are an entirely different matter. I remember with
fond admiration a tidy little man at the local Burger King 40
whom I overheard order a ham and cheese sandwich.

"A wha'?" the eruptive girl at the counter asked, pencil
poised over her computer card.

"I wish to order a ham and cheese sandwich," the man
repeated.                                                        45

dialogue

"I'm sorry, sir," the girl said, "but we don't carry ham
and cheese. All we got is what's on the board up there."

"Yes, I know," the man politely persisted, "but I believe
it is up there. See? The ham and cheese?"

The girl gaped at the menu board behind her. "Oh," she 50
finally exclaimed. "You mean a *Yumbo*. You want a
*Yumbo*."

"The ham and cheese. Yes."

conflict

"It's called a *Yumbo*, sir," the girl said. "Now, do you
want a Yumbo or not?"                                            55

The man stiffened. "Yes, thank you," he said through his

suspense

teeth, "the *ham* and *cheese*."

"Look," the girl shouted, "I've got to have an order here.
You're holding up the line. You want a *Yumbo*, don't you?
You want a *Yumbo*?"                                            60

But the tidy man was not going to say it, and thus were
they locked for a few more moments, until at last he stood
very straight, put on his hat, and departed intact.

1. Where does the writer first state his thesis?
2. How are the generalizations placed in relation to the specific details?
3. In the second illustration how does the writer indicate the stages of increasing tension between the counter girl and the man?
4. The first illustration contains no dialogue. Why is it unnecessary here?

*3-B*                A LOAF OF BREAD AND THE STARS
                         *Richard Wright*

Wright narrates this experience in his autobiography, *Black Boy* (1937), in which a
major point is his struggle growing up black in a white-dominated society.

One day I went to the optical counter of a department store to deliver a pair
of eyeglasses. The counter was empty of customers and a tall, florid-faced white
man looked at me curiously. He was unmistakably a Yankee, for his physical
build differed sharply from that of the lanky Southerner.

"Will you please sign for this, sir?" I asked, presenting the account book and   5
the eyeglasses.

He picked up the book and the glasses, but his eyes were still upon me.

"Say, boy, I'm from the North," he said quietly.

I held very still. Was this a trap? He had mentioned a tabooed subject and I
wanted to wait until I knew what he meant. Among the topics that southern    10
white men do not like to discuss with Negroes were the following: American
white women; the Ku Klux Klan; France, and how Negro soldiers fared while
there; Frenchwomen; Jack Johnson; the entire northern part of the United
States; the Civil War; Abraham Lincoln; U. S. Grant; General Sherman; Catholics; the Pope; Jews; the Republican party; slavery; social equality; Commu-    15
nism; Socialism; the 13th, 14th, and 15th Amendments to the Constitution or
any topic calling for positive knowledge or manly self-assertion on the part of
the Negro. The most accepted topics were sex and religion. I did not look at the
man or answer. With one sentence he had lifted out of the silent dark the race
question and I stood on the edge of a precipice.                              20

"Don't be afraid of me," he went on. "I just want to ask you one question."

"Yes, sir," I said in a waiting, neutral tone.

"Tell me, boy, are you hungry?" he asked seriously.

I stared at him. He had spoken one word that touched the very soul of me,
but I could not talk to him, could not let him know that I was starving myself    25
to save money to go north. I did not trust him. But my face did not change its
expression.

"Oh, no, sir," I said, managing a smile.

I was hungry and he knew it; but he was a white man and I felt that if I told
him I was hungry I would have been revealing something shameful.              30

"Boy, I can see hunger in your face and eyes," he said.

"I get enough to eat," I lied.

"Then why do you keep so thin?" he asked me.

"Well, I suppose I'm just that way, naturally," I lied.

"You're just scared, boy," he said.                                          35

"Oh, no, sir," I lied again.

I could not look at him. I wanted to leave the counter, yet he was a white
man and I had learned not to walk abruptly away from a white man when he
was talking to me. I stood, my eyes looking away. He ran his hand into his
pocket and pulled out a dollar bill.                                         40

"Here, take this dollar and buy yourself some food," he said.

"No, sir," I said.

"Don't be a fool," he said. "You're ashamed to take it. God, boy, don't let a thing like that stop you from taking a dollar and eating."

The more he talked the more it became impossible for me to take the dollar. 45 I wanted it, but I could not look at it. I wanted to speak, but I could not move my tongue. I wanted him to leave me alone. He frightened me.

"Say something," he said.

All about us in the store were piles of goods; white men and women went from counter to counter. It was summer and from a high ceiling was suspended 50 a huge electric fan that whirred. I stood waiting for the white man to give me the signal that would let me go.

"I don't understand it," he said through his teeth. "How far did you go in school?"

"Through the ninth grade, but it was really the eighth," I told him. "You see, 55 our studies in the ninth grade were more or less a review of what we had in the eighth grade."

Silence. He had not asked me for this long explanation, but I had spoken at length to fill up the yawning, shameful gap that loomed between us; I had spoken to try to drag the unreal nature of the conversation back to safe and sound 60 southern ground. Of course, the conversation was real; it dealt with my welfare, but it had brought to the surface of day all the dark fears I had known all my life. The Yankee white man did not know how dangerous his words were.

(There are some elusive, profound, recondite things that men find hard to say to other men; but with the Negro it is the little things of life that become hard 65 to say, for these tiny items shape his destiny. A man will seek to express his relation to the stars; but when a man's consciousness has been riveted upon obtaining a loaf of bread, that loaf of bread is as important as the stars.)

Another white man walked up to the counter and I sighed with relief.

"Do you want the dollar?" the man asked.                                          70

"No, sir," I whispered.

"All right," he said. "Just forget it."

He signed the account book and took the eyeglasses. I stuffed the book into my bag and turned from the counter and walked down the aisle, feeling a physical tingling along my spine, knowing that the white man knew I was really 75 hungry. I avoided him after that. Whenever I saw him I felt in a queer way that he was my enemy, for he knew how I felt and the safety of my life in the South depended upon how well I concealed from all whites what I felt.

---

1. Where does Wright place his chief expository remarks?
2. How is this placement different from that in the first example of narrative used for an expository purpose?
3. What would have been the effect if Wright had placed all of them at the very end? at the beginning?

*3-C*                              A NEW LIFE
                          *Carl Granville (student)*

It was 9:26 P.M. on December 11th, 1974. I had awaited this moment nine months. I had left work early to be by her side. She was always adamant that I should be there when it happened.

She had been in the labor room for almost ten hours. The endless screams from the woman in the next room made my wife become more and more 5 frightened. As gently as possible, I tried to calm her, but I myself had been having doubts. What if something went wrong? What if their lives were in danger? My fears were forgotten as the baby's head began to emerge. I felt a sparkling tingle throughout my body. What a moment! The birth of my child!

"Mr. Granville, you'll have to leave now." Pause.                             10

"Sir, you'll have to leave now." The voice was firm, official.

It was like being rudely interrupted in the middle of a wonderful dream, and a full minute elapsed before I realized what was happening. I started to speak, but seeing the futility of a protest, I dejectedly left the room. At 9:35 P.M. they whisked her off to the delivery room.                                          15

Here I am in the waiting room. There are three more expectant fathers present. One is anxiously wearing out the carpet, pacing up and down. Another seems nervously impatient. The third one, seated in a corner away from the rest, seems to be in a daze. I sit and try to read a book.

"This is your first?" asks the impatient one.                                20

"Uhh?"

"This your first?"

"Oh, yes . . . yes."

"This is my third. I got two girls already. Man, girls cost too much, but with my old lady always wrapped around me, what else can I do?"                    25

My sudden laughter disrupts the pacer and breaks the trance of the man in the corner.

"Oh, man," the talkative one goes on, "she's been in there for about a half-hour already. What the hell's keeping them this long?"

My analysis was right. He is impatient. Five minutes later the nurse 30 amnounces that he has girl number three. He shakes my hand gloomily and wishes me luck as he leaves. Immediately after, a very broad smile runs across the face of the man in the corner. He has just heard that his wife has given birth to an eight-pound boy.

I put down the book. "I hope I get a boy, too," I think. I start to imagine all 35 the fun we will have together. Why, when he's six, I'll only be twenty-six myself. He will be "wicked" but obedient. He will be just like his daddy. We will have such fun. Please, please, let it be a boy.

The pacer leaves to purchase a soda. We have exchanged only a few words so far. In his absence the nurse appears to announce that his wife gave birth to 40 a ten-pound boy. I find that his wife is the woman who was screaming. I greet him with the news as he returns, and his face lights up like a Christmas tree.

He startles me with a tremendous shout of glee. I cannot help feeling happy for him. The joy in his face is overwhelming. Now more than ever I want a boy.

The nurse appears again. "Mr. Granville, your wife gave birth to a girl. She weighs six pounds, eleven ounces." 45

The time is 10:11 P.M. For the second time tonight I feel throbs of depression. My wife is aware of this as I stand by her bed. She reminds me that I should be thankful that she and the baby came through in good health. I feel ashamed at my show of depression. Oh, but I so wanted a boy. How can I have much fun 50 with a girl? Try as I do, it's hard to shake off the depression that engulfs me. After half-heartedly joking with my wife for a while, I leave for home.

I buy myself a tall can of beer to celebrate my parenthood and I telephone my best friend to let him know the news. While I am chatting with him, a new thought dawns. What important difference, other than sexual, is there between 55 a boy and a girl? I mean, why can't I have as much fun with a girl as I think I will have with a boy? Why try to put people into pigeonholes? Why don't I give her a chance to prove herself?

The next day at 8:40 A.M. I present myself at the Kings County Hospital, maternity section. I am joyful with a vibrant new perspective, evident in my 60 bounce and spirit. I kiss my baby and look upon her not as a girl or boy, but as a living, capable, human being. I ask my wife's forgiveness for my behavior last night and tell her how much I love her for bringing us closer together through our baby.

Now, two years later, I could not be happier as a father. I have kept my 65 resolution to treat my daughter as a human being, which in turn has made me more appreciative of my wife. The fun that I have with my daughter goes way beyond my expectations; the joy she has brought into my life can never be described in mere words. She surely has had a positive effect in changing my attitude towards others, sex notwithstanding. As a matter of fact, I could not 70 care less whether my next baby is a boy or a girl.

I'll always treasure my daughter for this change in me, but right now all I can do is reflect on the beauty, the mystery, the sweetness, the power of life and love. Thank you, Chère, and you, too, Pauline.

1. Why does the author begin with verbs in the past tense and then shift to verbs in the present tense?
2. What do the references to the specific times and the descriptions of the other expectant fathers contribute? Why is the nurse only a voice?

---

*3-D*                   THE LOGICAL CAB DRIVER
                        *David Schoenbrun*

This anecdote appears in *As France Goes* (1957), which presents the writer's views on France and the French, gained from his long experience living there as a political correspondent for the *New York Times*.

The "intellectualism" of the French is found at every level of society. The café waiter, the taxicab driver, the restaurateur, the so-called "little people" of France are the most stimulating, if frequently exasperating, conversationalists in the world. Of them all, the most anarchistic and voluble is the taxicab driver. I deliberately provoke arguments with them—an easy thing to do—to see what they will say next. Of the hundreds of discussions in cabs one remains in my memory as uniquely, superbly French. It could not have occurred in any other country, except possibly in Brooklyn, where there exists a species of man akin in spirit if not in actual form to the French.

It was midnight in Paris and we were rolling along the Quai d'Orsay toward the Avenue Bosquet, where I live, on the left bank of the river Seine. As we came to the Pont Alexandre III the cab slowed down, for the traffic light was red against us, and then, without stopping, we sailed through the red light in a sudden burst of speed. The same performance was repeated at the Alma Bridge. As I paid the driver I asked him why he had driven through two red lights.

"You ought to be ashamed of yourself, a veteran like you, breaking the law and endangering your life that way," I protested.

He looked at me astonished. "Ashamed of myself? Why, I'm proud of myself. I am a law-abiding citizen and have no desire to get killed either." He cut me off before I could protest.

"No, just listen to me before you complain. What did I do? Went through a red light. Well, did you ever stop to consider what a red light is, what it means?"

"Certainly," I replied. "It's a stop signal and means that traffic is rolling in the opposite direction."

"Half-right," said the driver, "but incomplete. It is only an automatic stop signal. And it does not mean that there is cross traffic. Did you see any cross traffic during our trip? Of course not. I slowed down at the light, looked carefully to the right and to the left. Not another car on the streets at this hour. Well, then! What would you have me do? Should I stop like a dumb animal because an automatic, brainless machine turns red every forty seconds? No, monsieur," he thundered, hitting the door jamb with a huge fist. "I am a man, not a machine. I have eyes and a brain and judgment, given me by God. It would be a sin against nature to surrender them to the dictates of a machine. Ashamed of myself, you say? I would only be ashamed of myself if I let those blinking lamps do my thinking for me. Good night, monsieur."

Is this bad, is this good? Frankly I no longer am sure. The intellectual originality of the French is a corrupting influence if you are subjected to it for long. I never doubted that it was wrong to drive through a red light. After more than a decade of life in Paris, however, I find my old Anglo-Saxon standards somewhat shaken. I still think it is wrong to drive through a stop signal, except possibly very late at night, after having carefully checked to make sure there is no cross traffic. After all, I am a man, not a machine.

1. The writer wants us to see his experience as an illustration of his generalization that

the French have great intellectual originality. What narrative devices does he use to try to make us share his experience and hear and see the cab driver?

2. The writer could have told the anecdote in far fewer words if he had summarized much of what he and the driver said instead of reporting it in full. What would be lost in a shorter version?

3. Although the writer quotes five statements, he uses "said" only once (line 25). How does he indicate elsewhere the speaker and tone of voice?

---

3-E                              ON A COMMUTER TRAIN
                                      *Willie Morris*

This anecdote appears in *North Towards Home* (1967), Willie Morris's autobiographical account of his experiences growing up in a small Mississippi town and then working in New York. Throughout the book, he emphasizes the respect, or lack of it, shown by Americans toward each other. Although no thesis statement appears in this excerpt, Morris implies his dismay at the impersonality of life in a big city.

One afternoon in late August, as the summer's sun streamed into the car and made little jumping shadows on the windows, I sat gazing out at the tenement-dwellers, who were themselves looking out of their windows from the gray crumbling buildings along the tracks of upper Manhattan. As we crossed into the Bronx, the train unexpectedly slowed down for a few miles. Suddenly from 5 out of my window I saw a large crowd near the tracks, held back by two policemen. Then, on the other side from my window, I saw a sight I would never be able to forget: a little boy almost severed in halves, lying at an incredible angle near the track. The ground was covered with blood, and the boy's eyes were opened wide, strained and disbelieving in his sudden oblivion. A policeman 10 stood next to him, his arms folded, staring straight ahead at the windows of our train. In the orange glow of late afternoon the policemen, the crowd, the corpse of the boy were for a brief moment immobile, motionless, a small tableau to violence and death in the city. Behind me, in the next row of seats, there was a game of bridge. I heard one of the four men say as he looked out at the sight, 15 "God, that's horrible." Another said, in a whisper, "Terrible, terrible." There was a momentary silence, punctuated only by the clicking of the wheels on the track. Then, after the pause, I heard the first man say: "Two hearts."

1. Is Morris necessarily condemning the man who resumes the bidding?

2. Why does Morris repeat three times in one sentence that the scene was still, saying that everything was "immobile, motionless, a small tableau"?

3. An incident that presents such a dramatic contrast in behavior in such a short space may seem like a writer's attempt to find an easy way to impress readers. What of Morris's own role in this narrative and the fact that, like the card players, he is shut in a moving train and cannot be more than a spectator?

*3-F*                              CONFLICT
                        *Roger A. Painter (student)*

The writer begins by narrating three incidents to illustrate his point and lead to his
expository discussion. Note how the ending unifies the essay.

He came into the house quietly and made sure the door was locked. He
walked silently to his bedroom and turned the lamp on low-beam.
    "Where have you been?"
    "Mother, I've been out."
    "What were you doing?"                                                    5
    "Mother, I was out."
    "Who were you with?"
    "Mother, please go to sleep. I was out."
    "But what were you doing this late?"
    "Mother, if you didn't live here and I went to school here you wouldn't know  10
I was out and it wouldn't bother you."
    "But I'm worried."
    "I know, Mother. It is late. Good night."
                              •   •   •

    "Where were you?"
    "Hello."                                                                  15
His bicycle had jangled as he put the kickstand down and the sound brought
her to the door.
    "I was studying."
    "Have you had supper?"
    "Yes."                                                                    20
    "Where?"
    "At the Union."
    "I had supper for you."
    "I'm sorry. I tried to call."
                              •   •   •

    "You can't go to class in that outfit."                                   25
    "Why not?"
    "You have better shoes than that. Those things look like your parents don't
give you any money."
    "This is what I feel like wearing today."
    "You had better not leave with those shoes on."                          30
    "I'm almost late now—good-bye."
    "Change them."
    "Good-bye."
                              •   •   •

With these sketches I hope to illustrate the sometimes trivial, but nevertheless
real conflict from which I draw certain conclusions. Residing under the wings  35

of the hen in the postadolescent years may cause problems that, while seemingly only trivial at the time, collectively produce an amount of friction that makes smoke.

Living at home has advantages for the college student: automobile, cheap room and board, and a vast number of other benefits easily enumerated by most 40 parents. These things tend to build dependence on parents that is hard to break later on. At school, attendance is not taken in most classes, daily assignments are not collected, and students are, to a large extent, on their own. The campus students, in most cases, must keep a watch on their money supply, their time, and their actions, and in general must learn to get along without their parents. 45 This is a part of education that I miss.

I am rebellious, as is natural at my age, and, whereas the campus students take this feeling out in actions and bull-sessions with their friends, I take it out on my parents. This isolation and lack of communication with campus life is one of the greatest problems the "townies" have to cope with. The effort to fit 50 in socially is hampered by the fact that many campus organizations and activities are organized on the housing-unit basis: intramurals, dances, programs, and a large number of lesser things. But it is hard to justify a separate residence and its expense for these activities alone.

The questions and conflicts are many, and I think that the conflict of interest 55 will inevitably cause a break. If the break is hastened by prolonged and forced confrontation, it is less likely to be friendly. The on-campus student does not have the burden of forcing such a break, and I think this is much better. It is a real problem that I face, and it is not an easy one.

"What are you writing?" 60

"A rhetoric theme, Mother."


## ASSIGNMENTS

1. Think back to your earliest memories of school. What incident stands out most? Why? Compose a narrative about it in which you give your readers the details they need to be able to share the experience and relive it with you.

2. Choose a personal experience for which an old proverb such as "He who hesitates is lost," "A stitch in time saves nine," "A friend in need is a friend indeed," "Man proposes, God disposes," or "Penny-wise but pound-foolish" would make an appropriate title. Then narrate the experience briefly in such a way that your readers will see your point with little or no direct explanation from you.

3. Imagine that the editor of a magazine that tries to appeal to the "general reader" plans to use one of the photographs on pages 89–92 and has asked you to write a narrative of about 300 to 500 words for which the photograph would be an appropriate illustration. You may draw on your own experience, actual events, your imagination, or any combination of these.

4. Most well-known children's stories have strong moral points. Choose a familiar one such as "Little Red Ridinghood," "Cinderella," or "Jack and the Beanstalk" and

retell it with specific descriptive detail and as much suspense as you can create, building up to the moral point. Imagine that you will read your version to an intelligent, appreciative child about seven or eight years old.

5. Use the plot of the same story or a similar one, but this time give it a modern setting and logical explanations for any fantastic elements. Imagine that your readers will be people of your age and general interests.

6. Choose any fairly short television drama or comedy that you have enjoyed and that made a strong point. Retell it as a story, with full background detail.

7. Choose an editorial with which you agree and compose a short anecdote that illustrates its point in some way and that could therefore be used to introduce it.

8. Study the contribution that narrative makes to exposition in examples in other units, noting what elements of narrative technique have been used most successfully: Unit 1-C; Unit 4-D and E; Unit 5-A and C; Unit 8-F; Unit 9-E and G; Unit 10-E and H; Unit 11-E and H; Unit 12-C, D, F, and I; Unit 13-A, E, F, and G; Unit 14-C, D, and H; Unit 15-D and G; Unit 16-A, E, and F; Unit 17-A and I.

# UNIT 4

# *Characterization*

Throughout your life you will need the ability to judge the characters of others correctly. You will choose friends, instructors, student government officers, public officials, employers, employees, and a husband or a wife.

Characterization is a means of presenting, in written form, your interpretation of someone's personality. A letter home about your classmates, special date, faculty adviser, instructors; a report on the qualifications of a fellow student for a campus office; an answer to an examination question on a figure in history, current affairs, or fiction—all involve the same general mental process. Successful characterization, like description and narration, is basically a matter of selection. You must choose the large and small details that will make your reader see and understand the person you are describing. Often, a characterization attempts to interpret as well as to describe—to go beyond mere *showing* into the realm of *explaining*. Characterizations fall into two categories, depending on the subject and the writer's treatment: the individual and the type. Examples A, B, C, D, and E in this unit present individuals; F, G, and the paragraph in question 4 on Example G present types.

## *Characterization of an Individual*

The characterization of an individual requires particular details. Human interest, as we have seen with description and narration, lies in the concrete, the specific, rather than in the abstract, the general. We are more likely to be concerned about "Jane Blake" or "Jack Emmons" than about "the student."

Successful characterization may draw on many different sources of information about the person who is the subject. The physical appearance, favorite topics of conversation and manner of speaking, actions, beliefs, interests, habits, hobbies, relationships with others—these combine to reveal personality. But whatever your sources, remember that as readers we would rather be *shown* than *told*. Compare, for example, the following paragraphs. The first, about a famous football coach, attempts so much in so short a space that it becomes only a list of qualifying adjectives; they characterize, true, but are quickly forgotten because there are no details to give them vividness.

Knute Rockne had a clean mind and a healthy body, a clear vision and an indomitable will. He was famous for his driving energy, which showed in his every word and motion. He was dramatic, witty, and keen, and he knew human nature. These qualities raised him from the poverty of his immigrant boyhood to a position of wealth, culture, and nationwide fame.

The second, of a United States senator, is far more effective. By attempting less in more space and by adding comparison and incident to statement, it becomes much more vivid and memorable.

Henry Cabot Lodge was a gentleman, a scholar, and an elegant and persuasive figure in the United States Senate. As he strolled down the aisle of the Senate Chamber—slender, graceful, gray-haired, gray-bearded, the embodiment of all that was patrician—he caught and held the eye as might William Gillette on a crowded stage. He need not raise his voice, he need only turn for a moment and listen to a sentence or two of some colleague's florid speech and then walk indifferently on, to convince a visitor in the gallery that the speech was unworthy of attention. (Frederick Lewis Allen, *Only Yesterday.*)

## *Characterization of a Type*

The characterization of a type is an exposition of a *kind* of person rather than of an *individual*. It may be the businesslike setting up of qualifications for a position, such as a job, membership in an organization, candidacy for an office, nomination for an honor, eligibility for a scholarship; or it may be an artistically skillful portrayal, for enjoyment as well as for information, of the characteristics typical of a certain group of people, such as the student, the bank teller, the health-food enthusiast. Whatever the purpose, you should determine what the important characteristics are and present them coherently, developing each with details to complete the portrait. Sometimes you may wish to concentrate on a single feature of the type, such as the student's struggle to organize time efficiently, the bank teller's need to be impersonal about money, the health-food enthusiast's energy. Notice how the following paragraph about the writer, as a type, concentrates on the issue of happiness.

I should describe writers as a happy breed of men who are usually unhappy. The writer is either worried about something he has written or about something he is writing. If he isn't working at anything he's worried about that. He has his moments, of course, but they are not too frequent, and he knows very well that within a few hours he may be wondering what he ever saw in *that* paragraph. And one of the sad things about the whole process is that when he's jubilant he can foresee that he will shortly be discouraged but when he's discouraged he can't imagine being jubilant again. The outsider may well wonder why anyone persists in such a vocation. The insider knows that it's a compulsion, a sweet sorrow, that can't easily be exorcised. (Margaret Marshall, *Nations.*)

The characterization of a type tends to generalize—to deal only with such characteristics as are common to the entire group. Its subject will therefore be *the* student (as set off from other types—professors, salesclerks, parents), never *this* student.

## Choice of Subject

Choose as your subject an individual or a type about whom you know enough for an accurate and fairly complete analysis; most professional novelists, in creating characters, depend heavily on the qualities of people they have known. Although skilled observers of human nature can discover something interesting in even the most ordinary persons, you will find your work easier if you choose an individual or a type with an outstanding trait or ability around which you can arrange supporting details to produce a unified portrait. An individual such as an eccentric neighbor, a ne'er-do-well cousin, an ambitious classmate, or a determinedly independent grandparent can be the basis of a vivid characterization. Similarly, a colorful type such as the constant complainer, the health food enthusiast, or the crossword puzzle fan may provide a good subject.

## Methods of Characterization

**1. Use narrative liberally.** It is, as we have seen, one of the best ways of clarifying the abstract through the concrete. It shows the individual in action, and the small gesture may be as revealing as the large deed. Narrating how wealthy George Taylor wrote a one-dollar check for the United Fund is a far more effective way of revealing his stinginess than stating that he was stingy, just as showing Lodge in action, in the passage quoted, shows his aristocratic disdain far more successfully than would a statement that he was disdainful.

**2. Use several small incidents rather than one long one.** A personality is more completely and convincingly revealed by several varied examples of behavior than by a single big one; furthermore, a long narrative is likely to draw attention to itself as a story, overshadowing its main purpose here—the revelation of character through incident.

**3. Use dialogue.** It contributes to the narrative illusion of reality (page 45) and also shows not only what a person says but how that person talks. Our accents, vocabulary, grammar (or lack of grammar) may reveal much about our personalities, attitudes, and backgrounds. Note the amount of information about Irvine Lovelands' lack of education, his habits of thought and moral standards that Robert Louis Stevenson packed into this brief remark in *The Silverado Squatters:*

> A man, he told us, who bore a grudge against him, had poisoned his dog. "That was a low thing for a man to do now, wasn't it? It wasn't like a man, that, nohow. But I got even with him, I poisoned *his* dog."

**4. Use description sparingly.** You are likely to give physical appearance too much attention because it is much easier to catalog what meets the eye than to dig beneath the surface. Description has its place in a characterization, but only to show that outward appearance reveals or conceals inner qualities. Would you choose a roommate by height and weight or by disposition? Your answer indicates how relatively unimportant the outer person is. Yet a slovenly appearance or a habitual nervous twitch of the lips may well be worth mentioning as a significant indication of character.

**5. Use the opinions of others.** The reaction of the children, dog, or neighbors to someone's homecoming can reveal a great deal about that person. You can even draw a full picture of someone who never appears on the scene by focusing on the reactions of a variety of people. But more often this method is used in conjunction with other methods.

**6. Remember that your purpose is expository.** Keep clearly in mind the qualities of character that your analysis of your subject has shown are essential. These will guide you in determining which details and examples to include and which to omit. Never include illustrative materials for their own sake. They should always serve to bring out your larger, clearly defined, expository purpose.

## Organization

Whether you are characterizing an individual or a type, there is no single clear-cut pattern to be followed in organizing your material. The simplest arrangement is to choose a few outstanding traits and set them forth, with examples for each, in some logical order such as from the most obvious to the least. But such a plan is not necessarily the most effective. You may prefer the deductive pattern of stating all the characteristics first in general terms and then illustrating them in order; or the inductive one of giving your illustrations first and then drawing conclusions from them (often more interesting for readers because of its climactic strength); or you may merely give your illustrations, trusting your readers to draw the proper conclusions, which they can readily do if the illustrations are well selected. Almost any method of handling your material is allowable except tediously moralizing on the character's vices or virtues.

The only inescapable rule is that before you start writing you should carefully determine what you want to say, and then relate your material to that controlling idea. Beyond that, use whatever methods seem best for drawing a vivid and readable portrait, keeping in mind, of course, the law of emphasis—building up to an effective climax of event or idea.

## EXAMPLES

4-A                   THE DERELICT
                      *Willie Morris*

This paragraph is from *North Towards Home* (1967), an autobiographical account of a young, small-town southerner's first experiences living and working in New York City.

ANALYSIS

Description

Narration

Opinion of writer

Comparison

Narration

Dialogue

Along the sidewalks in our neighborhood roamed two old walkers who made their mark on the area. One was a bent-over old man who wore pince-nez; he carried an American flag, a Bible, and a megaphone. At almost any hour of the day you could hear him, standing on some 5 street corner nearby, delivering a feverish sermon on sin, redemption, and patriotism, or moving along the sidewalk with his dragging gait, shouting vengeance on every moving object in the vicinity, animal or vegetable. He was just as content trying to convert a Chevrolet pick-up truck as 10 he was in shouting his evangelical threats to the little Italian boys who congregated at the fruit stand on Lexington. There was a horror to this old man, to the echo of his grating voice coming down the narrow streets between the big buildings. Thin trickles of saliva would form on his mouth 15 and drip to the pavement; his moist insane proselytizing seemed as inexorable and illogical as the city itself, as its insane flow of vehicles and people. One Christmas morning, as my son played with his toys in the front of our apartment, I heard him from down the block, and through 20 a drab December mist I saw him shuffling along on 26th Street, solitary and mad; suddenly I felt sorry for him, alone on this Christmas day. I picked up a couple of cans of fancy sardines and rushed down the stairs, catching up with him on the sidewalk. "Merry Christmas," I said, the 25 first words I had ever spoken to him, and handed him the sardines. A puffed-up smile creased his face. He took the gift and said, "What is your religion, young man?" "I'm an old Mississippi Methodist," I replied. "Ah . . . Methodist," he said. "Then you don't believe in Jesus. Pity on you, 30 young man." And he walked away, gingerly putting the sardines in his coat pocket.

**4-B**

### MISS O
*Paul Ferrari (student)*

Of the many teachers I had in grade school, Miss O is the one I will never forget. She was the sternest instructor I ever had. She told us that we must have a solid foundation in algebra as preparation for high school, and she was going to use discipline to make sure we learned our math well.

She always dressed in pantsuits that accentuated her lean, sharp figure. Her 5 hair was cut short in a pixie style that brought her head to a point at the top of her towering, six-foot body. But her mannerisms were even more intimidating than her appearance.

Miss O was very domineering. Students had to line up outside her classroom and file in without uttering a word. She demanded that the day's lesson begin 10 immediately and continue until the last second of the period. If, while a pupil explained a homework problem at the chalkboard, there was an interruption— whether it was a necessary PA announcement or an unwanted disturbance from a student—she would impatiently tap her red pencil until her class could resume. When the interruption was over, she would hurry the pupil at the 15 board, saying "Okay, let's *go*," as if it were the student's fault that her class was disturbed.

Math was the only important subject, according to her. She frequently retained the class five extra minutes into the lunch period to teach one more lesson and then to give us even more homework. Everything had to be done her 20 way. She had her own format for the heading of a paper, for the way problems were written on the board, and even for the formation of the desks in rows. On the floor she had inked marks indicating where the left edge of each desk should be. If a desk was the slightest bit out of place she would reprimand the student sharply. Her room usually smelled of disinfectant. If someone wrote on a desk, 25 he could be found in her room at the end of the day, cleaning every desk. She had a special system of zeros. Zeros were for being late to class, for not doing homework, and for being unruly. An accumulation of zeros resulted in a drop in the grade for that marking period. She loved to give zeros, so much so that during class she kept her grade book open and her ominous red pencil ready. 30

If Miss O hadn't become a math teacher, she would have made a great army drill sergeant.

1. How has the writer organized his information?
2. Does the portrait seem exaggerated? Why—or why not?

---

*4-C*                   AMID BOUNTY, LONGING
                        *Leo Hamalian*

This essay was first published in the *New York Times* in 1976. With the benefit of hindsight, the writer tries to analyze his father's complex personality and his own psychological debt.

My father, like most Armenian survivors of the Turkish genocide, was a man who never wanted to leave home. Until he was forced to flee, he loved the place where he had been born and brought up. It was a milieu alien to the American mentality, and as a result my father never really adapted to the customs of this country. As I look back upon his memory, more in sadness than in the anger I 5 used to feel flaring so often in his presence, I think that his life was about the damage done to the human spirit by exile.

From the time that he set foot in the New World in 1911, an early victim of the Turkish pogroms against Christians, to the day of his lonely death in 1939, neither the chimera of the American Dream nor the bounty of material rewards 10 could numb the pain of a refugee who found himself uprooted in a strange land where he was forced to flourish or founder. He did all those things that transformed other transplanted Armenians into lovers of this land.

Yet I remember him as a ghost who gestures, talks, but utters no words, not even the smallest murmur, of that interior grief that I now realize he had held 15 within like a stone for 25 years.

He must have left recognizing the grim shadow that the future threw before him. Of a large family of prosperous peasants in the Lake Van area, only he and his sister got out of Turkey before the Turks got them, he to America, she to Egypt, where she lived out her days as a stateless person. But not even a futile 20 reality is easily replaced nor the wounds of separation quickly healed.

He tried to be a good American as he understood the idea. He became a photoengraver, took his family to picnics in Hudson Park, argued politics while he played backgammon with his cronies, attended church on 34th Street, and perhaps hoped that the Big Dream would materialize, as it did for so many 25 other Armenians. Instead, I suspect, it only emphasized his sense of loss. His emotional attachment to the place that had treated him like dirt was so massive, so monumental that he was almost blind to the bounty he had reaped in his new homeland.

Why did he resist resurrection when other Armenians were rising out of the 30 ashes of the Turkish tragedy? I am not sure I know, but I think that the stone of sorrow in his guts may simply have stayed stone. Nothing softened it, and this stonified sorrow showed itself in excessive sternness with his children. The more American we became, the more infuriated he became. We couldn't tell whether his anger was directed against America or against us. We felt that we 35 had somehow misbehaved by becoming what we had to become in face of the heavy claims made upon our malleable natures.

I think my father believed that he could regain, magically, some part of his past, even alleviate the pain of his exile if he could keep his children Armenian. Thus, he would triumph over the Turk, who had sought to destroy his Armenian 40 identity. So we spoke only Armenian at home, ate only Armenian food, and saw mainly Armenian friends. In those days, the nativist elements used the public school to disparage the cultural origins of foreigners; I must confess that I was an innocent but willing collaborator. I had no notion that my childish gestures of rebellion might have been torture to my father. 45

Now I think I know what was eating like acid at my father. Did he deserve the bounty and safety that the New World offered for the earning? Were those signs of success in reality the fruits of his failure as a man? Should he have stayed behind with his parents? Should he have left his sister? Should he have had the courage to confront his enemies, no matter what the cost to him? 50

I think my father felt guilty that he had escaped the fate of his family. Though he knew that he had avoided terror and even death, in one part of

himself he became persuaded that he had betrayed his family by not sharing
their destiny, that he had—this will sound irrational to all those but the survivors of concentration camps—survived at their expense.                           55

Thus far his insight took him, but no further. The act of sorting out and
comprehending these ambivalent feelings proved too much for this uneducated
though intelligent immigrant. And indeed why should he have been proud that
he had had to run away, even to save his life? This frame of mind was made
doubly difficult to endure by obtuse neighbors and America-firsters. He was in  60
America. He was safe. He was prospering. His children had opportunities. What
more did he want? Let the dead bury the dead. But my stubborn father could
not bring himself to congratulate himself for what he considered to be an act
of betrayal.

Fortunately, our society no longer puts pressure on immigrants to forget their  65
former associates, or to deny anything dear left behind. We deplore the bitter-
ness of a destiny that displaces people from their homes, that uproots and
deracinates, that creates a league of dislocated persons. Such people are no
longer debarred from the ranks of "good and true" Americans by virtue of their
tragic sense of life. We can be thankful that we have developed this dimension   70
of spiritual tolerance. I prize it, and my father, were he alive, would have prized
it.

1. The author is trying not only to describe his father as an individual but also to reach
   a deeper understanding of all that his father represents. What is meant by the statement at the end of the opening paragraph: "his life was about the damage done to
   the human spirit by exile"?
2. What does the author mean by calling the American dream a "chimera" in the
   second paragraph? What are "the ranks of 'good and true' Americans" in the last
   paragraph?
3. Why are so many of the author's remarks presented as questions?

*4-D*                                 LIFE AND DEATH
                              *Susan D. Schwartz (student)*

When I was eight we lived on the volcanic island of Stromboli off the western
coast of Italy. We lived in our own house, and each room had its own door to
the outside porch. We drank rain water stored in a clay jug, and an outhouse
was our only toilet. It was on Stromboli that I came to know an eighty-three-
year-old woman, Francesca Zame. She was one of the hundred and fifty people    5
in the small town of San Vicenzo, but she became very special for us.

One day, soon after our arrival, as I stood in the apricot tree picking apricots,
I saw Francesca coming up the dirt path toward our house. She walked with
eyes cast down, intent on what she was carrying in her apron. The apron, held
up to form a pocket, made a bumpy sag because of the weight in it. Her feet     10
scuffed the dirt as she walked, and a small cloud of dust formed around them.

Before she reached the gate, she called for my mother. Mama came as quickly as she could. Her stomach was so big that she had trouble running. She took Francesca's hand to help her inside the gate. Francesca gave her a full but gentle hug and kissed both cheeks. She looked up at Mama and told her how pretty she was. Arm in arm, they walked to the porch.

The porch was roofed with twigs. It stretched the full length of the four-room house. In front of the porch was a tin bucket on top of the water well. When Mama and Francesca reached the chairs on the porch, they both sat down very slowly, Francesca because of her age and Mama because of her large stomach. They talked as if they had not seen each other in thirty years.

Then Francesca unfolded her apron. Inside were large purple grapes and two fresh fish. She picked up one of the fish and waved it proudly in the air. Then she set it in Mama's hand and closed her fingers around it. While Mama stared at the fish, Francesca took one of the grapes, wiped it off with her palm, and pushed it into Mama's mouth. She took another grape and did the same thing, saying "You eat, is good for the bambino." She patted Mama's stomach and kissed her cheek once more.

Francesca treated Mama like a daughter: from that day on, she always brought things for Mama to eat—fresh fish and turnips, lettuce and tomatoes from her garden. She felt that there was nothing better than her fresh fish and vegetables. If Mama did not want them, Francesca forced them into her mouth and patted her big round stomach. Francesca never took no for an answer.

That day in the apricot tree, watching Francesca and Mama, I realized how much Francesca cared about life. She cared about it because she knew so much about death. On that volcanic island people could not know whether they and their families would be destroyed that day. Their life histories were divided into chapters by family deaths. They had learned to live day by day, making the most of each, savoring every detail of being alive.

That day I also realized how special Mama was. I was fascinated by her. Her skin was tight and smooth, and she became more huggable every day. She had a new smell, a fat smell, a round, clean smell that I had never known before. She reminded me of Santa Claus. She was more than a mother; she was everything. From that day on, I was very careful with Mama. We were very close.

I am no longer eight years old. The baby Mama was carrying then is now her eight-year-old daughter. We have not been in touch with Francesca since that summer, and Stromboli has had a major eruption. I wonder if Francesca still lives in her little house with her chickens and her garden. By now she would be in her nineties. I wonder if the apricot tree still bears fruit and if another child is learning from Francesca to care about life.

1. What specific details reveal Francesca's personality?
2. What general truths did the writer learn from watching Francesca? How are the specific details related to these truths?
3. What may be the writer's reason for mentioning the apricot tree again at the end?

*4-E*     BENJAMIN BANNEKER: ROOM TO DREAM AND DARE
*Lerone Bennett, Jr.*

This characterization comes from *Before the Mayflower: A History of the Negro in America* (1964) and gives the kind of factual information we expect from histories and encyclopedias. Banneker, the grandson of a slave, was a noted astronomer and mathematician in the early years of our country.

Benjamin Banneker, like Phillis Wheatley,° was a child of an age of birth pains. He was born in Maryland, the grandson of an Englishwoman and an African native. The Englishwoman, Molly Welsh, came to America as an indentured servant, worked her time out and bought a farm and two slaves. She freed the slaves and married one of them. Banneker's mother, Mary, was one of four 5 children born to this union. Banneker's father was an African native.

Banneker attended a local school with Negro and white children. Like Phillis Wheatley, he hungered and thirsted after books. His forte, however, was science—mathematics and astronomy. He became so proficient in these subjects that he was named to the commission which surveyed the territory which 10 became Washington, D.C. The Georgetown *Weekly Ledger* of March 12, 1791, noted the arrival of the commission. Banneker, the paper said, was "an Ethiopian whose abilities as surveyor and astronomer already prove that Mr. [Thomas] Jefferson's concluding that that race of men were void of endowment was without foundation." 15

Beginning in 1791, Banneker issued an annual almanac which has been compared with Benjamin Franklin's *Poor Richard's Almanac.* He also continued the study of astronomy and other scientific subjects.

His was an idyllic life. He lived on a farm, about ten miles outside Baltimore. A confirmed bachelor, he studied all night, slept in the morning and worked in 20 the afternoon. He washed his own clothes, cooked his own meals and cultivated gardens around his log cabin. He had an early fondness for "strong drinks," but later became a teetotaler.

His habits of study were odd, to say the least. Of a night, he would wrap himself in a great cloak and lie under a pear tree and meditate on the revolu- 25 tions of the heavenly bodies. He would remain there throughout the night and take to his bed at dawn.

A contemporary has left a portrait of the stargazer. "His head was covered with a thick suit of white hair, which gave him a very dignified and venerable appearance. . . . His dress was uniformly of superfine broadcloth, made in the 30 old style of a plain coat, with straight collar and long waistcoat, and broad-brimmed hat. His color was not jet-black, but decidedly Negro. In size and personal appearance, the statue of Franklin at the Library of Philadelphia, as seen from the street, is a perfect likeness. Go to his house when you would,

°Phillis Wheatley was brought up as a slave by a Boston family who, recognizing her abilities, gave her a good education. The collection of her poems, published in 1773, was the second book by a woman to be published in America and the first by a black woman.

either by day or night, there was constantly standing in the middle of the floor 35
a large table covered with books and papers. As he was an eminent mathematician, he was constantly in correspondence with other mathematicians in this
country, with whom there was an interchange of questions of difficult solution."

Banneker, unlike Wheatley, boldly lashed out at the injustices of the age. In
a famous letter of 1791, he reminded Thomas Jefferson that words were one 40
thing and slavery was another. "Suffer me to recall to your mind that time, in
which the arms of the British crown were exerted, with every powerful effort,
in order to reduce you to a state of servitude; look back, I entreat you . . . you
were then impressed with proper ideas of the great violation of liberty, and the
free possession of those blessings, to which you were entitled by nature; but, sir, 45
how pitiable is it to reflect, that although you were so fully convinced of the
benevolence of the Father of Mankind, and of his equal and impartial distri-
bution of these rights and privileges which he hath conferred upon them, that
you should at the same time counteract his mercies, in detaining by fraud and
violence, so numerous a part of my brethren under groaning captivity and cruel 50
oppression, that you should at the same time be found guilty of that most criminal act, which you professedly detested in others."

Banneker and Wheatley demonstrated, in their own ways, latent possibilities
in the burgeoning American Dream. To be sure, things were not rosy in this
period. But some men, a very few men, had room to dream and dare and hope. 55

1. What information does the author give to support the claim he makes in his opening
   sentence?
2. How does the author use specific detail, quotations, historical data, and comparison
   to develop his portrait of Banneker?

---

*4-F*             THE SURFER
                  *William Murray*

This characterization describes a type, not an individual. It comes from "Hanging
Five," an article on the pleasures of surfing published in *Holiday* magazine in 1967.
Another excerpt from the article appears as the first example in Unit 1.

If there is such a thing as an average surfer, he is between the ages of fourteen
and twenty-one and he lives within five miles of a beach. In Southern California
this isn't hard to do, because from Point Conception to the Mexican border, a
distance of 279 miles, there are nearly 300 established surfing spots; these range
from point and reef breaks, such as those at Malibu and Windandsea, to the 5
much more common beach breaks. It is the average surfer's duty and delight
to get to his favorite spot at least two or three times a week all year. Mundane
matters like school, parental opposition or the lack of an automobile will not
keep him from his rendezvous with the right wave. Nor will he be deterred by
such trifles as the objections of property owners, restrictions and local ordinances 10

on public beaches, and the icy waters of the California Current, which flows
south from the Gulf of Alaska and keeps water temperatures in the fifties all
winter. Even in January the aficionado will defy all authority, lightly shoulder
his board, seek out his favorite spot, don his rubber wet suit and spend hours,
often from dawn to dusk, perfecting his style on the prevailing swell.                    15

Most surfers are just nice kids from white middle-class families. They will
graduate from college, take jobs, get married and become fathers, and soon they
will be surfing once or twice a month, if at all. They will teach their children
how to surf, and they will retire gracefully to the outdoor barbecue, the bar and
the television set, captured by white collars and brown shoes. But there is        20
another class of surfer that is becoming more and more evident, a hard-core
minority of fanatics who are past their teens and for whom life has become an
endless summer in search of the perfect wave. It is this dedicated group, for
whom surfing is a metaphysic, that dominates the competitive scene, establishes
the pecking order on the beach and sets the styles for this new American sub-      25
culture based almost as much on language and looks as on skill in the water,
though the latter is still the basic prerequisite for status.

It's important to look the part. A surfer's hair doesn't have to be peroxide
blond, but it should be bleached and fluffy, and worn long. His eyeballs are
usually pink and his eyelids caked with salt, so that his expression often carries   30
a reptilian look—like that of the great green sea turtle. His lips tend to swell
and his skin is leathery. His shoulders are massive and his torso heavily muscled,
which makes his legs, especially when clad in the long Hawaiian shorts that are
currently the fashion, look undersized. Below his knees he is sure to sport surf
bumps, hard lumps of cartilage acquired from the constant pressure of kneeling    35
on a hard surface while paddling out to where the waves are breaking. He is
also likely to sport some colorful scars and to be missing a few teeth, mementos
of near-lethal encounters with hidden rocks, loose surfboards and other surfers.
This new 20th-Century Galahad would feel as naked without his bumps and
scars as a medieval jouster without his lance wounds.                               40

The style of dress is invariably casual, even away from the beach. Surfers are
usually barefoot, but have been known to flap around in thongs and tennis
sneakers. Long, gaily colored shorts are *de rigueur* on the sands, and are
replaced in the evenings by khakis, Levi's or tight slacks, usually worn with
long-tailed sports shirts, turtlenecks, open vests or windbreakers. The girls wear   45
practically nothing during the day, and the hippiest creations in the evenings,
when the partying starts. Take a panoramic picture of the crowd at any local
surfing spot and you'll immortalize a microcosm of this so-called beach look,
which consists of lots of brown flesh and shiny white teeth set off by dazzling
colors. The scene will be framed and peppered by the upright shields of the      50
surfers, for the boards gleam, too, in a variety of flashing lights. And the dis-
cerning will pick out the shields of the inner brotherhood by their much-waxed,
discolored, dented, bumped and scratched appearance, though at official contests the rulers of the waves will compete with new boards, often provided by
manufacturers eager for the right endorsement of their product.                    55

The surfer may live at home with his parents or he may share a pad with two or three other enthusiasts in some low-rent apartment development within hearing distance of the tides. If he takes a job for six months of the year, he'll qualify the rest of the time for the state's generous allotments of unemployment insurance. There is also the chance of making a buck or two out of surfing. Tournament champions are in demand to endorse various surfing products. And surfers may star in the dozens of profitable documentaries turned out every year by entrepreneurs such as Bruce Brown, whose film, *The Endless Summer*, has been packing them in at the art houses from coast to coast for months. Until recently, too, the wave warriors cropped up in the backgrounds of Hollywood's trashy beach movies. "The pictures are all phonies," one dedicated surfer said, "but I sure do like the bread."

1. How has the writer organized this characterization?
2. What generalizations do you find and where do they appear in the paragraphs?
3. Roughly how much of this is composed of generalized statements and how much of specific details to support them?

---

**4-G**           THE NORTH WOODS GUIDE
                    *J. Donald Adams*

This characterization of a type is from "Farewell to the North Woods Guide," an essay that appeared in the *Atlantic Monthly* in 1957. Adams wrote of his fear that such rugged individualists, experts in a life close to nature, were a vanishing breed and that their eventual disappearance would be a great loss.

Guiding at its best in the north woods deserves to be called a profession and an art. Consider the requirements: the guide must know his region the way a man knows his own house. He must be thoroughly familiar with the habits of fish and game and the uses of rod and gun. He must be a good cook and a first-rate woodsman, ingenious enough to make the best of the materials at hand. He should be an expert canoe-man. But the list doesn't end there. His value is much increased if he is a good companion, a man with whom you can sit around the fire when the day's sport is over, and with whom you can enjoy talking. He needs tact, and ability to bear with fools, and he must have a strong sense of responsibility.

The best of the breed are remarkable men, both in character and competence. I have never known a nervous or fretful man among them. Their balance is not only in their legs but in their minds as well. As most of us do not, they step, in Thoreau's phrase, to their own music. They are shrewd judges of character, because there is no quicker or more infallible way of discovering the faults in a man than to share his company on a camping trip. For years the experienced guide has observed people stripped to the essentials, shorn of the props which support them in their ordinary environment. The bluffer, the boas-

ter, the snob, the selfish egotist, the shirker, will all have betrayed themselves
after a day or two in the woods. If you can spend two weeks on the trail with  20
a man or woman without undue friction and disharmony, you can get on with
that person under any circumstances. That is one of my favorite laws of human
behavior.

A good guide is wise because he has learned to rock with the boat, to abide
by the laws of nature. He may not hear an oracle in the pine woods, as Emerson  25
did, but he is full of earthy wisdom. Schooled in making the best of what comes,
he steers a steady course between overconfidence and easy discouragement. He
knows that nature always evens up, always strikes a balance, except when man,
alone among the animals, disturbs it.

Out of this sense of balance comes that unforced, natural humor which is  30
usually his. No doubt there are exceptions, but I have never known a seasoned
guide who didn't have a sharp sense of the incongruous—the quality that lies
at the base of nearly all humor.

That beautifully competent skill of his didn't come out of books. It may be
that some people are born with a better sense of direction than others—you  35
don't have to go into the woods to see that demonstrated; but whatever the
guide's native capacity to orient himself may be, he has vastly strengthened it
by long and patient observation. He sees a host of things that we miss: the direction taken by tree branches; spots where the sun strikes longest; the conforma-
tion of the land; inlets and outlets that we might pass by. He knows this country  40
not in one season or two, but in all four, and is aware of every subtle change
that takes place.

Just as his broker client sniffs out trends in the market from the daily stock
listings, so he reads with ease the signs that point to a late or early season, where
the deer or moose will be heading, where the trout or landlocked salmon are  45
likely to be found. Given certain circumstances, certain conditions, he knows
what the reaction of wildlife will be. He is not guessing; he is drawing conclusions from a rich fund of long-assembled facts. He reminds me most, among
professional men, of the skillful surgeon: resourceful, ever ready to improvise,
always braced for an emergency, combining in rare degree exact knowledge  50
with the manual dexterity to implement it.

1. What words and phrases emphasize Adams's admiration for the typical guide?
2. What are the most important personal traits of the typical guide?
3. How has Adams organized the information? What transitional devices do you find?
4. Compare Adams's characterization of the guide with this purely descriptive paragraph. To what extent do the information and opinions in one support those in the
   other?

Here's the Maine guide. He wears what amounts to a uniform. It consists of a
wool shirt, preferably plain, nicely faded to soft, warm tones; dark pants, either
plus-fours, for some unknown reason, or riding breeches; wool socks and the sole-
less, Indian-type moccasin, or high laced boots. He carries a bandana in his hip
pocket and may or may not wear another knotted around his neck. But he must

wear a battered felt hat, with a collection of salmon flies in the band, and he must wear it with an air; and he must wear a hunting knife day and night; and he must look tough and efficient. If he has high cheek bones and tans easily, that is his good luck. He can then admit to part-Indian ancestry, accurately or not. Indian blood is an item highly esteemed by "sports." (Louise Dickinson Rich, *We Took to the Woods*, 1942.)

## ASSIGNMENTS

1. Review Examples B through E and list the chief characteristics of each individual presented as the main subject. Have the authors merely stated what the characteristics are or have they illustrated them with details, incidents, speeches, and the opinions of others to make them vivid and believable?

2. Imagine that a casting director has asked your help in selecting people for small character parts in various movies and has given you the photographs (pages 89–92) that show faces clearly. Choose two faces and write an essay of about 300 words describing the kinds of characters that they will probably suggest to most audiences and explaining why you think so.

3. Write a 300–500 word characterization of an individual whom you find interesting and know well enough to describe in detail. Check your rough draft against the suggestions listed in "Characterization of an Individual," earlier in this unit, to make sure that you have taken advantage of all the methods appropriate to developing your characterization.

4. Write a characterization of a type, choosing your own subject: not *a* particular professor but *the* professor, truck driver, rock guitarist, grandparent, straight-A student, neighborhood pharmacist, and so on. Treat your subject as a single individual, but be sure to include only qualities that are common to the type and that distinguish it from other types, not those that individualize a person within a type.

5. All the authors of the examples in Unit 3 use some characterization. Which of the characters seemed most vivid to you? Why? What methods did the authors use?

# UNIT 5

# *Words*

"Open, Sesame!" said Ali Baba, and the door of the robbers' cave obeyed. Folk and fairy tales throughout the world give similar examples of the power of words. "Spell," meaning to say the letters of a word, comes from "spell," a magic formula. The accurate use of words will not give you magical powers, but it is essential for your primary purpose—communicating your meaning. A forceful use of words is essential for your secondary purpose—catching and holding your reader's attention.

The earlier units on composing in general, description, narration, and characterization, included recommendations to choose appropriate words. This unit will concentrate on them.

## *Levels of Language*

Compared to the other widely spoken languages of the world, English has an unusually large number of words that are **synonyms** or near-synonyms of each other. But synonyms are hardly ever truly interchangeable. The **denotations**—the dictionary definitions—of two words may be exactly the same; but their **connotations**—the associated meanings they have acquired through use—are rarely the same. For example, *female* is one of the dictionary definitions for *woman* and *woman* for *female*, but someone who says "Two females sat in the car" probably has a very different opinion of them from someone who says "Two women sat in the car." Similarly, both *noted* and *notorious* can be defined as *well-known*, and they even come from the same Latin root, but they connote two very different kinds of reputation.

Our many synonyms and varying connotations give us a choice of levels on which to write, from the very formal to the very informal. Colloquial English is informal—the level most of us use when writing and speaking to friends. The vocabulary and the sentence structure are relatively simple and may include many contractions, some slang, and some regional and dialect words. A college or unabridged dictionary will tell you if a word is colloquial, dialectal, or slang—and therefore perhaps not appropriate in a formal paper.

Scholarly and technical English includes whatever specialized words and phrases are appropriate to the particular subject. The sentences have standard English structures but are often relatively long with many subdivisions.

Standard English (or "standard edited English") is somewhere between colloquial and scholarly English. It has the kinds of words and sentence structures used by writers for the more serious publications meant for the general reader—big city newspapers, national circulation magazines, and textbooks like this one.

Consider these versions of a single request:

> Leave us go (ungrammatical/dialectal)
> Let's split (slang)
> Let's go (informal)
> Let us go (formal)

Each will be appropriate at some time, including the ungrammatical version if you are quoting a speaker who used it. Whatever level you choose, be consistent. A sudden shift will startle your readers and make them wonder if you have changed your purpose. Good English is appropriate English—appropriate to the occasion, to the subject, and especially to the intended reader.

## *Dictionaries*

The more words you know well, the better you will be able to choose the ones appropriate to your particular needs. A good dictionary is as necessary for a writer as ink and paper. Keep one beside you when writing. A pocket-sized edition can help with spellings when you write in class, and an unabridged edition—every library has at least one—will help you with complicated problems. But the college edition is the one you should have on your desk—small enough to be picked up with one hand but detailed enough to answer most of your questions about words.

There are three widely respected American dictionaries. In alphabetical order they are

*American Heritage,* published by Houghton Mifflin
*Webster's New Collegiate,* published by G. & C. Merriam
*Webster's New World,* published by Collins-World and Simon & Schuster

Each has over 150,000 entries, gives much the same kind of information on each word, and has much the same kind of additional material on punctuation, the history of the language, and so on. Also, they are nearly the same in size, weight, and price. Examine all three carefully before you choose. Decide which seems to have the most readable type, the most understandable abbreviations, and the clearest diagrams and illustrations. A comparison of their entries for "infer" and "irregardless" will give you a good indication of their differences in presentation and degree of conservatism.

Ask for them by the names of their publishers as well as by their titles, particularly the two "Webster's." There are many dictionaries, some relatively worthless, that use Noah Webster's name, so that "Webster's" in the title guarantees nothing. Remember also to check the copyright date on the back of the title page so that you can be sure of getting the latest edition.

Whichever dictionary you buy, study its opening pages carefully for directions on using it. Each has its own system for presenting information and its own methods of abbreviation. Here is the entry for *pleasure* in *Webster's New World Dictionary:*

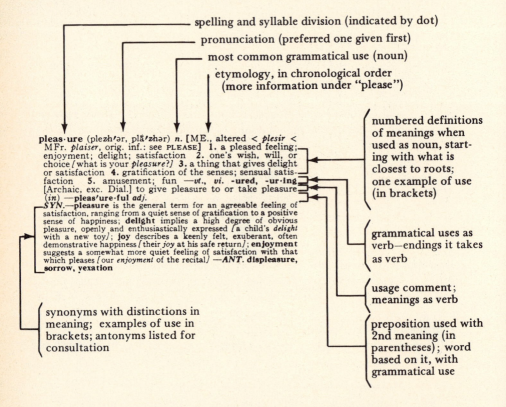

spelling and syllable division (indicated by dot)

pronunciation (preferred one given first)

most common grammatical use (noun)

etymology, in chronological order
(more information under "please")

numbered definitions
of meanings when
used as noun, starting with what is
closest to roots;
one example of use
(in brackets)

grammatical uses as
verb—endings it takes
as verb

usage comment;
meanings as verb

preposition used with
2nd meaning (in
parentheses); word
based on it, with
grammatical use

synonyms with distinctions in
meaning; examples of use in
brackets; antonyms listed for
consultation

**pleas·ure** (plezh′ər, plā′zhər) *n.* [ME., altered < *plesir* < MFr. *plaiser,* orig. inf.: see PLEASE] **1.** a pleased feeling; enjoyment; delight; satisfaction **2.** one's wish, will, or choice [what is your *pleasure?*] **3.** a thing that gives delight or satisfaction **4.** gratification of the senses; sensual satisfaction **5.** amusement; fun —*vt.,* *vi.* **-ured, -ur·ing** [Archaic, exc. Dial.] to give pleasure to or take pleasure (*in*) —**pleas′ure·ful** *adj.*
*SYN.*—**pleasure** is the general term for an agreeable feeling of satisfaction, ranging from a quiet sense of gratification to a positive sense of happiness; **delight** implies a high degree of obvious pleasure, openly and enthusiastically expressed [a child's *delight* with a new toy]; **joy** describes a keenly felt, exuberant, often demonstrative happiness [their *joy* at his safe return]; **enjoyment** suggests a somewhat more quiet feeling of satisfaction with that which pleases [our *enjoyment* of the recital] —*ANT.* **displeasure, sorrow, vexation**

To find more synonyms for a word than your dictionary includes, consult a *thesaurus,* or "treasury" of synonyms. The best known, *Roget's Thesaurus,* is published in a variety of editions. When you choose a word from a thesaurus, always check your dictionary as well to be sure that the word has the connotations you want. You may find *fluent, voluble, glib,* and *flippant* listed together, but although speakers will thank you for calling them fluent, they will not be much pleased to be called voluble and will certainly take offense at being called glib or flippant.

## Specific, Concrete Words

For most of your nonspecialized writing, in college and later, "standard English" will be appropriate. But this does not mean that you must limit yourself to "safe," dull words. The more precise and economical your word choice is, the more likely it is to be clear and forceful. As mentioned in the section of Unit 2 on "diction and the five senses," a specific word like *shuffle* or *trudge* or *saunter* is not only briefer than *walk slowly* but is also more precise and therefore more effective. Notice how Shana Alexander piles up specific words for a dramatic and humorous effect in this paragraph:

> Instead of harrying, chivying, threatening with travel taxes and otherwise cramping the tourist's style, I think we ought to coddle, cosset, encourage, advise, underwrite and indemnify him in every possible way. Huge herds of vigorous, curious, open-eyed Americans freely roaming the world are, it seems to me, quite possibly a vital national resource today as at no other time in our history. . . . I am for tourists of any and all kinds: sneakered and sport-shirted and funny-hatted, pants-suited and pajamaed and jetsetted, knapsacked and bearded, festooned with Instamatics and phrase books and goofy sunglasses, traveling scientists and schoolteachers and schoolchildren and trade missions, Peace Corpsmen, ballet corps, opera companies and symphony players, tennis players, footballers, junketeering congressmen and highballers—all of them to be set wandering and peering and snooping and migrating and exploring and studying and just mooching all over the face of the globe. (Shana Alexander, "The Real Tourist Trap," *Life*.)

## Figures of Speech

Comparisons of all kinds can help to make the unfamiliar seem familiar for your readers and can bring the abstract and general to life by relating it to the concrete and specific. To show a reader how hot a room was, you could simply state the fact, "The room was 98° Fahrenheit," but a straightforward comparison would help the reader to see that you wanted to emphasize the heat: "The room was as hot as an oven."

A figure of speech might be more memorable because, instead of making a logical, literal comparison, it is imaginative. There are several kinds; among the most common and useful are the following:

**1. Simile:** "The room was like an oven." The room and the oven are compared, but the writer takes for granted that the reader thinks of an oven as hot, whereas in "The room was as hot as an oven" this point is included.

**2. Metaphor.** "The room was an oven." The room and the oven are presented as one thing, but the writer assumes that the reader knows they are not.

**3. Implied metaphor.** "The room baked us." Ovens are enclosed spaces used for baking, but they are not mentioned. The writer assumes that the reader will make the connection.

**4. Extended metaphor.** "The room was an oven that baked our conversation dry, and the soufflé of fantastic ideas on which we had hoped to feast was now only a burnt crust." The association of heat and an oven is carried through several related applications to describe the psychological effect of heat.

**5. Hyperbole.** "The temperature of the room felt like 1000°." The extreme exaggeration emphasizes the point.

**6. Understatement.** "With the thermometer at 98°, we can safely describe the room as warm." Understatement is the opposite of hyperbole, but the reader is expected in both cases to realize that the statement should not be taken literally. A variation on understatement uses a negative for the same effect, as in "With the thermometer at 98°, the room was not underheated."

**7. Personification.** "Like a fevered invalid, the room enclosed us in a smothering embrace." The room is described as though it had the characteristics of a human being.

Figurative language can stimulate your reader's imagination and make your writing more memorable, but you must use it cautiously. To borrow an old simile, it is like seasoning on food—a little can go a long way.

Avoid the *mixed metaphor*, a combination of comparisons that do not fit together. A political speaker recently claimed, "My ace in the hole is that I'm not a bull in the china shop swinging a meat axe." Avoid clichés, comparisons that have grown stale through overuse, such as "green as grass," "busy as a bee," or "old as the hills," unless you can breathe new life into them as in "He seemed as busy as a bee, but we never saw any honey." Avoid comparisons that may call up inappropriate associations, as in "With a good manager the business sprouted like potatoes in a damp cellar." This is partly appropriate because potatoes do indeed sprout quickly in a damp cellar, but most readers will think of damp cellars as unpleasant and will probably go on to imagine the potatoes as rotting.

**Euphemisms** are related to figurative language. They are words or phrases that let us soften a harsh or unpleasant or embarrassing fact. We have a variety of expressions to describe physical acts we would rather not name directly. For example, rather than say we are going to the toilet, we may say we are going to the bathroom or the john or the rest room, but "toilet" itself is an old euphemism—check its etymology. Many people are reluctant to say that someone has died and prefer saying that he has passed away. Old people are now called senior citizens, and garbage collectors are sanitary engineers. Use such expressions when you think your readers would be offended by more accurate words, but also be on guard against words that conceal the truth. Someone who steals information from our government for a foreign one is a spy, but we call someone who steals information for us an intelligence agent. Is being terminated from your job really easier than being fired? Is an experienced car in better condition than a used car? Don't be afraid to call a spade a spade, or even, sometimes, a shovel.

## Short, Simple Words

In general, use short, simple words in standard English. Use longer, more complicated, or technical ones only when they are absolutely necessary to make your meaning clear. More and more often, critics are complaining of the pompousness of much modern writing and of the confusions that result. Some branches of the federal government and some businesses are trying to simplify the language of their reports and contracts, but we still have a long way to go. Theodore Bernstein, an editor of the *New York Times* and author of several books on writing, calls such pompousness "windyfoggery" and illustrates it with this anecdote:

Dr. William B. Bean, who in the *Archives of Internal Medicine* often tilted a lancet at the writing operations of his fellow healers, has passed on the story of a New York plumber who had cleaned out some drains with hydrochloric acid and then wrote to a chemical research bureau, inquiring, "Was there any possibility of harm?" As told by Dr. Bean, the story continues:

"The first answer was, 'The efficacy of hydrochloric acid is indisputably established but the corrosive residue is incompatible with metallic permanence.' The plumber was proud to get this and thanked the people for approving of his method. The dismayed research bureau rushed another letter to him saying, 'We cannot assume responsibility for the production of a toxic and noxious residue with hydrochloric acid. We beg leave to suggest to you the employment of an alternative procedure.' The plumber was more delighted than ever and wrote to thank them for reiterating their approval. By this time the bureau got worried about what might be happening to New York's sewers and called in a third man, an older scientist, who wrote simply, 'Don't use hydrochloric acid. It eats hell out of pipes.'" (Theodore M. Bernstein, *The Careful Writer*, 1973.)

Bernstein goes on to say that specialized terminology is, of course, appropriate in technical writing, but "windyfoggery, which often is technical jargon gone wrong and blanketed in blurriness, is not useful to any purpose."

Be concise. Use only as many words as you need to convey your meaning effectively. Omit any that are not necessary, even simple ones. Why, for example, write "It is my opinion that the team won the game due to the fact that they tried really hard" when you can write "I think that the team won because they tried hard"? When you are afraid that your essay is not long enough, do not stretch it with extra words. Find more material—more examples, more details. These will strengthen what you say; extra words will only dilute it.

"Clutter" (Unit 6-D) gives more advice on how to strengthen your writing by leaving out words you don't need.

## EXAMPLES

These examples differ sharply in style, but all the writers have chosen precise, concrete words and economical phrases to strengthen their points.

**5-A**                    THE FLIGHT OF REFUGEES
                           *Ernest Hemingway*

Hemingway has had more influence on contemporary prose than any other modern writer. Sometimes he went to extremes in simplifying word choice and sentence structure and in using understatement, but his news reporting provides excellent examples of forceful simplicity. In the following, a complete news dispatch headed "Barcelona: 3 April 1938," he describes several hours in the Spanish Civil War. Notice his concentration on facts, his choice of details, and the rare indications of his emotions.

It was a lovely false spring day when we started for the front this morning. Last night, coming into Barcelona, it had been grey, foggy, dirty and sad, but today it was bright and warm, and pink almond blossoms coloured the grey hills and brightened the dusty green rows of olive trees.

Then, outside of Reus, on a straight smooth highway with olive orchards on 5 each side, the chauffeur from the rumble seat shouted, "Planes, planes!" and, rubber screeching, we stopped the car under a tree.

"They're right over us," the chauffeur said, and, as this correspondent dived head-forward into a ditch, he looked up sideways, watching a monoplane come down and wing over and then evidently decide a single car was not worth turn- 10 ing his eight machine-guns loose on.

But, as we watched, came a sudden egg-dropping explosion of bombs, and, ahead, Reus, silhouetted against hills a half mile away, disappeared in a brick-dust-coloured cloud of smoke. We made our way through the town, the main street blocked by broken houses and a smashed water main, and, stopping, tried 15 to get a policeman to shoot a wounded horse, but the owner thought it was still possibly worth saving and we went on up toward the mountain pass that leads to the little Catalan city of Falset.

That was how the day started, but no one yet alive can say how it will end. For soon we began passing carts loaded with refugees. An old woman was driv- 20 ing one, crying and sobbing while she swung a whip. She was the only woman I saw crying all day. There were eight children following another cart and one little boy pushed on a wheel as they came up a difficult grade. Bedding, sewing-machines, blankets, cooking utensils and mattresses wrapped in mats, sacks of grain for the horses and mules were piled in the carts and goats and sheep were 25 tethered to the tailboards. There was no panic, they were just plodding along.

On a mule piled high with bedding rode a woman holding a still freshly red-faced baby that could not have been two days old. The mother's head swung steadily up and down with the motion of the beast she rode, and the baby's jet-black hair was drifted grey with the dust. A man led the mule forward, looking 30 back over his shoulder and then looking forward at the road.

"When was the baby born?" I asked him, as our car swung alongside. "Yesterday," he said proudly, and the car was past. But all these people, no matter where else they looked as they walked or rode, all looked up to watch the sky.

Then we began to see soldiers straggling along. Some carried their rifles by 35 the muzzles, some had no arms. At first there were only a few troops, then finally there was a steady stream, with whole units intact. Then there were troops in trucks, troops marching, trucks with guns, with tanks, with anti-tank guns and anti-aircraft guns, and always a line of people walking.

As we went on, the road choked and swelled with this migration, until, 40 finally, it was not just the road, but streaming alongside the road by all the old paths for driving cattle came the civilian population and the troops. There was no panic at all, only a steady movement, and many of the people seemed cheerful. But perhaps it was the day. The day was so lovely that it seemed ridiculous that anyone should ever die. 45

Then we began seeing people that we knew, officers we had met before, soldiers from New York and Chicago who told how the enemy had broken through and taken Gandesa, that the Americans were fighting and holding the bridge at Mora across the Ebro River and that they were covering this retreat and holding the bridgehead across the river and still holding the town. 50

Suddenly, the stream of troops thinned and then there was a big influx again, and the road was so choked that the car could not move ahead. You could see them shelling Mora on the river and hear the pounding thud of the guns. Then there came a flock of sheep to clog the roads, with shepherds trying to drive them out of the way of the trucks and tanks. Still the planes did not come. 55

Somewhere ahead, the bridge was still being held, but it was impossible to go any farther with the car against that moving dust-swamped tide. So we turned the car back toward Tarragona and Barcelona and rode through it all again. The woman with the newborn baby had it wrapped in a shawl and held tight against her now. You could not see the dusty head because she held it tight 60 under the shawl as she swung with the walking gait of the mule. Her husband led the mule, but he looked at the road now and did not answer when we waved. People still looked up at the sky as they retreated. But they were very weary now. The planes had not yet come, but there was still time for them and they were overdue. 65

1. What words describe how crowded the road was? How specific are they? What words describe other actions of any kind? colors? sounds?
2. What reaction from the reader does the writer seem to want?
3. In paragraph 5 why list the kinds of things piled on the carts instead of saving space by calling them "household effects" or "portable possessions"? What distinction may be drawn between "crying" and "sobbing"?
4. Are there any words that you could remove without changing the meaning and effect of the description?

---

**5-B**　　　　　ON SOCIETIES AS ORGANISMS
　　　　　　　　　*Lewis Thomas*

These paragraphs are from an essay first published in the *New England Journal of Medicine* and then in *The Lives of a Cell* (1974), a collection of Dr. Thomas's essays. The writer, a noted research scientist, is fascinated by the behavior of living things of

all kinds, from the parts of a single cell to human beings. He begins the essay by pointing out that although we often compare the behavior of humans to that of insects,
scientists object to any interpretation of insect behavior in human terms.

The writers of books on insect behavior generally take pains, in their prefaces,
to caution that insects are like creatures from another planet, that their behavior
is absolutely foreign, totally unhuman, unearthly, almost unbiological. They are
more like perfectly tooled but crazy little machines, and we violate science
when we try to read human meanings in their arrangements.                    5

It is hard for a bystander not to do so. Ants are so much like human beings
as to be an embarrassment. They farm fungi, raise aphids as livestock, launch
armies into wars, use chemical sprays to alarm and confuse enemies, capture
slaves. The families of weaver ants engage in child labor, holding their larvae
like shuttles to spin out the thread that sews the leaves together for their fungus  10
gardens. They exchange information ceaselessly. They do everything but watch
television.

What makes us most uncomfortable is that they, and the bees and termites
and social wasps, seem to live two kinds of lives: they are individuals, going
about the day's business without much evidence of thought for tomorrow, and  15
they are at the same time component parts, cellular elements, in the huge,
writhing, ruminating organism of the Hill, the nest, the hive. It is because of
this aspect, I think, that we most wish for them to be something foreign. We do
not like the notion that there can be collective societies with the capacity to
behave like organisms. If such things exist, they can have nothing to do with us.  20

Still, there it is. A solitary ant, afield, cannot be considered to have much of
anything on his mind; indeed, with only a few neurons strung together by
fibers, he can't be imagined to have a mind at all, much less a thought. He is
more like a ganglion on legs. Four ants together, or ten, encircling a dead moth
on a path, begin to look more like an idea. They fumble and shove, gradually  25
moving the food toward the Hill, but as though by blind chance. It is only when
you watch the dense mass of thousands of ants, crowded together around the
Hill, blackening the ground, that you begin to see the whole beast, and now you
observe it thinking, planning, calculating. It is an intelligence, a kind of live
computer, with crawling bits for its wits.                                    30

At a stage in the construction, twigs of a certain size are needed, and all the
members forage obsessively for twigs of just this size. Later, when outer walls
are to be finished, thatched, the size must change, and as though given new
orders by telephone, all the workers shift the search to the new twigs. If you
disturb the arrangement of a part of the Hill, hundreds of ants will set it vibrat-  35
ing, shifting, until it is put right again. Distant sources of food are somehow
sensed, and long lines, like tentacles, reach out over the ground, up over walls,
behind boulders, to fetch it in.

Termites are even more extraordinary in the way they seem to accumulate
intelligence as they gather together. Two or three termites in a chamber will  40
begin to pick up pellets and move from place to place, but nothing comes of it;
nothing is built. As more join in, they seem to reach a critical mass, a quorum,

and the thinking begins. They place pellets atop pellets, then throw up columns and beautiful, curving, symmetrical arches, and the crystalline architecture of vaulted chambers is created. It is not known how they communicate with each 45 other, how the chains of termites building one column know when to turn toward the crew on the adjacent column, or how, when the time comes, they manage the flawless joining of the arches. The stimuli that set them off at the outset, building collectively instead of shifting things about, may be pheromones [odors] released when they reach committee size. They react as if 50 alarmed. They become agitated, excited, and then they begin working, like artists.

The phenomenon of separate animals joining up to form an organism is not unique in insects. Herring and other fish in schools are at times so closely integrated, their actions so coordinated, that they seem to be functionally a 55 great multi-fish organism. Flocking birds, especially the seabirds nesting on the slopes of offshore islands in Newfoundland, are similarly attached, connected, synchronized.

Although we are by all odds the most social of all social animals—more interdependent, more attached to each other, more inseparable in our behavior than 60 bees—we do not often feel our conjoined intelligence. Perhaps, however, we are linked in circuits for the storage, processing, and retrieval of information, since this appears to be the most basic and universal of all human enterprises. It may be our biological function to build a certain kind of Hill.

[Thomas then quotes the claim of a scholarly journal that small contributions to knowledge published for other scholars to use achieve "a corporate, collective power that is far greater than one individual can exert."]

With some alteration of terms, some toning down, the passage could describe 65 the building of a termite nest.

It is fascinating that the word "explore" does not apply to the searching aspect of the activity, but has its origins in the sounds we make while engaged in it. We like to think of exploring in science as a lonely, meditative business, and so it is in the first stages, but always, sooner or later, before the enterprise 70 reaches completion, as we explore, we call to each other, communicate, publish, send letters to the editor, present papers, cry out on finding.

1. What specific words describe actions? living things?
2. Where does Thomas use figurative language? What seems to be the purpose?
3. What distinctions does Thomas make among words in a kind of list at the end of his first sentence, in the sentence beginning in line 7, and in the sentence beginning in line 59?
4. Can you shorten any of Thomas's sentences by changing or omitting words without at the same time changing the meaning and effect?
5. The sentences vary in length from short (under 10 words) to long (over 30 words). Where and how does this variation emphasize Thomas's main points?
6. Check the etymology, denotation, and connotation of these words: *launch, ruminating, neuron, ganglion, forage, tentacle, termites, pellets, quorum, explore.*

**5-C**                              FAREWELL, MY LOVELY
                                        *E. B. White*

  These paragraphs are from an essay first published in the *New Yorker* (1936) with
which White was connected for many years. Richard L. Strout suggested the idea, and
so White signed the essay "Lee Strout White." In it, he pays tribute to the car most
responsible for starting the "age of the automobile." Writing nine years after the last
Model T was built, he had to assume that few of his readers strove drove a Model T. Note
how he combines factual information with warm emotion, and formal word choice
with colloquialisms.

WORD CHOICE        The Model T was distinguished from all other makes of
                   cars by the fact that its transmission was of a type known
metaphor           as planetary—which was half metaphysics, half sheer fic-
                   tion. Engineers accepted the word "planetary" in its epi-
                   cyclic sense, but I was always conscious that it also meant   5
                   "wandering," "erratic." Because of the peculiar nature of
                   this planetary element, there was always, in Model T, a
metaphor            certain dull rapport between engine and wheels, and even
                   when the car was in a state known as neutral, it trembled
                   with a deep imperative and tended to inch forward. There   10
                   was never a moment when the bands were not faintly
personification    egging the machine on. In this respect it was like a horse,
simile             rolling the bit on its tongue, and country people brought to
                   it the same technique they used with draft animals.
                      Its most remarkable quality was its rate of acceleration.   15
                   In its palmy days the Model T could take off faster than
                   anything on the road. The reason was simple. To get under
precise verbs      way, you simply hooked the third finger of the right hand
                   around a lever on the steering column, pulled down hard,
                   and shoved your left foot forcibly against the low-speed   20
                   pedal. These were simple, positive motions; the car
precise verbal     responded by lunging forward with a roar. After a few sec-
                   onds of this turmoil, you took your toe off the pedal, eased
precise verbs      up a mite on the throttle, and the car, possessed of only two
                   forward speeds, catapulted directly into high with a series   25
                   of ugly jerks and was off on its glorious errand. The abrupt-
                   ness of this departure was never equalled in other cars of
                   the period. The human leg was (and still is) incapable of
metaphor           letting in a clutch with anything like the forthright aban-
                   don that used to send Model T on its way. Letting in a   30
                   clutch is a negative, hesitant motion, depending on delicate
                   nervous control; pushing down the Ford pedal was a sim-
metaphor           ple, country motion—an expansive act, which came as nat-
simile             ural as kicking an old door to make it budge.
metaphor              The driver of the old Model T was a man enthroned.   35

margin notes:

metaphor

colloquialisms
metaphor

metaphor

simile
personification

metaphor

implied metaphor

simile

The car, with top up, stood seven feet high. The driver sat
on top of the gas tank, brooding it with his own body.
When he wanted gasoline, he alighted, along with everything else in the front seat; the seat was pulled off, the
metal cap unscrewed, and a wooden stick thrust down to  40
sound the liquid in the well. There were always a couple
of these sounding sticks kicking around in the ratty sub-
cushion regions of a flivver. Refuelling was more of a social
function then, because the driver had to unbend, whether
he wanted to or not. Directly in front of the driver was the  45
windshield—high,  uncompromisingly  erect.  Nobody
talked about air resistance, and the four cylinders pushed
the car through the atmosphere with a simple disregard of
physical law.

During my association with Model T's, self-starters were  50
not a prevalent accessory. They were expensive and under
suspicion. Your car came equipped with a serviceable
crank, and the first thing you learned was how to Get
Results. It was a special trick, and until you learned it (usually from another Ford owner, but sometimes by a period  55
of appalling experimentation) you might as well have been
winding up an awning. The trick was to leave the ignition
switch off, proceed to the animal's head, pull the choke
(which was a little wire protruding through the radiator)
and give the crank two or three nonchalant upward lifts.  60
Then, whistling as though thinking about something else,
you would saunter back to the driver's cabin, turn the
ignition on, return to the crank, and this time, catching it
on the down stroke, give it a quick spin with plenty of
That. If this procedure was followed, the engine almost  65
always responded—first with a few scattered explosions,
then with a tumultuous gunfire, which you checked by racing around to the driver's seat and retarding the throttle.
Often, if the emergency brake hadn't been pulled all the
way back, the car advanced on you the instant the first  70
explosion occurred and you would hold it back by leaning
your weight against it. I can still feel my old Ford nuzzling
me at the curb, as though looking for an apple in my
pocket.

The lore and legend that governed the Ford were  75
boundless. Owners had their own theories about everything; they discussed mutual problems in that wise, infinitely resourceful way old women discuss rheumatism.
Exact knowledge was pretty scarce, and often proved less
effective than superstition. Dropping a camphor ball into  80
the gas tank was a popular expedient; it seemed to have a

*implied metaphor*

tonic effect on both man and machine. There wasn't much
to base exact knowledge on. The Ford driver flew blind.
He didn't know the temperature of his engine, the speed
of his car, the amount of his fuel, or the pressure of his oil   85
(the old Ford lubricated itself by what was amiably
described as the "splash system"). A speedometer cost
money and was an extra, like a windshield-wiper. The
dashboard of the early models was bare save for an ignition
key. . . . Whatever the driver learned of his motor, he   90
learned not through instruments but through sudden
developments. . . .

*implied metaphor*

One reason the Ford anatomy was never reduced to an
exact science was that, having "fixed" it, the owner

*extended metaphor*

couldn't honestly claim that the treatment had brought   95
about the cure. There were too many authenticated cases
of Fords fixing themselves—restored naturally to health
after a short rest. Farmers soon discovered this, and it fitted
nicely with their draft-horse philosophy: "Let 'er cool off
and she'll snap into it again."   100

*metaphor*

Sprinkled not too liberally among the millions of amateur witch doctors who drove Fords and applied their own
abominable cures were the heaven-sent mechanics who

*implied metaphor*

could really make the car talk. These professionals turned
up in undreamed-of spots. One time, on the banks of the   105
Columbia River in Washington, I heard the rear end go

*implied metaphor*

out of my Model T when I was trying to whip it up a steep
incline onto the deck of a ferry. Something snapped; the
car slid backward into the mud. It seemed to me like the

*implied metaphor*
*metaphor*

end of the trail. But the captain of the ferry, observing the   110
withered remnant, spoke up.

"What's got her?" he asked.

"I guess it's the rear end," I replied, listlessly. The captain leaned over the rail and stared. Then I saw that there
was a hunger in his eyes that set him off from other men.   115

"Tell you what," he said, carelessly, trying to cover up

*colloquialism*

his eagerness, "let's pull the son of a bitch up onto the boat,
and I'll help you fix her while we're going back and forth
on the river."

We did just this. All that day I plied between the towns   120
of Pasco and Kennewick, while the skipper (who had once
worked in a Ford garage) directed the amazing work of

*implied metaphor*

resetting the bones of my car.

Springtime in the heyday of the Model T was a delirious
season. Owning a car was still a major excitement, roads   125

hyperbole

colloquialism

simile

implied metaphor

metaphor

were still wonderful and bad. The Fords were obviously conceived in madness: any car which was capable of going from forward into reverse without any perceptible mechanical hiatus was bound to be a mighty challenging thing to the human imagination. Boys used to veer them 130 off the highway into a level pasture and run wild with them, as though they were cutting up with a girl. Most everybody used the reverse pedal quite as much as the regular foot brake—it distributed the wear over the bands and wore them all down evenly. That was the big trick, to wear 135 all the bands down evenly, so that the final chattering would be total and the whole unit scream for renewal.

The days were golden, the nights were dim and strange. I still recall with trembling those loud, nocturnal crises when you drew up to a signpost and raced the engine so 140 the lights would be bright enough to read destinations by. I have never been really planetary since. I suppose it's time to say goodbye. Farewell, my lovely!

1. What words describe specific actions?
2. Where does White use figurative language and what is the effect?
3. Where and how does he explain technical terms?
4. How does the word choice show that White is being both serious and humorous?
5. The sentences vary in length from short (under 10 words) to long (over 25 words); where and how does White use this variation to emphasize his points?
6. Can you shorten any of the sentences by changing or omitting words without at the same time changing the meaning and effect?

---

**5-D**                    CHALLENGE
                        *Jesse Jackson*

These paragraphs come from the Reverend Jackson's speech to an audience composed primarily of black high school and college students at the 1979 convention of Operation PUSH. Note his use of colloquial language.

The reason I have so much faith in this generation of young people is because down through the years student involvement has made a difference in social change. During the McCarthy Era, students fought the threat of free speech being taken away from us. When Rosa Parks found herself in anguish she went to Dr. King who was a student who led that great struggle somewhere between 5 Selma and Montgomery. Students met a struggle and made a difference. The reason some of us can't make sound decisions is that we've been sidetracked. Some by violence, some by sex, some by lack of opportunity. I tell the story over and over again, how do you measure a man. You can't look at some cow-

boy definition of a man. You're not a man because you got notches on your belt; 10
you're not a man because you can violate somebody; you're not a man because
you can push somebody else down; you're not a man because you can kill
somebody.

You're a man because you can heal somebody. You're not a man because you
can make a baby; you're a man because you can raise a baby and provide for 15
a baby and produce for a baby. That makes you a man. Young sisters, there's
another side to that story. You can't measure yourself by your bosom—you've
got to do it by your books. You've got to have something in your mind. There's
nothing that's more perverted than to see somebody with a fully developed
bottom and a half developed brain. You've got to check out your mind. I got a 20
little message that says—the buses are not leaving now; so just sit down and be
cool. The buses are not leaving so just sit down and be cool. We have this situation for many of us do not want to face the reality and the options of our lives.
So when we begin to remind you about sex, we're not being unreal. Someone
said "Rev., you don't understand about sex—there's a thrill in sex." I understand 25
there's a thrill. I've got five children; I understand thrill, I'm not unaware of
that. Except, I also know this; that when people all around you tell you that you
can't do something and you can do it, and you do it—that's a thrill. When you
graduate from high school, that's a thrill. When you come across that stage and
have a Medical Degree or a Law Degree, that's a thrill. When you make a 30
touchdown, that's a thrill. When you do your best against the odds and make
it when everybody around you says you couldn't make it, that's a thrill. When
you end up going to college instead of to jail, that's also a thrill. And all I'm
saying is that we should not have a one-thrill syndrome; all of life can be thrill-
ing if you develop your mind, develop your body and develop your soul. Say 35
amen.

1. What specific, concrete words are used?
2. Where is repetition used for emphasis?
3. Can you condense any of the sentences by changing or omitting words or phrases
   without at the same time changing the meaning and effect?

---

5-E                          A METAPHOR USED TWICE
                                *Jacob Bronowski*

In *Science and Human Values* (rev. 1965), the writer, a scientist and philosopher,
argues that creative scientists and creative artists share the same goal, to discover unity
in the variety of experience, and both often devote years to uncovering the full significance of a single idea. He illustrates this with two brief quotations from Shakespeare's
plays. These paragraphs are given here mainly for the skilled analysis of Shakespeare's
metaphor, but note Bronowski's own word choice.

What is a poetic image but the seizing and the exploration of a hidden likeness, in holding together two parts of a comparison which are to give depth

each to the other? When Romeo finds Juliet in the tomb, and thinks her dead, he uses in his heartbreaking speech the words,

> Death that hath suckt the honey of thy breath. 5

The critic can only haltingly take to pieces the single shock which this image carries. The young Shakespeare admired Marlowe, and Marlowe's Faustus had said of the ghostly kiss of Helen of Troy that it sucked forth his soul. But that is a pale image; what Shakespeare has done is to fire it with the single word honey. Death is a bee at the lips of Juliet, and the bee is an insect that stings; 10 the sting of death was a commonplace phrase when Shakespeare wrote. The sting is there, under the image; Shakespeare has packed it into the word honey; but the very word rides powerfully over its own undertones. Death is a bee that stings other people, but it comes to Juliet as if she were a flower; this is the moving thought under the instant image. The creative mind speaks in such 15 thoughts.

More than ten years later Shakespeare came back to the image and unexpectedly made it concrete, a metaphor turned into a person in the drama. The drama is *Antony and Cleopatra;* the scene is the high tower; and to it death comes in person, as an asp hidden among figs. The image of the asp carries, of 20 course, many undertones; and most moving among these is Cleopatra's fancy, that this death, which should sting, has come to her to suck the sweetness. Cleopatra is speaking, bitterly, tenderly, about the asp:

> Peace, peace:
> Dost thou not see my Baby at my breast, 25
> That suckes the Nurse asleepe.

The man who wrote these words still carried in his ear the echo from Juliet's tomb, and what he added to it was the span of his life's work.

1. In the first paragraph, how appropriate are these words to the writer's point: *seizing, shock, fire, packed, rides?*
2. Check the etymology and various meanings of *fancy* and *image;* how is each word used here?

## ASSIGNMENTS

1. Write a paper of about 300 words on the word choice and figurative language in the description of the jet engine (Unit 2-C).
2. Revise one of your earlier essays by replacing vague words with precise, concrete ones and by omitting words that you do not need.
3. Read a column by a sports writer or listen to a radio sports announcer who you think makes events exciting; then write an essay discussing how particular words and phrases made the action seem vivid.
4. Compose a three-minute radio commercial for something you like very much, such

as a particular product, a performer, a movie, a political leader. Assume that your commercial will be broadcast only on your campus.

5. Rewrite the commercial you composed for assignment 4, but this time assume that it will be broadcast on a regular station. What changes must you make for the different audience?

6. Choose something inanimate, such as a pair of shoes, a bicycle, a stone, or a river, and in 200 to 300 words describe it as if it were a specific kind of animate creature, anything from a one-cell animal to a human being.

## Additional Assignments: Photographs

The photographs on the following pages may suggest subjects for your class discussions and writing assignments. Several of the assignments that follow appear also in the "Assignments" sections of earlier units. They are repeated here because you may now see them in a different light.

1. Choose one photograph and compare and contrast your opinions and interpretations with those of your classmates. What differences in opinion do you find? What seem to be the reasons for the differences? Present your answers to these questions in an essay of about 250 words.

2. Choose another photograph. What in it catches your attention most? Why? Compose a paragraph of about 150 words explaining your answers to these questions. Imagine that your readers will be from one of the following groups and indicate which group you have chosen: (a) people living and working in small towns; (b) people living and working in large cities; (c) elderly people; (d) students in your college; (e) tourists from foreign countries who want to learn about American life.

3. Choose one of the photographs and compose a detailed description of it in about 250 words. Imagine that you will read your description to another student who is suffering from temporary eye trouble and who wants to be able to follow class discussion of the photograph.

4. a. Choose two photographs that have something in common in subject or mood. In about 300 words, explain to one of the groups of readers listed in question 2 in what ways the photographs are similar.
   b. Choose two photographs that clearly differ in subject or mood. In about 300 words, explain to the same or another group of readers how these differ.

5. Imagine that the editor of a magazine that tries to appeal to the "general reader" plans to use one of the photographs and has asked you to write a narrative of about 300 to 500 words for which the photograph would make an appropriate illustration. You may draw on your own experience, actual events, your imagination, or any combination of these.

6. Imagine that a casting director has asked your help in selecting people for small character parts in several movies and has given you the photographs that show people's faces clearly. Choose two faces and write an essay of about 300 words describing the sorts of characters that you think they will suggest to an audience and explaining why you think so.

7. a. Choose a photograph and compose a title and a statement of about 50 words that could be used with it in a magazine or newspaper that tries to appeal to one of the groups listed in question 2.
   b. Compose another title and statement for the same photograph but with one of the other groups of readers in mind.

Hoops, de Wys

Hoops, de Wys

Serbin, de Wys

Dorothea Hahn (student)

Edward Hasuner/NYT Pictures

Rudy L. Klaiss/NYT Pictures

Teresa Sabala/NYT Pictures (Census Bureau—computer disk files)

# PART TWO

## Aids in Organizing

The trained mind relies on several patterns to organize thoughts logically. You must learn these so that you can help your readers to see the relationships among your main points. The assignments in Parts Two and Three will give you practice in a variety of patterns. Those in Part Two are relatively simple.

Unit 6 discusses the outline, the skeletal arrangement of ideas according to a formal pattern. It will help you to master and retain the ideas of other writers. It will also help you to plan your own writing. The outline not only condenses material but makes the relative importance of the parts visibly clear.

Unit 7 discusses the summary, the carefully proportioned condensation of your reading that you will often use in answering examination questions and making reports.

Unit 8 examines the chronological pattern, the straightforward order of time, already discussed in Unit 1, where it was applied to a sequence of events. Unit 8 shows how it can be applied to the steps of a process.

Unit 9 examines the use of comparison to reveal likenesses and differences. For this you have a choice of two basic patterns, the opposing and the alternating, each creating a different emphasis on the subject matter. This unit also examines a special form of comparison, the analogy, used to explain an unfamiliar or complex subject.

Unit 10 examines the problem of classification—the division of a group into the kinds or classes of which it is composed. This requires operating from a given principle and making a logical arrangement of the resulting parts.

All the assignments in Parts Two and Three are valuable exercises in the use of particular patterns. But you must remember that they are only exercises. They have much the same relationship to the real business of writing as practicing scales has to singing an aria. You will later find yourself combining several of these patterns in a single essay, for when the trained mind is faced with a complex writing problem, it turns naturally and skillfully from one pattern to another, or uses one within another, in any combination that best serves the particular purpose.

# UNIT 6

# The Outline

The outline lets you see a whole essay or lecture at a glance. It not only records the main ideas—any notes can do that—it also shows their relative importance and their relationships with each other. It can therefore give you essential help in studying and writing. Compare the usefulness of these two versions of the same information:

1. This presents it in a rough summary—

   History is divided into two periods—prehistoric, before writing, and historic, after writing. Prehistoric, known by remaining weapons and utensils, is divided into four stages: Old Stone (rude and primitive), New Stone (more advanced), Copper-Bronze (first use of metals), and Iron. Historic age is much better known through written records.

2. This presents it in a rough outline—

   History is divided into two periods:
      Prehistoric—before writing—known by weapons and utensils
         Old Stone (rude and primitive)
         New Stone (more advanced)
         Copper-Bronze (first use of metals)
         Iron

     Historic—after writing—much better known, through written records

The formal outline is merely a conventional, labeled arrangement of logical indentations like those shown in the second version. It may be more elaborate and precise than you can work out in detail while listening to a lecture, but you can apply the general principles even when in a hurry. Besides helping you to see how the writers and lecturers organized their main ideas, it will help you to organize your own. Every time you plan a paper, you will have occasion to work out a brief outline like that in Unit 1, "The Fundamentals of Writing." The longer the piece of writing is expected to be, the more detailed your planning should be. There are two common forms of outline: the topic outline and the sentence outline.

## Topic and Sentence Outlines

In both topic and sentence outlines, each heading, subheading, and sub-sub-heading is based on the relative importance of the parts of the material, without regard to paragraphing. The number of paragraphs in an essay has no necessary relation to the number of main sections of the thought of the essay. Some important points may require several paragraphs, others only one or two, depending on the complexity of the material to be presented. But in an outline the material is arranged logically, according to various degrees of importance, through a careful system of designations and indentations. The two kinds of outline differ only in the way each unit of thought is expressed. In the topic outline, a word or phrase indicates an item; in the sentence outline, each item is presented in a complete sentence. The topic outline is easier to write and is usually adequate for small plans for which you need only a reminder of the material and ideas involved. But for complex schemes, for material that you may put aside for some time, and above all for plans that someone else must read and evaluate, the sentence outline is far superior. Moreover, expressing each item in a complete sentence forces you to think through your material more thoroughly and will therefore make writing the paper easier.

## Outline Structure

Your success in outlining depends on your logic in choosing and arranging items. You must break down a whole into its main parts and then break each of these coordinate parts into its parts, and so on.

**Designation.**   The customary symbols to mark the parts are these:

Roman numerals (I, II, etc.) for main divisions
Capital letters (A, B, etc.) for secondary points
Arabic numerals (1, 2, etc.) for third-degree points
Lower-case letters (a, b, etc.) for fourth-degree points

You will not often need the fifth and sixth degrees, but when you do, indicate the fifth by Arabic numerals and the sixth by lower-case letters, each enclosed in parentheses.

**Indentation.**   All points of the same rank must be parallel down the page, each one beginning at the same distance from the left-hand margin. Indicate each subordinate rank by indenting it slightly to the right. With this method, all the Roman numerals for the main divisions will be the same distance from the left margin, all the capital letters for the secondary points will be indented slightly farther than the Roman numerals, and so on. If each degree is indented the equivalent of about three letters, you should have enough space left for the subpoints of the fourth degree and even for those of the fifth and sixth degrees, if you have any.

Make sure that the symbols stand out so that the relationships will be clear. The following arrangement is poor because the second line of each of the longer items (I and A) is at the same margin as the symbol for the item:

I. The Aztec Indians had early attained a very remarkable degree
of civilization.
    A. Their surviving buildings indicate a considerable knowledge
of architecture.
    B. Their ancient weapons are made with great skill.

This next arrangement makes the symbols stand out, and therefore the relationship of the parts is clear:

I. The Aztec Indians had early attained a very remarkable degree
   of civilization.
    A. Their surviving buildings indicate a considerable knowledge
      of architecture.
    B. Their ancient weapons are made with great skill.

## The Reading Outline

Making an outline is an excellent way to study anything you read, and later the outline will help you review it quickly.

**1. What is the main idea?** Read the entire piece through carefully—you would outline a book by chapters or other manageable units, not as a whole. Then reduce its central meaning to a single comprehensive sentence. This is the main idea or thesis, and should always appear at the head of your outline, for it represents the "essay as a whole." This thesis sentence should express content, not purpose, and should be long enough to indicate the major divisions of your plan. Omit all unnecessary expressions, such as "the author says."

**2. What are the main divisions of the author's thought?** These are the major sections into which the lesser points are grouped. If you find eleven, say, or seventeen, reconsider. You are probably "failing to see the forest because of the trees in the way" and are treating small details as important items. A single chapter or essay cannot manage so many main points—probably, in fact, not more than a half-dozen at most. Remember that there will be at least two, however; since outlining is a process of breaking down, a one-point outline is not an outline at all. If at first you think you have only one, it is the main idea, and you must break it down into points I, II, and so on.

**3. Make the main points comparable.** The material of each should have about the same level of importance as that of the others. If not, that point does not deserve equal rank in the outline. Whenever possible, make such equality clearly evident through parallel wording (see A and B under I in the examples at the top of this page).

**4. Break down each main section into its own smaller parts.** Thus you arrive at the secondary divisions, which you indicate by capital letters and an indented position.

**5. Finish outlining each main section before moving on.** It is better not to start on items of the third rank, however, until you have worked out all the second-rank items for that section, or on the fourth until the third is completed, and so on. Otherwise, you may lose perspective and give too much importance to trifling points. Be sure that within every level your points are logically of equal importance, and continue to indicate the fact not only by similar symbols and indentations but, wherever possible, by parallel wording as well.

**6. Make your outline follow a deductive order.** Proceed from the general to the particular, from the main point to the subpoints beneath it. Even if the author has deliberately reversed the order of the material for emphasis, giving the particulars first and arriving at the main point only through them, your outline must nevertheless present the author's points deductively.

**7. Omit everything irrelevant to the main plan.** Rhetorical questions, figures of speech, elaborate descriptions, repetitions for effect—reduce them all to the basic points they illustrate or emphasize. The college lecturer who advised students, "Take down the point I am trying to make, not the funny story I tell you in making it," was right—although you might mention such a story in its properly subordinate position as a subpoint under the superior point it illustrates.

**8. Use as many levels as you find suitable.** The purpose of your outline will determine how much detail you should include. For example, you may or may not choose to list under a point the three subpoints composing it, but if you mention one subpoint you are duty bound to give the others of the same rank.

**9. Avoid the meaningless single subpoint.** If the information on a point is not divisible into at least two subpoints, it has no subpoint at all. For instance, if the only example that you are going to give under the main heading "A. Trees" is "1. Oak," your main heading should be "A. Oak trees," because you do not have a subpoint. There is only one exception to this rule. If you have information for two or more subpoints under one heading (for example, "A. Dogs, 1. Beagles, 2. Poodles, 3. Boxers") but for only one under a matching heading, you may list that as "1" under "B" (for example, "B. Cats, 1. Siamese") to show that it is parallel with the subpoints under A and not with the more general heading of "A." Otherwise, incorporate the example into your statement of its superior point.

**10. Check your work to see that it is entirely logical.** Remember that your main-idea sentence must cover, briefly but definitely, the thought contained in the main points of the essay, and point "I" must read so as to include logically its own "A," "B," and "C," and so on. Similarly, each set of subpoints must add up to the main point under which it appears: "a," "b," and "c" must compose "1"; "1" and "2" must compose "A"; "A" and "B" must compose "I"; and "I," "II," "III" (plus the Introduction and Conclusion) must compose the main idea. (Sometimes a change in wording can correct a flaw in logic. If "a," "b," and "c" fit logically under "2," but "d" does not, you may be able to keep "d" by narrowing its scope or by enlarging the scope of "2" to include it.)

**11. Be consistent.** Whichever type of outline you choose for a particular purpose, do not mix it with the other type. Do not use single words or phrases to present any items in a sentence outline. Do not use any sentences in a topic outline.

## The Writing Outline

The outlines that you make to guide you in your own writing will be essentially the same as those you have made of your reading. The logic involved in the two is the same. Just as your reading outline is your version of the framework on which someone else has constructed an orderly essay or report, your writing outline is the framework on which you will construct your own. But here, instead of a completed work to take apart, you have the raw materials to put together: the ideas, facts, and opinions based on your own experiences, your reading, or the remarks of others. How to gather and organize material when making a preliminary outline for your own writing has already been discussed in Unit 1 (pages 10–12). For the formal structure of the outline, all the suggestions given for the reading outline also apply.

If your writing outline will be for your eyes alone, you may, of course, find a rough form adequate, but if others will read it to judge your plans or as a guide to your paper, you should follow the formal structure with great care.

## EXAMPLES

For your convenience, the paragraphs of the following essay are numbered. In both the sentence and the topic outlines given after the essay, these numbers are in the margin to emphasize the relationship between each outline and the essay.

*6-A* THE FIFTH FREEDOM
*Seymour St. John*

This essay was first published in the *Saturday Review* in 1955, but the writer's criticism of American education is still widely applicable. Note, for example, the 1977 plea for students' "right to fail" in William Zinsser's essay (Unit 14-C).

[1] More than three centuries ago a handful of pioneers crossed the ocean to Jamestown and Plymouth in search of freedoms they were unable to find in their own countries, the freedoms we still cherish today: freedom from want, freedom from fear, freedom of speech, freedom of religion. Today the descen-

dants of the early settlers, and those who have joined them since, are fighting 5
to protect these freedoms at home and throughout the world.

[2] And yet there is a fifth freedom—basic to those four—that we are in
danger of losing: *the freedom to be one's best*. St. Exupery describes a ragged,
sensitive-faced Arab child, haunting the streets of a North African town, as a
lost Mozart: he would never be trained or developed. Was he free? "No one 10
grasped you by the shoulder while there was still time; and nought will awaken
in you the sleeping poet or musician or astronomer that possibly inhabited you
from the beginning." The freedom to be one's best is the chance for the development of each person to his highest power.

[3] How is it that we in America have begun to lose this freedom, and how 15
can we regain it for our nation's youth? I believe it has started slipping away
from us because of three misunderstandings.

[4] First, the misunderstanding of the meaning of democracy. The principal
of a great Philadelphia high school is driven to cry for help in combating the
notion that it is undemocratic to run a special program of studies for outstanding 20
boys and girls. Again, when a good independent school in Memphis recently
closed, some thoughtful citizens urged that it be taken over by the public-school
system and used for boys and girls of high ability, that it have entrance requirements and give an advanced program of studies to superior students who were
interested and able to take it. The proposal was rejected because it was undem- 25
ocratic! Out of this misunderstanding comes the middle-muddle. Courses are
geared to the middle of the class. The good student is unchallenged, bored. The
loafer receives his passing grade. And the lack of an outstanding course for the
outstanding student, the lack of a standard which a boy or girl must meet, passes
for democracy. 30

[5] The second misunderstanding concerns what makes for happiness. The
aims of our present-day culture are avowedly ease and material well-being:
shorter hours; a shorter week; more return for less accomplishment; more soft-
soap excuses and fewer honest, realistic demands. In our schools this is reflected
by the vanishing hickory stick and the emerging psychiatrist. The hickory stick 35
had its faults, and the psychiatrist has his strengths. But the trend is clear: *Tout
comprendre c'est tout pardonner* [To understand everything is to excuse every-
thing]. Do we really believe that our softening standards bring happiness? Is it
our sound and considered judgment that the tougher subjects of the classics and
mathematics should be thrown aside, as suggested by some educators, for doll- 40
playing? Small wonder that Charles Malik, Lebanese delegate at the U.N.,
writes: "There is in the West" [in the United States] "a general weakening of
moral fiber. [Our] leadership does not seem to be adequate to the unprecedented challenges of the age."

[6] The last misunderstanding is in the area of values. Here are some of the 45
most influential tenets of teacher education over the past fifty years: there is no
eternal truth; there is no absolute moral law; there is no God. Yet all of history
has taught us that the denial of these ultimates, the placement of man or state

at the core of the universe, results in a paralyzing mass selfishness; and the first
signs of it are already frighteningly evident.                                    50

[7] Arnold Toynbee has said that all progress, all development come from
challenge and a consequent response. Without challenge there is no response,
no development, no freedom. So first we owe to our children the most demanding, challenging curriculum that is within their capabilities. Michelangelo did
not learn to paint by spending his time doodling. Mozart was not an accom- 55
plished pianist at the age of eight as the result of spending his days in front of
a television set. Like Eve Curie, like Helen Keller, they responded to the challenge of their lives by a disciplined training: and they gained a new freedom.

[8] The second opportunity we can give our boys and girls is the right to
failure. "Freedom is not only a privilege, it is a test," writes De Nöuy. What 60
kind of a test is it, what kind of freedom where no one can fail? The day is past
when the United States can afford to give high school diplomas to all who sit
through four years of instruction, regardless of whether any visible results can
be discerned. We live in a narrowed world where we must be alert, awake to
realism; and realism demands a standard which either must be met or result in 65
failure. These are hard words, but they are brutally true. If we deprive our
children of the right to fail we deprive them of their knowledge of the world
as it is.

[9] Finally, we can expose our children to the best values we have found. By
relating our lives to the evidences of the ages, by judging our philosophy in the 70
light of values that history has proven truest, perhaps we shall be able to produce that "ringing message, full of content and truth, satisfying the mind,
appealing to the heart, firing the will, a message on which one can stake his
whole life." This is the message that could mean joy and strength and leadership—freedom as opposed to serfdom.                                              75

## 6-B     SENTENCE OUTLINE OF "THE FIFTH FREEDOM"

The numbers in brackets near the left margin correspond to the paragraph numbers
in the essay. Within the outline, the italicized sentences in brackets are not part of the
outline; they give explanations of the outline structure.

**Main idea:** Besides the four freedoms we cherish, there is a fifth, the freedom to
be one's best, which we are in danger of losing through our misunderstandings but which we must preserve and pass on to our children by
challenging them.

[1]            I. Today we cherish four freedoms.
                 A. The pioneers came to America to find them.
                    1. One is freedom from want.
                    2. Another is freedom from fear.
                    3. Another is freedom of speech.                          5
                    4. Another is freedom of religion.

[*These are a common kind of subpoint, a simple enumeration. Here they are written out more fully than in
the essay, to satisfy the requirements of the sentence
outline.*]                                                                    10

    B. Today we fight to protect them.
    [*A and B are parallel subpoints as cause and effect of the
introductory statement; note the balanced wording.*]

[2]    II. The fifth freedom is freedom to be one's best.
    [*Now the subject of the essay, indicated by the title, begins;*  15
*the first main section prepared the way for it.*]
    A. It is basic to the other four.
    B. We are in danger of losing it.
    [*The incident of the Arab child, being only an illustration,
may be omitted from a brief outline.*]                                         20

[3–6]    III. We   are   losing   this   fifth   freedom   through   three
misunderstandings.
[*A question like the one that begins ¶3 is rhetorical and
should never appear in the outline in that form. Here, moreover, half the answer doesn't appear until the next point,*  25
*beginning in ¶7.*]

[4]    A. The first misunderstanding is of the meaning of democracy.
    1. We think that democracy in education means gearing all
courses to the middle level.
    2. We reject special programs and schools for superior stu-  30
dents as undemocratic.
    a. In Philadelphia a special program for superior stu-
dents was attacked.
    b. In Memphis a proposed special school for superior stu-
dents was rejected.                                                           35
    [*Here, a and b are examples supporting 2 which in
turn supports A and therefore should be included,
unlike the illustration in II. Notice both the continued reduction of the original wording and the par-
allel sentence structures for parallel points.*]                              40

[5]    B. The second misunderstanding is of the meaning of happiness and results from our stress on comfort rather than on
accomplishment.
    1. Our schools try to excuse children rather than discipline
them.                                                                          45
    2. They try to amuse children rather than educate them.
    [*Details such as shorter hours and metaphors such as
the hickory stick are omitted, the outline stripping the
essay down to its bare ideas.*]

[6]    C. The third misunderstanding is of ultimate values.         50
    1. These values have been denied in recent teacher
education.
    a. Eternal truth is denied.
    b. Absolute moral law is denied.
    c. The existence of God is denied.                             55

*[Subpoints at this level could be omitted, but if we include one we must include all.]*

  2. The inevitable result in mass selfishness is already evident.

[7–9]  IV. To assure our children the freedom to develop, we must chal- 60 lenge their abilities.
*[Toynbee's statement is a further illustration so that we can omit it from the outline.]*

[7]  A. We can give them a demanding curriculum.
  1. Michelangelo did not learn to paint by doodling.  65
  2. Mozart did not become a pianist by watching television.
  3. They, like Eve Curie and Helen Keller, were challenged by disciplined training.
  *[1 and 2 are negative examples and 3 is positive, but they are on the same level.]*  70

[8]  B. We can give them the right to failure.
  *[De Nouy's statements, like Toynbee's, can be omitted.]*
  1. We must not give high school diplomas without regard to merit.
  2. We must be realistic about failure to meet standards and 75 must teach our children realism.
  *[Again, 1 is a negative statement and 2 a positive one, but they are parallel points.]*

[9]  C. We can give them the best values we know.
  1. We can show them what history has taught us to be true. 80
  2. These truths may inspire us to make a "ringing message" that could mean true freedom for them.
  *[Although 1 is the means and 2 is the end in view, they are parallel points under C.]*

Note the following points about the preceding outline:

**1.** The statement of the main idea makes specific reference to the four main points and is therefore a one-sentence *summary* of the essay; but it does not attempt to jump a level and include any of the supporting points.

**2.** The four sentences stating the main points, I, II, III and IV, when taken together, form a slightly longer summary of the essay. We can, in turn, expand this by including the sentences for points A, B, and C.

**3.** These summaries would seem stiff if compared to the summary of the essay on page 112. Sentence designations in the outline have replaced the transitions used in the summary, and the effort to keep parallel points in parallel wording has eliminated sentence variety. As a piece of writing, the summary is obviously better; but as a view of the writer's organization, the outline is better.

**4.** Starting with the lowest level of subpoints (in this example, designated "a," "b," and so on), check for two things: first, to see that all statements having designations of the same level are actually comparable in importance; second, to see that all subpoints, at every level, are actually logical under the superior point of which they are the divisions.

*6-C*         TOPIC OUTLINE OF "THE FIFTH FREEDOM"

**Main idea:** Besides the four freedoms we cherish there is a fifth, the freedom to be one's best, which we are in danger of losing through our misunderstandings but which we must preserve and pass on to our children by challenging them.

[1]                    I. Four cherished freedoms—from want, from fear, of speech, of religion
                          A. Sought by early settlers.
                          B. Protected by our efforts today
[2]                   II. Fifth freedom—to be one's best                                    5
                          A. Basic to other four
                          B. In danger of being lost
[3–6]                III. Three misunderstandings of fifth freedom
[4]                       A. Democracy
                             1. Education geared to middle level                            10
                             2. Special education for superior students considered undemocratic
[5]                       B. Happiness
                             1. Children excused, not disciplined
                             2. Children amused, not educated                               15
[6]                       C. Values
                             1. Denial of all ultimate values
                             2. Mass selfishness as result
[7–9]                IV. Challenge necessary for children's development
[7]                       A. Demanding curriculum                                           20
                             1. Michelangelo
                             2. Mozart
                             3. Eve Curie and Helen Keller
[8]                       B. Right to failure
                             1. High school diplomas on merit only                          25
                             2. Realistic view of failure
[9]                       C. Our best values
                             1. Teachings from history
                             2. Inspiration to be truly free                                30

Compare this topic outline with the sentence outline preceding it. What differences do you see in wording and arrangement? The brevity here results not only from using fewer words in each item but from using fewer low-order subpoints. Although a topic outline can have as many subdivisions as a sentence outline, in practice it usually has fewer.


*6-D*                      CLUTTER
                       *William Zinsser*

Often, what you plan to outline will not have convenient transitional markers like "First," "Second," and "Finally" to guide you to the divisions and subdivisions of the material. The third chapter from *On Writing Well* (1980), quoted here in full, lacks such markers, but often the first sentence of a paragraph is a guide to that paragraph's relation to the rest of the discussion. Zinsser develops here the claim he made earlier in his book that "Clutter is the disease of American writing. We are a society strangling in unnecessary words, circular constructions, pompous frills and meaningless jargon."

The numbers and letters in the margin correspond to those of the topic outline that follows.

I.

[1] Fighting clutter is like fighting weeds—the writer is always slightly behind. New varieties sprout overnight, and by noon they are part of American speech. It only takes a John Dean testifying on TV to have everyone in the country saying "at this point in time" instead of "now."   5

II.
  A.
    1.
    2.

[2] Consider all the prepositions that are routinely draped onto verbs that don't need any help. Head up. Free up. Face up to. We no longer head committees. We head them up. We don't face problems anymore. We face up to them when we can free up a few minutes. A small detail, 10 you may say—not worth bothering about. It *is* worth bothering about. The game is won or lost on hundreds of small details. Writing improves in direct ratio to the number of things we can keep out of it that shouldn't be there. "Up" in "free up" shouldn't be there. Can we picture anything 15 being freed *up?* The writer of clean English must examine every word that he puts on paper. He will find a surprising number that don't serve any purpose.

  B.
    1.
    2.

[3] Take the adjective "personal," as in "a personal friend of mine," "his personal feeling" or "her personal 20 physician." It is typical of the words that can be eliminated nine times out of ten. The personal friend has come into the language to distinguish him from the business friend, thereby debasing not only language but friendship. Someone's feeling *is* his personal feeling—that's what "his" 25 means. As for the personal physician, he is that man so often summoned to the dressing room of a stricken actress so that she won't have to be treated by the impersonal physician assigned to the theater. Someday I'd like to see him identified as "her doctor." 30

[4] Or take those curious intervals of time like the short minute. "Twenty-two short minutes later she had won the final set." Minutes are minutes, physicians are physicians, friends are friends. The rest is clutter.

  C.

[5] Clutter is the laborious phrase which has pushed out 35 the short word that means the same thing. These locutions are a drag on energy and momentum. Even before John Dean gave us "at this point in time," people had stopped saying "now." They were saying "at the present time," or

"currently," or "presently" (which means "soon"). Yet the 40
idea can always be expressed by "now" to mean the
immediate moment ("Now I can see him"), or by "today"
to mean the historical present ("Today prices are high"), or
simply by the verb "to be" ("It is raining"). There is no
need to say, "At the present time we are experiencing 45
precipitation."

III.

A.

[6] Speaking of which, we are experiencing considerable
difficulty getting *that* word out of the language now that
it has lumbered in. Even your dentist will ask if you are
experiencing any pain. If he were asking one of his own 50
children he would say, "Does it hurt?" He would, in short,
be himself. By using a more pompous phrase in his professional role he not only sounds more important; he blunts
the painful edge of truth. It is the language of the airline

B.

stewardess demonstrating the oxygen mask that will drop 55
down if the plane should somehow run out of air. "In the
extremely unlikely possibility that the aircraft should experience such an eventuality," she begins—a phrase so oxy-
gen-depriving in itself that we are prepared for any disaster, and even gasping death shall lose its sting. As for those 60
"smoking materials" that she asks us to "kindly extin-
guish," I often wonder what materials are smoking. Maybe
she thinks my coat and tie are on fire.

C.

[7] Clutter is the ponderous euphemism that turns a slum
into a depressed socioeconomic area, a salesman into a 65
marketing representative, a dumb kid into an underachiever and garbage collectors into waste disposal personnel. In New Canaan, Conn., the incinerator is now the
"volume reduction plant." I hate to think what they call
the town dump.                                                    70

D.

[8] Clutter is the official language used by the American
corporation—in the news release and the annual report—
to hide its mistakes. When a big company recently
announced that it was "decentralizing its organizational
structure into major profitcentered businesses" and that 75
"corporate staff services will be aligned under two senior
vice-presidents" it meant that it had had a lousy year.

[9] Clutter is the language of the interoffice memo ("The
trend to mosaic communication is reducing the meaning-
fulness of concern about whether or not demographic seg- 80
ments differ in their tolerance of periodicity") and the language of computers ("We are offering functional digital
programming options that have built-in parallel reciprocal
capabilities with compatible third-generation contingen-
cies and hardware").                                              85

E.

[10] Clutter is the language of the Pentagon throwing dust in the eyes of the populace by calling an invasion a "reinforced protective reaction strike" and by justifying its vast budgets on the need for "credible second-strike capability" and "counterforce deterrence." How can we grasp 90 such vaporous double-talk? As George Orwell pointed out in "Politics and the English Language," an essay written in 1946 but cited frequently during the Vietnam years of Johnson and Nixon, "In our time, political speech and writing are largely the defense of the indefensible.... Thus 95 political language has to consist largely of euphemism, question-begging and sheer cloudy vagueness." Orwell's warning that clutter is not just a nuisance but a deadly tool did not turn out to be inoperative. By the 1960s his words had come true in America.                                                100

IV.

[11] I could go on quoting examples from various fields—every profession has its growing arsenal of jargon to fire at the layman and hurl him back from its walls. But the list would be depressing and the lesson tedious. The point of raising it now is to serve notice that clutter is the 105 enemy, whatever form it takes. It slows the reader and robs the writer of his personality, making him seem pretentious.

A.

[12] Beware, then, of the long word that is no better than the short word: "numerous" (many), "facilitate" (ease), "individual" (man or woman), "remainder" (rest), "initial" 110 (first), "implement" (do), "sufficient" (enough), "attempt" (try), "referred to as" (called), and hundreds more.

B.

Beware, too, of all the slippery new fad words for which the language already has equivalents: overview and quantify, paradigm and parameter, input and throughput, peer 115 group and interface, private sector and public sector, optimize and maximize, prioritize and potentialize. They are all weeds that will smother what you write.

C.

[13] Nor are all the weeds so obvious. Just as insidious are the little growths of perfectly ordinary words with 120 which we explain how we propose to go about our explaining, or which inflate a simple preposition or conjunction into a whole windy phrase.

1.

[14] "I might add," "It should be pointed out," "It is interesting to note that"—how many sentences begin with 125 these dreary clauses announcing what the writer is going to do next? If you might add, add it. If it should be pointed out, point it out. If it is interesting to note, *make* it interesting. Being told that something is interesting is the surest way of tempting the reader to find it dull; are we not all 130

2.

stupefied by what follows when someone says, "This will

interest you"? As for the inflated prepositions and conjunctions, they are the innumerable phrases like "with the possible exception of" (except), "for the reason that"
(because), "he totally lacked the ability to" (he couldn't), 135
"until such time as" (until), "for the purpose of" (for).

V.       [15] Clutter takes more forms than you can shake twenty
sticks at. Prune it ruthlessly. Be grateful for everything that
you can throw away. Re-examine each sentence that you
put on paper. Is every word doing new and useful work? 140
Can any thought be expressed with more economy? Is anything pompous or pretentious or faddish? Are you hanging
on to something useless just because you think it's
beautiful?

[16] Simplify, simplify.                                    145


*6-E*                TOPIC OUTLINE OF "CLUTTER"

**Main idea:** To write effectively we must reduce clutter in our use of language.

[1]          I. Problem of rapid growth of clutter
            II. Redundancies
[2]              A. Prepositions
                    1. Unnecessary ("head up")
                    2. Illogical ("free up")
[3–4]            B. Adjectives
                    1. Unnecessary ("his personal feeling")
                    2. Debasing meaning ("personal friendship")
[5]              C. Longer words and phrases
[6]         III. Euphemisms and jargon to conceal unpleasant truths
                 A. Physical pain
                 B. Danger
[7]              C. Social discrimination
[8–9]            D. Bad business news
[10]             E. Government action
            IV. Other redundancies
[11–14]          A. Long words and phrases ("numerous" for "many")
                 B. Fad words ("optimize")
                 C. Ordinary words
[15]                1. Unnecessary explanations
[16]                2. Inflated prepositions and conjunctions
             V. Need for ruthless editing: simplify


1. In "The Fifth Freedom" every paragraph received an outline designation either of
the first or second level (I and II, and III. A, B, C, and IV. A, B, and C). How does
the relationship between the paragraphs and the outline designations of "Clutter"
differ from this?
2. What are the reasons for the differences?

3. Why do paragraphs 4 and 9 have no corresponding designations in the outline?
4. How is paragraph 13 related to the rest of the essay?
5. In the outline II.A and II.B are subdivided, but II.C is not. Why?
6. Make a sentence outline of "Clutter."

## ASSIGNMENTS

1. Before you start work on outlining the ideas in an essay, test your knowledge of numbering and arrangement and your sense of logical relationships by putting into proper topical outline form the items in the following unorganized list. Use as many main points and as many degrees of subordination as the material seems to you to require, but limit yourself to these words.

| | | | |
|---|---|---|---|
| caves | meat | sandals | chicken |
| clothing | tents | Irish potatoes | fruit |
| sausage | vegetables | pork | sneakers |
| potatoes | lemons | boots | shelter |
| food | suits | oranges | hats |
| cabins | cottages | hamburger | beans |
| apples | lima beans | sweet potatoes | houses |
| sauerkraut | cole slaw | slippers | corn |
| pineapple | bacon | grapefruit | beef |
| caps | bungalows | berets | headgear |
| footwear | navy beans | T-bone steaks | cabbage |

   a. Assuming common agreement as to the definition of each term, there can be no disagreement as to two aspects of the completed arrangement: the items that will appear in a single group at a given level (such as oranges, lemons, etc.) and the subpoints that will appear under a given main point (such as oranges, lemons, etc., under fruit); for this much is logically inherent in the material.
   b. However, the arrangement of the items within a single group at any level will vary according to purpose. Consider, for example, the differing orders of the five items under the larger heading of fruit that may result, depending on whether the issue is size, color, type, price, scarcity, area of production, popularity, or nutritive value. Justify, according to some such purpose, the order within each group in your own arrangement. Will the same purpose determine the order within each?
   c. Under what main idea might all these items appear?
2. Choose a magazine article, a book chapter, or an essay from a unit in this book and compose an outline of each type based on it. These should be good for your first efforts: Unit 1-B, Unit 2-H, Unit 4-F and G, Unit 10-B, F, and H. These are more challenging: Unit 2-G; Unit 3-C and D; Unit 4-C and E; Unit 9-F; Unit 11-E and G; Unit 12-I; Unit 13-F; Unit 14-E; Unit 16-F.
3. Check your outlines carefully with the directions given earlier in this unit. Make sure that they are consistent in logic and structure and give a faithful breakdown of the original.

# The Summary

As a beginning college student, you may wish that you could write shorthand and capture every word in your lecture courses. It is a needless wish. As a matter of fact, if you do know shorthand you will be unwise to try to take down a whole lecture, word for word. You would have to spend valuable time later transcribing and would rob yourself of valuable practice in summarizing.

The many details that fill our daily lives constantly force us to condense them in some way so that we can retain what is most significant. In college, you must not only take lecture and reading notes but also summarize much of your reading, and perhaps write synopses of plays or novels. Outside, you will want to get the gist of a speech, a news report, an article on current affairs, a new technical work in your own professional field. You may use an outline, a skeleton form of summarizing (Unit 6), or you may condense the essential material into readable paragraph form, writing what is variously called an abstract, a digest, a précis, or a summary.

The summaries in popular magazine digests are not often the best models for practical purposes; aimed at maximum reader appeal, they usually consist only of selected chunks of the original (the more dramatic bits), skillfully glued together by editorial transitions, and are abridgments rather than true summaries. To record briefly the essence of the information that an author has presented in detail, you may be wise to sacrifice reader interest in favor of a more sober and better-balanced type of condensation.

**1. Select only the main points.** Good writers use all kinds of devices to impress their main issues on a reader. They repeat them, perhaps several times, in different words; they use figures of speech; they fill their articles with descriptive details and narrative examples. In writing a summary, you must pick your way through all these rhetorical devices to arrive at concise statements of the essential ideas only.

**2. Determine the length of a summary by your needs.** You may reduce a 500-page book to a tenth of its length, or you may state its theme in a single sentence, depending on how much detail you require. The longer the material to be summarized, however, the shorter the summary is likely to be, in proportion, since all the material must be reduced to manageable form. Your instructor may suggest a summary of a certain length or proportion.

**3. Paragraph according to your material, not the author's.** The number of paragraphs in the summary bears no relationship to the number in the original essay but should be determined by the rules of good paragraph development. The result may well be, as we shall see later, the use of one paragraph for each of the main points of the essay.

**4. Apportion your space fairly according to the material.** A more or less literal reproduction of one or more important paragraphs in an essay is not a summary (unless, of course, the author has included summarizing paragraphs of which you may take advantage). The summary should be the essay in miniature, a condensation of the whole, not a selection of bits and pieces.

**5. Avoid, in general, the author's phrasing and sentence structure.** A summary involves no question of plagiarism, since it does not pretend to be original in any sense. But if you depend too much on the author's phrasing and sentence structure, you may find yourself with a neatly written copy of the material rather than with a brief summary of its content. Putting an idea into your own words is the surest way to prove your understanding of it.

**6. Do not, however, write a paraphrase.** A paraphrase is the translation of another work into simpler words and sentences. Like any careful translation, it includes every thought. This may make the meaning of the original clearer, but the process of simplifying will almost certainly make it longer. Remember, a summary is a condensation—a shorter form of the original.

**7. Read through the entire work before you begin to summarize it.** If it is long, you will find that jotting down notes on the main points will help you later. Then, when you can see it as a whole, decide which are the author's essential points and which lesser points you should include to make the essential ones clear. In choosing lesser points, always keep in mind your reader's needs and the intended length of your summary.

**8. Write your summary from the author's point of view.** As much as possible, keep the flavor, the tone, of the original. Especially avoid such expressions as "the author says," and concentrate on a clear-cut phrasing of *what* he or she says. Compare the information value of these two sentences summarizing Example D on page 252:

**a.** Mark Twain discusses the meaning of the word *lagniappe*.
[*This adds little to what the title and author lines tell us.*]

**b.** Lagniappe, a Spanish word we picked up in New Orleans, means something extra thrown in for good measure.
[*This tells us not merely that he said something, but what he said, from the first-person point of view used in the essay.*]

**9. Omit all extraneous comments.** The summary is no place to record your own opinion of the material condensed. Such comments as "The author says that he thinks socialized medicine a good thing, but I disagree with him" are criticisms and are entirely out of place here. "Socialized medicine is a good thing" followed by a digest of the material offered in support of this opinion is all that belongs in the summary, which should be a condensation of the facts and opinions presented by the author—nothing more.

Be faithful to the author's emphasis and interpretation. You may find some of the author's lesser points more interesting than the main points, but a good summary is not your version of the author's material. It should be a miniature version of the original.

## EXAMPLES

The following three summaries are all of "The Fifth Freedom," which appears in the preceding unit (pages 99–101), where it is also outlined. Compare these summaries with each other and with the sentence and topic outlines to determine the advantages and disadvantages of each as a way to reduce material to its essential elements.

### 7-A    SUMMARY OF "THE FIFTH FREEDOM"

This summary reduces the essay to one-fourth its original length.

More than three centuries ago a few pioneers came to America in search of the freedoms we still cherish: freedom from want, freedom from fear, freedom of speech, and freedom of religion. Today their descendants and others are fighting to protect those freedoms everywhere. But there is a fifth freedom, basic to these four, that we are in danger of losing—the freedom to be one's 5 best through the opportunity of developing to one's highest power. (¶¶ 1–2)

This freedom is in danger because of three misunderstandings. The first is about the meaning of democracy. This misunderstanding has defeated attempts to give special opportunities to superior students. The second is about what makes for happiness. Our culture's stress on material well-being has been 10 reflected in the schools by too little discipline and too easy subjects. The third is about the importance of values. The recent denial of such ultimates as eternal truth, absolute moral law, and the existence of God is already reflected in increasing mass selfishness. (¶¶ 3–6)

To preserve the fifth freedom, we must do three things. First, we must give 15 our children the most challenging curriculum of which they are capable, for only a disciplined training produces great people. Second, we must give them the right to fail, for only through standards that make for success or failure can they learn what real life is like. Third, we must give them the best values that history has given us; these will assure them of freedom. (¶¶ 7–9)    20

1. What supporting details are omitted in the summary?

2. Why is the first paragraph of the summary as long as the last although the original material that it condenses is only half the length of that condensed in the last paragraph?

---

## 7-B ONE-PARAGRAPH SUMMARY OF "THE FIFTH FREEDOM"

This summary reduces the essay to slightly more than one-tenth its original length.

We are still fighting today to protect what the pioneers sought in America three centuries ago: freedom from want and fear, and of speech and religion. Basic to these, a fifth freedom—to be one's best by developing to one's highest power—is now endangered by three misunderstandings: of the meaning of democracy, the nature of happiness, and the importance of moral values. As a 5 result, all our standards have deteriorated alarmingly. To preserve this freedom, we must give our children the most challenging curriculum possible, the right to fail, and exposure to the highest moral values.

## 7-C ONE-SENTENCE SUMMARY OF "THE FIFTH FREEDOM"

This summary reduces the essay to less than one-twentieth its original length.

To preserve the traditional four freedoms for our children, we must also preserve a fifth, freedom to be one's best through full development, which we must safeguard by intellectual challenges, realistic testing, and high moral standards.

## ASSIGNMENTS

1. Study the three summaries carefully, comparing each with the original essay and with each other. Note in each what is saved in space and what is lost in detail.
2. Turn back to one of the essays in an earlier unit and summarize it in one sentence. Then summarize it in about 200 words. What have you been able to include in the longer summary that you had to omit in the shorter one? In writing the longer summary, consider your paragraphing carefully. The number of paragraphs you use will not necessarily be related to the number in the original material, but it may indicate the number of main points in the original.
3. As assigned by your instructor, reduce other essays in this book to a single sentence—the author's "thesis," or main idea. Which are more difficult to summarize and why?

# UNIT 8

## Process

A frequent purpose of expository writing is to explain a procedure. This may take the form of specific direction-giving (telling the readers how to do something that they presumably want to do) or of more general information-giving (telling the readers how something that is interesting in itself is done). The same basic organizational pattern is used in each, but the styles of presentation differ.

### Giving Directions

Directions are all around us, from the simple "Stop" on a street sign to the intricacies of parliamentary procedure explained in *Robert's Rules of Order*. We find them in cookbooks and laboratory manuals, on seed packets and instruction sheets accompanying new appliances. They are the basis of much education both in school and out, and you will frequently find yourself in the role of teacher.

On any level, direction-giving requires extraordinary care. The first requirement is clarity. Although many other types of expository writing are merely to satisfy the curiosity of the readers or add to their general knowledge, the explanation of a procedure usually leads them to action. If they cannot follow your direction-giving easily and accurately, it will be worthless. It is essential not only that you know your subject well but also that you keep your readers' needs constantly in mind.

**1. Choose a suitable subject.** It should be some process that you have actually done yourself—if your information is secondhand, your readers will probably do better to learn it directly from the source. Be sure, furthermore, that the subject is one on which it is possible to give real "directions" that reasonably intelligent readers can expect to follow with success. The advice to "choose a small subject and develop it thoroughly" applies here; directions that are too condensed may be worse than none at all. In choosing a subject, consider both the length of the paper you plan to write and the time you have available for writing it.

**2. Give complete details.** You are something of a specialist in the subject in which you are giving directions, or you would not have chosen it. But you are writing for those who wish to learn, not for those who already know. When specialists discuss their specialties with ordinary people, they often have difficulty putting themselves in another's place. The experienced chef, in giving a recipe, may omit a detail that other chefs would take for granted, but without it the amateur will struggle in vain to re-create the culinary masterpiece. Always assume your readers to be ignorant of your subject (they probably are), and leave no blanks. On the other hand, don't antagonize them by "talking down" unnecessarily.

**3. Define special terms.** Words that you take for granted, from the height of your experience, may be a real stumbling block to "general readers," people with ordinary intelligence and curiosity but little or no knowledge of your subject. Every field has its own peculiar vocabulary—special words, or special meanings attached to familiar ones, which seem to the uninitiated like a foreign language. Words and phrases such as "empennage," "shim" and "clarify the butter" will be immediately understood by the aeronautical engineer, the carpenter, and the cook, respectively, and may be used freely by one craftsman in writing for others of that craft. But when you write for general readers, you must be on your guard, carefully defining such terms whenever you cannot omit them or substitute more familiar ones.

**4. Give reasons for the steps involved.** Clear directions carefully followed may result in a successful conclusion even though followed blindly, but intelligent readers will be grateful for a running explanation of *why* a certain step is necessary as well as *how* it is to be taken. The explanation may save them from trying dangerous shortcuts. "Always work with the knife blade turned away from you so that you will not cut yourself if it slips." "Let the milk cool before adding the beaten egg, which otherwise will cook into lumps before you can stir it in."

**5. Include negative directions.** It is often important to warn readers what *not* to do, with a brief mention of the reasons. "Do not hold the compass near any metal object, such as your belt buckle, because it may fail to register accurately." "Never allow the glass that has contained cyanide to be used for any other purpose, because it cannot be entirely cleaned of the poison." Your science instructor and laboratory manual will give further illustrations of negative advice.

**6. Use illustrative aids.** Never let your directions remain vague or general if you can find a way to be definite and concrete. A hurriedly sketched map is more useful than a page of written instructions on how to go somewhere; a simple sketch or diagram accompanying the text may do much to clarify a complicated procedure. Verbal images such as "The standard gearshift is arranged in an H pattern" are valuable descriptive aids in direction-giving.

## Giving Information

Not all accounts of processes, however, are intended to give readers directions by which they may themselves perform the process. We are interested in many operations that we never expect to perform or even to witness. From *Robinson Crusoe* to the feature article in today's magazine, literature has been filled with accounts of such operations, and readers have flocked to them, not to get directions for themselves, but to satisfy their curiosity and add to their general knowledge.

For every process (welding, dissection, engine repair, cooking) that you will learn from directions so that you can perform it, there will be a dozen (the working of the party system, the operation of the law of supply and demand, the procedures of a legislature) that you will want explained only so that you can understand how they are done. Similarly, in conversation, in examination and report writing, and in many other circumstances, you will be required to explain a process in which you may never have been directly involved.

The demands that writing such informative papers make upon you differ in some details from those of direction-giving.

**1. Your subject may be something you have not done.** In fact, it may well be something that no one person can do. But it should still be something with which you are thoroughly familiar. If you have lived in a mining district, you probably need not have been a miner in order to give a reader an accurate account of the mining process. A first trip through a steel mill, if you have a lively interest, some previous knowledge, and a good guide, might conceivably supply you with enough material for an interesting though relatively general account of how steel is made.

**2. Your subject may be a relatively long, involved process.** Compare the subject of "how to make a steel casing," a process that one person can perform, with "how steel is made," a process requiring elaborate equipment and many workers. With the first, you would give your readers specific directions that they could follow. With the second, which your readers would not expect to repeat on their own, you would give far less detail.

## Organization in Giving Directions or Information

Since time is always involved in doing things, the pattern of both types of process paper is necessarily the simplest one—chronological. Asked how to get to City Hall, you may reply, "Continue east to the first traffic light, then turn left and go three blocks." In explaining any process involving more than a single step, you would be foolish to wrench the steps out of their natural time sequence.

The sequence of parts, then, takes care of itself in this type of expository writing, but you must choose how to group them within the sequence. You will be faced with a multitude of small, separate steps to group into a few clear, manageable units. You should undertake this planning before you begin the actual writing of the essay. An orderly plan will guide you as you write, and it will guide your readers later. Four suboperations of five steps each, for instance, are far easier to follow and remember than twenty single steps.

However familiar you may be with the process of starting a new lawn, for example, you must first think through the decisions and motions involved in that procedure. You may decide that these steps should be mentioned:

1. Weeding
2. Digging to loosen soil
3. Liming
4. Fertilizing
5. Raking to distribute chemicals
6. Seeding
7. Raking to distribute seed
8. Rolling
9. Watering

When you look over your list, however, you may find that these steps are not equal in importance and that they can be grouped into a few main units, each consisting of a number of related steps.

I. Preparing the soil
  A. Weeding
  B. Digging to loosen soil
II. Adding chemicals
  A. Liming
  B. Fertilizing
  C. Raking to distribute chemicals
III. Planting seed
  A. Seeding
  B. Raking to distribute seed
  C. Rolling
IV. Watering

You are at last ready to start writing. Cover the bones of this skeleton plan with the flesh of words and phrases. Your plan should never stick out unpleasantly through the body of your finished prose, as though your paper were only a sentence outline. It should instead give your readers a pleasant sense of meaningful order. Determine the amount of space needed for each main division and develop your paragraphs accordingly. Use transitional devices to hold them together and especially to clarify any shift from one division of your subject to another, but vary these devices. Do not overdo the easy but monotonous "then" and "the next step."

## *Reader Interest*

To write the everyday cookbook variety of direction-giving, in which space is at a premium, you need only clarity and good logical order. Someone wishing to operate a washing machine in a laundromat wants no more than brief, clear, numbered directions. But in a process essay, you may often prefer to use special devices to gain reader interest.

Consider, for instance, what attitude you should take toward your material— what tone to adopt for the particular audience that you intend to reach. In direction-giving you need not limit yourself to the formal "One does this" or the more direct and personal "Do that." You may instead present your directions in a personal narrative and, by saying something like "I did this," add human interest. Rather than plunging directly into the first step of the procedure, you may begin in a leisurely fashion—with an account of how you came to be familiar with the process, or why you consider it worth doing. Instead of ending with the final step, you may give an account of the results of the procedure and their significance—not an essential part of direction-giving as such but often adding reader interest.

In the paper informing us of a process rather than giving us directions for doing it, the pressure to be interesting increases. Although the reader who wants to know how to do something may be entirely satisfied with simple, clear directions, the reader who wants general information may turn away from an account that is not lively as well as intelligible. Here is your chance to use fully the arts of description, narration, and characterization as aids to exposition. Enliven your account of how steel is made by vivid descriptions of the furnaces and what goes on in them, with sketches of the people who operate them, or with your own personal reactions to the scene, so that your readers feel that they are there, sharing the experience with you. And give special thought to composing an attention-getting beginning and a memorable ending.

## *EXAMPLES*

The first four selections exemplify direction-giving, and the remaining three information-giving. Notice the differences among them in the use of detail and in the degree to which the writers try to catch the interest of readers.

*8-A*                              BAKED BEANS

This is a standard recipe from a cookbook.

Soak 2 cupfuls of dry beans overnight. In the morning, boil until soft, and drain. Put them into a covered bean pot with ¼ lb. salt pork. Mix into ½ cup of boiling water the following: ½ tsp. baking soda, ¼ tsp. mustard, ¼ cup molasses, and salt and pepper to taste. Pour over beans, adding enough more water to

cover. Bake for 6 hours in a slow oven, uncovering during the last half hour to 5
brown.

**8-B**                        BAKING BEANS
                          *Louise Dickinson Rich*

This selection comes from *We Took to the Woods* (1942), an autobiographical
account of the author's experience after she and her husband left their city home for
what they hoped would be the "simple life" in Maine.

Now about the baking of the beans. Baked beans have to be baked. That
sounds like a gratuitous restatement of the obvious, but it isn't. Some misguided
souls boil beans all day and call the lily-livered result baked beans. I refrain
from comment.

We use either New York State or Michigan white beans, because we like 5
them best, although yellow-eyes are very popular, too. I take two generous cups
of dry beans, soak overnight and put them on to boil early in the morning.
When the skins curl off when you blow on them, they're boiled long enough.
Then I put in the bottom of the bean pot, or iron kettle with a tight-fitting
cover, a six-by-eight-inch square of salt pork with the rind slashed every quarter 10
of an inch, a quarter of a cup of sugar, half a cup of molasses, a large onion
chopped fairly fine, and a heaping teaspoonful of dry mustard. This amount of
sugar and molasses may be increased or cut, depending on whether you like
your beans sweeter or not so sweet. This is a matter every man has to decide
for himself. The beans are dumped in on top of this conglomerate, and enough 15
hot water is added to cover, but only cover. The baking pot should be large
enough so there's at least an inch of freeboard above the water. Otherwise
they'll boil over and smell to high heaven. Cover tightly and put into a medium
oven—about 350° is right. They should be in the oven by half past nine in the
morning at the latest, and they should stay there until supper time, which in 20
our family is at six.

So far there is no trick in making good baked beans. The trick, if it can be
dignified by such a term, lies in the baking, and like a great many trade tricks,
it consists only of patience and conscientious care. You have to tend the beans
faithfully, adding water whenever the level gets down below the top of the 25
beans, and you have to keep the oven temperature even. If you're lazy, you can
put in a lot of water and not have to watch them so closely. But to get the best
results, you should add only enough water each time to barely cover the beans.
This means that you'll give up all social engagements for the day, because you
can't leave the baby for more than half an hour at a time. I think the results 30
are worth it—but then, I haven't anywhere special to go anyhow. My beans are
brown and mealy, and they swim in a thick brown juice. They're good. I always
serve them with corn bread, ketchup and pickles.

1. Where and how does the writer give her opinions?
2. In Example A, if anything were omitted from the directions, they would be incom-

plete. What could be omitted here and still leave us with adequate directions for baking beans? What would such omissions do to the overall effect?

**3.** Check the etymology, denotation, and connotation of *gratuitous* (line 2), *conglomerate* (line 15).

---

8-C                              TAKING CARE OF CONTACTS
                                  *Marjorie Sybul (student)*

Except for the light touch just before the end, this is straightforward direction-giving.

ANALYSIS

I. General
problem

A. General
procedure #1
B. General
procedure #2

Contact lenses are a big investment. Before you decide to buy a pair, you should realize that hard contact lenses require much more care than does an ordinary pair of glasses. A definite procedure must be followed daily for your own safety. Unlike a pair of glasses that is casually put 5 on and taken off, contact lenses must be prepared for insertion and, when not in use, must be stored in a liquid. You must use two special solutions: a wetting agent to prepare the lenses for insertion, and a soaking agent to keep the lenses pliable. 10

II. Specific
procedures: nine
steps before
insertion

Before touching your contact lenses, wash your hands thoroughly; bacteria trapped between the lens and the eye can cause infection. Then uncap the bottle of wetting solution and set it aside. Close the sink drain to prevent the loss of a lens if you accidentally drop it. Open the left chamber 15 of the lens case. The concave surface of the lens will be facing you. Touch the lens very gently; it will stick to your wet finger. Place it between your thumb and forefinger, and carefully rinse it with water. Now, holding the lens at its edges, squeeze one drop of wetting solution on each side. 20 Rub the lens gently and rinse again. Put another drop on the concave surface. The lens is now ready for insertion.

III. Specific
procedures: four
steps for insertion

At first, inserting the lens will seem very difficult, but, like many other things, it becomes easier with practice. Balance the lens on the tip of your middle finger and 25 slowly raise your finger to your eye. At the same time, be sure to cup your other hand underneath to catch the lens should it drop from your finger. Look straight ahead and bring the lens to your iris. At the slightest touch, the lens will pop into place. Now follow the same procedure with 30 the other lens.

IV. Specific
procedures: six
steps for removal

Removing the contact lens is fun. First open the appropriate chamber of your lens case. Then bend your head down and place one cupped hand under your eye. With

the other hand, pull the outer edge of your eyelid to one 35
side as though you were imitating the shape of an Oriental
eye. Blink, and the lens will pop into your hand. Place the
lens in the lens case with the concave side facing you.
Squeeze a few drops of soaking solution over it and close
the chamber. The soaking solution will be rinsed away the 40
next time you reinsert the lens.

V. Benefits

A. Benefit #1

B. Benefit #2

C. Benefits #3 and 4

This entire procedure takes only a few moments, and
every step must always be followed. There are several large
benefits. When any of your lensless friends happen to see
you popping your lenses in or out, they are sure to be 45
impressed and fascinated by your courage and will probably gasp and groan. When you meet another lens wearer,
you will immediately have a great bond in common and
will be able to swap stories about the time you lost a lens
in the middle of the decisive game in a tennis match or on 50
a crowded dance floor. More seriously, the small sacrifice
in time and effort required to learn these procedures and
follow them faithfully will be more than repaid by the
great improvement in your appearance and in your
peripheral vision.                                              55

## 8-D  HOW TO MAKE AN ICE CREAM SODA
### Charles Dippold (student)

In contrast to the preceding example, this has two purposes: to inform readers on
making an ice cream soda and to make them laugh at the exaggerated picture of the
"ideal" soda.

As a former Amalgamator of Aqueous Solutions of Carbonic Acid, I can state
with authority that the ice cream soda is the acme of the soda jerker's art. Sun-
daes, cokes, and shakes are all secondary; anyone can ladle syrup over ice cream
or mix charged water and syrup to make a coke, but it takes long experience
and inspired artistic endeavor to blend together the few simple ingredients of 5
that masterpiece of the profession, the ice cream soda. As in any art, individual
technique varies, but like any artist, I believe mine to be the most satisfactory.

To begin with, a glass must be chosen. The ideal glass is tall, with thick sides
to prevent breakage, and with a heavy base to prevent tipping. It should be
conical in shape, since a cone has only one-third the volume of a cylinder of 10
equal height and base, while appearing almost as large.

Equipped with the proper glass, one now chooses the syrup. I personally prefer chocolate, but with any flavor the procedure is the same. The proper amount
must be judged by the soda jerker. It is generally between two and three ounces,

depending upon the size of the glass and one's individual taste. A dab of stiff 15
whipped cream is flipped upon the syrup by a dexterous tap of the spoon on the
edge of the glass, and then one is ready for the most important step, adding the
water.

The object is to produce a light, frothy, homogeneous mixture of charged
water and syrup. To do this perfectly, the fine stream must be used. At some 20
fountains, quality must be sacrificed to speed and the coarse stream substituted,
but since we are considering the ideal soda, we may disregard this practice. One
places the glass under the faucet, slowly moving the handle forward to allow
the soda water to fizz out with increasing velocity, and rotating the glass carefully to insure a complete mixture of water and syrup. When the glass is about 25
two-thirds full, the water is shut off and the soda is ready for the addition of the
ice cream.

Two small scoops are better than one large one, since a large one blocks the
bottom of the glass so that all of the liquid cannot be removed with the straw.
The scoops must be well rounded to prevent their disintegration in the liquid. 30
The ice cream is carefully slipped in, to avoid splashing; and now the soda is
ready for its crowning glory, the cap.

Slowly and carefully the charged water is again added in a fine stream, the
object being to produce as high a cap as possible without causing it to run over.
If the stream strikes the floating ice cream, the water will splash out violently. 35
This is particularly embarrassing if it lands on a customer sitting in front of the
faucet. However, a really great soda jerker has so coordinated his hand and eye
by constant practice that he skillfully guides the stream into the glass without
splashing. When the cap has reached the highest possible point, the water is
turned off, the artist quickly seizes a spoon, and both soda and spoon are non- 40
chalantly set before the customer in one graceful motion.

What a joy it is to behold! Beads of moisture form on the cool sides, and
through the foamy mass one may discern the white lumps of ice cream floating
like beautiful water lilies. The top, streaked with brown lines of chocolate, rises
like some snow-capped mountain, inviting the epicure to partake of this nectar 45
and ambrosia, the ice cream soda.

1. Besides giving the piece unity of content by sticking to his subject, the writer has
   given it unity of tone by his consistently mock-serious approach. Does this make the
   piece more interesting or is it annoying?
2. Given the necessary equipment and materials, could you make a good soda with
   only his directions to guide you, or would you be better off with a strictly informative list of steps?
3. How many paragraphs are devoted to actual direction-giving? What do the others
   accomplish? Are they worthwhile?
4. How many paragraphs begin with a transitional device? How many end with one,
   preparing us for the next paragraph?
5. At what point does the author give reasons for doing as he directs? At what point
   does he warn of what will happen otherwise?

*8-E*        HOW DICTIONARIES ARE MADE
               *S. I. Hayakawa*

This is a complete subdivision of a chapter in *Language in Thought and Action* (4th edition, 1978). The author is a semanticist, a specialist in the development and changes in the meanings of words.

It is an almost universal belief that every word has a "correct meaning," that we learn these meanings principally from teachers and grammarians (except that most of the time we don't bother to, so that we ordinarily speak "sloppy English"), and that dictionaries and grammars are the "supreme authority" in matters of meaning and usage. Few people ask by what authority the writers 5 of dictionaries and grammars say what they say. The docility with which most people bow down to the dictionary is amazing, and the person who says, "Well, the dictionary is wrong!" is looked upon with smiles of pity and amusement which say plainly, "Poor fellow! He's really quite sane otherwise."

Let us see how dictionaries are made and how the editors arrive at defini- 10 tions. What follows applies, incidentally, only to those dictionary offices where first-hand, original research goes on—not those in which editors simply copy existing dictionaries. The task of writing a dictionary begins with the reading of vast amounts of the literature of the period or subject that it is intended to cover. As the editors read, they copy on cards every interesting or rare word, 15 every unusual or peculiar occurrence of a common word, a large number of common words in their ordinary uses, and also the sentences in which each of these words appears, thus:

> pail
> The dairy *pails* bring home increase of milk
> Keats, *Endymion*
> I, 44–45

That is to say, the context of each word is collected, along with the word itself. For a really big job of dictionary writing, such as the *Oxford English* 20 *Dictionary* (usually bound in about twenty-five volumes), millions of such cards are collected, and the task of editing occupies decades. As the cards are collected, they are alphabetized and sorted. When the sorting is completed, there will be for each word anywhere from two or three to several hundred illustrative quotations, each on its card. 25

To define a word, then, the dictionary editor places before him the stack of cards illustrating that word; each of the cards represents an actual use of the word by a writer of some literary or historical importance. He reads the cards carefully, discards some, re-reads the rest, and divides up the stack according to what he thinks are the several senses of the word. Finally, he writes his def- 30 initions, following the hard-and-fast rule that each definition must be based on what the quotations in front of him reveal about the meaning of the word. The editor cannot be influenced by what he thinks a given word ought to mean. He must work according to the cards, or not at all.

The writing of a dictionary, therefore, is not a task of setting up authoritative 35 statements about the "true meanings" of words, but a task of recording, to the best of one's ability, what various words have meant to authors in the distant or immediate past. The writer of a dictionary is a historian, not a lawgiver. If, for example, we had been writing a dictionary in 1890, or even as late as 1919, we could have said that the word "broadcast" means "to scatter," seed and so on; 40 but we could not have decreed that from 1921 on, the commonest meaning of the word should become "to disseminate audible messages, etc., by wireless telephony." To regard the dictionary as an "authority," therefore, is to credit the dictionary writer with gifts of prophecy which neither he nor anyone else possesses. In choosing our words when we speak or write, we can be guided by 45 the historical record afforded us by the dictionary, but we cannot be bound by it, because new situations, new experiences, new inventions, new feelings, are always compelling us to give new uses to old words. Looking under a "hood," we should ordinarily have found, five hundred years ago, a monk; today, we find a motorcar engine.

50

1. What larger expository purpose than is indicated by the title does this selection serve? Where is it discussed? Write a sentence that expresses what you believe to be the main idea of the whole essay.
2. Which paragraphs actually tell how dictionaries are made? Make a numbered list of the main steps in the process.

---

*8-F*  DEATH AND BURIAL ON YAMACRAW
*Pat Conroy*

This excerpt comes from *The Water Is Wide* (1972), a book describing the writer's year as a teacher on the little island of Yamacraw, off the coast of South Carolina. Two other excerpts from this book are Unit 2-F and Unit 12-B. Here, the account of a particular death and burial reads like pure narrative. But in content it is plainly intended to explain a typical death and burial on the island.

In March there was a death on the island. Like most deaths on Yamacraw, it came with unforeshadowed swiftness; there was no lingering or gradual wasting away or bedside farewells. A heart attack felled Blossom Smith on a Saturday, an islander raced to Ted Stone's house, Stone immediately radioed for a rescue helicopter from Savannah. Blossom was carried to an open field near the night- 5 club, where half the island gathered around her wailing and praying. The helicopter appeared, landed rapidly and efficiently, received the motionless Blossom into the dark angel with the rotating wings, lifted into the sky in a maelstrom of debris and air, then disappeared over the top of the trees. It was

all very quick, very impressive, and very futile. Blossom died that night in 10
Savannah surrounded by strangers and the ammonia smells of a death ward.

Death meant the cessation of all activity on the island and, though school was
in session, no children appeared at the door on the day of the funeral. Though
it was a time of intense emotional sorrow, a funeral was also an important social
event. Relatives in Savannah and Hilton Head hired an excursion boat to trans- 15
port mourners to the island. The immediate family was fed and consoled. The
old women of the island sat around and reminisced about their girlhood. They
also wondered out loud who was going to be called to the Lord's bosom next.

Early Tuesday morning a contingent of island men went to the "colored cemetery" to dig a grave. Two dapper undertakers accompanied the body from 20
Savannah on the excursion boat. The whole proceeding exuded the air of a
ritual performed so many times that everyone knew exactly what was expected
and everyone had a part to play. As I drove to the cemetery, I was taken aback
by the number of mourners who had come to the island. The road leading to
the cemetery was thick with well-dressed black people slowly walking toward 25
the open hole that would serve as Blossom's final resting place.

Many of my students were already at the gravesite when I arrived. They
looked faintly bewildered by the fuss and rising sadness. The procession of people continued unbroken through the woods. Most of them talked animatedly,
laughed with mild restraint, and seemed to be enjoying the festival beneath the 30
trees. Several relatives threw their arms around each other in greeting. But all
grew rather silent as they neared the deep, rooted scar gouged out of the earth
near a large, straight pine tree in the cemetery. Three saplings, freshly cut, lay
perpendicular across the open grave. Beside the grave, her face powdered and
rouged in death, her body neatly dressed, her hands folded across her small 35
bosom, her casket decorated with ludicrous frills, lay Blossom Smith.

Behind the big pine trees, a vast and greening marsh stretched for a mile
before it paused for the river. Magnolia trees towered and presided over the
ceremony. The cemetery was hauntingly beautiful. Yamacraw's lone deacon,
a bespectacled man named William Brown, bowed his head reverently to begin 40
the ceremony. "Jesus took you from us. He took you to be with him." His voice
was plaintive, immensely evocative, and profoundly sad. His sermon was almost
a cry, a lament from one who did not understand death, but who accepted it
as a calling of man by his creator, a manifestation of a larger, unfathomable,
mysterious, yet loving presence in the universe. 45

Then everyone present walked beside the open coffin and viewed Blossom
for the last time. A chorus of older women sang a spiritual with voices of
ancient, incomparable sorrow. The column moved slowly, laboriously, as each
mourner paused to look deeply into the image of death. Some reached out and
lightly touched Blossom's face. Others looked at her, then covered their eyes 50
and wept. Some spoke to her aloud and bade farewell as though she would be
gone for only a short time. Some became slightly hysterical and had to be com-
forted by a team of women who seemed to be present for that purpose. Some

spoke the name of Jesus aloud. Some stared at Blossom, then joined the grieving
chorus that rallied new voices with every breath.                                    55

Flowers abounded beside the casket, carefully tended by the two undertakers, who seemed to encourage the atmosphere of sorrow and hysteria by their
dramatic presentation of each new part of the ceremony. Most of the flowers
were plastic, a vivid example of a twentieth-century incursion of Yamacraw.
Aunt Ruth's husband had been the island undertaker before his death. He had   60
fashioned pine coffins in a shed near his house. He would have none of the tacky
death chambers wrought by factories and peddled by the oily undertakers of
Savannah. Death on the island was cleaner and less packaged when he was
alive. The plastic flowers, with their senseless bid for immortality, added an
ugliness to the ceremony hard to define.                                             65

•      •      •

After every single person filed by the open casket and responded appropriately to the sight of Blossom's lifeless body, an old lady stepped out of the crowd
holding a small girl not more than three years old. To my utter disbelief, the
woman very slowly passed the girl over the casket into the arms of a waiting
man. The little girl looked down and saw Blossom's dead face and became hys-   70
terical. Three times the girl was passed over Blossom's body, and her screaming
grew louder each time. I was horrified but did not feel that it would be enthusiastically applauded if I rushed in and rescued the girl. I seemed to be the only
one upset by this ritual. I learned later that the little girl was Blossom's grand-
daughter, who had lived with Blossom before she died. To protect the girl from   75
Blossom's spirit returning from the grave to haunt her, the girl had to be passed
over Blossom's body three times. Thus freed, the girl disappeared into the crowd
still screaming.

A little while later, the singing having subsided and the weeping having
become softer, the two undertakers gave a signal to the six men who acted as   80
pallbearers. The six men lifted the casket and placed it on the saplings that lay
across the grave. They then looped ropes around the casket and lifted it slightly
into the air. Several other men slid the saplings out of the way. The casket was
then lowered into the hole. Four men started shoveling dirt. At this time there
was a stirring among the crowd. A palmetto tree near the marsh was rattling   85
and shaking as though a powerful wind was blowing through it. Only there was
no wind blowing and no other trees around it were affected. A few women
screamed and the entire crowd shrank back to size up the significance of the
event. I tried to explain scientifically what I was witnessing and found no ready
or easy explanation. The palmetto then grew still again, and I heard someone   90
behind me say, as in a prayer, "That's Blossom tellin' us she still around."

1. What are the chief actions by the mourners in the "process" of the funeral?
2. Where and how does the writer indicate his opinions and emotions?
3. What suggests that the writer was not pleased by the two undertakers?

**4.** What is the etymology and meaning of each of the following words and how is it used by the writer? *maelstrom, debris, cessation, contingent, dapper,* and *exuded* (¶1–¶3); *presided* (¶5).

## ASSIGNMENTS

1. Look through the selections in this unit for examples of the four points of view from which directions can be presented: the first-person "I (or we) do this," the second-person "You do that," the indefinite third-person "One should do thus and so," and the impersonal passive "Such and such should be done." Compare the effects produced. Will your choice of method be governed by your material, your attitude toward it, or your reader?

2. Most of these selections have strictly informative titles. Try supplying more stimulating ones for some of them (see Unit 1, pages 21–22).

3. For a direction-giving paper do not choose an involved subject such as how to cure inflation or a complicated procedure like how to play bridge, but rather some simple process for which you can give directions that will actually direct. You need not limit yourself, however, to a procedure that can be done perfectly on the first attempt; you may assume the necessity for repeated practice, as in how to perform the crawl stroke.

   Suitable subjects include how to perform a card trick, use a jigsaw, prepare a favorite dish, cast for trout, treat a snakebite, learn to ride a bicycle, write a theme, paddle a canoe, sail a boat, go waterskiing or skin diving, repair a leaky faucet or an electrical connection, shoot free throws, make an archer's bow, build a model airplane, caddy, run a trap line, develop films, drive a car, administer artificial respiration, conduct a business meeting. These topics, however, like those in other units, are meant merely as *suggestions*, to be used if you wish, but preferably to remind you of other suitable ones on which you may be even better equipped to write. When you have chosen a subject,

   **a.** Present it as a list of numbered steps (page 117).

   **b.** Make a rough outline in which you arrange these steps logically into larger related units (page 117).

   **c.** Write out the procedure as briefly as possible, limiting yourself to a simple straightforward account of how to do it and working from this outline.

   **d.** Write a second essay in which you add as much reader interest as you can—this will involve decisions as to the purpose of your paper, the kind of reader to whom it is addressed, and the attitude you wish to assume toward your subject.

4. For your informative process paper choose a subject that is so familiar to you that you can explain it accurately and interestingly to those less well informed. Remember that you can choose a larger field than for item 3, since you will not need to go into the exact details necessary to direction-giving. Suggested topics: How a drug store is run (compare "How to Make an Ice Cream Soda" in scope), how a fish (bird, insect, animal) lives, how an election is conducted, how calves (chickens, pigs) are raised, how something is mined or grown or harvested, how some business is run, how an airplane flies, how a ball team is managed, how a factory process (such as the manufacture of lead pencils) is carried on, how a newspaper is published, how

a paper route is managed, how an amateur play is produced, how puppets are handled.

Your subject chosen, proceed as before: think through your material and jot down the important phases of the procedure in their proper sequence; determine the larger units into which they fall and make a rough outline; decide on your attitude toward your material—your purpose in presenting it. As an account of something with which you have had some experience, your paper will probably be cast into the form of a first-person narrative like several in this unit. But do not be distracted into writing pure narration; an account of how a summer camp is run should not be sidetracked, for example, into the more exciting story of a near-drowning that once occurred there.

5. Examine the use of the process-paper approach to material in the following examples in other parts of this book: Unit 1-A; Unit 2-A and C; Unit 12-B and D; Unit 13-C, D, and G; Unit 15-F.

# Comparison

In Unit 5 we saw how comparison used in the form of rhetorical devices could add vividness and clarity. Comparison as a pattern of thought involves holding up two similar but not identical objects, situations, people, ideas, and so on, to determine in detail their likenesses and differences. We follow this pattern in selecting brand-name goods, in determining contest winners, in choosing a candidate or a way of life—in any situation that involves weighing and judging.

Whenever you are faced with an important choice, you view the various possibilities carefully, noting their similarities and, even more important, their differences, since it is through the latter that you will ultimately reach a decision. Which toothpaste to buy? Which college to attend? Even, which person to marry?—a toothpaste with fluoride or one without? a community college or a four-year one? intelligent, charming, but unreliable X or intelligent, unimaginative, but dependable Y?

In college writing assignments and examinations, you will often be asked to reach conclusions on a choice of objects, people, issues, or theories by comparing them. Your purpose in writing the essay of comparison may only be to determine similarities and differences, or it may be to convince your readers of the superiority of one of the things you are presenting. Whatever your subject and purpose, the general mental process will be the same.

## Content

**1. Choose two things as your subject.** More than two may be involved in your original view, but since you usually eliminate choices by holding them up in successive pairs, your subject remains essentially a matter of alternatives at any one point. In reaching a decision as to which of several automobiles to buy, for example, you will probably narrow your choice by weighing and eliminating until you arrive at the two likeliest, which you will then compare exhaustively to each other.

**2. Choose two things alike but different.** They must be alike enough to be actually comparable, different enough to make the comparison fruitful through contrast. Two cars of the same make and year and model may have certain differences, despite standardized production, but such variations are usually tiny. On the other hand, although an automobile and a tricycle are vehicles, they are too dissimilar to make any attempt at comparison worthwhile.

**3. Make your treatment of the two things similar.** If you mention a certain type of detail about one, be sure to include it or to note the lack of it in your discussion of the other. If leg room is important in your choice of cars, for example, consider it in both the cars you are comparing.

## Organization

The logical order for material in the process, as we saw in the preceding unit, is chronological. In the essay of comparison, however, two plans for organization are appropriate. One is usually called the opposing pattern, and the other the alternating pattern.

**1. Opposing pattern.** Suppose you decide to compare education as you experienced it in high school with what you have found in college. Probably you will be concerned primarily with painting a vivid picture of life in each area, and your paper will consist of two main divisions: education in high school and education in college. Where you place the parts will ordinarily depend on which you wish to stress—the more important one should be last.

Since you wish to compare the two, you must, in developing them, examine essentially the same phases of experience in each. Your subpoints under each main division, then, are likely to be similar—for example, activities, teachers, classes. Determine the order of these subpoints logically and then maintain it under each heading. If you decide that you wish to emphasize your experience in college, your skeleton outline may look like this:

  I. Education in high school
    A. Teachers
    B. Classes
    C. Activities
 II. Education in college
    A. Teachers
    B. Classes
    C. Activities

As you write, you may merely paint two pictures, leaving your readers to draw their own conclusions; or you may often refer, in your second picture, to the points of contrast with the first; or you may write a conclusion that will tie them together and make clear your purpose in treating both in the same paper.

**2. Alternating pattern.** If, however, you wish to emphasize the details of the comparison instead of the larger differences, you will find an alternating arrangement more useful. In this, the levels of the points are the reverse of those used earlier; the aspects of each way of life are stressed and the area is subordinated. Your previous subpoints become main divisions; your main divisions, subpoints under each. Your skeleton outline will then look like this:

I. Teachers
   A. High school
   B. College
II. Classes
   A. High school
   B. College
III. Activities
   A. High school
   B. College

Which of the two orders you use for a given paper will probably be less a matter of choice than a requirement of your particular subject. For the topic of high school versus college, the first would probably be better since it emphasizes the contrast between the two pictures as a whole. But when you wish to stress the particular points of a comparison—one beach resort versus another, for instance, as to climate, hotels, and amusements—the second type of pattern would be better. If you completed the discussion of one resort before you started on another, the details of the first might have faded from your readers' minds before they were halfway through the second.

These two patterns can be seen in operation on a small scale in the following paragraphs. The first, attempting to distinguish between two often confused objects by stressing their differences, uses the opposing pattern.

> The beginner has some trouble in distinguishing the planets from the stars, but the following difference in appearance may help. The stars are so distant that they shine only as points of light even through the largest telescopes. In consequence, their light is unsteady because of disturbances in the Earth's atmosphere, such as the rising of warm currents and the falling of cold currents. Thus the stars twinkle. The planets, on the other hand, are very much nearer—so near that with the exception of Pluto they show as discs in our large telescopes, and not as single points of light. Therefore their light is not so much affected by disturbances in our atmosphere. It is usually said that planets do not twinkle, but shine with a steady light. (Clyde Fisher, *Exploring the Heavens*.)

Brief as this paragraph is, it demonstrates the relationship of parts in the opposing pattern clearly:

| Sentence 1: | Introduction. Planets and stars |
|---|---|
| 2: | I. Stars |
| | A. Very distant |
| 3 and 4: | B. Result—twinkling |
| 5: | II. Planets |
| | A. Less distant |
| 6 and 7: | B. Result—steady light |

The treatment of both parts of the subject is so brief that there is no paragraph break (as might have been expected) when the second is introduced in sentence 5, but still "on the other hand" is a valuable transition between the two. Notice, too, the balance of "in consequence" (sentence 3) and "therefore" (sentence 6), transitions introducing in each part the comparable material on results.

The even briefer paragraph that follows is an equally clear example of the alternating pattern. Here, two people are compared detail by detail.

> Irène was, like Eve, a brilliant, courageous bearer of the great Curie name, yet in every other respect the two sisters were far apart. Where Eve was a Gaullist, Irène was pro-Communist. Eve was chic and smart; Irène lived in a gray chemist's smock. Eve traveled the world and mingled with the mighty; Irène's world was the laboratory of the Curie Institute and she mingled with molecules and atoms, whose power was less visible if mightier. (David Schoenbrun, *As France Goes.*)

In outline form the pattern is clearly seen:

Sentence 1:      Introduction. Irène and Eve Curie
       2:       I. Politics
            A. Eve—Gaullist
            B. Irène—pro-Communist
       3:      II. Dress
            A. Eve—fashionable
            B. Irène—workaday
       4:     III. Experience
            A. Eve's—wide and important
            B. Irène's—narrow but more important

To see more clearly how the effects of these two methods of organizing comparisons differ, rewrite each of these sample paragraphs according to the other pattern. The changes you find will be greatly multiplied in longer pieces.

Each pattern has limitations. The opposing pattern is not suitable for papers of more than a thousand words. Readers would forget the first part of the subject long before they finished the second. But a writer may use the opposing pattern briefly at many points in a paper or book of any length. The alternating pattern may have the monotony of a swinging pendulum if many of the parts are the same length. The pattern is most effective when the alternation varies from a contrast within a sentence, to one between sentences, and to one between paragraphs, depending on what is most appropriate for the particular material.

## Analogy

An analogy is a special kind of comparison. Like the figures of speech we examined in Unit 5, its only purpose is to make something vivid and understandable. Unlike most figures of speech, however, an analogy is always based on several points of comparison. Also, since the purpose is always practical, it appeals primarily to our sense of logic rather than to our emotions.

A familiar analogy is the description of a pump to explain the heart: the heart with its valves forcing blood through the body is compared to a pump with its valves forcing water through a system of pipes. These are two very different things—one anatomical, the other mechanical—but the relationship of their parts is comparable at point after point, and the working of the complex and unfamiliar becomes clearer through analogy with the relatively simple and familiar.

Analogies can be particularly helpful in translating measurements of some kind into familiar terms. For example, an advertisement for an airline caught the eye with "Last week we moved Chicago to Dallas." The advertisement continued: "In an average week, U.S. scheduled airlines carry three-and-a-half million passengers an average of 800 miles. That's the equivalent of picking up every man, woman, and child in Chicago and transporting them to Dallas." The advertisers made their point.

Do not expect an analogy to prove anything. The action of a pump can be used to explain that of the heart, but it does not follow that a heart is a machine whose parts can be replaced easily or that a plumber could perform open-heart surgery successfully.

## Balanced Sentence Structure

A construction that will give you special help in writing a comparison is the balanced sentence. It emphasizes the similarity of ideas by presenting them in similar grammatical patterns, as in "government of the people, by the people, and for the people." When the ideas are contrasting, the balance is called *antithesis* because the first part states a point, or thesis, which the second opposes or contradicts to some degree by a contrast. Two examples are "Give me liberty or give me death" and "Let us never negotiate out of fear, but let us never fear to negotiate"—sentences in American history as memorable for expression as for thought. Note the examples of antithesis in the selections that follow, especially in A, B, and the last two paragraphs of D.

## EXAMPLES

These examples all have some form of the alternating pattern. You will find it far more useful than the opposing pattern because it fits a greater variety of purposes and can be applied in varying degrees. Note in the examples the extent to which the writers use the aids discussed in the earlier units—description, narration, characterization, and precise word choice.

*9-A*                              THE SEVENTH CONTINENT

These paragraphs are from a travel agency's brochure on cruises to Antarctica. Notice that as the paragraphs grow longer, we move from a single sentence covering both regions to separate sentences for each, and then to more than one sentence.

Antarctica differs from the Arctic regions, which are better known to us and easier to reach. The North Pole is crossed daily by commercial airlines, whereas not a single commercial airliner operates over Antarctica.

The Arctic is an ocean covered with drifting ice and hemmed in by the continents of North America, Asia and Europe. The Antarctic, on the other hand, 5 is a continent as large as Europe and the United States put together, and surrounded entirely by oceans—the Atlantic, the Indian and the Pacific.

More than a million persons live within 2,000 miles of the North Pole and the area is rich in forest and industry. There are animals and birds of many varieties. Within the same distance of the South Pole, there are no settlements 10 apart from scientific stations which are entirely dependent on outside supplies for every need. There is not a single tree and not a single animal. It takes 70 to 80 years to grow an inch of moss.

1. What do these two regions have in common that makes them comparable? In how many and what respects are they compared?
2. Rewrite this description as a comparison organized in the opposing pattern.
3. Explain the advantages and disadvantages of the two patterns in presenting this particular information.
4. What transitional devices did you use to link the parts of your comparisons? What devices are in the example?

---

*9-B*                          TOLSTOY'S CONTRADICTIONS
                                    *Henri Troyat*

After two introductory sentences, this short paragraph from an article in the *Literary Guild Magazine* (1968) is the ultimate in balanced construction: all the remaining sentences match, each forming an antithesis whose parts are marked with "He preached" and "but he. . . ."

Who is Tolstoy? For me, he suffered his whole life long from an inability to match his thoughts with his actions. He preached asceticism and chastity, but he gave his wife thirteen children. He preached the joys of poverty, but he never lacked for anything. He preached the need for solitude, but he was the most surrounded and the most adulated man of his times. He preached hatred 5 of the government, but he never suffered any curtailment of his freedom, while his followers went into exile.

1. Rewrite this paragraph to make a comparison in the opposing pattern.
2. Explain the advantages and disadvantages of the two patterns in presenting this particular information.

---

*9-C*             THE DOWNFALL OF CHRISTMAS
*William Kirchoff (student)*

Not all essays of comparison are patterned as neatly as the first two, which show the alternating pattern in its clearest and simplest form. In longer pieces, the pattern can be used more freely, as shown in this example and the ones that follow. The same questions apply, however, to their organization and sentence structure.

ANALYSIS
General topic

       Christmas is gone. The American people have stood Christmas up against a wall and executed it, and from its grave a ghost has arisen. Strangely enough, this ghost is also named Christmas. This new Christmas is different, much different, from the one I knew not too long ago. Most of 5 the things that to me meant Christmas are gone. A little change here and a little change there have made Christmas a ghost of its former self.

I. First example
  A. Then

       A noticeable change has taken place in the tree. As I remember our trees, they were green, a green that could 10 not only be seen, but smelled. The ornaments were bright, but not gaudy. The lights were few and plain. I remember I used to have a favorite light each year, one that was in just the right place, and just the right color. All this sentiment was old-fashioned, though, and America was pro- 15 gressive. Manufacturers told us that we must always keep ahead of the Joneses and that we must always be new and

  B. Now

unique. It is now no longer fashionable to have a green tree. One must have a silver one, a white one, a pink one, or a blue one. One must have a tree with music tinkling 20 from a hidden music box. The ornaments are no longer simple. They are now all hideous sizes and shapes, splashed with color, signifying nothing. They are all silver and sparkle, and no sentiment. The lights must bubble, flash, blink, glimmer, and do a million other things. The Christmas tree 25 is now an over-glorified monstrosity that smells suspiciously like machine oil.

II. Second example
  A. Then
  B. Now

       Christmas songs have likewise undergone a disastrous change. It seems that no one was satisfied with "Silent Night." Now we have such pieces of trash as "I Saw 30 Mommy Kissing Santa Claus" and "Santa Rides a Strawberry Roan." Then there is the song that has done the most toward ruining Christmas, and that is "Santa Baby." It is my opinion that that is the lowest depth to which any song-writer can stoop. The modern songwriter is succeeding in his attempts to make a farce out of Christmas songs.

**III. Third example**
  **A. Then**
  **B. Now**

Poor old Santa has really been through the mill. He is no longer the kindly old gentleman who puts candy in children's stockings. He is now the man in the nylon acetate beard and the red satin costume (which sells for twelve dollars and ninety-five cents at most downtown stores) who tells children to buy such and such from this or that store. He is now the man who comes riding into town surrounded by twenty-five Hollywood models in skimpy costumes, about a month early. Like everything else, Santa has gone commercial.

**IV. Fourth example**
  **A. Then**
  **B. Now**

Even the Christmas season is different. Instead of a day or a week, it is now a month long and growing every year. It starts when Santa arrives in town accompanied by television and movie stars. It gets well under way when Santa is starred on some program and tells gullible children what to buy and from whom. The person who sponsors his show must feel very proud of himself.

**V. Individual illustration**

Merry Christmas, everybody; Peace on Earth, good will toward men, and see whose house decorations can be the gaudiest. Mr. Smith is full of Christmas spirit. His house has 200 strings of light bulbs spelling out the first verse of "Jingle Bells." It looks as if no one will have a white Christmas, except Mr. Jones, who sprays his whole front lawn with 50 gallons of artificial snow.

**Conclusion**
  **Summary of "now"**

Well, in short, that is the Christmas of today, a mere ghost of the Christmas that used to be. All the feelings are gone. Like almost everything made in this country, it smells and tastes like tin cans. It looks like a gaudy fireworks display, and sounds like Tin Pan Alley. Worst of all, the feeling of Christmas is like the feeling of any other holiday when no one works. The one day of the year that was set aside for tradition is ruined by the American people who know no tradition. One day out of three hundred and sixty-five, and we had to go and ruin it. Christmas is gone. It died when the true meaning of Christmas was all but forgotten, when Rudolph the red-nosed reindeer took the place of Dasher, when Mommy kissed Santa Claus, when a chorus girl in a low-cut evening gown sang "Silent Night" with a glycerin tear in her eye.

1. Why are the "now" sections longer?
2. Is the writer's use of colloquial words and phrases appropriate to his purpose?

*9-D*            NO MORE MOON-JUNE: LOVE'S OUT
                      *Richard Stengel*

This complete essay was first published on the Op Ed page of the *New York Times* (August 1979) with a note stating that the writer is not married. Watch how he weaves background information on his subject into the alternating pattern of his comparison.

Romantic love is a supreme fiction, marriage for love the consequence of that fiction, and divorce the painful evidence of that initial delusion.

The history of romantic love is the continuing ironic testimony of the power of our minds to mesmerize our bodies, while romantic marriage is the most recent and least successful evolutionary stage in the history of matrimony.    5

Now that the Census Bureau has estimated that more than one in three marriages will end in divorce, it is apparent that the solution to the troubled state of matrimony is a return to the tradition of arranged marriages.

The sentimental sanctity of love was the invention of the Provençal poets of the 12th century, and they saw it as the exotic refinement of a bored aristocracy.   10 Since then, however, love has democratized itself and is no longer the luxury of a courtly minority but the expectation of every man and woman. Indeed, the joys of romantic love are the birthright of every American, for the Framers of the Declaration of Independence declared "the pursuit of happiness" to be the inalienable right of all men and women.                                                   15

Love, though, is neither a right nor an instinct, but a learned form of behavior; it is not a spontaneous feeling but an artificial ritual. It is a response that we have learned from literature, and its contemporary handmaidens, the news media.

As lovers, we are all actors—we imagine ourselves most spontaneous when   20 we are most imitative. We learn how to love from movies, television, novels, magazines and advertisements. We learn to adore love, to idolize love, to fall in love with love.

To most Americans, love is romantic love. It is a drive or state of tension induced by our prevailing romantic myths. The lover's nourishment is the   25 expectation of bliss. Love is a competitive and covetous game: competition for a mate brings out the best in an individual. To be alone is not considered a self-imposed choice but evidence of failure in the contest of love.

During the Industrial Revolution, arranged romantic marriages succumbed to individual love matches. The monotony of work and the impersonality of the   30 city led people to escape monotony in personal relations and retreat from impersonality to the "emotional fortress" of marriage. Urbanization caused the "privatization" of marriage so that the intimacy of wedlock became a sanctuary from a world where all intimacy was excluded.

Yet, romantic marriage was the cradle of its own demise. More and more   35 pressure was forced on marriage to be "a haven in a heartless world." As the temptations of the outside world were becoming more varied, the standards of marital fidelity became more exigent. Opportunity multiplies, morality

declines: The pressure on marriage increased geometrically. Between 1870 and
1920 the number of divorces multiplied fifteenfold.                                    40

In the past, when society was more structured, married partners were exter-
nally oriented, and did not have to rely exclusively on each other for emotional
gratification. They could find that elsewhere. Romantic passion had always
existed *outside* of marriage but it had nothing to do with wedlock. Contemporary society forces couples to depend on each other for permanence and sta-  45
bility, functions that were formerly provided by a large familial and social
network.

Today, marriage has not lost its function; it suffers from a surfeit of functions.
The marriage partner must not only be a lover, but a friend, a colleague, a
therapist, and a tennis partner. Indeed, the standards of romantic marriage—  50
unquestioned fidelity and undiminished passion—are merely an ideal to be
approximated, not a universal precept to be obeyed.

Traditionally, the selection of mates has been determined by social, political
and economic considerations directed either toward establishing new ties or
reaffirming old ones. Every arranged marriage was the formation of a new  55
society—a merger of a network of familial and social relationships. Marriage
was a duty. Its *raison d'être* was procreation. Children were best raised in a
congenial home, and a congenial home was best created by a reasonable
arrangement between congenial people. Marriage was contracted according to
a principle other than the self-interest of the participants, and emotional satis-  60
faction was neither the origin nor purpose of marriage.

The concept of arranged marriage is based on a positive view of human
nature. Its guiding principle is that marriage requires a more durable foundation than romantic love, that wisdom is more important in the choosing of a
partner than passion, and that everyone can find something to "love, honor, and  65
cherish" in anyone else.

Romantic love, however, is fundamentally narcissistic; we either choose
someone who resembles ourself, the self we'd like to be or think we are, or we
choose someone who complements us. The former is incestuous, the latter
entropic. If love means touching someone outside of ourselves, then romantic  70
love is solipsistic while arranged marriage is altruistic.

Romantic love allows us the reverie of imagining what the other person is
like, whereas arranged marriage forces us to acknowledge truly another human
being. Instead of falling in love with an ideal-image, an arranged marriage
teaches us how to live with an actual individual. The myth of romantic love  75
teaches us how to fall in love. Perhaps when marriages are arranged, we will
learn *how* to love.

1. What transitional devices does the writer use and where are they?
2. Summarize this example in about 150 words, using the opposing pattern of
   organization.
3. Check the etymology, denotation, and connotation of each of these words: *romantic, sanctity, matrimony, myth, covetous, sanctuary, exigent, surfeit, precept, raison d'être, narcissistic, entropic, solipsistic, altruistic, reverie.*

**3.** From what you have observed, do you agree with the author's claim in the fifth paragraph that love is "a learned form of behavior . . . not a spontaneous feeling"? What is your opinion of his opinions on the benefits of an arranged marriage?

---

*9-E*                          WHO AM I?
                    *Caroline Bajsarowicz (student)*

Which "me" shall I be today? This question confronts me every time I stand before my closet searching for something to wear.

Shall I dress like a JAP, a "Jewish American Princess"? (This style has become very popular around my affluent suburban neighborhood.) I could wear my black formal pantsuit and exquisitely colored scarf, a gold pendant, a charm 5 bracelet, and 14-carat gold hoop earrings. My richly colored, dark brown platform shoes and coordinating handbag would accentuate this polished outfit. My short brown hair would be blown dry so that it could lie perfectly. Then in front of my vanity mirror, I'd spend an hour polishing my nails, spraying a light mist of my favorite perfume, and most important, applying my cosmetics: first foun- 10 dation and blush, then eyeshadow and mascara. This outfit, with my dark green pants coat trimmed with fur, gives me the appearance of a high class snob. I become the stereotyped "rich student." (I have also been called a bitch when I dressed like this.)

At the other end of the closet there is a distinct odor of pine trees and outdoor 15 freshness. My faded blue jeans with the old turtle patch in the center of twenty other brightly colored patches hang here on a peg. With them I wear a stained red T-shirt two sizes too large, old white sweat socks, and dirty hiking boots. My hair is generally tousled and hidden under a blue bandanna. I pay no special attention to my appearance and use no nail polish or makeup. I throw on a 20 shocking, bright green down jacket and pull on a pair of blue and gold checked mittens. My ghastly outfit presents me as a nonconformist.

Like the contents of my closet, the contents of my small but cluttered bedroom show my two personalities. All my brushes, cosmetics, and powders are neatly arranged on a large, mirrored vanity next to my bed. The bed is draped 25 with a lacy orange bedspread and is covered by a dozen stuffed animals. The three scalloped shelves above my bed are filled with my collections of dolls, figurines, and souvenirs. Across the room, there is a modern, bright yellow sewing chest. But above this hangs a poster of a snowcapped mountain and a cloudless blue sky. Under my bed, hidden by the sides of the bedspread, is a down 30 sleeping bag. My green Trailways backpack hangs next to my handbag. In my photo album, a picture of my friends at a beer party is pasted next to a photograph of an altar of ice carved on a cliff.

My dual personality complicates my social life. Half of me gets along with most of the other students. I attend the many functions sponsored by the uni- 35 versity, cheer for our sports teams, attend club meetings, and spend Friday nights dancing in the Rathskeller at the weekly Beer Blasts. I ask myself, though,

"Is this what everybody calls fun? Is this having a good time?" I may be smiling, laughing, joking, and acting out the gestures of amusement so that I'll seem to fit in with the group of people I'm with, but part of me doesn't want to be there. 40 There are so many more constructive activities I'd rather be doing, such as learning about musical instruments, making a needlepoint pillow, or taking a solitary walk through a park.

At summer orientation for freshmen, when we were given a list of all the clubs and sports in the university, I had many problems deciding which ones I 45 wanted to join. The more popular clubs, such as the sororities, appealed to me because I could meet so many girls in the school. I would have such privileges as exclusive rights to a table in the cafeteria and free passage into the Panhellenic Suite. But I also wanted to join the Outing Club. Although it has only four members, they appreciate those other things I like.                                                     50

I'm a freshman with only three years left before I must answer that infamous question, "What do you want to be when you grow up?" I have spent many long hours trying to decide. How I would love to fulfill my mother's dream by marrying a wealthy doctor. My husband and I would live in an upper-middle-class, suburban neighborhood and own a boat, two cars, and several pairs of 55 skis. Probably, we would compete with the Joneses. Every time our neighbors bought something or went on a vacation, we'd buy something bigger and go to a more exclusive resort or on a more exotic cruise. It would be comfortable to settle down to familiar routine with only superficial worries.

But the rebellious me doesn't want this routine. That part of me would much 60 rather go through life without ever settling down. Some people may say this free style of living is that of a bum or hippie, but I want to be independent and unrestrained so that I can see the many splendors of this world. The rebellious me doesn't want to be tied down with a job or a home, nor does it want to worry about the Joneses.                                                                                         65

How can these two very different personalities exist in one person? I have three years left to find the answer. . . .

1. Why does the author give somewhat more attention to her conventional "rich student" self than to her rebellious self?
2. Why does the author give the descriptive details of her clothes and room first rather than the larger problem she faces?

---

*9-F*                          NEW AND OLD STEREOTYPES
                                    *Addison Gayle, Jr.*

These paragraphs conclude *The Way of the New World; The Black Novel in America* (1975). Note how the writer sometimes implies the characteristics of one group by describing the other negatively instead of describing both in full. For example, when Gayle says that the writers whom he admires "were no scavengers," he is in effect saying that the other writers were scavengers.

Nothing would be more desirable than to end this study on such a positive note, to herald the arrival of the black writer in the persons of Killens, Gaines, and Kelley as constituting a final victory over white nationalism, to pronounce once and for all the death knell of the old stereotypes, images, and metaphors which enslaved the minds of generations of Blacks. Yet to do so would be to 5 engender false optimism. For images, metaphors, and symbols of black life are as much a part of the present as of the past. The stereotypes of Harris, Page, and Dixon, of Van Vechten, Mailer, and Styron live again in movies and television fantasies written by Blacks, performed in by Blacks, and supported and sustained by Blacks. The list is almost too numerous to mention: *Superfly, Mel-* 10 *inda, Shaft, Coffy,* "The Flip Wilson Show," "Sanford and Son," and "The Red Ball Express" represent only the most flagrant examples.

These, the new imagists, because for the most part they are Blacks, are more immune from criticism than the imagists of old. They ignore criticism from the black community and are content to exist as the ventriloquist dummies of their 15 more sophisticated masters irrespective of the damage wrought by their actions. One thinks of the novelists, of Charles Chestnutt and Sutton Griggs, of Richard Wright and William Smith, of Ann Petry and Zora Hurston; they were men and women who, despite flaws in perception which often limited their vision, believed in the sanctity of the black spirit, who sought, through their art, to 20 elevate a race of people. These were no scavengers, ignoring the worth and dignity of a people; they were not brainless narcissists unable to realize that their own dignity and sense of achievement were tied in, inseparably, with that of their people. They would have held no truck with those who created and performed in the *Superflys* and the *Melindas*, would not have joined with those 25 who, here, in this period of the twentieth century, attempt to recreate the stereotypes of old—the darky entertainer, docile child, or brute Negro. Like John Killens, they were dedicated to preserving the historical artifacts of a people and would have demanded films based upon the lives of Frederick Douglass, Malcolm X, Sojourner Truth, and Harriet Tubman, films that reveal the dignity 30 of a people whose travels have extended from the middle passage to twentieth-century America.

There is no correlation to be made, however, between the black sycophants of the present time and the novelists, past and present, and thus, the renaissance wrought by the Black Aestheticians, the new sense of historical vision in the 35 works of black poets and novelists, the progress made in gaining control over the images, symbols, and metaphors of black life are threatened by men and women of little talent and far less intelligence, whose objective is not to inform but to disparage, not to create positive images, but to recreate negative ones of the past, to glamorize the hustler and the hipster, to elevate ignorance and 40 downgrade intelligence in a world in which intelligence, knowledge, and understanding are paramount for a people who must yet break the bonds of oppression.

And thus there is little cause for optimism. One is gratified, of course, at the progress of the black novel from 1853 to the present, and the maturity of the 45 novelists supports Fuller's assertion of a new Black Renaissance; one knows, however, that the final battle against the imagists continues, and that the new propagandists are more often Black than white; one watches their "artistic" offerings, listens to their infantile rationalizations, is dismayed at their inability to dedicate themselves to what is noble and beautiful in a race of people and 50 one, despairingly, recalls the lines from a Baraka poem, "Will the machine gunner please step forward?"

1. According to Gayle, what are the chief characteristics of the writing and films of the "new imagists"?
2. What does Gayle indicate, directly or indirectly, were the characteristics of the writing he admires?
3. How does Gayle use repetition to emphasize the contrast between the two groups of writers?
4. Check the etymology, denotation, and connotation of these words and phrases: *stereotype, engender, sustained, flagrant, imagists, scavenger, narcissists, hold truck with* (colloquial), *artifacts, middle passage, sycophants, disparage, propagandists.*

---

9-G             THE BOY WHO CAME TO SUPPER
*Russell Baker*

This complete essay was first published in the *New York Times* (August 1980). The writer is a syndicated newspaper columnist, long known for his humorous observations on life in the United States. Note how he combines his references to dinner and supper in almost every paragraph.

For a long time I used to eat supper. "Supper's at 5 o'clock and you'd better be here," my mother would say. We lived in the rural South then, but later we moved to New Jersey and kept right on eating supper, though sometimes it was as late as 6 o'clock.

In fact, I was still eating supper at the age of twenty-two when I started 5 working for an Eastern newspaper. Since it was a morning paper the work hours extended from 3 P.M. to midnight with an hour off to eat, and at 7 P.M. an editor habitually notified me that it was all right to go to dinner.

Since all the other reporters racing for the first martini were also going to dinner, I went to dinner, too. In this way I gradually became a dinner eater, 10 though the transition was confusing. On days off, since I was still living at home, my mother insisted that I eat supper, though it was often served as late as 7 P.M. now.

For a year or two, I remained in this transitional stage—a dinner eater at the office, a supper eater at home. Since I was eating dinner five nights a week and 15 supper only twice, however, the dinner habit began to enslave me and tensions developed at home.

"When are we going to have dinner?" I would ask my mother. "Supper will be ready as soon as I finish frying the potato cakes," she would say. We were drifting apart. Something basic we had once shared had now eroded. I was moving into another world, the world of the dinner eaters, while she was firmly anchored in the world of supper eaters. I left home and have been an incorrigible dinner eater ever since.

This distinction between Americans who eat supper and those who eat dinner is one of the most striking divisions in the national life, yet nobody has ever persuasively explained the difference between the parties, though many sociologists have tried.

Andy Rooney, for example, holds that it defines the difference between political parties. Democrats eat supper before sundown, he states, while Republicans eat it at 8 P.M. and call it dinner.

If this is so, how does he explain why headwaiters in New York keep me waiting at the bar past 10 P.M. while influential Democrats arriving in limousines are promptly ushered to the dinner table I thought I had reserved for 8:30?

Calvin Trillin has a theory that the distinction has something to do with American regionalism. His three tests for identifying an Eastern city are: "a place where nobody on the City Council ever wears white patent-leather shoes, where there are at least two places to buy pastrami" and "where just about everybody eats supper after dark and calls it dinner."

Trillin's theory is not supported by my experience in Newark, N.J., and Baltimore—indisputably Eastern cities, in which I lived for fifteen years among people who almost universally ate supper. In fact, the notion that anybody could eat dinner at the end of the day, except in the movies, never occurred to me until the age of twenty-two.

Until then, in my experience, dinner was eaten only once a week, always at 3 o'clock on Sunday afternoon. When somebody invited you to dinner you assumed it would be eaten at midafternoon on Sunday and the menu would be chicken. Having seen Jean Harlow and Wallace Beery in "Dinner at Eight," I realized there were unique people who put on tuxedos and gowns to eat dinner at the hour when normal people were taking their prebedtime cocoa, but the idea that I might ever doll up in order to tuck into the potato cakes seemed as far-fetched as the possibility of picking up Claudette Colbert on a Greyhound bus.

When I was in the transitional stage, learning to eat dinner with veteran journalistic dinner eaters, I first assumed that dinner was distinguished from supper by the beverage that came with it. Supper had always been accompanied by iced tea, a glass of milk or, in cold weather, a cup of coffee, all of which were designed to wash down the potato cakes. At dinner, the prevailing drink seemed to be gin, which was designed to help you forget you were eating potato cakes.

This may explain why I was converted so easily, but it does not explain anything more profound, since deeper investigation showed that many supper eaters partake regularly of beer, and even bourbon with ginger ale, while many dinner eaters are content with soda water, a few ice cubes and a slice of lime.

Long investigation of this division among Americans forces me to dismiss as myths such popular theories as: (1) that blue-collar people eat supper while establishment people eat dinner; (2) that people with good digestion eat supper while people prone to gastric distress eat dinner; and (3) that people with hearty appetites are supper eaters while people with jaded palates are dinner eaters who are really just going through the motions so they will have an excuse to lap up the wine. 65

My studies have produced only two illuminating facts: first, that a real supper 70 eater wouldn't be caught dead with a Cuisinart in the kitchen; second, that dinner eaters are five times less likely than supper eaters to faint dead away if you serve them an artichoke.

1. What characteristics of "supper" and "dinner" does the writer use as the basis for the comparison?
2. How and where does the writer use specific details to support his points? How and where does he use narrative?
3. Most of the essay is in standard English, but occasionally the writer uses a colloquial expression, such as "wouldn't be caught dead" in the last paragraph. What others can you find and what may be the writer's purpose in using them?
4. Distinguish between these synonyms for *idea: notion, thought, opinion, concept.* What is the etymology of *jaded* and how does it differ from *tired* in meaning? What is the origin of *bourbon* as a name for whiskey?

## ASSIGNMENTS

1. Write an essay of comparison, choosing as your subject two things enough alike to be comparable but with enough differences to make the comparison worthwhile. There are two chief types of topics: (1) a comparison based on periods of time—"then and now" or "now and later," and (2) a comparison based on two coexistent things—"this and that."

   Suggestions for the first type: horse and automobile, washboard and washing machine, clothing styles, early and contemporary cars, kindergarten and grade school, high school and college, your parents' childhood and yours.

   Suggestions for the second type: gasoline and diesel engines, city life and suburban life, suburban life and farm life, community colleges and universities, football and soccer, a camping vacation and a resort vacation, your home and that of a friend, your bedroom and that of a brother or sister, a book or play and the movie version, two different singers, two makes of automobile, two breeds of dogs, two TV situation comedies, two TV news analysts.

   After choosing a subject, decide which type of organization will be better for it, and make an outline showing the main points and subpoints you intend to develop.
2. Discuss the use of comparison in examples in other units, notably Unit 2-G; Unit 3-C; Unit 4-C; Unit 5-B; Unit 11-A and C; Unit 12-D and F; Unit 14-G.

# UNIT 10

# *Classification*

The many forms of plant and animal life may at first glance appear chaotic, but the biologist sees in them a high degree of order. This order is due to an elaborate system of classification. All life is first grouped into a few primary divisions called phyla; each phylum is in turn subdivided into smaller groups called classes; each class is subdivided into orders; and so on down through the family, the genus, the species, the variety. This system brings order out of chaos, enabling the biologist to consider any plant or animal in its proper relationship to all the rest.

Anthropologists similarly classify people according to races; businesses divide their creditors into various degrees of risk; instructors group their students, at the end of each term, into the levels provided by the prevailing marking system. Sometimes we overdo the job of neat pigeonholing and distort our picture of material that does not readily respond to such treatment. Nevertheless, accurate knowledge depends greatly on the clarifications provided by the process of classification.

## Content

To classify any group formally and completely would involve taking into consideration every representative of that group and breaking down classes into subclasses and so on until the ultimate in division had been attained. For most purposes, however, it is sufficient to consider only the important classes into which we can divide a given subject and to treat only its principal groups and perhaps subgroups. An essay on musical instruments, for example, meant for the general reader need not have classifications covering every rare or ancient piece but may consider only those commonly used by the modern orchestra. Once the writer has divided and grouped them into kinds and described the outstanding instruments of each kind, the task of classification is, for practical purposes, complete. The purpose of such an essay is usually not total thoroughness; the writer uses classification as an aid in bringing out some other point in an orderly but pleasing manner.

**1. Choose a limited group as your topic.** It should be small enough so that you can, in a brief paper, go into some detail in describing the subgroups. "People" is too much to handle; "taxi drivers" might do nicely.

**2. Choose a group with three or more subgroups.** There are, of course, classifications with only two classes, but they will give you much the same training in organization as the essay of comparison discussed in the preceding unit. Classifying people into "types I like and those I dislike" is an example of a limited and rather pointless division of a subject that is too large.

**3. Consider a personal and original development.** Many classifications already exist; for example, scientists regularly classify meteorites into three types according to the nature of their composition: iron, iron and stone, and stone. But you may get—and give—more enjoyment with an original approach such as that of the girl who classified "dates" according to the reasons for her choices into the "boy-across-the-street" type, the "he-has-a-blue-sports-car" type, and the "we-enjoy-each-other" type. Your instructor will perhaps guide you here with a specific requirement depending on whether fact or opinion is your goal. But if you look for an original classification, beware of the "good–bad–average" kind, which is likely to produce less originality than it may appear to promise.

**4. Choose and use a single principle of classification.** Your principle will determine the classes to be discussed. Engines may be classified according to maker, use, speed, number of cylinders—but only one at a time. An attempt to classify drivers into women drivers, truck drivers, and good drivers is no classification at all, merely a loose and purposeless discussion. The topic "women drivers" announces that the principle guiding the division is sex; "truck drivers" changes the principle to the type of vehicle driven; and "good drivers" changes it once more, this time to driving skill. Actually, there are the beginnings here of three distinct classifications:

a. According to sex (women, men—one of these two-part and ready-made schemes)
b. According to vehicle driven (truck, taxi, passenger car)
c. According to proficiency (good, bad, average)

**5. Do not permit your classes to overlap.** In the scheme just discussed, for example, a truck driver might also be both a woman and a good driver.

**6. Make your classification reasonably complete.** As mentioned earlier, your essay need not be exhaustive, but it should appear sufficiently complete for your purpose. In classifying hunting dogs by breed, you might leave unmentioned certain rare varieties, but you would be obliged to consider all those commonly known. To discuss horror movies you dislike and those you tolerate, you must include those you enjoy; then your classification, based on the principle of your own attitude, would be satisfactorily complete.

**7. Introduce subclasses as needed.** If there are finer divisions of any of the subgroups into which you divided your original group, you may wish to include them. In classifying students according to religious faiths—for example, as Jews,

Catholics, Protestants, Moslems, and so on—you may want to subdivide at least the Protestants according to the principal denominations, such as Methodist, Presbyterian, or Baptist. But be sure to keep such a subgrouping in its place, and do not allow yourself or your reader to confuse it with the larger classification on which your paper is based.

## *Organization*

The several main classes (categories) forming your classification will, of course, constitute the principal divisions of your plan; the only remaining question is the order in which you can best treat them. Sometimes this order is natural—inherent in your subject—leaving you no choice; sometimes you will have to decide among several possibilities, all logical. Choose the one that best suits your purpose and is likely to be clearest to your readers.

To write of students according to their college year, you would probably use a chronological order starting with freshmen, going on to sophomores and juniors, and finishing with seniors. If you classify them according to religions, you might follow the chronological order in which these were founded. More probably, however, you would arrange the groups according to numerical size on your campus or in the nation. Or perhaps you will choose an order based on your own interest in the various religions, saving until last the one you consider most interesting or important so that you can make a strong final impression on your readers. What you think will best attract your readers' interest will help you to choose which to place first.

As to your discussion of each class, note that as in the comparison theme, your outline divisions indicate comparable topics and therefore should receive similar treatment. Study the following brief paragraph:

> The distinctions I am making among three different kinds of culture—*post-figurative*, in which children learn primarily from their forebears, *cofigurative*, in which children and adults learn from their peers, and *prefigurative*, in which adults learn also from their children—are a reflection of the period in which we live. Primitive societies and small religious and ideological enclaves are primarily postfigurative, deriving authority from the past. Great civilizations, which necessarily have developed techniques for incorporating change, characteristically make use of some form of cofigurative learning from peers, playmates, fellow students, and fellow apprentices. We are now entering a period, new in history, in which the young are taking on new authority in their prefigurative apprehension of the still unknown future. (Margaret Mead, *Culture and Commitment.*)

Notice that the three kinds of culture Mead names are listed in her first sentence as a parallel series, each named, then followed by an "in which" definition. The three sentences that follow take up these kinds in the same order, explaining where each is found. Not all essays of classification will or should show such complete balance, especially the longer and more informal ones. But similar treatment is inevitable: the preceding quotation is the opening paragraph of a small book that is divided into three chapters, "The Past," "The Present," and "The Future," which develop the author's thoughts about these three kinds of culture one by one in the order in which she introduces them. These long chapters do not, of course, match in wording—but they do in purpose and accomplishment.

If as a writer you classify, you must recognize the need to give roughly the same treatment to each of your categories. If you write on the American Kennel Club's official classification of dogs (a somewhat arbitrary sorting into six groups: sporting, hound, working, terrier, toy, nonsporting), and if you give information on breeds, uses, and popularity for sporting dogs, your reader will expect you to cover the same areas, probably in the same order, for the other five categories. Note that the first section suggested—breeds—will involve the kind of subclassification that a classification often includes (see item 7 in the discussion of "Content").

## Reader Interest

Tedious as an outline may appear, it is a valuable aid in making a logical, orderly essay. But remember not to let it obtrude awkwardly. Your finished theme should have a pleasing variety within the orderly arrangement. A formal classification that never goes beyond the outline stage remains a mere listing under appropriate heads and subheads and appeals only to readers already interested in the subject. Make your classification, like your papers on previous assignments, both readable and logical. Never let yourself or your reader lose sight of the essential underlying order, but use every means available to make your writing appeal.

## EXAMPLES

Your chief concern in this unit will be to observe, in each selection, the subject being classified, the principle used, the number of classes that result, and the order in which they are presented. Also notice the transitions that hold together the discussions of the various classes.

**10-A**                    BOOK OWNERS
                        *Mortimer J. Adler*

This excerpt comes from an essay, "How to Mark a Book," first published in the *Saturday Review* in 1940.

There are three kinds of book owners. The first has all the standard sets and best-sellers—unread, untouched. (This deluded individual owns woodpulp and ink, not books.) The second has a great many books—a few of them read through, most of them dipped into, but all of them as clean and shiny as the day they were bought. (This person would probably like to make books his own, but is restrained by a false respect for their physical appearance.) The third has a few books or many—every one of them dog-eared and dilapidated, shaken and loosened by continual use, marked and scribbled in from front to back. (This man owns books.)

1. What is the principle of classification involved here? Do these three classes constitute a "reasonably complete" discussion of the subject?
2. Notice the almost perfect parallelism of the treatment of the three classes, similar to the kind of balance we found in the development of the essay of comparison. But like the antitheses of Example B in Unit 9, this could not be sustained at length. Compare the high degree of organization here with the greater freedom in the longer selection that follows.
3. Check the etymology, denotation, and connotation of *deluded* and *dilapidated*.

*10-B*                      THE ONES LEFT BEHIND
                      *Rebecca Lanning (student)*

The Cullowhee Exodus, so much a part of the average WCU student's Friday life, begins around noon and by three o'clock is in full swing. Almost everyone who can possibly do so has wedged himself into a homeward-bound car, leaving behind only those who couldn't find a ride, those who feel they have too much studying to do, and those rare and inexplicable souls who seemingly enjoy a weekend on a temporarily almost deserted campus.

The most bitter of those left behind are the No-Way-Homers. These are made up of individuals unlucky enough to have a four-o'clock class and to find no driver willing to wait until 4:50, and those who live too far away from the university to be able to travel there and back in a weekend. These two groups spend their weekend with appropriate differences: the first complaining endlessly about the stupidity of the computer that gave them such a lousy schedule, the second moaning to anyone within earshot of the folly of having any institution for higher education located so far from civilization.

The largest group of these campus weekenders, the Studiers, are less bitter than the No-Way-Homers but more disgusted. In fact, they are running over with disgust because, having wrestled with the books all week, they must now continue the match throughout the weekend. Most of the Studiers are chronic procrastinators; some are the lucky people to whom Professor Smith has given one of his little over-the-weekend take-home fifty-question "opportunity" quizzes; and the rest are the students of Sandbox 2331, who were informed in class on Friday of a term paper due the following Monday.

On Saturday afternoon the library is full of sleeping Studiers who had stayed awake far into Friday night. Some of them were scheduling their Saturday study time; others were plotting the arsenic murder of Professor Smith and his ilk. Quickly the weekend flies by, and with it the intentions of the Studiers, who when questioned later about how they spent their time, mutter something unintelligible about how much work they accomplished. In all truth, however, the only thing they really did was getting ready to get ready to study.

Neither bitter nor disgusted is the third, final, small, and entirely atypical group of those remaining behind, the Enjoyers. These rare people seem actually to relish life on an almost empty campus. They spend the entire weekend looking cool and detached as they sit drinking cokes in the Town House or strolling along the ivy-bordered walks, showing off their wonderful dispositions and making enemies right and left. The Enjoyers are considered by everyone else to be either remarkably school-spirited or downright crazy—but maybe they actually do enjoy the atmosphere of a simulated Siberia.

Time marches on (to coin a phrase), and soon it is Monday. Back troop the rest of the student population, and the No-Way-Homers, the Studiers, and the Enjoyers all blend into the renewed hustle and bustle for another busy college week. One thought, however, runs continually through most of their minds: "Just wait till next weekend; wild horses couldn't keep me here."

1. What determines the order of the three major classes?
2. Point out the subclasses mentioned in ¶¶ 2, 3, and 4.

---

### 10-C   MENTAL DEPRESSION: THE RECURRING NIGHTMARE
#### *Jane E. Brody*

The following excerpt, which was published in the *New York Times* (1977), forms the first two-thirds of an article by a writer who regularly covers health news. The rest of the article describes various treatments for depression.

ANALYSIS
Introduction

Major class #1

Major class #2

The feeling is familiar to almost everyone—nothing seems satisfying, things don't work out, you can't get yourself to do much of anything and your mental landscape is bleak. It's called depression, and few of us get through life without experiencing it at one time or another.

Many things can get a person "down," including the weather (midwinter doldrums are an annual event for some), the letdown after the excitement and activity of the holidays, insufficient sleep, too much work and too little time in which to get it done. The ordinary everyday "blues" are fortunately usually brief and self-curing and, although they take the edge off life, are not terribly incapacitating.

However, for millions of Americans, depression is a far more serious, sometimes even life-threatening, situation. Most serious depressions are reactions to stressful life events—loss of a job or a spouse, serious financial setback, a serious illness or injury, the end of a love affair. After a reasonable number of weeks or months, most such depressions usually lift and the world and life begin to seem 20 brighter.

Major class #3

But for some people, depression is a recurring phenomenon that is provoked by events that others seem to weather with little difficulty or get over very quickly. And for others, depression happens "out of the blue," unrelated 25 to any particular situation, and totally incapacitates the victims. Many accomplished people suffered from severe depression, including Sigmund Freud, Abraham Lincoln, Nathaniel Hawthorne, Winston Churchill and the astronaut, Edwin E. Aldrin. 30

Importance of major class #3

The National Institute of Mental Health estimates that each year between 4 and 8 million Americans suffer depressions severe enough to keep them from performing their regular activities or compelling them to seek medical help. Perhaps 10 to 15 million others have less severe 35 depressions that interfere to some extent with the performance of normal activities.

All told, depression is clearly "the mental illness of the '70's," rivaling schizophrenia as the nation's number one mental health problem and currently increasing signifi- 40 cantly among people below the age of 35.

Theories on causes of major class #3

Some experts say the social tensions of the times—the erosion of trust, diminished personal impact, unrealistically high expectations for success, disintegration of the family, 45 social isolation and loss of a sense of belonging to or believing in some stable, larger-than-self institution—foster a society especially prone to depression.

Subclasses of #3
Subclass #1

Recognizing depression, should it strike you or someone you know, can sometimes be very difficult. In its classic, 50 undisguised form, depression has three main characteristics:

Sub-subclass #1

¶Emotional—A dull, tired, empty, sad, numb feeling with little or no pleasure from ordinarily enjoyable activities and people; 55

Sub-subclass #2

¶Behavioral—Irritability, excessive complaining about small annoyances or minor problems, impaired memory, inability to concentrate, difficulty making decisions, loss of sexual desire, inability to get going in the morning, slowed reaction time, crying or screaming, excessive guilt feeling; 60

Sub-subclass #3

¶Physical—loss of appetite, weight loss, constipation, insomnia or restless sleep, impotence, headache, dizziness, indigestion and abnormal heart rate.

Subclass #2    But in many cases, the symptoms of depression are "masked," disguised in a form that makes recognition by 65 the depressed person, his family, friends and even his physician difficult. "The exhausted housewife, the bored adolescent and the occupational underachiever are often suffering from depression just as truly as the acutely suicidal patient or the one who refuses to get out of bed," according 70 to Dr. Nathan Kline, a New York psychiatrist.

The patient with disguised depression may complain of headache, backache or pains elsewhere in the musculoskeletal system. He may have a gastrointestinal disorder, such as chronic diarrhea, a "lump" in the throat, chest pain 75 or a toothache.

Or his depression may be disguised in sexual promiscuity, overeating, excessive drinking or various phobias.

Depression in children is usually masked, presenting symptoms like restlessness, sleep problems, lack of attention 80 and initiative.

In addition to stressful events that cause depression (called "reactive" or "exogenous" depression), and unknown internal, probably biochemical, causes (called "endogenous" depression), depression can result from 85

Other causes of major class #3    organic diseases, including viral and bacterial infections, such as hepatitis, influenza, mononucleosis and tuberculosis; hormonal disorders, such as diabetes and thyroid disease, and such conditions as arthritis, nutritional deficiencies, anemia and cancer.    90

1. Why is "Masked" not listed as a fourth classification of the symptoms of depression, after "Emotional," "Behavioral," and "Physical"?
2. What distinction is the author drawing between "emotional" and "behavioral" symptoms?

---

## 10-D    THE SOUTH AFRICANS
### *E. J. Kahn, Jr.*

The following paragraphs are from *The Separated People* (1968), a study of South Africa, and were first published in the *New Yorker*.

The peculiar composition of South Africa's population . . . has given the country its character and its controversiality. There are four principal kinds of South Africans. Largest in number and least in influence are its twelve and a half million black-skinned people. There are almost two million others, of mixed blood, who are known as "Colored." Their skins range in hue from white to 5 black, but whatever a Colored man's color, his rights are meager. There are slightly more than half a million Asiatics, most of them of Indian ancestry and all of them second-class citizens. First class is reserved for three and a half million Whites, who, as they never forget, constitute the largest concentration of white people in Africa. Johannesburg, the Republic's main metropolis, with a total population of 1,250,000, has the biggest white population of any city on the continent. Johannesburg also has the biggest black population. It is in large part because of such unique distinctions that contemporary South Africa is so uniquely vexed.

The mere identification of the various categories of South Africans can confuse outsiders. The Whites—who rarely have anyone else in mind when they use the term "South African"—are often known as "Europeans," although in fact most of them have firm African roots; some of their family trees were planted in African soil a dozen generations ago. (The few Japanese in South Africa also rate as Europeans, because most of them are businessmen and it suits the South African government to treat them—although Chinese do not get the same break—as honorary Whites.) In the Transvaal province—wherein are located both Johannesburg and Pretoria, the country's administrative capital—"non-European" means "non-White." In the province of the Cape of Good Hope, however, wherein lies Cape Town, the country's legislative capital (the highest judicial body sits in still another province, at Bloemfontein in the Orange Free State), the only non-Whites considered non-European are the Coloreds, most of whom live in the Cape. Throughout South Africa the darkest and most downtrodden of its residents are called either Africans, as they themselves prefer to be designated, or Bantu, as the government prefers to designate them (in many African languages, "Bantu" means "people"), or natives, or kaffirs, a word of Arabic origin that means infidels and is akin to the American "niggers." Only bigots and Africans use "kaffir."

South Africa is extremely conscious of the variety and disparity of its inhabitants. Where else on earth would the head of a government refer, as Prime Minister Balthazar John Vorster did in the winter of 1967, to "my country and my *peoples*"?

1. This selection suggests some of the need for and difficulties of classifying. What is the principle of classification here?
2. How do you account for the order in which the classes are presented? Could it have been reversed?
3. Check the etymology, denotation, and connotation of *unique*. How does it differ from *unusual* and *rare*?

---

10-E                        **OUTER LIMITS**
*Jane Panzeca (student)*

A good student need not be on the honor role or a whiz at taking tests. He or she must, however, view learning as a way to expand and grow as a human being and as a way to contribute to society.

There are four basic types of students: Regurgitators, Magicians, Sluggards, and Generators. The Regurgitators are the ones who cough up information as 5 it was dictated to them. They do well on tests but never offer an opinion or idea of their own. The Magicians are the deceivers; they view schooling as a means of getting a high-paying job. They are the master cheaters who pull top grades from midair but who perform a disappearing act when the going gets tough. The Sluggards are habitually lazy. They lack motivation and regard school as 10 useless. They must be pushed to learn, even though they have the ability to do well. The Generators are the dedicated students who take part in all class discussions. They see learning in a different light. Although they are not all honor students, they are curious and in touch with the world around them. They will view even the most common things differently from their peers.                    15

If one representative of each group were taken by an instructor to a stream and asked to throw a pebble into the water and then to express a thought, each would react differently. The Regurgitator might say, "Well, what is *your* opinion?" The Magician might reply, "Are we going to be asked this on a test?" The Sluggard might say, "*I'*m not going to throw the stone; you throw it for me!" 20 The Generator might reply, "I get the idea! It reminds me of an earthquake. The rock hitting the water generates ripples. Earthquake waves are like the vibrations in the water."

A student who is curious and interested will see even very ordinary devices in a provocative way. For such a student, learning is like the pebble causing 25 circular waves, a never-ending process; for, after all, learning has no limits.

*10-F*                          FOUR KINDS OF TALKING
                                    *Desmond Morris*

These paragraphs are taken from *The Naked Ape* (1967) in which the author, a zoologist and anthropologist, examines animal behavior to shed light on human behavior.

Talking evolved originally out of the increased need for the cooperative exchange of information. It grew out of the common and widespread animal phenomenon of nonverbal mood vocalization. From the typical, inborn mammalian repertoire of grunts and squeals there developed a more complex series of learnt sound signals. These vocal units and their combinations and recombi- 5 nations became the basis of what we can call *information talking*. Unlike the more primitive nonverbal mood signals, this new method of communication enabled our ancestors to refer to objects in the environment and also to the past and the future as well as to the present.

To this day, information talking has remained the most important form of 10 vocal communication for our species. But, having evolved, it did not stop there. It acquired additional functions. One of these took the form of *mood talking*. Strictly speaking, this was unnecessary, because the nonverbal mood signals

were not lost. We still can and do convey our emotional states by giving vent
to ancient primate screams and grunts, but we augment these messages with 15
verbal confirmation of our feelings. A yelp of pain is closely followed by a verbal
signal that "I am hurt." A roar of anger is accompanied by the message "I am
furious." Sometimes the nonverbal signal is not performed in its pure state but
instead finds expression as a tone of voice. The words "I am hurt" are whined
or screamed. The words "I am furious" are roared or bellowed. The tone of 20
voice in such cases is so unmodified by learning and so close to the ancient
nonverbal mammalian signaling system that even a dog can understand the
message, let alone a foreigner from another race of our own species. The actual
words used in such instances are almost superfluous. (Try snarling "good dog,"
or cooing "bad dog" at your pet, and you will see what I mean.) At its crudest 25
and most intense level, mood talking is little more than a "spilling over" of
verbalized sound signaling into an area of communication that is already taken
care of. Its value lies in the increased possibility it provides for more subtle and
sensitive mood signaling.

A third form of verbalization is *exploratory talking*. This is talking for talk- 30
ing's sake, aesthetic talking, or, if you like, play talking. Just as that other form
of information-transmission, picture-making, became used as a medium for aesthetic exploration, so did talking. The poet paralleled the painter. But it is the
fourth type of verbalization that we are concerned with in this chapter, the kind
that has aptly been described recently as *grooming talking*. This is the mean- 35
ingless, polite chatter of social occasions, the "nice weather we are having" or
"have you read any good books lately" form of talking. It is not concerned with
the exchange of important ideas or information, nor does it reveal the true mood
of the speaker, nor is it aesthetically pleasing. Its function is to reinforce the
greeting smile and to maintain the social togetherness. It is our substitute for 40
the social grooming of other primates. By providing us with a nonaggressive
social preoccupation, it enables us to expose ourselves communally to one
another over comparatively long periods, in this way enabling valuable group
bonds and friendships to grow and become strengthened.

1. Can you justify the use of only two paragraphs to develop four points?
2. Compare the effectiveness, for the average reader, of the rather general and technical definition of information talking with the vivid examples illustrating mood
   talking. Notice, too, the sentence-long adjectives under grooming talking. Are they
   formal or informal in tone?
3. Check the etymologies and meanings used here of these words: *repertoire, primate,*
   *augment, aesthetic, grooming.*
4. Some of Morris's words and phrases might be classified as "technical jargon" (see
   Unit 5), for example, *nonverbal mood vocalization, inborn mammalian repertoire,*
   and *nonverbal mammalian signaling system.* What does he mean by these terms?
   Can you express the meaning of any of them more simply without using more
   words?

## *10-G*   AMERICAN MAGAZINES AND AMERICAN CULTURE
### *Peter McGrath*

This excerpt forms three-quarters of an article that appeared in *New Society* (July 1980). It begins with the recent rescue from bankruptcy of *Harper's*, a highly respected, 130-year-old magazine. The writer uses his classification of successful magazines to support his opinions on the dangers of current American attitudes.

Last year *Harper's* lost more than $1.5 million according to prospective buyers who claim to have seen its books. It had a long-term subscription liability reported at $4 million, and an unfavourable contract with an advertising sales agency. Its circulation of 300,000 made it one of the five best-read magazines of its kind. But its kind was the wrong kind, from an advertiser's point of view. 5

The fact is that general-interest magazines have about as much of a future in the American market as Socrates would have as a talk-show host on commercial television. No matter how good the material, the audience will never be suitable for advertisers. *Harper's* once indulged in demographic testing and found it had an elite readership: good education, high income, nice homes in Scarsdale 10 and Chevy Chase. But no one could figure out what these people were interested in consuming, other than ideas. They had money, but were they whisky drinkers or wine buffs? Sports car drivers or eminently sensible owners of Volvo estate wagons? The *Harper's* readership didn't define itself with anything like enough precision. 15

Thirty years ago, when magazines were fewer in number, and the field was dominated by a few fat general-interest publications—the *Saturday Evening Post*, *Life*, *Look*, and *Collier's*, now all gone, though two have been revived in different form—defining your readers wasn't so important. Your competition was other general-interest magazines. But in the past ten years, partly because 20 prime-time television has priced itself beyond the reach of all but the richest advertisers, the magazine business has been thriving. Therefore crowded. Therefore competitive.

And the business has changed. If you want to start a magazine today, you target a particular readership. You appeal to a particular interest, defining it as 25 narrowly as possible. For instance: it is not narrow enough to concentrate on women simply, as *Redbook* does; there must be magazines for liberated women (*Ms.*), career women with children (*Working Mother*), even fat women—*Big Beautiful Woman*, introduced earlier this year. It's not enough that there are general sports magazines like Time Incorporated's excellent *Sports Illustrated;* 30 there must be separate magazines for each separate sport—*Golf Digest* has a million readers, and its chief competitor *Golf* has over 700,000. . . .

Among the magazines with revenues of at least $2.7 million last year, more than a dozen are devoted to automobiles. There are six more for motorcyclists alone, and these are subdivided according to the split between road and trail 35 bikers. A magazine called *Pickup, Van and 4WD* (for four-wheel drive), took in as much money as *Harper's* did—about $5,150,000—but did so with a circulation 75,000 lower.

How? Because its readership is so easily defined. They want the tiny refrig- 40 erators that fit inside vans, and the compact stereo systems you can conceal in the wall panels of your truck. They want the plexiglas tops that convert a pickup truck into a camper. With *Pickup, Van and 4WD,* as with *Big Beautiful Woman,* an advertiser knows exactly what he's getting. . . .

Even literate readers segment themselves in this way. There is now a boom in science magazines; one of these, *Science 80,* was started by the hyper-schol- arly American Association for the Advancement of Science and features ads for high-tech items like a Sony radio with a "memory scan" device that lets you hear exactly 3.5 seconds of each of eight preselected stations before you have to make your choice.

. . . There is no reading public any more; there are only markets. Once upon 50 a time a man would start a magazine because he thought he had some idea worth hearing, or knew of some writers worth reading. Publishing was almost a missionary activity, and the intimate relationship that readers had with mag- azines testified to this. People knew the exact day of the week or month their magazines came out on—hence names like *Saturday Review*—and would look 55 forward to those dates as one would look forward to the visit of a friend. And as they turned the pages, they would find voices that were personal, even eccen- tric, but always distinctive and familiar—think of H. L. Mencken at *American Mercury,* or Walter Lippmann at the early *New Republic.*

Today's entrepreneur, though, starts a magazine out of no inner compulsion. 60 He simply spots a market that isn't being served. Do affluent, suburbanite professionals in their mid-forties with 2.2 children lack a publication to call their own? For them there will be *Prime.* Are flat dwellers neglected in a country that makes a fetish of home ownership? They will need *Apartment Life,* which has a current circulation of over 830,000. The modern publisher picks his sub- 65 ject according to its advertising possibilities, and gradually the line between advertising and editorial content begins to disappear.

But whose fault is this? Certainly not the advertisers; they're only seizing an opportunity. Not the publishers—you can't demand that a man lose money, though you might applaud him when, like Martin Peretz at the *New Republic,* 70 he does so for the sake of keeping a point of view in circulation.

The market favors single-interest magazines because Americans have become a single-interest people. It's no coincidence that this age of publications like *Pickup, Van and 4WD* is also an age of so-called "single-issue" politics.

Single-issue politics is the politics of the anti-abortion groups, of the gun own- 75 ers who oppose limits on access to the weapons. For such people there is one standard and one only by which to judge a politician: his stand on the issue they care most about. One slip and he's dead, no matter how much they may like his record in other areas. In 1978, Senator Dick Clark, a liberal Democrat from Iowa, was astonished to find liberal Democrats voting against him simply 80 because he supported federal aid for abortions for the poor; he lost to a lack- lustre candidate he was expected to beat easily. This year the pro-abortion pol- itician is an endangered species.

The problem with single-issue politics is that it distorts the democratic pro-

cess. In the tug-of-war for politicians' hearts and minds, it gives an advantage 85
to people whose views are narrow. It favors conflict over consensus, rigidity over
flexibility. It mocks the man who tries to make of his opinions a coherent whole.
At bottom, it is authoritarian.

Single-issue politics is a product of single-interest culture. And this culture, of
which today's magazines are so accurate a reflection, is individualism's ultimate 90
achievement, pluralism gone berserk. The American ideology encourages people to pursue their own happiness in their own way, but there's a point beyond
which a narrow pursuit of happiness, of one's own personal interests, under-
mines the system that makes it all possible. As Robert Frost once remarked in
an interview, the reason "we've got a good arrangement here" is that "we're 95
minding our own business a certain amount, and we're minding each other's
business a certain amount." If Americans don't start minding each other's business a little more, they're going to find no business left to mind.

1. What principles of classification does the writer use?
2. What may be his reasons for choosing them?
3. What transitional devices do you find?
4. How well does he support his conclusion? Do you agree with it?
5. Check the etymology, denotation and connotation of each of these words: *elite,
   buffs, entrepreneur, consensus, berserk.*

---

### 10-H        BUSINESS STATUS—HOW DO YOU RATE?
#### *Enid Nemy*

This article, given here almost complete, appeared in the *New York Times* (August
1980). The writer's tone is half-joking; how accurate do you think her observations are?

You arrive for a business appointment. First you spend 20 minutes in the
waiting room, leafing through January's *Reader's Digest* and the April *New
Yorkers.* Then the receptionist tells you to go in—the first corridor on the right,
the fifth door on the left.

Right then, you should know that you don't rate. According to unofficial 5
office protocol, you're a one or two on a scale of 10. Not quite the bottom of
the totem pole—a zero wouldn't have been granted an appointment at all—but
next thing to it.

Still, if it's any comfort, you may find that the person with whom you have
the appointment isn't a 10 either, or even a six or seven. His rating, or hers, may 10
be just as pathetic as your own.

There are two distinct aspects to business status. The first encompasses the
actual office space you occupy, and the second is how you are treated and
greeted when you arrive in someone else's office for an appointment.

In the matter of office space, it is as well to know that anyone without an 15 office, that is, a physical space with walls, is probably not worth wasting time on. This includes all or most newspaper reporters.

Cubicles also aren't worth much. At most, they're half a step up, but that's only if they have doors. Cubicles without doors are considered about as impressive as Princess telephones. 20

It is, however, in the genuine private offices that the status game is played seriously. For example, it's a good thing to be on friendly terms with men and women who have suites of rooms on high floors. Executives of this ilk can be very useful. As can the occupants of large corner offices with two walls of windows or, at the very least, with lots of windows, or even one big window. 25

Windows, in fact, apparently are as essential to office prestige as Christmas is to retailing. Even at the United Nations, where legend has it that the building was designed so that there could be no corner offices, the expanse of glass in individual offices is said to be a dead giveaway as to rank. Five windows are excellent, one window not so great. 30

In addition to a lofty floor number and windows, a carpet is another feature to look for. At a certain corporate level, offices almost always have carpets. If they don't, the assumption is that the occupants don't wish to have them. But they practically all do, so there is rarely need to assume.

As though all this weren't enough, some cities have additional hierarchical 35 clues. There are Washington officeholders who would hang their heads in shame if they didn't have a big flag and a personally inscribed picture of the President. And areas, best unnamed, where an office without a bar and refrigerator is, well, naked.

As for visiting other offices, the signals are equally clear. An important visitor 40 is not kept waiting after his presence is made known. He is met and escorted to the inner office by a private secretary. That is about as well as most people can do, other than the few who rate the big gun himself or herself coming out to the reception area to do the escorting personally. This treatment usually entails a similar kind of farewell—the caller is escorted right out to the elevator by his 45 host.

Assuming that one doesn't rate the biggie greeting, but the scene of the appointment is finally reached, what happens then? It's a bad sign if the person is talking on the telephone and indicates with a casual wave of a hand that you be seated. Better, much better, if the telephone conversation is terminated 50 immediately, and the greeting is done by a figure at least on its feet.

The nuances are endless. For example, once a business meeting has begun, it's a sign of the visitor's importance if there are no interruptions. This generally means that the outside office has been told to hold telephone calls. If calls are accepted, the situation still isn't hopeless so long as the conversation is confined 55 to saying that the call will be returned later.

If you're kept waiting in the reception area, told how to find the right office yourself, are faced with a hand holding a telephone and another hand waving you to a chair and are constantly interrupted by long telephone conversations, be advised: There is nowhere to go but up. 60

1. The writer has two main classes; how does she arrange the subclasses of each?
2. Check the etymology, denotation, and connotation of *protocol* and *entails*.
3. What is the effect of the writer's occasional use of such colloquialisms as *dead give-away, big gun,* and *biggie?* What other colloquial words and phrases do you find?

## ASSIGNMENTS

1. For an essay of classification you have a wide choice of subject matter. For example, you may write of classes already existing in guns, boats, airplanes, engines, welding processes, ways of preparing food, swimming strokes, trees, crops, cattle, pets, advertising, music, musical instruments, mathematics, curricula. Some of these subjects also lend themselves to more original handling, depending on the principle of classification you adopt and on the attitude you take toward the material. But more likely to demand originality of treatment are subjects such as love, patriotism, weather, television commercials, books, movies, fraternities.
2. You may especially enjoy a personal and original classification of some limited group of people: students, teachers, "dates," pledges, grandparents, salespeople, customers, employers, dog lovers, service-station attendants, taxi drivers, bridge players, pilots, amateur fishermen, news commentators, ball players, sports fans, dancers, hitchhikers.
3. Having chosen your subject, decide on a single principle of classification and keep it firmly in mind as you jot down the classes that you will include, making sure that they represent a reasonably complete treatment of the subject. Next, determine the most effective order in which to present these several classes, and then make a brief outline, indicating not only the classes and their order, but, with subpoints, the kind of information that you will include under each. (Remember that the information should be approximately the same and presented in approximately the same order for each class.)
4. Study the use of classification in the examples in other units: Unit 13-B, ¶3, and F, ¶5; Unit 14-E, ¶4; Unit 16-G, ¶2.

# PART THREE

## Aids in Reasoning

Although the earlier parts of this book required that you use reasoning, they emphasized organization and arranging material in patterns to show the relationships and relative importance of the parts. We shall now examine the intellectual processes that bring order to the act of thinking itself.

Unit 11 considers analysis, finding the parts, whether of a mechanism or of a problem, that compose the whole. Analysis is similar to classification, discussed in Unit 10, but it may be more complex than classification and has far broader implications. It is not only simple division but also dissection to discover root principle.

Unit 12 considers the relationships of cause and effect that are among the chief sources of the order through which we understand events around us.

Unit 13 considers induction, the process of arriving at generalizations by examining particulars. This process, essential to the development of modern science, is called the scientific method, but as a method of reasoning it reaches far beyond the laboratory.

Unit 14 considers the complementary process of deduction, the earliest method of reasoning to have been brought to perfection. Here, using generalizations reached by the inductive method, we exercise the pure logic of the syllogistic process in arriving at the truth about particulars.

Unit 15 considers definition—thinking through to the meaning of a term. Formally, definition includes the logical processes of deciding first in what class the term belongs and then what particular characteristics distinguish it from all others of that class. But definition may go far beyond this formal exercise. It has been left until last in this part of the book because it may combine any or all of the ways of writing and reasoning considered in the earlier units—from description through deduction.

The logical processes in all the units in this section are ways of reasoning rather than of organizing, and you will have ample opportunity in the assignments to draw on the aids and patterns you have practiced in Parts One and Two.

# UNIT 11

## Analysis

When your chemistry instructor gives you an unknown substance, you are expected to analyze it—to break it down into the elements composing it. You have used a similar process every time you tried to discover the sections into which a topic logically falls. Much of your education, in fact, is discovering the parts that make the whole or memorizing them as presented by your textbooks and instructors: "The government of the United States consists of three branches: the executive, the legislative, and the judicial," or "Successful writing requires attention to content, organization, and mechanics." But analysis is a logical process with applications reaching far beyond the college laboratory or classroom. Every problem to be solved, every situation requiring thought must be analyzed and its components discovered so that a solution or conclusion may be intelligently reached.

### Division

The simplest kind of analysis is a form of division—we split a subject in the way we section an apple, to make it yield comparable parts. The results are not like those of classification (Unit 10), however, because they come from breaking down a single thing rather than a group. Apples in the mass may be classified— into sizes, colors, varieties; but one apple will be divided into halves or quarters. We use division when we think of a year as twelve months or of a day as morning, afternoon, and evening. We use it when we think of the world as composed of continents, or of a nation as composed of states.

### Dissection

The process that we shall for convenience call dissection operates on a deeper level of analysis than division. Dissection yields not similar sections of the apple but its different components: skin, flesh, core, stem. Some subjects lend themselves to either kind of breakdown. We divided the day into comparable time periods, but we can dissect it into logical rather than chronological components: classes, outside activities, recreation (see pages 10–12). Many subjects that can be analyzed by dissection would not lend themselves to division. A pencil could be dissected into graphite, wood, and paint, or divided into inch-long pieces; but although you can easily dissect your radio, you cannot divide it.

The analytical process, as you can guess, goes far beyond apples and radios, however. You may use it, of course, in the relatively simple matter of explaining the parts of which a given mechanism is composed (it will then be similar to the simple informative type of description discussed in Unit 2), but you may also use it in the far more difficult task of discovering the issues in a complex problem. You may be interested in listing the components of a diesel engine or in setting forth what you believe to be the elements of Homer's greatness as an epic poet. In either task the process of analysis by dissection is essentially the same.

## Enumeration

How often in expository discourse we find such expressions as these:

Three questions remain to be considered.
Five possible courses of action exist.
Two reasons for his failure appear.
Several misconceptions must be corrected.

Analysis by division or dissection involves determining the number of parts or phases of the subject and discussing them one by one. How many there are will be determined largely by the circumstances of the subject, but there are limits. There will never be less than two, since by definition analysis implies a breaking down; and there are rarely more than five or six, as a larger number becomes unwieldy. Reasonable completeness, in analysis as in classification (page 146, item 6), will suffice.

Here, too, it is of prime importance to choose a principle to guide you through the breakdown of your subject so that your result will be neatly ordered pieces making up a logical whole. Whether they are parts of a simple mechanism or abstract qualities making up a reputation, they must be comparable. The tone is not an item in enumerating the parts of a radio, although it is the result of the parts; nor is the title of general one of the qualities of Washington's character that you may list as constituents of his greatness. It is essential that you recognize elements logically similar and omit the unrelated.

The order of the parts you finally choose as suitable will be determined, of course, by the usual patterns of arrangement for emphasis (see page 11). Because the parts are comparable, you may often find that numbers make the best transitions: "1," "2," "3" or "first," "second," "third," and so on (the forms "firstly," "secondly," "thirdly" are no longer popular). Other transitions like "next" and "another" may also serve to emphasize your arrangement.

## Focusing on a Problem

Analysis need not stop with an enumeration of parts. As a logical process it is also applicable to problem solving. To find a solution, you must discover the exact nature of the problem; to discover its nature, you must break it down into its component parts. Whether you are hunting for an error in your bank balance, choosing a career, or settling one of the world's major ills, the general procedure will be the same.

You may make a preliminary analysis in order to eliminate any aspects of the subject that are irrelevant to your view of the problem, just as when, asked to determine the chemical composition of an unknown substance, you rule out rapidly the more unlikely possibilities. Martin Luther King described doing this in *Stride Toward Freedom*. Having found three ways in which oppressed people might react to oppression—by acquiescence, violence, and nonviolent resistance—he ruled out the first two as unsuitable and concentrated on the third. You may analyze the psychological pressure on the average student, for instance, into the academic, economic, and social aspects, and decide to eliminate the first two from your discussion in order to devote yourself to the third as the one over which the student has most control. You will then proceed to break down the chosen part of the problem into its subordinate parts (dormitory life, dating, extracurricular activities, etc.), and on the basis of these parts, clearly stated, you will work through to a logical solution of the problem.

Although such an analysis is often applied to problem solving, it does not necessarily include a solution. It may imply an answer, or it may merely lay bare the issues for the reader's consideration; clarification is the central purpose of the analytical process.

## Statement of Root Principle

To help your readers understand the parts of an analysis and see how they fit together, you may well begin with a summing-up instead of a breaking-down—with a setting forth of the root principle, the essence, the key to the whole subject. This procedure may not seem to be "analysis" at all, in the sense in which we have been using the word; but in a wider sense it is one of the most valuable parts of this logical process. Analysis may mean not only dissection, a breakdown into parts, but reduction to bare essentials—to a simpler form. Such a reduction is likely to precede the normal taking-apart process (especially in the handling of abstract and complex subjects) to give the dissection clarity and purpose.

A writer might, for example, begin an analysis of the depression of the thirties by reducing that great economic phenomenon to a basic description, such as starvation in the midst of plenty, before breaking it down into its causes, results, manifestations, or whatever other aspects interest the writer. The root principle will serve as a unifying guide among the aspects. One writer reduces the greatness of Lincoln to the fact that he was able to make such a reduction out of the confusion of his time:

> The greatness of Lincoln consisted precisely in the fact that he reduced the violence and confusion of his time to the essential moral issue and held it there against the cynical and worldly wisdom of the merchants of New England and the brokers of New York and all the rest who argued for expedient self-interest and a realistic view. (Archibald MacLeish, *A Time to Act*)

## EXAMPLES

*11-A*                    THE STRUCTURE OF A COMET
                              *C. C. Wylie*

This example of objective description, analyzing a comet, is taken from *Astronomy, Maps and Weather* (1942), a book intended for the general reader.

The head of a comet is a hazy, faintly shining ball. This head, or *coma*, is the essential part of the comet and gives it its name. Inside the coma there is usually, but not always, a *nucleus*. The nucleus is formed as the comet approaches the Sun and is seen as a starlike point near the center of the coma. Naked-eye comets always, and telescopic comets often, form a *tail* as they approach the Sun. 5 The tail is formed by matter streaming off in a direction opposite to the Sun. Usually the tail attains its maximum length and brightness a little after the comet passes perihelion.

In volume, comets are the bulkiest members of the solar system. The head, or coma, is rarely smaller than the Earth in diameter, and for one or two comets 10 the diameter of the head has surpassed that of the Sun. The length of the tail of a spectacular comet may be as much as one hundred million miles, or about the same as the distance of the Earth from the Sun.

The mass of any comet is exceedingly small—so little that it cannot be measured directly. Calculations from the amount of light reflected indicate that the 15 mass of Halley's Comet, one of the most spectacular, was a little less than that of the rock and dirt removed in excavating the Panama Canal. From its mass and volume the density of the head of Halley's Comet was estimated as being equivalent to twelve small marbles per cubic mile. It is believed that the head of a comet is composed of dust and small particles surrounded by gas. The den- 20 sity of the tail of a comet is almost inconceivably small. For Halley's Comet the density has been calculated as equivalent to one cubic centimeter of air at sea level pressure expanded to two thousand cubic miles.

1. What principle of organization has the writer used?
2. Can you think of a different method of organization that would make the material as clear?

**3.** What similarities and differences do you find in purpose, organization, and general style between this example and Unit 2-D, Unit 4-F, and Unit 9-A?

**4.** Check the etymology and denotation of *perihelion*.

**5.** Where and how does Wylie use figures of speech to make his description clear?

---

***11-B***      WHAT WINNING AND LOSING REALLY ARE
           *Michael Novak*

This essay, which is here complete, first appeared in the *New York Times* (1976) and then as part of a book, *The Joy of Sports.*

Vince Lombardi has become a demon to some unbelievers. He is known for the sentiment, "Winning isn't everything; it's the only thing" and for his supposed ruthless authoritarianism.

Are these what he believed and practiced? If so, how did he believe and practice them? 5

One of the most graceful essays ever written about him is included in Howard Cosell's *Cosell.* He calls it "Lombardi: Ask His Players." In fact, few men have won so much love and devotion from those who have worked for them.

Why, then, the antagonism?

For one thing, the enlightened seldom notice the power and authority in the 10 games they play. At CBS, or at *The New York Times*, or at *Newsweek*, authority is now a bowl of Jell-O. The style, however, is seldom as direct as on a practice field.

Second, a coach is a teacher. He doesn't just hire a bunch of pros and have them "do their thing." He has to give the team unity, a style, a signature. He 15 has to bring each individual to the highest peak of his craft for each performance. Excellence is much more tightly demanded in football than in journalism, if only because there are only 14 games of 60 minutes each in which to be as perfect as one can.

Third, class and ethnic styles of exercising authority must be taken into 20 account. Football coaches deal with young men of many backgrounds and emotional histories. Most of the players they deal with are in their 20's; the oldest (except for a rare George Blanda) are in their 30's. There are angers and furies in coaches, but the players soon learn how to interpret them, how to discern whether they are fed by personal animosity, pettiness, resentment or only 25 honest passion. One learns in life how to adjust to barks, epithets and rages, just as one learns the underlying states of soul that prompt them.

Lombardi, it is said, could shed tears openly and be as tender as a child; the range of emotions open to Italian males is considerably larger than the range allowed upper-class Anglo-Saxon males. There was no need for Lombardi to be 30 a cool, laconic Humphrey Bogart, Paul Newman or Cary Grant.

Lombardi is also praised for the wide range of his sympathies. He treated individuals very differently. He nursed Bart Starr along, glowed with pleasure at the antics of Paul Hornung, bellowed with rage at certain hulking lineback- ers. His record with blacks, Cosell notes, was remarkable for its honesty and color blindness.

Finally, the record shows, few coaches had the streak of humor that often lighted Lombardi's face and presence. He could laugh at himself and mock his own intensity. His teams knew how to laugh. Can a man who laughs so easily be as cold, tyrannical and unintelligent as his unrelievedly serious critics allege?

If life is not a football game, neither is it a morality play between the enlight- ened and the unenlightened. Those with conservative convictions are often, in execution, amazingly tolerant and compassionate; those with liberal convictions are often, in execution, machinelike, arrogant and unbending. The human being is endlessly complex, immeasurably rich in variation. In particular, foot- ball coaches, whom psychologist describes as in the main, "authoritarian per- sonalities," may be more fair and just in their dealings with individuals than are sweetly liberal psychologists. So, Lombardi.

Of course, winning *is* the only thing—as an attitude, a desire, a spirit. In football, winning means excellence, defeating the demons of error and fate. Winning means outwitting everything that climate, occasion, injuries, opposing strategies and chance can throw in one's way. Winning means being as perfect under fire as humans can be. Losing means somehow, through one's own fault, not having prepared enough.

"Winning is the only thing" does not mean "win at all costs, by any means, fair or foul." Nor does it mean that losing is without dignity. Every team, even the Green Bay Packers at their best, loses sometimes.

It means that losing is, in the end, one's own responsibility. One's own fault. It means that there are no excuses.

"Winning is the only thing" is capable of sinister interpretations. But it is also capable of expressing the highest human cravings for perfection. Winning does not simply mean crushing one's foes, but being the best one can possibly be— and conquering the fates and adversities that are stronger forces even than opposing teams.

Winning is both excellence and vindication in the face of the gods. It is a form of thumbing one's nose, for a moment, at the cancers and diseases that, in the end, strike us all down, every one of us, even spirits as alive as Vince Lombardi's.

We miss you, Vince.

1. The author uses enumeration to emphasize the organization of part of this essay. How does he use questions to emphasize larger sections of it?
2. How does the author use the repetition of certain words and phrases for emphasis?
3. How convincing, in your opinion, is the author's argument that "Of course, winning *is* the only thing"?
4. How do the etymologies of *sinister, excellence,* and *vindication* help to explain Novak's use of these words?
5. What details, what specific, concrete words, and what figures of speech does Novak use to make his analysis vivid?

*11-C*                    MOTHERHOOD IN BONDAGE
                              *Adrienne Rich*

This essay, which is complete here, first appeared in the *New York Times* (1976).
The writer is a noted poet.

ANALYSIS

Introduction

Every great new movement in human consciousness
arouses both hope and terror. The understanding that
male–female relationships have been founded on the status
of the female as the property of the male, or of male-dom-
inated institutions, continues to be difficult for both women 5
and men.

General problem

It is painful to acknowledge that our identity has been
dictated and diminished by others, or that we have let our
identity depend on the diminishment and exploitation of
other humans. This idea still meets with the resistance that 10
has always risen when unsanctioned, long-stifled realities
begin to stir and assert themselves.

Specific area #1

Resistance may take many forms. Protective deafness—
the inability to hear what is actually being said—is one.
Trivialization is another: the reduction of a troubling new 15
complexity to a caricature, or a clinical phenomenon.

example

A literary critic, reviewing two recent anthologies of
women's poetry, declares that "the notion that the world
had been put together exclusively by men, and solely for
their own benefit, and that they have conspired together 20
for generations to discriminate against their mothers and
sisters, wives and daughters, lovers and friends, is a neurosis
for which we do not yet have a name." It is striking that,
even in his denial, this writer can describe women only as
appendages to men.                                            25

Specific area #2

In her forthcoming history of birth control in America,
the Marxist historian Linda Gordon writes, "For women
. . . heterosexual relations are always intense, frightening,
high-risk situations which ought, if a woman has any sense
of self-preservation, to be carefully calculated" (*Woman's* 30
*Body, Woman's Rights: A Social History of Birth Control
in America.*) The power politics of the relations between
the sexes, long unexplored, is still a charged issue. To raise
it is to cut to the core of power relations throughout society,
to break down irreparably the screens of mystification 35
between "private life" and "public affairs."

Specific area #3

But even more central a nerve is exposed when motherhood is analyzed as a political institution. This institution—which affects each woman's personal experience—is
visible in the male dispensation of birth control and abor- 40

Examples:

tion; the guardianship of men over children in the courts
and the educational system; the subservience, through most
of history, of women and children to the patriarchal father;
the economic dominance of the father over the family; the
usurpation of the birth process by a male medical estab-   45
lishment. The subjectivity of the fathers (who are also sons)
has prescribed how, when, and even where women should
conceive, bear, nourish and indoctrinate their children.
The experience of motherhood by women—both mothers
and daughters—is only beginning to be described by   50
women themselves.

Examples:

Until very recently, the choice to be or not to be a
mother was virtually unavailable to most women; even
today, the possibility of choice remains everywhere in jeopardy. This elemental loss of control over her body affects   55
every woman's right to shape the imagery and insights of
her own being. We speak of women as "nonmothers" or
"childless"; we do not speak of "nonfathers" or "childless
men." Motherhood is admirable, however, only so long as
mother and child are attached to a legal father: mother-   60
hood out of wedlock, or under the welfare system, or lesbian motherhood are harassed, humiliated or neglected. In
the 1970's in the United States, with 26 million children of
wage-earning mothers, eight million in female-headed
households, the late 19th-century stereotype of the   65
"mother at home" is still assumed as the norm—a "norm"
that has, outside of a small middle-class minority, never
existed.

Dissection

In trying to distinguish the two strands—motherhood as
*experience,* one possible and profound experience for   70
women, and motherhood as enforced identity and as political *institution*—I myself only slowly began to grasp the
centrality of the institution, and how it connects with the
dread of difference that infects all societies.

Under that institution, all women are seen primarily as   75
mothers; all mothers are expected to experience motherhood unambivalently and in accordance with patriarchal
values; and the "nonmothering" woman is seen as deviant.

Since the "deviant" is outside the law, and "abnormal,"
the pressure on all women to assent to the "mothering" role   80
is intense. To speak of maternal ambivalence; to examine
the passionate conflicts and ambiguities of the mother–
daughter relationship, and the role of the mother in indoc-
trinating her daughters to subservience and her sons to
dominance; to identify the guilt mothers are made to feel   85

for societal failures beyond their control; to acknowledge that a lesbian can be a mother and a mother a lesbian, contrary to popular stereotypes; to question the dictating by powerful men as to how women, especially the poor and nonwhite, shall use their bodies, or the indoctrination of 90 women toward a one-sided emotional nurturing of men, is to challenge deeply embedded phobias and prejudices.

Conclusion        Such themes anger and terrify, precisely because they touch us at the quick of human existence. But to flee them, 95 or trivialize them, to leave the emotions they arouse in us unexamined, is to flee both ourselves and the dawning hope that women *and* men may one day experience forms of love and parenthood, identity and community that will not be drenched in lies, secrets and silence.

1. What distinctions does Rich imply exist between motherhood as experience and motherhood as political institution?
2. What does she list as actions that conventional society may label "deviant"? Why would these actions appear to be a threat to convention?
3. What do the etymologies of these words contribute to make their modern meanings clear: *usurpation, jeopardy, wedlock, unambivalently, deviant?*

---

*11-D*            TWO IMPERATIVES IN CONFLICT
*Richard Shoglow (student)*

There is some evidence in the world that the phenomenon called the "territorial imperative," or something very like it, exists, and this can lead to pessimistic conclusions about the future of the human race. Ardrey, in his essay called "Of Men and Mockingbirds," points out some evidence to support the idea of "territoriality." For instance, he reports on twenty-four different prim- 5 itive tribes in various separate areas around the world. Although they were unable to learn from each other, they all formed similar social bands occupying specific permanent territories. This showed the unlearned, perhaps genetic, need of human beings for their own territory.

A second example of these territorial instincts is, I think, in the Middle East 10 today. The situation there is a struggle for possession of an area. Both the Israelis and the Palestinians are in battle over this territory—one to keep it and the other to obtain it. Both regard this land as necessary for their existence and as belonging to them.

Among my neighbors and even in my own family, I have seen further evi- 15 dence of a territorial imperative. My father, for instance, was very worried when a neighbor decided to build a boathouse near the property boundary of our house. Although we had plenty of land to spare, my father was worried about losing a little part of it. I have seen arguments between neighbors about

trees that cross property boundaries and even disputes over whether a boundary  20
marker had been moved a foot or so. If this phenomenon is instinctive, innate,
it is therefore inevitable that people must clash for living space. The increasing
pressure of a growing population and a severely limited world space may lead
to a catastrophic battle, such as a nuclear war, that could mean the end of the
world.  25

But while the potential for disaster may exist in our territorial imperative,
there is some evidence that a "social imperative" may also exist. This "social
imperative"is our ability to share and to cooperate with our fellow human
beings. If this exists, then there is hope for our future. Maybe many of our
problems will be solved eventually. Ardrey's article mentions that there are  30
some animals, such as the elephant, the antelope, and the gorilla, who have no
territorial bond. These animals wander constantly, moving where food can be
found. They have no wars. There is no competition over a particular territory.
They move together, sharing the space and the food. The Middle East dispute
is in an uneasy equilibrium as both sides, with the help of negotiators, search  35
for a compromise solution that can bring peace. If their "territorial imperative"
gets the better of either of them, a terrible conflict may erupt, but as long as
both sides are willing to cooperate, they can avoid war. If traditional enemies
can really join and share for the betterment of mankind, perhaps there can be
a more optimistic view of man's future.  40

We are born with a genetic structure that helps to determine the adjustment
we make in this world. But we are also subject to the influences of our social
environment. We can learn new behavior and we can modify our predisposi-
tions. If this were not true, all constructive influences such as education would
be worthless. I believe—or at least hope—that we will learn to modify our  45
genetic need for territory by accepting the modern reality. We all inhabit the
same rapidly shrinking earth populated by a rapidly rising number of people.
We must share and cooperate, because there is no other way.

1. This essay was written in response to one of the readings assigned in the course.
   What use does the writer make of analogy, narration, and comparison in his analysis
   of the "territorial imperative"?
2. By what methods does he analyze the "social imperative"?
3. The writer refers to his own individual experience and also to a major international
   problem. What is the effect of this use of both small-scale and large-scale examples?

---

*11-E*      WHY THEY MOURNED FOR ELVIS PRESLEY
              *Molly Ivins*

This example, a complete news article, first appeared in the *New York Times* (1977).

Why did 25,000 people stand for hours in an almost unbearable heat, in a
truly unbearable crush, trying to get a glimpse of a rock-and-roll singer? Why
did so many drive all night, take plane trips they couldn't afford, set out from

half a continent away without money or comforts or plans, solely to attend the
funeral of Elvis Presley? 5

The people who came to mourn offered only one reason: "Because," they
said over and over, "we love him."

Those who make it their business to explain such phenomena offered a multitude of reasons. Mass hysteria, they said. Ghoulishness. Suppressed sexual
yearnings. An acting out of class antagonisms. Nostalgia for lost innocence and 10
youth. They attributed it to generational identification, to Freudian repression,
to a mad media overkill.

But if some observers seemed condescending or embarrassed by the open
displays of sentimentality, mawkishness and love, Mr. Presley's fans saw nothing
to be ashamed of in glorying in their sorrow. They were not offended by an 15
instant commercialization of their grief, by the T-shirts reading "Elvis Presley,
In Memory, 1935–1977" that were on sale for $5 in front of Mr. Presley's
mansion.

The Memphis police, whose courtesy was remarkable, carefully carried water
out to the waiting fans, gently carried away the fainters, and played with the 20
children. When fans emerged distraught after viewing Mr. Presley's body, the
police walked up to them, put an arm around their shoulders and walked away
with them, talking soothingly until the fans were calmer.

The police became unpopular at one point, when they shut out at least 10,000
waiting fans on Wednesday evening. "Why are you treating us like this?" 25
shouted a man as he was pushed away from the gate. "Why do you have all
those helicopters and cops here?"

"We're afraid of a riot," replied a sheriff's deputy.

The fan was outraged, "You don't understand," he said. "We're not troub-
lemakers, we didn't come here to . . . we're, we're *family*. We came because 30
we love him."

One seldom expects the country's President to adequately note the passing of
a rocker, but Jimmy Carter's assessment of Elvis Presley's appeal—"energy,
rebelliousness and good humor"—is remarkably close to the mark. When he
started out in the 1950's he looked like a hood, he sang sensually. Part of his 35
appeal in the 1970's was our remembering what we thought was "sexy" back
then. Underneath that greaser hairdo, he had the profile of a Greek god.
Besides, our parents didn't like him, so what could be better? And the music?
Well, the music can be left to the music critics, who by and large seem to think
it's pretty good. A teenage foot that never tapped to "Heartbreak Hotel" in the 40
50's probably belonged to a hopeless grind.

A large proportion of the mourners in Memphis were the girls who once
screamed and cried and fainted at Elvis Presley concerts in the 1950's. They
grew up, but they never got over Elvis.

The idols of one's adolescence tend to endure—you never forget how you 45
worshipped them. There is never anyone quite so wonderful as the people who
were seniors when you were a freshman. And the intense crushes of adolescent
girls helped create the phenomenon of Elvis Presley.

The fans who came to Memphis, especially the women, tended to have been

Elvis fans "from the beginning." Many of them said they had married right out 50
of high school and that their last memories of girlhood are of passionate feelings
about Elvis Presley—"My first love."

"I told my husband he'd always be second to Elvis." "I loved him then and
I love him now." They never stopped being Elvis fans. They kept up their Elvis
Presley scrapbooks. They went to his concerts and grabbed the scarves he used 55
to give away, and had them framed. Some of them seemed to realize that it
was, perhaps, a little silly, but he seemed to represent the only rebellion they
ever knew, the dreams of their youth.

Oh, there were some who came to Memphis because "it's what's happening,
man." Just to be there, to be seen, to see, without caring. But for the most part, 60
Memphis was awash with genuine emotion for three days. It is too easy to dismiss it as tasteless. It is not required that love be in impeccable taste.

1. According to the author, what reasons did some observers give for the arrival of
   25,000 people from all over the country in Memphis to pay their last respects to
   Elvis Presley?
2. What additional reasons does the author find for the large number of mourners?
3. What descriptive and narrative touches does the author use to bring out her main
   point and to make the scene vivid?

---

*11-F*                          SPLITTING THE WORD
                                 *Anthony Burgess*

These paragraphs begin the chapter on words in *Language Made Plain* (1964), a
book explaining the basic principles and terminology of linguistics to the general
reader. A phoneme is any one of the smallest units of sound of which words are composed and which distinguish one word from another. In English these are often not
indicated by spelling. For instance, the phonemic difference between *though* and
*those* is the *z* sound in *those*.

For the moment—but only for the moment—it will be safe to assume that
we all know what is meant by the word "word." I may even consider that my
typing fingers know it, defining a word (in a whimsical conceit) as what comes
between two spaces. The Greeks saw the word as the minimal unit of speech;
to them, too, the atom was the minimal unit of matter. Our own age has learnt 5
to split the atom and also the word. If atoms are divisible into protons, electrons,
and neutrons, what are words divisible into?

Words as things uttered split up, as we have already seen, into phonemes, but
phonemes do not take *meaning* into account. We do not play on the phonemes
of a word as we play on the keys of a piano, content with mere sound; when 10
we utter a word we are concerned with the transmission of meaning. We need
an appropriate kind of fission, then—one that is *semantic,* not *phonemic.* Will
division into syllables do? Obviously not, for syllables are mechanical and met-

rical, mere equal ticks of a clock or beats in a bar. If I divide (as for a children's reading primer) the word "metrical" into "met-ri-cal", I have learned nothing 15 new about the word: these three syllables are not functional as neutrons, protons, electrons are functional. But if I divide the word as "metr-; -ic; -al" I have done something rather different. I have indicated that it is made of the root "metr-," which refers to measurement and is found in "metronome" and, in a different phonemic disguise, in "metre," "kilometre," and the rest; "-ic," which 20 is an adjectival ending found also in "toxic," "psychic," etc., but can sometimes indicate a noun, so that "metric" itself can be used in a phrase like "Milton's metric" with full noun status; "-al," which is an unambiguous adjectival ending, as in "festal," "vernal," "partial." I have split "metrical" into three contributory forms which (remembering that Greek *morph-* means "form") I can call 25 *morphemes*.

1. How does the author use analogy? metaphor?
2. Why does he use "fission" in the third sentence of the second paragraph instead of "division" or "splitting"?
3. Why does the author mention dividing words into syllables since he immediately says that doing so gives him no new information about the words?

---

*11-G*            THREE LANGUAGES IN A NOVEL
                        *Addison Gayle, Jr.*

This excerpt is from *The Way of the New World: The Black Novel in America* (1975). The author is a noted black scholar and professor of literature.

*Dunsfords Travels Everywheres* is almost the complete novel. So well has the consolidation between form and content been executed that the novel resembles a well-constructed dream. Language is the key to unraveling the dream, and [William Melvin] Kelley utilizes three language systems in order to tell his narrative. There is the standard English used by the narrator, setting the 5 tone of the novel and describing various incidents. There is the language of experimentation, found in the works of such writers as James Joyce and Melvin Tolson, which characterizes the dreamlike surrealistic world and contrasts reality and illusion. There is, finally, the rich language of the Harlem community, spoken by Carlyle and Hondo, pointing to racial homogeneity even within 10 Diversity: "Carlyle sat back, smiled at Ma Buster. 'Just steadying the ship, Ma. . . . We'll have us a good time, Ma. We'll get some fried clams and fries and have a little party, just the three of us, and him too, if he wants. . . . We'll drop off Hondo and send your man home, and have a little party, just us. . . .'"
All three language systems contain their own legends and myths, hold their 15 own allegorical content; each is reflective of cultural plurality.
Cultural plurality is the key phrase necessary in any attempt to understand the over-all meaning of *Dunsfords Travels Everywheres*. In the Cafe of One

Hand, in the city of Atzuoreurso and Jualoreurso, exists a cultural system bearing analogy to that of the Americans. Each segment of the society is defined by 20
the clothes it wears, and each opts for sameness over diversity, for cultural
hegemony instead of cultural plurality. Therefore, each surrenders his identity,
chooses similar life-styles to those of each other. The same holds true for Dunsford and Wendy. For Wendy, the end result is self-hatred—a Black involved
in the slave trade—and finally, death. For Dunsford, salvation is possible 25
because he has not forgotten elements of a language system which speaks to the
question of diversity and non-conformity, is capable of retaining contact with
his cultural past. Thus his travels, which take him through the cultural capitals
of the Western world, lead inevitably back to Harlem, where cultural democracy, not cultural hegemony, is the prevailing factor.                              30

In *A Different Drummer* and in *Dunsfords Travels Everywheres*, Kelley is
cognizant of a black cultural history which his characters either know or must
discover. Caliban, intuitively, has always known that the cultural system which
defined him was not that of the Euro-American imagists. Dunsford, on the other 35
hand, must discover his cultural heritage anew, and in so doing undertake the
journey to a black identity. Eventually the journey will lead outside the definition of the West, away from images and symbols that represent Western man,
and toward those, rich and enduring, in the African/Black heritage. At the end
of the novel he has come to partial awareness, has made his break, tenuous 40
though it may be, with the paraphernalia of imagistic language handed down
from the West and gained a new perception of himself.

1. How does the author use classification to make his point?
2. What examples of comparison do you find as part of the author's method of
   analysis?
3. Check the etymology, denotation, and connotation of *surrealistic, hegemony, plurality*. Who is Caliban?

---

*11-H*    THE BAD AND WORSE SIDES OF THANKSGIVING
          *The New Yorker*

This example is taken from an unsigned satire published in the "Notes and Comments" section of the *New Yorker* (November 1978).

At last, it is time to speak the truth about Thanksgiving. The truth is this: it
is not a really great holiday. Consider the imagery. Dried cornhusks hanging on
the door! Terrible wine! Cranberry jelly in little bowls of extremely doubtful
provenance which everyone is required to handle with the greatest of care!
Consider the participants, the merrymakers. Men and women (also children) 5
who have survived passably well through the years, mainly as a result of living
at considerable distances from their dear parents and beloved siblings, who on

this feast of feasts must apparently forgather (as if beckoned by an aberrant Fairy Godmother), usually by circuitous routes, through heavy traffic, at a common meeting place, where the very moods, distempers, and obtrusive personal habits that have kept them happily apart since adulthood are then and there encouraged to slowly ferment beneath the cornhusks, and gradually rise with the aid of the terrible wine, and finally burst forth out of control under the stimulus of the cranberry jelly! No, it is a mockery of a holiday. For instance: *Thank you, O Lord, for what we are about to receive.* This is surely not a gala concept. There are no presents, unless one counts Aunt Bertha's sweet rolls a present, which no one does. There is precious little in the way of costumery: miniature plastic turkeys and those witless Pilgrim hats. There is no sex. Indeed, Thanksgiving is the one day of the year (a fact known to everybody) when all thoughts of sex completely vanish, evaporating from apartments, houses, condominiums, and mobile homes like steam from a bathroom mirror.

Consider also the nowhereness of the time of the year. The last week or so in November. It is obviously not yet winter: winter, with its death-dealing blizzards and its girls in tiny skirts pirouetting on the ice. On the other hand, it is certainly not much use to anyone as fall: no golden leaves or Oktoberfests, and so forth. Instead, it is a no man's land between the seasons. . . .

Consider for a moment the Thanksgiving meal itself. It has become a sort of refuge for endangered species of starch: sweet potatoes, cauliflower, pumpkin, mince (whatever "mince" is), those blessed yams. Bowls of luridly colored yams, with no taste at all, lying torpid under a lava flow of marshmallow! And then the sacred turkey. One might as well try to construct a holiday repast around a fish—say, a nice piece of boiled haddock. After all, turkey tastes very similar to haddock: same consistency, same quite remarkable absence of flavor. But then, if the Thanksgiving pièce de résistance were a nice piece of boiled haddock instead of turkey, there wouldn't be all that fun for Dad when Mom hands him the sterling-silver, bone-handled carving set (a wedding present from her parents and not sharpened since) and then everyone stands around pretending not to watch while he saws and tears away at the bird as if he were trying to burrow his way into or out of some grotesque, fowllike prison.

What of the good side to Thanksgiving, you ask. There is always a good side to everything. Not to Thanksgiving. There is only a bad side and then a worse side. For instance, Grandmother's best linen tablecloth is a bad side: the fact that it is produced each year, in the manner of a red flag being produced before a bull, and then is always spilled upon by whichever child is doing poorest at school that term and so is in need of greatest reassurance. Thus: "Oh, my God, *Veronica*, you just spilled grape juice [or "plum wine" or "tar"] on Grandmother's best linen tablecloth!" But now comes worse. For at this point Cousin Bill, the one who lost all Cousin Edwina's money on the car dealership three years ago and has apparently been drinking steadily since Halloween, bizarrely chooses to say, "Seems to me those old glasses are *always* falling over." To which Auntie Meg is heard to add, "Somehow I don't remember *receivin'* any of those old glasses." To which Uncle Fred replies, "That's because you and George

decided to go on vacation to *Hawaii* the summer Grandpa Sam was dying."
Now Grandmother is sobbing, though not so uncontrollably that she cannot
refrain from murmuring, "I think that volcano painting I threw away by mis-  55
take got sent me from Hawaii, heaven knows why." But the gods are merciful,
even the Pilgrim-hatted god of cornhusks and soggy stuffing, and there is an
end to everything, even to Thanksgiving. Indeed, there is a grandeur to the
feelings of finality and doom which usually settle on a house after the Thanksgiving celebration is over, for with the completion of Thanksgiving Day the  60
year itself has been properly terminated—shot through the cranium with a
high-velocity candied yam. At this calendrical nadir, all energy on the planet
has gone, all fun has fled, all the terrible wine has been drunk.

But then, overnight, life once again begins to stir, emerging, even by the next
morning, in the form of Japanese window displays and Taiwanese Christmas  65
lighting, from the primeval ooze of the nation's department stores. Thus, a new
year dawns, bringing with it immediate and cheering possibilities of extended
consumer debt, office-party flirtations, good—or, at least, mediocre—wine, and
visions of cheapskate excursion fares to Montego Bay. It is worth noting, perhaps, that this true new year always starts with the same mute, powerful mythic  70
ceremony: the surreptitious tossing out, in the early morning, of all those horrid
aluminum-foil packages of yams and cauliflower and stuffing and red, gummy
cranberry substance which have been squeezed into the refrigerator as if a reën-
actment of the siege of Paris were expected. Soon afterward, the phoenix of
Christmas can be observed as it slowly rises, beating its drumsticks, once again  75
goggle-eyed with hope and unrealistic expectations.

1. What subdivisions does the writer make in analyzing the subject? Can you think of
   others that would also be appropriate?
2. Would a different sequence for presenting the material be equally clear and
   effective?
3. Check the etymology, denotation, and connotation of *forgather, aberrant, distempers, pirouetting, no man's land, yams, torpid, repast, pièce de résistance, grotesque, bizarrely, nadir, surreptitious, phoenix.*
4. How and where does the writer use figures of speech, narration, and characterization to complete the satire?

## ASSIGNMENTS

1. The simplest subjects for analysis by dissection are definite objects such as a fountain
   pen or mechanical pencil, a sailboat, a tennis court, a football team—in all of which
   the parts are easily discoverable. More challenging is the analysis of an institution
   (school, church, government) or a work of art (a poem, a painting, a symphony), in
   which the existing parts are less readily discernible.
2. Use the analytical process to solve some problem, such as a strongly felt but perhaps
   hitherto unexamined like or dislike of your own (for a person, a course, a custom),

the popularity of something (a sport, a fad, a curriculum), the success of something or someone (a program, a campaign, an individual).

3. Approach through a statement of root principle the analysis of a leader, a form of government, war, peace, success, the American way of life.

4. Whatever subject you choose or whatever approach you decide on, keep your purpose clearly in mind. A textbook, for example, can be analyzed as an object by dissecting the physical parts of which it is composed, or it can be analyzed by dissecting the content. But do not confuse two purposes: a red cover is not to be mentioned in the same breath with a clear-cut literary style.

5. Analysis is such a common method by which the mind works that you can find it illustrated to some extent in every unit in this book. It operates most conspicuously in Unit 16, where you will find it essential to support an argument, in Unit 17 for critical writing, and in Unit 18 for the research paper. Study its use in the next unit in all the examples, particularly in E, F, G, and H.

# Cause and Effect

In this unit we shall examine the motivating forces that have combined to produce a certain result, or the results that have been produced or that may be produced by such forces. This kind of thinking is analytical, like that examined in Unit 11, because the causes of effects and the effects of causes are not always readily evident. The special features of this kind of analysis require a unit devoted to them.

A student, hurrying to class, falls flat on a campus walk. The effects are immediately apparent: his books scatter, his breath is knocked out of him, his slacks are ripped, and he is generally disheveled. He picks up himself and his property, arrives in the classroom looking flustered, and explains "I had an accident—I fell down." Asked what caused it, he adds, "Nothing—I just fell." But if he examined the circumstances carefully he would find some cause, or causes. Perhaps a slab of pavement, raised slightly by a tree root, tripped him; perhaps waving vigorously to a friend threw him off balance; perhaps he was uncoordinated from lack of sleep. Whatever the reason or combination of reasons, a cause must have existed.

If, driving to the campus, you hit another car, one cause is clear, wherever the blame may lie—two objects tried to occupy the same space at the same time. The point is that no events just "happen"; they are part of the vast pattern of cause and effect—effects becoming causes of other effects in an endless chain. Whatever the immediate cause of your car crash, the accident itself will cause still further effects—delay, a bent fender, maybe a traffic ticket, and so on. One of our most common logical problems is to discover the true causes behind the effects, or to trace from the causes the actual effects that have resulted or that probably will result. They may be single, as when cough medicine brings relief; they may be numerous, as when the use of an antibiotic has to be discontinued because of side effects. They may be closely related, as is a gun shot to the wound, or separated by time, as is contact with poison ivy from the next day's blisters. The connection of cause and effect may be clearly evident, or it may be revealed only after careful analysis. But it is always there.

You have been learning to find your way through this complicated world of causes and effects since early childhood, when you discovered that fire was hot and knives were sharp and crying won you sympathy. Certain causes led you not only to come to college but to choose this one, and you were probably already thinking of higher education in terms of its effects on your future. If you look over the papers you have written for this course, you will undoubtedly find examples of cause and effect; in this unit you will be asked to write a paper that concentrates upon this relationship. But first we should look at some of the fallacies—the wrong beliefs—involved.

**1. Do not mistake a time relationship for a cause.** This confusion results in the popular *post hoc* fallacy (named from the Latin *post hoc, ergo propter hoc*, meaning "after this, therefore because of this"). This fallacy is responsible for the origin of many of our superstitions. A black cat crosses our path, and bad luck follows; therefore a black cat is believed to have caused the bad luck. Breaking a mirror, walking under a ladder, and so on—these belong to the mythology of our culture and are attempts to explain something whose true cause is unknown or too unpleasant to be faced. Certainly, we might see these as causing bad effects if we were scratched by the cat or cut by the mirror or spattered with paint; but, as intelligent people, we would look for other, plausible causes of any *unrelated* misfortune that follows. Before we can attribute a series of storms to atomic tests, we need much more research. The tests *may* prove to be a contributing cause, but they may not—after all, we had bad storms long before the atom was split. Note the continuing debate among scientists over the links between some foods and cancer.

**2. Do not mistake for a cause something actually unrelated.** Akin to the *post hoc* fallacy is the assumption that two things that usually happen at the same time must have a causal relationship—for instance, popular opinion holds that leaves turn color in the fall because of the first frost of fall, although scientists insist that the change usually precedes the frost. A causal relationship is often attributed to many pure coincidences: someone who seems to be following you down a lonely street may merely be going in the same direction at the same speed.

**3. Do not settle for one cause if there are more.** One effect may have been produced by multiple causation. Comic books may contribute to juvenile delinquency, but so do many other social forces. If a normally cheerful man appears surly, he may have had an argument with his neighbor about the neighbor's dog, received an unexpectedly large telephone bill, been criticized by his boss, had a flat tire on the way to work, or be coming down with a cold. More probably, a combination of these causes has affected him—the proverbial last straw did not break the camel's back all by itself.

**4. Distinguish between immediate and remote causes.** Asked why you are here in college, you could truthfully answer, "Because my father and mother married," but the inquirer is probably concerned with more recent causes directly connected with the effect in question.

**5. Be sure the cause could produce the result.** If a large dog is left unwatched in the kitchen and three pounds of baloney disappear, the dog is a likely suspect—particularly if, as with the disappearance of the teapot and spoons in Huxley's essay (Example I in this unit), there is other circumstantial evidence as well, such as distended ribs and a greasy muzzle and paws. On the other hand, a small puppy may be exonerated, not from lack of motive but of capacity.

**6. Allow for causes that may nullify predicted effects.** Corn needs rain, but a heavy rainfall does not assure farmers of a good crop; it may instead prevent them from planting in time or, if heavy enough, may drown the corn they have already planted. Wage increases do not necessarily result in more buying power; they may instead contribute to an increase in the cost of living.

**7. Avoid predicting contradictory effects.** The campaign promises of politicians to lower taxes and also expand the public works program are not taken seriously by experienced voters.

**8. Do not mistake cause for effect or effect for cause.** Some medieval philosophers believed that the great European rivers sprang up where the great cities were built; the modern historian sees the process in reverse. The old farmer who said, "If I'd known I was going to have such nice children, I'd have picked a better mother for 'em," might also stand correction.

**9. Avoid the pitfall of rationalization.** In the search for causes and effects, especially the causes of your own opinions or the effects of your own actions, you may be tempted to use false or superficial explanations that let you avoid facing the truth. For instance, drivers involved in car accidents often blame road conditions or mechanical failure, denying their own carelessness; and students may excuse their failure to study adequately by pleading that the assignment was too long or that they needed sleep, rather than admit their laziness.

## EXAMPLES

*12-A*                    LIVING ON THE ALTIPLANO
                         *Georgie Anne Geyer*

These paragraphs are taken from a travel article in the *Atlantic Monthly* (1967).

The Altiplano, that high plain which balances at 14,000 feet like a slate between the two spectacular black ridges of the Andes, has formed and influenced the life of the Incas more than anything else. Its thin stern air has even affected the bodies of the Indians, giving them larger lungs to bear the strain and more red corpuscles to stand the cold.                               5

It is a stunning part of the world, with broad barren valleys and purple mountains dotted by floating clouds that can suddenly erupt in convulsive showers. Historians say that the very barrenness of the land and its prohibitiveness are what prodded the Incas into their astonishing accomplishments. They had to use every piece of land, to terrace and burrow and organize and work together, 10 to be able to live there.

1. The author mentions several possible effects of living on the Altiplano. Which ones can be tested scientifically to determine whether or not there is a genuine cause-and-effect relationship and which can only be a matter of opinion? Why?
2. What difference in wording is there in presenting the provable effects and the ones that are opinion?

---

*12-B*                          DEATH OF AN ISLAND
                                    *Pat Conroy*

These paragraphs are from *The Water Is Wide*, an autobiographical account of the author's year on a small island off the coast of South Carolina. Unit 2-F and Unit 8-F are also about the island.

ANALYSIS
Effect
     [Yamacraw] is not a large island, nor an important one, but it represents an era and a segment of history that is rapidly dying in America. The people of the island have changed very little since the Emancipation Proclamation. Indeed, many of them have never heard of this procla- 5 mation. They love their island with genuine affection but

Cause
have watched the young people move to the city, to the lands far away and far removed from Yamacraw. The island is dying, and the people know it.

Background
     In the parable of Yamacraw there was a time when the 10 black people supported themselves well, worked hard, and lived up to the sacred tenets laid down in the Protestant ethic. Each morning the strong young men would take to their bateaux and search the shores and inlets for the large clusters of oysters, which the women and old men in the 15 factory shucked into large jars. Yamacraw oysters were world famous. An island legend claims that a czar of Russia once ordered Yamacraw oysters for an imperial banquet. The white people propagate this rumor. The blacks, for the most part, would not know a czar from a fiddler crab, but 20 the oysters were good, and the oyster factories operating on the island provided a substantial living for all the people. Everyone worked and everyone made money.

Cause
     Then a villain appeared. It was an industrial factory situated on a knoll above the Savannah River many miles 25 away from Yamacraw. The villain spewed its excrement

Effect
into the river, infected the creeks, and as silently as the pull of the tides, the filth crept to the shores of Yamacraw. As every good health inspector knows, the unfortunate con-

Effect
sumer who lets an infected oyster slide down his throat is 30 flirting with hepatitis. Someone took samples of the water around Yamacraw, analyzed them under a microscope,

Effect

and reported the results to the proper officials. Soon after this, little white signs were placed by the oyster banks forbidding anyone to gather the oysters. Ten thousand oysters 35 were now as worthless as grains of sand. No czar would order Yamacraw oysters again. The muddy creatures that had provided the people of the island with a way to keep

Effect

their families alive were placed under permanent quarantine. 40

Cause

Since a factory is soulless and faceless, it could not be moved to understand the destruction its coming had wrought. When the oysters became contaminated, the

Effect

island's only industry folded almost immediately. The great migration began. A steady flow of people faced with 45

Effect

starvation moved toward the cities. They left in search of jobs. Few cities had any intemperate demand for professional oyster-shuckers, but the people were somehow assimilated. The population of the island diminished considerably. Houses surrendered their tenants to the city and 50

Effect

signs of sudden departure were rife in the interiors of deserted homes. Over 300 people left the island. They left reluctantly, but left permanently and returned only on sporadic visits to pay homage to the relatives too old or too stubborn to leave. As the oysters died, so did the people. 55

1. Here the relationship of cause and effect is plainly visible. Where does it start?
2. List the sequence of effects that follow the initial cause of trouble.
3. What words suggest that the writer feels certain that his analysis of the cause-and-effect relationship is correct?
4. Check the etymology, denotation, and connotation of *tenets, intemperate, assimilated, sporadic (bateaux,* the French for *boats,* is borrowed from the French settlers of Louisiana).

---

*12-C*                        THE DECISIVE ARREST
                           *Martin Luther King, Jr.*

In these paragraphs from his book, *Stride Toward Freedom* (1958), Dr. King shows a real cause that has been obscured by more obvious but false ones. Note that here he tries to explain only why Mrs. Parks broke the law; she was not the *cause* of the great bus strike but rather, as King wrote later, a "precipitating factor." The immediate effect was her arrest, but this in turn touched off a series of larger effects that are still operating.

On December 1, 1955, an attractive Negro seamstress, Mrs. Rosa Parks, boarded the Cleveland Avenue Bus in downtown Montgomery. She was returning home after her regular day's work in the Montgomery Fair—a leading department store. Tired from long hours on her feet, Mrs. Parks sat down in the

first seat behind the section reserved for whites. Not long after she took her seat, 5
the bus operator ordered her, along with three other Negro passengers, to move
back in order to accommodate boarding white passengers. By this time every
seat in the bus was taken. This meant that if Mrs. Parks followed the driver's
command she would have to stand while a white male passenger, who had just
boarded the bus, would sit. The other three Negro passengers immediately com- 10
plied with the driver's request. But Mrs. Parks quietly refused. The result was
her arrest.

There was to be much speculation about why Mrs. Parks did not obey the
driver. Many people in the white community argued that she had been
"planted" by the NAACP in order to lay the groundwork for a test case, and at 15
first glance that explanation seemed plausible, since she was a former secretary
of the local branch of the NAACP. So persistent and persuasive was this argument that it convinced many reporters from all over the country. Later on,
when I was having press conferences three times a week—in order to accommodate the reporters and journalists who came to Montgomery from all over 20
the world—the invariable first question was: "Did the NAACP start the bus
boycott?"

But the accusation was totally unwarranted, as the testimony of both Mrs.
Parks and the officials of the NAACP revealed. Actually, no one can understand
the action of Mrs. Parks unless he realizes that eventually the cup of endurance 25
runs over, and the human personality cries out, "I can take it no longer." Mrs.
Parks's refusal to move back was her intrepid affirmation that she had had
enough. It was an individual expression of a timeless longing for human dignity
and freedom. She was not "planted" there by the NAACP, or any other organization; she was planted there by her personal sense of dignity and self-respect. 30
She was anchored to that seat by the accumulated indignities of days gone by
and the boundless aspirations of generations yet unborn. She was a victim of
both the forces of history and the forces of destiny. She had been tracked down
by the *Zeitgeist*—the spirit of the time.

1. What words show that Dr. King feels certain that his analysis of the cause-and-effect
   relationship is correct?
2. Check the origin of the word *boycott*.
3. How does the connotation of *plausible* differ from that of its synonym *credible*?
   How do the etymologies of *intrepid* and *aspiration* help us to understand their
   meanings?

---

**12-D**                       DIX HILLS: THE GROWN-UPS' TOY
                               *Donna Satriale (student)*

Note the writer's attention to both immediate and long-term effects.

My first glimpse of Dix Hills was from the back seat of my mother's '62
Falcon as we drove from one model home to another. Dead, brown leaves dan-

gled from the twisted branches of scrawny trees. The ground was a smear of
coagulated mud, rippled in places and strewn with rivulets. It sucked my sneakers from my feet as I walked past the naked skeletons of houses until we came  5
to the one which Dad said was ours. We went there often, as if we were visiting
a sick relative in the hospital.

We were one of the first families to move in. My sister and I thrived among
the pounding hammers and roaring bulldozers. The unfinished houses invited
us to romp in them. Every empty lot was our playground. We were French  10
explorers discovering exotic lands, archaeologists digging up the ruins of an
ancient Palestinian city, medieval knights conquering a fortress, and messengers
struggling through the Egyptian desert. Dix Hills was a land of make-believe
where a child's creative imagination could expand.

A shabby cornfield marked the end of our pebbly street. Carefree, we  15
sprinted between the bristly stalks, playing tag and hide-and-seek as if the field
were ours and it was the only place on earth. We lost shoes, toys, and hair
ribbons there. Sometimes we lost ourselves, dozing between the mounds with
the silver sunlight filtering through the corn.

As time went on we found that we had to go farther and farther away to  20
play in the empty housing lots. More families were constantly moving in. Shiny,
civilized moving vans replaced the ferocious bulldozers, velvety sod carpeted
our digging sites, and cars interrupted our kickball and hop-scotch games. The
cornfield was plowed under, and more houses were built.

Across the street was a dense patch of woods, and we began to play there.  25
Mighty forts were built, traps set, and holes dug. We climbed trees and swung
on vines, scratching our arms and legs. Afterwards, we were afraid to go home
because we were coated with dirt and were often the victims of "creeping crud"
or poison ivy. But they knocked down our forts, our trees, and our woods to
expand the parking lot for the public library.  30

Because the library was so close, we did a lot of reading. We read about far-
away places where children played in untouched cornfields and open woods—
children who were not trapped in suburbia.

It wasn't long until everything was frosted with an upper-middle-class snob-
bery. Dix Hills was suddenly ripped from the hands of the children and given  35
to the grown-ups. There was nothing left for the children to do except to play
the adults' games. Cliques and clubs formed even among the children. It was
no longer "My Pop can lick your Pop," but "My father makes $45,000 a year,
what does your father make?"

Today, there are no children playing kickball in the street. They are in air-  40
conditioned houses watching "Sesame Street" or swimming in private, fenced-
in pools. The neighbors rarely communicate, and when they do the falseness of
their artificial smiles shines from their gleaming capped teeth. It is a quiet community, and the people like it that way. For me, it is too quiet. It is sterile.

1. Compare this presentation of changes in a place with the presentation of changes in
   Example B in this unit.

**2.** Could this writer have made more extensive use of the alternating pattern of comparison to emphasize the cause-and-effect theme underlying her material?

---

*12-E*             WHY PEOPLE ARE PREJUDICED
                      *William Nilsson (student)*

Many words have been written about the various racial and religious aversions still extant among large segments of the population. Thinking people everywhere have stressed the evils of prejudices, have shown them to be illogical and unfounded, have demonstrated the harm they do and the benefits to be derived from abandoning them. It occurs much less often that someone endeav- 5
ors to point out objectively the reasons why people have prejudices and seeks out the primary roots from which prejudices stem. Perhaps it is only through an examination of these fountainheads of prejudice that any ultimate solution can be arrived at.

A good starting point might be a definition of the word. A prejudice may be 10
defined as a preconceived aversion to a person, place, or thing without adequate acquaintance with said person, place, or thing. A good example of a common prejudice is the dislike for certain foods. In many cases this can be proved to be based completely on preconceived ideas. I know a woman who says that she dislikes cheese, but on several occasions she has eaten it in sauces and liked it 15
when she didn't know it was there. A certain man who professes an intense dislike for a particular kind of meat has eaten it many times without complaint when his wife told him it was something else. Such dislikes can often be traced to childhood impressions. The child who hears his father scorn salad as "rabbit food" will often adopt this dislike purely through suggestion and not because of 20
any taste aversion. The small child whose mother bribes him with rewards for eating certain foods will come to think of them as something unpleasant. Parental attitudes and example, therefore, are among the most significant factors in the development of prejudices. Certainly they also play a major role in the fostering of racial and religious bias. The child who hears his parents speak dis- 25
paragingly of certain racial and religious groups, associating them with dishonesty, boorishness, and other undesirable character traits, will accept these ideas without much question. After all, don't Mother and Father know what is right?

Another source of prejudice is feelings of inferiority. The person who claims to dislike symphonic music, painting, or serious literature invariably knows little 30
about them and has never made any effort to become acquainted with them. He will usually tell you that such things are for snobs and "highbrows," or are boring. What he is really expressing is his feelings that he is somehow intellectually incapable of appreciating them. Since such a feeling of inferiority is naturally unpleasant, he counteracts it by decrying and belittling that which he 35
believes he cannot learn to understand.

Still another reason for prejudice may be found in man's basic fear of the unknown, the unfamiliar. Immigrant groups, newly arrived in the United

States, usually settle in neighborhoods where there are many other people who speak their language. Because of linguistic limitations, they develop a clannish- 40 ness which an American might easily interpret as hostility. They keep strange customs that may make him ill at ease in their company and give him that uncomfortable feeling of "not belonging." He may wonder if they are talking about him when they speak a language he doesn't understand.

Economic factors, too, may have a strong influence on prejudices. A certain 45 group may be feared as a threat to the economic security of another. The Chinese and Japanese, up to recent times, have been bitterly resented on the West Coast because their willingness to work for low wages caused unemployment and a lower standard of living among native Americans in the area. On the other hand, it may be very profitable for one group to keep another one in 50 an inferior status. One of the main reasons for the well-to-do Southerner's long desire to keep the Negro from full equality was his unwillingness to lose a source of cheap labor, a loss which has followed the Negro's increasing awareness of his rights, both economic and social. An idea of the importance of economic factors in fostering prejudice can be derived from an examimation of work- 55 men's compensation insurance statistics, which show the unbelievably low wages paid to Negroes by, for example, Southern lumber camp owners.

The question that may follow from this is why the occasional lynchings and other acts of violence against Negroes in the South were usually done not by the well-to-do but by the extremely poor "white trash" who derive no profit from 60 Negroes' labor. These people must do backbreaking toil themselves in order to eke out the barest living. This uncovers still another cause of prejudice, the need of a scapegoat, the need of an outlet for hostilities and frustrations built up by a life of fruitless toil for meager returns. It was this same emotional need that the Nazis used to stir up popular sentiment against the Jews in a Germany 65 impoverished by World War I and the injustices of the Versailles Treaty. It was this need that was taken advantage of by wealthy Polish and Russian landlords in Czarist times whenever peasants showed signs of discontent with their economic lot. The peasant's hostilities were diverted by blaming his poverty on the Jews, thus providing a tangible something to vent his grievances on, and touch- 70 ing off the notorious pogroms.

Bad example acquired in childhood from parents and other adults, innate feelings of inferiority, distrust of the unknown and unfamiliar, fear of economic competition, desire for profit through exploitation, the need for a scapegoat— these are the main sources from which prejudices spring. While this essay does 75 not attempt a solution of the problem, it does suggest that such a solution cannot be a simple one, with the causes of prejudice so numerous, so diverse, and so deep-seated.

1. How does the writer lead up to a statement of his general topic at the end of the first paragraph?
2. In his second paragraph how does he make the examples of his definition lead to a cause of prejudice? In the rest of the essay how much space does he devote to examples to support his analysis of causes?

3. What transitional words and phrases does the writer use? How is the final paragraph related to the rest of the essay?

---

12-F

## ON BEING A TWIN
### *Jeremy Seabrook*

In these paragraphs—two-thirds of an essay from *New Society* (June 1977)—the writer describes the effects of family attitudes.

If you are a twin, people behave as though you are not worth making a relationship with; and they recoil, sensing that there is no reserve of feeling within you which you could possibly expend on them. They are interested, but polite. They say, "Oh, is he like you?" You can watch them adjust to the possibility of a replica of the individual they have just met; and you feel your sense of unique- 5 ness assailed. They ask if you feel pain and joy on behalf of each other. If he is suffering, do you feel a pang? Can you bear to be apart? Perhaps if we had been identical twins, this might have been true.

It has been nothing like that. But it does have some curious and even frightening consequences. My twin has always been there. This may seem a very 10 banal and obvious thing to say; but he was there as a presence, and not as a person. It's only now that we are well into our thirties, that we have begun to exist for each other.

Our family made the same assumptions about us that are common in the general response to twinning. The first was that there is a sense of symmetry in 15 nature and that human characteristics are distributed in compensating opposites: the absence of a feature in one of us was made good by the presence of another, which, in turn, is taken from the other twin. There was a division of human qualities between us soon after birth, like a fairy-tale christening, at which all the members of the family bestowed a gift upon us, or in some cases, 20 a curse. It seems to have occurred to no one that the same features might have been present in both of us. As soon as one of us displayed the faintest trace of a human characteristic, a compensating one had to be found for the other. Our natures were built by our relatives, an elaborate and ingenious construct which it has taken half a lifetime to demolish. 25

It was clear from the beginning that my brother was a good child who didn't cry. All that was left for me was to be bad; but to make up for it they decided that I would be clever. However, this implied that Jack would be dull; so it was decreed that he would be practical, skilled with his hands—which he became. This caused me to be clumsy and maladroit; and to make up for this I was given 30 a loving disposition, which I faithfully set about developing—even though I occasionally sensed guiltily that it wasn't true, and I longed to express my hatred of Aunt Maud and my loathing of bunny rabbits.

Our whole personalities were created rather than allowed to develop, and the pace was forced. When one of us gave any sign of a preference or an ability, 35 there was a rush to seek out its opposite for the other.

This meant that over time we became, each for the other, an object of great mystery. The other was always endowed with what we didn't have, with what we lacked. My twin was a reproach to me for all the things I could never be. He was the beautiful one; and this meant, not simply that I was plain, or even 40 tolerably neutral in my appearance, but that I was ugly. For many years I observed people overcome what I imagined was their revulsion before they could even bear to talk to me. But if I was bright, this implied that my brother was not merely average, or even quite clever, but that he was backward. And we obliged in carrying out these determinants whispered over our cradle by the 45 malevolent adults. It was promptly discovered—in early infancy somehow— that my brother would never be able to read or write. Later, when I went to the grammar school, he was consigned to the C stream in the secondary modern. These roles pursued us far into adult life; and it wasn't until he was in Germany doing national service that my brother realized, with wonder, that he 50 was writing to his girl friend every day, letters he was amazed to find linguistically competent and marvellously rich in ideas.

· · ·

So we grew, slightly deformed, like trees that have a common root, but have no room to grow to their full height side by side. He was a shadow cast over my childhood. I have a photo of us at the age of about seven. We are holding 55 hands in front of the lilac bush, and we are dressed identically. I have no recollection of the picture having been taken; only I am incredulous that we could ever have held hands. He was always there, with his beautiful violet eyes, silent and reproachful over his model-making, building aeroplanes with strips of frail balsa wood, exuding a smell of pear drops from the adhesive he used. Once or 60 twice he did make a clumsy attempt to relate to me. When Gran died, he tried to put an arm round me; when he was fourteen, he tried to talk to me about loneliness. Terrified, I fled. It was like being molested by a stranger.

But now that we are grown up and our lives are separate in every way, we sometimes don't meet for a year or more at a time—there remains, curiously, 65 an ache and an absence. There is a sense of emptiness where he should have been and never was. I feel at times strangely incomplete. The space he occupied has remained vacant. It seems to me now that much of my adult life has been spent looking for people who resemble—not him but myself; a belated and doomed search for things I ought to have shared with my twin. I remain with 70 a corrosive fear of being alone; and yet with others I feel inadequate, half a person. But it is half a person with no complement.

1. In the second paragraph what does the writer mean by "My twin has always been there"? Why does he repeat the thought in the next-to-last paragraph?
2. What use does the writer make of analysis, narrative, analogy, and other forms of comparison? of concrete detail?
3. Check the etymology, denotation, and connotation of *banal, ingenious, maladroit, malevolent, incredulous, corrosive.*

*12-G*                                      NEW-BORN MOTHER
                                            *Marina Warner*

This essay, here almost complete, first appeared in the London *Observer* (July 1977).
In *Alone of All Her Sex*, the writer, a novelist and poet, studies the changing roles of
women as shown in changing beliefs about the Virgin Mary.

"Talking babies" is bad form. Dinner party chat can wander around giving
up smoking, the quality of the food . . ., the shortcomings of public transport
and other yawns. But talking babies is beyond the pale. The rearing of children—and one can call it motherhood, since women continue to do it in far
greater numbers than men—has low status and is therefore boring. Women 5
apologise: "I'm just a mother," because they think it would be more interesting
if they weren't. Working mothers submit to public values too and expect greater
acknowledgement of the job, not the mothering.

Not that I am going over to the Mediterranean view which decrees child-
bearing the destiny and only fulfilment of women; that too is a constricting 10
prejudice. But to see the work of a mother in the crucial years of infancy when
character is formed as a sequence of dirty nappies [diapers] is the equivalent of
reviewing a love affair in terms of changing the bed sheets. The drudgery is
present, of course: but having a baby is still the grandest rite of passage I have
had to suffer.                                                               15

The birth of a child hurls the mother—and the father—into a strange universe, moving powerfully according to its own laws, its inmost nature knowable
only by participation, incommunicable to the uninitiate. Inside the womb, the
baby has a certain degree of reality, as it beats and kicks, playing its own battery
of drums, executing its big top feats under one's ribs. But this gives only a 20
presentiment.

When the child, warm, wet, slippery, crying out, face crumpled from the
sudden burst into the light, first wriggled in my arms on my belly I knew I had
been taken over—it was unmistakable—by something that immediately made
all the difference. I had crossed a boundary of existence, just like the baby. And 25
for my husband, standing there beside the delivery couch, the attachment to
the child was that moment made as fast. The passage to parenthood is instant,
ferocious and irrefutable; it comes on you like being winded.

This is not to say that it is love alone. The new world inspires rage and fear
as well. The exhaustion of the first few weeks is hallucinatory. There are terrible 30
tiny moments of grief, and the terror of loss, of harm, of failure. I have a friend
who regularly sleepwalks, looking for her baby on the floor where she is certain
she has fallen: I have woken crying out, "No, not that, no!" certain that one of
us has rolled over and suffocated ours—when he lies safely asleep in his cot.

The pleasures of it have, at a more intense level, the quality of delight in 35
finding a new aptitude: the exhilaration of first floating, realising one can swim,
perhaps the wonder of a child standing free on his own legs for the first time.
So much of mothering is involuntary, motivated at a level deep down, perhaps
in the very DNA.

There is the phenomenon that took me entirely by surprise, that I had never 40
heard of previously: the spontaneous spurting of milk. Sometimes, when my son
cries, I feel the milk rise spontaneously in response. There is a scientific explanation for this: sympathy flowing between mother and infant releases oxytocin,
a chemical which amongst other things is responsible for milk "let-down." But
like most scientific explanations, it leaves the mystery intact.   45

The symbiosis between infant and mother is fostered by intimacy in the first
few hours and days, so several studies have reported; therefore one can say perhaps that maternal responses are learned rather than innate. But they *feel*
instinctive. The baby's needs, rhythms, emotions hold sway not just over the
practical side of life, but over the psychical as well. I swore for instance that I 50
would never make googoo eyes or squeal nonsense at any baby of mine. He or
she would learn to listen to grown-ups behaving naturally. But immediately, I
raised my voice, widened my eyes and gabbled. This instinct has its reasons,
again the studies have found. Newborn babies focus more easily on staring eyes,
and they hear more clearly sounds at a higher pitch. The child is master of the 55
man.

It is only after I had been thrown into this new world of experience that I
found friends talking about it too, telling me how they had felt with their first-
born. Had I never listened before? I don't think it was only that. Motherhood
is like a street gang in a ghetto: you learn the rules only after you've joined.   60

Its physiology alone is still misunderstood through prejudice and lack of
inquiry. And it seems to me now not just an irony but a tragedy that, through
the mistake of confusing sexual equality with sexual identity and the fear of
betraying the feminist cause, the many other dimensions of this central female
difference continue to be hidden from history and beggared of honour.   65

1. Does Warner's view of motherhood coincide in any way with that of Adrienne Rich
   (Unit 11-C)?
2. Where does Warner use specific, concrete words to make her points vivid? comparisons of any kind, including figures of speech?
3. Check the etymology and meanings of these words and phrases: *beyond the pale,
   rites of passage, irrefutable, symbiosis, fostered, beggared of honor.*

---

**12-H**                      THE ROLE OF RACE
                            *Kenneth B. Clark*

These paragraphs form most of the second half of an essay published in the magazine section of the *New York Times* (October 1980). The writer, a frequent spokesman
for black Americans, is Distinguished Professor Emeritus of Psychology at the City
University of New York. He begins the essay by arguing that the majority of black
Americans still live in poverty, despite civil rights gains, because too many people think
that class discrimination is now the chief cause of black poverty and fail to see the
continuing force of racial prejudice.

The present inability of black political and civil-rights leaders to cope with the persistent and deepening problems of American racism has many causes. Within the last decades there has been an abrupt loss of most of the major and charismatic black leaders. Martin Luther King, Jr., was assassinated just as he was seeking more effective methods to deal with the bedeviling problems of 5 Northern and urban racism. Whitney M. Young Jr., of the National Urban League, died suddenly as he was developing plans to make corporate leaders more sensitive and responsive to their pragmatic self-interest in seeking the goals of racial justice. Roy Wilkins retired after a long and productive tenure as leader of the N.A.A.C.P., and his successor, Benjamin Hooks, has not demon- 10 strated a similar capacity. With the retirement of James Farmer, the Congress on Racial Equality soon became a separatist cult virtually indistinguishable from the racists whom the organization had fought so courageously. Malcolm X was murdered as he was seeking a way to become a rational and effective ally of other civil-rights leaders.                                               15

The erosion of the civil-rights leadership cannot be explained only by the death and retirement of the early black leaders. Ironically, the very success of the civil-rights movement has deprived it of many of its potential leaders. Some of the most effective civil-rights lawyers were appointed to the Federal courts, thus taking them away from the battlefront. Thurgood Marshall, Robert L. 20 Carter, Spottswood W. Robinson, 3d, and Constance B. Motley can—and do— contribute to the quest for racial justice as examples of personal achievement and as direct guardians of democracy within our judicial system, but they can no longer do so as activists.

More than 5,000 black officials have been elected within the last ten years 25 throughout the nation, demonstrating that the almost total racial exclusion within the American political system has ended. But this gain is finite; black elected officials either do not have the power or have not yet found the formula to improve the educational, economic and housing status, and the quality of life, of the black underclass. And they have, at least temporarily, been removed 30 from the pool of potential civil-rights leaders.

The same conclusion must be reached concerning those blacks who have made it into the middle class by means of jobs in corporate America. Many of these new black managers and executives are assigned to such race-related, "created" areas as "community affairs" and "special markets." They are rarely 35 found in line positions concerned with developing or controlling production, supervising the work of large numbers of whites or competing with their white "peers" for significant promotions. In these created jobs, blacks lack the kind of security that goes with line positions; they are kept on by the sufferance of white governmental and corporate decision makers.                                      40

These black employees jeopardize what little power they have if they seek to exercise it too aggressively in behalf of other blacks. It is generally understood by blacks in these positions, and by their white "benefactors," that the cause of personal racial justice can best be served if blacks demonstrate that they are "objective," "balanced," "moderate" and not too pushy on racial issues. As a 45 consultant to private corporations on affirmative action, I have often observed that, with some noticeable exceptions, black affirmative-action officers of corporate and educational institutions are more likely to be cautious in the performance of their roles than many whites in similar positions.

Many black directors on corporate boards seem similarly unable or unwilling 50 to become actively involved in promoting employment and staffing practices beyond racial tokenism. They find it difficult and awkward to jeopardize their personal gains and the affable acceptance of their white colleagues, and they appear to have little power to influence decisions relating to blacks of the white-controlled corporations or institutions with which they are identified. Some 55 blacks have even stated publicly the premature and wishful belief that their status and positions in these corporations and institutions are unconnected to the fact that they are black.

Even the more insightful of these successful blacks have not yet found the formula for communicating to whites that the presence of experienced and 60 thoughtful blacks in genuine decision-making positions can bring a dimension and perspective that could improve the quality of the decision-making operation itself. Unqualified racial justice within a corporation or an educational institution strengthens the structure and function of that institution and gives solidity to the overall economy.                                                    65

Yet another negative side effect of racial progress has been a new and imminent risk of serious intraracial turbulence that has further eroded the position of the nation's traditional black leadership. Underclass blacks who observe the apparent success of middle-class blacks can readily compare it with the chronic failures of their own lives. Traditional resentment and hostility toward whites 70 can extend to resentment and hostility toward successful blacks. Past American racism was democratic in that it tended to reject and exclude all blacks without regard to intelligence, education, talents or personal character. The struggle for racial justice could be conducted with a minimum of intraracial class conflict. With the recent success of the civil-rights movement, however, some blacks 75 appear not only to have escaped exclusion, but even to have been embraced by white society. A few black males are invited to join private clubs as a sign of institutional maturity—or as a means of making the white members of these suddenly integrated clubs worthy of consideration for judicial or other public office. Some blacks are able to purchase homes or rent apartments in previously 80 all-white neighborhoods and suburbs. But the masses of the black underclass remain entrapped in deteriorating ghettos. When they vent their frustrations and desperation in spasmodic eruptions, they are told by black middle-class leaders that this will only make matters worse. Such advice from the representatives of the black middle class to the "nothing-to-lose" black underclass can 85 be expected to elicit and intensify the latent group self-hatred common to oppressed groups. An example of this was the cool—if not hostile—reaction Andrew Young and Jesse Jackson received when they sought to reason with blacks in Miami after the recent uprising in that city.

The dynamics, threats and challenges of today's struggle for unqualified 90 racial justice may well require a new kind of black leadership. There are serious questions whether the charismatic individual leaders who played so important a role in recent decades are appropriate for the modern era. There are uncertainties as to whether the structure and function of the traditional civil-rights organizations can cope with the problems spawned by their past successes. The types of strategy and action that the present requires may demand a new coalition of political, community, religious and academic leadership among blacks. The danger is that a vehicle to bring about such a coalition is not currently available, and it needs to be developed and put into use before it is too late.

... From the Emancipation Proclamation to the present, there has been a repetitive cycle of hope, progress, frustration, turbulence, violence and seeming regression. We now seem to be in the frustration phase. ... The challenge to the nation's leadership, white and black, is to restrain a new wave of turbulence and regression, and to create a new era of hope and visible progress on the path to equal justice for all Americans.

1. What causes does Clark list for the failure of black leaders to solve present problems? What support does he offer for his claims?
2. What transitional words and phrases does he use?
3. Does he offer any solution to the problems he describes?
4. Check the etymology, denotation, and connotation of *charismatic, pragmatic, sufferance, jeopardize, imminent, intraracial, chronic, elicit, latent.*

---

## 12-I.  THE METHOD OF SCIENTIFIC INVESTIGATION
### *Thomas H. Huxley*

This example is a famous lecture on the scientific method by the nineteenth-century writer who helped to publicize Darwin's theory of evolution and was noted for his ability to clarify difficult abstract concepts, largely through the use of simple narrative examples. This example is placed at the end of this unit because it not only shows cause and effect but also makes the logical processes of induction and deduction remarkably clear. These processes, the subject of the next two units, are closely related to the logic of cause and effect.

The method of scientific investigation is nothing but the expression of the necessary mode of working of the human mind. It is simply the mode at which all phenomena are reasoned about, rendered precise and exact. There is no more difference, but there is just the same kind of difference, between the mental operations of a man of science and those of an ordinary person, as there is between the operations and methods of a baker or of a butcher weighing out his goods in common scales, and the operations of a chemist in performing a difficult and complex analysis by means of his balance and finely graduated weights. It is not that the action of the scales in the one case, and the balance in the other, differ in the principles of their construction or manner of working;

but the beam of one is set on an infinitely finer axis than the other, and of course turns by the addition of a much smaller weight.

You will understand this better, perhaps, if I give you some familiar example. You have all heard it repeated, I dare say, that men of science work by means of induction and deduction, and that by the help of these operations, they, in 15 a sort of sense, wring from Nature certain other things, which are called natural laws, and causes, and that out of these, by some cunning skill of their own, they build up hypotheses and theories. And it is imagined by many, that the operations of the common mind can be by no means compared with these processes, and that they have to be acquired by a sort of special apprenticeship to the 20 craft. To hear all these large words, you would think that the mind of a man of science must be constituted differently from that of his fellow men; but if you will not be frightened by terms, you will discover that you are quite wrong, and that all these terrible apparatus are being used by yourselves every day and every hour of your lives. 25

There is a well-known incident in one of Molière's plays, where the author makes the hero express unbounded delight on being told that he had been talking prose during the whole of his life. In the same way, I trust that you will take comfort and be delighted with yourselves, on the discovery that you have been acting on the principles of inductive and deductive philosophy during the same 30 period. Probably there is not one here who has not in the course of the day had occasion to set in motion a complex train of reasoning, of the very same kind though differing of course in degree, as that which a scientific man goes through in tracing the causes of natural phenomena.

A very trivial circumstance will serve to exemplify this. Suppose you go into 35 a fruiterer's shop, wanting an apple—you take up one, and, on biting it, you find it is sour; you look at it, and see that it is hard and green. You take up another one, and that too is hard, green, and sour. The shopman offers you a third; but, before biting it, you examine it, and find that it is hard and green, and you immediately say that you will not have it, as it must be sour, like those 40 that you have already tried.

Nothing can be more simple than that, you think; but, if you will take the trouble to analyze and trace out into its logical elements what has been done by the mind, you will be greatly surprised. In the first place, you have performed the operation of induction. You found that, in two experiences, hardness and 45 greenness in apples went together with sourness. It was so in the first case, and it was confirmed by the second. True, it is a very small basis, but still it is enough to make an induction from; you generalise the facts, and you expect to find sourness in apples where you get hardness and greenness. You found upon that a general law, that all hard and green apples are sour; and that, so far as it goes, 50 is a perfect induction. Well, having got your natural law in this way, when you are offered another apple which you find is hard and green, you say, "All hard and green apples are sour; this apple is hard and green, therefore this apple is sour." That train of reasoning is what logicians call a syllogism, and has all its various parts and terms—its major premise, its minor premise, and its conclu- 55 sion. And, by the help of further reasoning, which, if drawn out, would have to be exhibited in two of three other syllogisms, you arrive at your final determination, "I will not have that apple." So that, you see, you have, in the first place, established a law of induction, and upon that you have founded a deduction, and reasoned out the special conclusion of the particular case. Well now, sup- 60 pose, having got your law, that at some time afterwards, you are discussing the qualities of apples with a friend: you will say to him, "It is a very curious thing—but I find that all hard and green apples are sour!" Your friend says to you, "But how do you know that?" You at once reply, "Oh, because I have tried them over and over again, and have always found them to be so." Well, if we 65 were talking science instead of common sense, we should call that an experimental verification. And, if still opposed, you go further, and say, "I have heard from the people in Somersetshire and Devonshire, where a large number of apples are grown, that they have observed the same thing. It is also found to be the case in Normandy, and in North America. In short, I find it to be the uni- 70 versal experience of mankind wherever attention has been directed to the subject." Whereupon, your friend, unless he is a very unreasonable man, agrees with you, and is convinced that you are quite right in the conclusion you have drawn. He believes, although perhaps he does not know he believes it, that the more extensive verifications are—that the more frequently experiments have 75 been made, and the results of the same kind arrived at—that the more varied the conditions under which the same results are attained, the more certain is the ultimate conclusion, and he disputes the question no further. He sees that the experiment has been tried under all sorts of conditions, as to time, place, and people, with the same result; and he says with you, therefore, that the law 80 you have laid down must be a good one, and he must believe it.

In science we do the same thing; the philosopher exercises precisely the same faculties, though in a much more delicate manner. In scientific inquiry it becomes a matter of duty to expose a supposed law to every possible kind of verification, and to take care, moreover, that this is done intentionally, and not 85 left to a mere accident, as in the case of the apples. And in science, as in common life, our confidence in a law is in exact proportion to the absence of variation in the result of our experimental verifications. For instance, if you let go your grasp of an article you may have in your hand, it will immediately fall to the ground. That is a very common verification of one of the best established 90 laws of nature—that of gravitation. The method by which men of science established the existence of that law is exactly the same as that by which we have established the trivial proposition about the sourness of hard and green apples. But we believe it in such an extensive, thorough, and unhesitating manner because the universal experience of mankind verifies it, and we can verify it 95 ourselves at any time; and that is the strongest possible foundation on which any natural law can rest.

So much, then, by way of proof that the method of establishing laws in science is exactly the same as that pursued in common life. Let us now turn to another matter (though really it is but another phase of the same question), and 100 that is, the method by which, from the relations of certain phenomena, we prove that some stand in the position of causes towards the others.

I want to put the case clearly before you, and I will therefore show you what I mean by another familiar example. I will suppose that one of you, on coming down in the morning to the parlor of your house, finds that a teapot and some spoons which had been left in the room on the previous evening are gone—the window is open, and you observe the mark of a dirty hand on the windowframe, and perhaps, in addition to that, you notice the impress of a hobnailed shoe on the gravel outside. All these phenomena have struck your attention instantly, and before two seconds have passed you say, "Oh, somebody has broken open the window, entered the room, and run off with the spoons and the teapot!" That speech is out of your mouth in a moment. And you will probably add, "I know there has; I am quite sure of it!" You mean to say exactly what you know; but in reality you are giving expression to what is, in all essential particulars, an hypothesis. You do not *know* it at all; it is nothing but a hypothesis rapidly framed in your own mind. And it is an hypothesis founded on a long train of inductions and deductions.

What are those inductions and deductions, and how have you got at this hypothesis? You have observed, in the first place, that the window is open; but by a train of reasoning involving many inductions and deductions, you have probably arrived long before at the general law—and a very good one it is— that windows do not open of themselves; and you therefore conclude that something has opened the window. A second general law that you have arrived at in the same way is that teapots and spoons do not go out a window spontaneously, and you are satisfied that, as they are not now where you left them, they have been removed. In the third place, you look at the marks on the windowsill, and the shoemarks outside, and you say that in all previous experience the former kind of mark has never been produced by anything else but the hand of a human being; and the same experience shows that no other animal but man at present wears shoes with hobnails in them such as would produce the marks in the gravel. I do not know, even if we could discover any of those "missing links" that are talked about, that they would help us to any other conclusion! At any rate the law which states our present experience is strong enough for my present purpose. You next reach the conclusion, that as these kinds of marks have not been left by any other animals than men, or are liable to be formed in any other way than by a man's hand and shoe, the marks in question have been formed by a man in that way. You have, further, a general law, founded on observation and experience, and that, too, is, I am sorry to say, a very universal and unimpeachable one—that some men are thieves; and you assume at once from all these premises—and that is what constitutes your hypothesis—that the man who made the marks outside and on the windowsill, opened the window, got into the room, and stole your teapot and spoons. You have now arrived at a *vera causa*—you have assumed a cause which, it is plain, is competent to produce all the phenomena you have observed. You can explain all these phenomena only by the hypothesis of a thief. But that is a hypothetical conclusion, of the justice of which you have no absolute proof at all; it is only rendered highly probable by a series of inductive and deductive reasonings.

I suppose your first action, assuming that you are a man of ordinary common sense, and that you have established this hypothesis to your own satisfaction, will very likely be to go off for the police, and set them on the track of the burglar, with the view to the recovery of your property. But just as you are starting with this object, some person comes in, and on learning what you are about, says, "My good friend, you are going on a great deal too fast. How do you know that the man who really made the marks took the spoons? It might have been a monkey that took them, and the man may have merely looked in afterwards." You would probably reply, "Well, that is all very well, but you see it is contrary to all experience of the way teapots and spoons are abstracted; so that, at any rate, your hypothesis is less probable than mine." While you are talking the thing over in this way, another friend arrives, one of that good kind of people that I was talking of a little while ago. And he might say, "Oh, my dear sir, you are certainly going on a great deal too fast. You are most presumptuous. You admit that all these occurrences took place when you were fast asleep, at a time when you could not possibly have known anything about what was taking place. How do you know that the laws of Nature are not suspended during the night? It may be that there has been some kind of supernatural interference in this case." In point of fact, he declares that your hypothesis is one of which you cannot at all demonstrate the truth, and that you are by no means sure that the laws of Nature are the same when you are asleep as when you are awake.

Well, now, you cannot at the moment answer that kind of reasoning. You feel that your worthy friend has you somewhat at a disadvantage. You will feel perfectly convinced in your own mind, however, that you are quite right, and you say to him, "My good friend, I can only be guided by the natural probabilities of the case, and if you will be kind enough to stand aside and permit me to pass, I will go fetch the police." Well, we will suppose that your journey is successful, and that by good luck you meet with a policeman; that eventually the burglar is found with your property on his person, and the marks correspond to his hand and to his boots. Probably any jury would consider those facts a very good experimental verification of your hypothesis, touching the cause of the abnormal phenomena observed in your parlor, and would act accordingly.

Now, in this supposititious case, I have taken phenomena of a very common kind, in order that you might see what are the different steps in an ordinary process of reasoning, if you will only take the trouble to analyze it carefully. All the operations I have described, you will see, are involved in the mind of any man of sense in leading him to a conclusion as to the course he should take in order to make good a robbery and punish the offender. I say that you are led, in this case, to your conclusion by exactly the same train of reasoning as that which a man of science pursues when he is endeavoring to discover the origin and laws of the most occult phenomena. The process is, and always must be, the same; and precisely the same mode of reasoning was employed by Newton and Laplace in their endeavors to discover and define the causes of the movements of the heavenly bodies, as you, with your own common sense, would employ to detect a burglar. The only difference is, that the nature of the inquiry being more abstruse, every step has to be more carefully watched, so that there may not be a single crack or flaw in your hypothesis. A flaw or crack in many 195 of the hypotheses of daily life may be of little or no moment as affecting the general correctness of the conclusions at which we may arrive; but, in a scientific inquiry, a fallacy, great or small, is always of importance, and is sure to be in the long run constantly productive of mischievous, if not fatal, results.

Do not allow yourselves to be misled by the common notion that an hypoth- 200 esis is untrustworthy simply because it is an hypothesis. It is often urged, in respect to some scientific conclusion, that, after all, it is only an hypothesis. But what more have we to guide us in nine-tenths of the most important affairs of daily life than hypotheses, and often very ill-based ones? So that in science, where the evidence of an hypothesis is subjected to the most rigid examination, 205 we may rightly pursue the same course. You may have hypotheses and hypotheses. A man may say, if he likes, that the moon is made of green cheese: that is an hypothesis. But another man, who has devoted a great deal of time and attention to the subject, and availed himself of the most powerful telescopes and the results of the observations of others, declares that in his opinion it is 210 probably composed of materials very similar to those of which our own earth is made up; and that is also only an hypothesis. But I need not tell you that there is an enormous difference in the value of the two hypotheses. That one which is based on sound scientific knowledge is sure to have a corresponding value; and that which is a mere hasty random guess is likely to have but little 215 value. Every great step in our progress in discovering causes has been made in exactly the same way as that which I have detailed to you. A person observing the occurrence of certain facts and phenomena asks, naturally enough, what process, what kind of operation known to occur in Nature applied to the particular case, will unravel and explain the mystery? Hence you have the scien- 220 tific hypothesis; and its value will be proportionate to the care and completeness with which its basis has been tested and verified. It is in these matters as in the commonest affairs of practical life: The guess of the fool will be folly, while the guess of the wise man will contain wisdom. In all cases, you see that value of the result depends on the patience and faithfulness with which the investigator 225 applies to his hypothesis every possible kind of verification.

1. In the example of the apple, what steps are the basis for the conclusion?
2. In the example of the teapot, what steps are the basis for the conclusion?
3. What is the basis for rejecting the suggestion by the first friend? by the second friend?
4. Check the etymology, denotation, and connotation of *mode, phenomena, graduated, beam, axis, induction, deduction, hypothesis, theories, syllogism, premise, verification, hobnailed, unimpeachable, presumptuous, suspended, supposititious,*

*abstruse, fallacy;* what is the singular form of *phenomena?* of *hypotheses?* (Note that *apparatus* may be either singular or plural).

5. What use does Huxley make of narrative, of analogy, and of comparison to make his points clear?

## ASSIGNMENTS

1. Everyone has prejudices—strong feelings on some subject, for or against, which exist without much thought or reason (see Example E in this unit). If you have noticed a prejudice held by one of your friends, ask what your friend believes to be its cause; then examine the answer and decide whether it is reasonable or whether your friend has been guilty of rationalization. Try the same experiment with a prejudice of your own (areas of taste, religion, politics, and race are good hunting grounds).

2. Choose some incident in your own life that at first seems to have been pure "accident," and search for causes. Consider all possibilities, rejecting those that do not bear up under scrutiny and explaining why you believe others to be the true ones.

3. Determine what you believe to be the cause or causes of one of your present strong interests or hobbies. Then test the validity of your conclusions by checking them against the list of warnings on pages 181–82.

4. Examine some local phenomenon—a campus tradition, a dating custom, an excessive or a deficient interest in some kind of activity (from sports to studies), the presence or absence of the honor system—and try to determine the cause or causes behind it.

5. Write an essay with a title such as "I Changed My Mind" or "I Used to Think So" in which you organize your material into three sections: your original attitude toward something (a sport, activity, profession, person); the cause of your change of mind; your present attitude. Devote most of your attention to the cause of the change and its effects.

6. Choosing as your subject some situation, policy, or plan on your campus, write an essay predicting what the outcome will be. For example, what effects can logically be expected to follow an increase in tuition or enrollment? a change in entrance or degree requirements? the relaxation or tightening of rules regarding class attendance, drinking, visiting hours in dormitories?

7 Missionaries are sometimes used by psychologists as examples of "mixed motives," their choice of vocation presumably having been inspired not only by a desire to spread their religious beliefs but also, perhaps, by an interest in travel, a desire for adventure, a yearning for power and prestige, even a thought for financial security; and the effects of their choice are doubtless as numerous and varied. Make a thorough analysis of the causes that led you to come to college or to choose a particular college or to choose your vocation, if you have already done so. Then analyze similarly the many effects of your choice, both those that may already have occurred and those that may reasonably be predicted. Write an essay embodying your findings.

# UNIT 13

# *Induction*

One of the oldest and most common activities of the mind is what is popularly called "drawing a conclusion." This is nothing more or less than arriving at what one takes to be a general truth by observing particular events. This process is an important source of children's knowledge of the world about them even before they have learned to speak; a baby given a spoonful of too-hot oatmeal immediately "concludes" from this experience that all spoonfuls of oatmeal will be equally painful. Only through additional experience, patiently and even forcibly provided, can the baby be convinced otherwise.

What the baby has done is to use—and abuse—the logical process of induction. In this method of reasoning we observe a certain thing to hold true in a number of similar situations, and we then generalize from them to conclude that it will be true in all similar situations. Such reasoning is an extremely important source of knowledge, but we must remember that the validity of a general "law" established in this way is always dependent on the number and appropriateness of the instances that support it. Used properly, the inductive process has been the principal tool in the tremendous advances made by modern science; abused, it has been the source of many of our popular misconceptions and prejudices.

If, on moving into a new community, we find that the school buildings are in good condition, that the teaching staff is well qualified and remains year after year, that the local parent–teacher organization has a large membership and frequent, well-attended meetings, and that a high percentage of the graduates go on to college and succeed there, we may safely infer that the community offers good educational opportunities for children. We have thus used the inductive method, informally, to reach a general conclusion that is almost certainly sound. But if, on a shopping trip, we have the misfortune to be cheated by a Swiss storekeeper and, having brooded over the injustice, we assert that all Swiss are thieves, we have established nothing but a prejudice. The conclusion is unwarranted because it is based on completely inadequate evidence.

At best, the inductive method gives only probability. The fact that the sun has always risen does not prove that it always will, although the likelihood is great enough for us to plan the future in terms of it. Even the scientist cannot examine every existing instance before establishing a generalization on the basis of observation, although Francis Bacon, father of the inductive method, hoped to do so. As nonspecialists we can do a much less thorough job than the scientist—so much less that our generalization may have to be qualified from "all" to "most," from "always" to "usually." But it may still be sufficiently valid to be useful and convincing within its limits.

Evidence to support an inductively established generalization may take numerous forms. It may be the result of your experience through experiment or observation. It may be facts and figures drawn from your reading—even scientists draw from the reported research of others as well as from the results of their own. It may be the opinions of others, discovered through reading, questionnaires, or interviews. Whatever it is, you must try to determine its reliability. You would not depend on advertisements for the complete truth about a product, or expect a chemist to give an authoritative opinion on a ballet. An automobile company once used the slogan, "Ask the man who owns one," but if a man has never driven another make, his opinion of his own car is worth little compared to the results of a consumer organization's exhaustive tests of many makes and models.

Induction is such a common mental process that you have undoubtedly often used it informally in writing and thinking. In this unit, however, you are asked to give particular attention to induction as a logical procedure—to its powers and its dangers—and to write a paper that, whatever other methods of reasoning or whatever patterns of organization you may use, is based primarily on the inductive process of drawing a justifiable general conclusion from a sufficient number of admissible particulars.

**1. Do not decide in advance what your conclusion will be.** Your object is to arrive at whatever truth emerges from the evidence, not to select evidence to fit your previous idea of the truth, which may prove to be mistaken. It is true that to give your collection of evidence purpose and direction, you should have an inkling of what the results of your investigation will prove, just as scientists may begin with a hypothesis, a tentative formulation of the truth they are working to establish. But like scientists, you must be willing to abandon your preconceptions, if the facts fail to uphold them, in favor of what they actually establish. You may start to investigate the effect of extracurricular activities on student grades with the impression that the time spent in such activities necessarily interferes with scholarship. But perhaps the relaxation they provide actually makes a student study more effectively. Your final generalization must be whatever the evidence supports.

**2. Do not shift ground.** Although you should maintain an open mind as to the outcome of your observations, you must not lose sight of the problem that you are investigating. In trying to determine the effect of extracurricular activities on grades, for instance, you must not allow yourself to be sidetracked to the interesting question of the value of extracurricular activities in creating a well-rounded individual, which is quite another matter. Sticking to the subject often involves, for your sake and the reader's, a preliminary definition of exactly what you mean by the terms you use.

**3. Include a reasonable number of instances.** Drawing conclusions does not mean jumping to them. Hasty generalizations, the fallacy most frequently found in inductive reasoning, is the making of general statements on the basis of insufficient evidence. Your conclusions about the effect of extracurricular activities on grades will have little general validity if you base your observations on only three or four students. What constitutes a "reasonable" number of instances will depend partly on the subject: an investigation of whether city or rural backgrounds have produced more presidents of the United States could easily include all the presidents, but a similar study of American doctors could reasonably be done through a sampling. The number of instances needed will also depend on your intention. For practical purposes, you will not need nearly as many as scientists do; their studies may require hundreds of instances, but your inductive essay may need only a few well-chosen ones. Further, you need not give the details of all the instances but only the evidence drawn from them.

**4. Use fair instances.** Do not fail, through carelessness or prejudice, to get a representative sampling. Those who take public opinion polls avoid this error by elaborate techniques for getting fair samples of opinion. If you are studying the effects of activities on the grades of students in general, do not limit your examples to those with high or low grades, but make a cross section. Do not conclude, because of a number of student arrests for speeding, that the police are prejudiced against students unless you can prove that other speeding drivers are not being arrested. The more carefully you guard against any evidence of prejudice, any loading of the dice, in your choice and analysis of instances, the more reliable and convincing will be your conclusions.

**5. Do not neglect negative instances.** Charles Darwin, the great nineteenth-century British naturalist, is said to have kept special records of any evidence that tended to disprove the hypothesis concerning evolution that was guiding his research, on the grounds that he could easily remember the data that supported his theory but needed to keep reminding himself of the existence of contrary evidence. If the negative instances prove not to be typical, disregard them. Otherwise they may make you modify your final generalization from "all students" to "most" or "many."

**6. Word your conclusion to fit your particulars.** You must never generalize beyond what the evidence warrants. The fact that you may not be able to arrive at an unqualified conclusion as to "all" students does not, however, rule out the use of the inductive process; there is often a virtue in suggesting significant trends even though you cannot prove an altogether consistent pattern. But limit your generalizations to your evidence: with percentages, or with such words (carefully chosen to represent your evidence as accurately as possible) as *nearly all, probably, usually, likely*—or *possibly, sometimes, few, seldom, rarely*. (See "The Language of Uncertainty," Example B in this unit.)

**7. Make sure that any analogy you use is apt.** Remember that analogies (see Unit 9) are never evidence, merely rhetorical devices used to clarify. In inductive reasoning they are sometimes used on the assumption that if two things are alike in certain respects, they are also alike in others. But their value depends on how apt and reasonable they are. The fact that swimming, being a skill, requires much practice as well as an understanding of the strokes and muscles involved may aptly illustrate the point that writing (also a skill, though of a very different sort) cannot be mastered only by a study of grammar and rhetoric but also requires much practice. But a country doctor's need for a car is too far removed from the international scene to make clear to the reader that a nation needs its own merchant marine, though both situations involve transportation.

## *Organization*

You may have found the word *inductive* used by teachers and in textbooks to indicate a pattern of organization for a paragraph or a whole composition. Used in this rhetorical sense, it refers to a method of leading up to a climax by presenting the particulars first and by keeping until the last, for emphasis, whatever general statement is being made. In other words, the inductive method or organization is so named because it follows the pattern the mind must take in reasoning inductively, which is, as we have seen, that of working from the supporting instances to the general conclusion that may be drawn from them. In such an arrangement the "topic sentence" of the paragraph or the "main idea" of the entire paper is expressed in the final statement, where it makes a special impression on the reader, who is accustomed to the more usual order, which places it first.

*There is, however, no necessary connection between induction as a method of reasoning and as a pattern of organization.* An enumeration of details summed up in a final statement, rhetorically, does not necessarily involve the inductive process of generalizing logically from particulars. The following is addition, not induction:

> Any time we look out, we see grackles and starlings on the lawn; and flickers, goldfinches, catbirds, and cowbirds are frequent visitors. This morning a bluejay came to our birdbath, and before he left, he had been joined by two robins and several sparrows. A wren is nesting in a wren house on our porch. In all, we have recorded more than twenty different species here this spring.

Of more importance to you here, a paper based on inductive reasoning does not have to present its instances first and then its generalization. True, this is the order in which your mind must have worked to reach a conclusion. But having reached it, you may choose to begin your paper with the conclusion instead of saving it until the end. This is called the *deductive pattern* of organization. In it, you state your generalization first so that it will help your readers to understand more easily the particulars of the supporting evidence and the steps you used.

> We have had a very poor football team this year. We lost our first two games
> of the season by heavy margins. The third game was a tie, but we then lost the
> next three. Even though we won the last game, we were outplayed in all but the
> first quarter.

Notice that although the deductive *pattern* is used here, the *reasoning* is
inductive: the results of the seven games are used as particulars to establish the
generalization that we have had a very poor team. The same material, *arranged*
inductively (by moving the general statement from the beginning to the end),
would read as follows:

> We lost our first two football games this year by heavy margins. The third game
> was a tie, but we then lost the next three. Even though we won the last game, we
> were outplayed in all but the first quarter. We have had a very poor team this
> year.

The pattern has been changed, but the kind of reasoning remains the same.

The term *induction* as used here does not mean a pattern for organizing
ideas but a method of sound reasoning that may be the basis of many kinds of
writing. An essay based on careful inductive reasoning may make use of one or
several of the patterns discussed in earlier units—classification, comparison,
analysis—in the development of its thesis. So long as your inductive reasoning
is sound, its conclusions will be recognized and respected, whatever order you
choose for presenting your material.

## EXAMPLES

For the best example of inductive reasoning, go back to Huxley's "The
Method of Scientific Investigation" (Unit 12-I) and reread the first six
paragraphs.

*13-A*                THREE INCIDENTS
                *The New Yorker*

This essay, given here complete, appeared unsigned in the *New Yorker* (September
1980).

I am fully aware that anecdotal evidence is no longer, if it ever was, in good
scientific repute. Nevertheless, in the course of the past few months I have been
witness to three aberrations of nature that seem to me to be worth noting. They
suggest, if nothing else, that, contrary to much received understanding, man is
not the only form of life that is capable of making a fool of itself. The first of 5
these incidents occurred in the spring, just under the eaves on our front veranda.
There is a fixture up there, a galvanized-iron box about the size and shape of a
thick paperback book (it has something to do with the outdoor lights), that forms
a kind of shelf. I came out on the veranda one morning in time to see a bird—

a little red-breasted house finch—make a landing there on the top of the box 10
and deposit a beakful of grass. I stood on tiptoe and craned my neck, and saw
the beginnings of a nest. It was in many ways an excellent nesting site—dry,
airy, nicely sheltered. But it was also as slippery as glass. And, as I watched, a
gust of breeze came along and the nest slid off and blew away in pieces. Well,
that, I thought, is that. The bird, however, thought differently. It went to work 15
again, retrieving the scattered grasses, and started another nest. Another
doomed nest, I should say. Because another little breeze came along and scattered that nest, too. But the finch was undismayed. I watched it start still
another nest, and I watched that nest blow away. That was enough for me. I
went on with my own affairs. But every now and then through the rest of the 20
day I went over to the door or the window and looked out. The finch was always
there—sitting on the box, fluttering away, swooping back with a wisp of grass.
And there was still nothing more than the pathetic beginnings of a nest.

The second incident occurred in the house, in the attic. I went up there a
couple of weeks ago to look for something or other. I was feeling my way 25
toward an old chest of drawers when something odd caught my eye. It was a
strand of ivy espaliered on the wall above the little end window. It was two or
three feet long, its leaves were a sickly yellowy green, and it had forced itself,
at God knows what exertion, through a tiny crack in the window frame from
the life-giving sunlight into the deadly dusk of the attic. 30

And then, just the other day, I was out weeding the garden and sat down on
the bench to rest and noticed an anthill at my feet. There was much coming
and going around the hole—a stream of foraging workers. I leaned down and
watched a worker emerge from the hole, race away through the grass, pounce
on a tiny something—a seed, maybe, or an egg or a minuscule creature—and 35
head quickly back toward the hole. Only, it headed in the wrong direction. It
raced this way and that, back and forth, farther and farther away from home.
I had to get up from the bench to follow it. I finally lost it, in a weedy jungle,
a good eight feet (the equivalent, perhaps, of a couple of miles) from where it
wanted to be. I went back to the bench and sat down again and wondered. It 40
might be possible, I thought, to somehow see the strivings of the finch as an
example of determination, an iron procreative perseverance. And the ivy: its
suicidal floundering, too, might be explained—as an evolutionary thrust, an
urge (like that of some aquatic organism feeling its way up a beach) to try a
new environment. But the ant! There was no way of rationalizing that: the phe- 45
nomenon of a worker ant—an ant bred exclusively to forage for its queen—
unable to find its way home. It shook and shattered the concept of a knowing
and nurturing instinct, of a computerized infallibility, in nature. I felt a tug of
something like sympathy for that errant ant. And also for the finch and the ivy.
They gave me a new vision of nature: a nature unmechanized, a nature vul- 50
nerable, a nature appealingly natural.

1. The writer gives the three incidents chronologically—in the order in which they
   occurred. Do you find any additional reason for this sequence?

2. Where does the writer use specific, concrete details? specific, concrete words?
3. Check the etymology, denotation, and connotation of *aberrations, received understanding, espaliered, foraging, minuscule.*

---

*13-B*                THE LANGUAGE OF UNCERTAINTY
                        *John Cohen*

These paragraphs from an essay that first appeared in *Scientific American* (1957) report the results reached inductively through experiments. The conclusions, therefore, have a firmer base than informal observation.

ANALYSIS
Conclusion
Examples

Analysis of example

Uncertainty pervades our lives so thoroughly that it dominates our language. Our everyday speech is made up in large part of words like *probably, many, soon, great, little.* What do these words mean? "Atomic war," declared a recent editorial in the London *Times,* "is likely to ruin 5 forever the nation that even victoriously wages it." How exactly are we to understand the word *likely?* Lacking any standard for estimating the odds, we are left with the private probability of the editorial writer.

Analysis of
conclusion

Such verbal imprecision is not necessarily to be con- 10 demned. Indeed, it has a value just because it allows us to express judgments when a precise quantitative statement is out of the question. All the same, we should not and need not hide behind a screen of complete indefiniteness. Often it is possible to indicate the bounds or limits of the quan- 15 titative value we have in mind.

Classification of data

The language of uncertainty has three main categories: (1) words such as *probably, possibly, surely,* which denote a single subjective probability and are potentially quantifiable; (2) words like *many, often, soon,* which are also 20 quantifiable but denote not so much a condition of uncertainty as a quantity imprecisely known; (3) words like *fat, rich, drunk,* which are not reducible to any accepted number because they are given values by different people.

Method of analysis of
data

We have been trying to pin down, by experimental stud- 25 ies, what people mean by these expressions in specific contexts, and how the meanings change with age. For instance, a subject is told "There are many trees in the park" and is asked to say what number the word *many* means to him. Or a child is invited to take "some" sweets from a bowl 30 and we then count how many he has taken. We compare the number he takes when alone with the number when one or more other children are present and are to take some sweets after him, or with the number he takes when instructed to give "some" sweets to another child. 35

Category #1:

Results of analysis
Example

Examples

Category #2:
Results of analysis

Examples

Category #3:
Results of analysis

Examples

First, we find that the number depends, of course, on the items involved. To most people *some friends* means about five, while *some trees* means about twenty. However, unrelated areas sometimes show parallel values. For instance, the language of probability seems to mean about 40 the same thing in predictions about the weather and about politics: the expression *is certain to (rain,* or *be elected)* signifies to the average person about a 70 per cent chance; *is likely to,* about a 60 per cent chance; *probably will,* about 55 per cent. 45

Secondly, the size of the population of items influences the value assigned to an expression. Thus, if we tell a subject to take "a few" or "a lot of" beads from a tray, he will take more if the tray contains a large number of beads than if it has a small number. But not proportionately more: if 50 we increase the number of beads eightfold, the subject takes only half as large a percentage of the total.

Thirdly, there is a marked change with age. Among children between six and fourteen years old, the older the child, the fewer beads he will take. But the difference 55 between *a lot* and *a few* widens with age. This age effect is so consistent that it might be used as a test of intelligence. In place of a long test we could merely ask the subject to give numerical values to expressions such as *nearly always* and *very rarely* in a given context, and then measure his 60 intelligence by the ratio of the number for *nearly always* to the one for *very rarely.* We have found that this ratio increases systematically from about 2 to 1 for a child of seven to about 20 to 1 for a person twenty-five years old.

1. The writer gives the results of the experiment, not all the data on which they were based (presumably these are available on request). Are the results convincing without the data?
2. What is the principle of classification of the general subject in ¶3? What is the principle of the classification of the results of the analysis in ¶5–7?
3. Check the etymology, denotation, and connotation of *quantitative, subjective, quantifiable, denote, contexts.*

---

**13-C**             THE CHILD IN JANUARY
*Gordon D. DeLetto (student)*

All forms of activity lead to boredom when performed on a routine basis. We can see this principle at work in people of all ages. On Christmas morning, children play with their new toys and games. But the novelty soon wears off, and by January those same toys can be found tucked away in the attic. The

world is well stocked with half-filled stamp albums and unfinished models, each 5
standing as a monument to someone's waning interest. When parents bring
home a pet, their child gladly grooms it. Within a short time, however, the
burden of caring for the animal is shifted to the parents. Adolescents enter high
school with enthusiasm but are soon looking forward to graduation. A similar
fate befalls the young adults going on to college. How many adults, who now 10
complain about the long drives to work, eagerly drove for hours at a time when
they first obtained their licenses? Before people retire, they usually talk about
doing all of the interesting things that they never had time to do while working.
But soon after retirement, the golfing, the fishing, the reading and all of the
other pastimes become as boring as the jobs they left. And, like the child in 15
January, they go searching for new toys.

1. Why has the author arranged his data in a chronological pattern?
2. What criticism of people is implied by the author's use of the analogy of the behavior of children with toys?

---

**13-D**           THE PASSING OF LITTLE GIBBS ROAD
                   *Connie Keremes (student)*

My neighborhood is dying. The houses know it. They creak and groan at the
slightest breeze. The trees know it. Their bare limbs rasp dryly together in the
wind. The people know it. They gaze out of dusty windows and sigh at the
falling leaves.

The houses in my neighborhood are ancient and dilapidated. Many years ago, 5
they were fine, well-cared for buildings with fresh paint and neat lawns. Now,
however, the houses, more than fifty years old, have become quite tumbledown.
They are simply too old and weathered to endure another fierce winter. The
houses are sagging structures. They never seem to stand straight but, rather,
they lean heavily to one side as if they might topple over at any moment. The 10
rotting beams and frames groan under the weight of roofs which look like
patchwork quilts of mending slate. The shingled fronts are discolored from
many winters of snow and ice. Several shingles have come loose from many of
the houses and, left unrepaired, creak back and forth in the wind. Every stoop
and walk is crumbling and cracked. A few homeowners have placed potted 15
plants on the stoops in an attempt to hide the many cracks—but the plants
make the deep fissures all the more apparent. The houses appear more pathetic
than ugly in their dilapidation, for their squeaking paint-chipped doors and
groaning frames seem to say these once fine homes will soon crumble to dust.

The houses are not alone in their deterioration, for the trees are also decaying. 20
At one time, the trees along my street were tall and leafy, but now they are
bent and twisted with age. The tops of many trees have been sawed off because
their branches had been tangling the telephone wires. Such trees have now
become rotting stumps overrun with burrowing insects. Those trees which are

standing are gnarled and diseased. Vandals have carved obscenities in the trunks 25
of several trees, boldly leaving their names and dates beside the deed. A few
leaves cling to the twisted branches, but for the most part the trees are barren.
They bend low as the wind whines through their bare limbs. These wasted old
trees will easily be uprooted by the first strong blast that blows this year. They
undoubtedly will not survive the winter. 30

The people themselves seem to be wasting away. Only very old people live
in the neighborhood, for the children who once lived there have all grown up
and moved away. No one ever moves into the neighborhood—only out. The
old people who live here are very frail. They walk slowly along the cracking
sidewalks, their kerchiefed heads bent against the gusty winds. In passing each 35
other along the street, the old people no longer smile or stop to talk, but merely
nod grimly and continue along their way. They lack the strength to climb up
on their roofs to patch a hole or fasten a loose shingle, and as a result their
houses become progressively more dilapidated. Aware of their failing strength
and inability to make repairs on the decaying neighborhood, the old people 40
resign themselves to staying indoors and staring dully out at the leaves that swirl
across the cracking sidewalks and past the gnarled trees. There is nothing left
for them to do but to watch the neighborhood die.

1. The subject and main point here are similar to those of Examples B and D in the
   preceding unit. What differences and similarities do you find in the three authors'
   methods of presentation?
2. Why does the author save her discussion of the people until the last?

---

**13-E**  OCCASIONS OF HOPE
*Phyllis Theroux*

This essay, here complete except for a brief autobiographical introduction, first
appeared in the *New York Times* (August 1977).

It is sometimes said that we Americans are in danger of losing all sense of
ritual, unless one wants to count a weekly dash to McDonald's as a meaningful
routine. But the birthday party shows no sign of decline, although the point of
it tends to change as life proceeds. Children, for instance, think that on their
birthday—oh cruel, illusory kickoff to nowhere—they will step from brown 5
grass onto green, which is how I used to envision the state line between California and Nevada. An adult tends to switch the colors around.

Children step toward the cake with the assumption that love is a right, honor
is a natural sequel, and respect (for the honoree) absolutely essential. The adult
has seen that combination fall upon hard times too often to take it for granted. 10
And contrary to that irritating slogan some born-again adults coined, "Today is
the first day of the rest of your life," the birthday child says, "Nonsense, today
is the *only* day, and if you aren't nice to me on all the others, I won't invite you
to my next party."

The difference in views may lie in different attitudes toward death. For a child, death is a non-existent bookend that disguises itself as growth, freedom, and the day one finally gets permission to have one's ears pierced. Only later does it come to us that life is not an infinite series of octaves, that there will be a last note just as there was a first. Where once we strained to disconnect from one bookend, we now drag our feet toward the other. A birthday reminds us of the distance we've covered in spite of ourselves.

Yet I wonder if this accounts for all of our feelings about birthdays.

There is also an element of self-consciousness that adults are notoriously capable of carrying around that keeps us from wanting what we want, for fear of not getting, much less deserving it. Think of the child again, waiting for the party to begin. With what outrageous expectation does he pace the floor. No wonder he goes berserk at the first ring of the doorbell. Think now of the adult sitting somewhat uncomfortably in the living room, not knowing quite how to respond when the guests pump his hand, being embarrassed at the toasts, grateful that anyone came at all, but relieved when the party is over. If children are distinguished by their disappointment over being one present short of what they expected, adults are often distinguished by their inability to know how to measure up to the occasion. In both instances we have difficulty handling the ritual, at least as it applies to ourselves.

There was one particular birthday that I celebrated that points up the dilemma. I assembled the guest list, planned the menu, figured out what was going to happen, and could hardly wait to turn it into a reality. But in the interim I had mentally had the party a hundred times, feasted my eyes upon all the people I loved, thrown them together in combinations of twos and threes, stood back and watched them get to know each other, and had a wonderful time. Too wonderful.

About a week before my actual birthday, a friend telephoned to make sure that she had the right date, since I had never sent out invitations. It was then that I realized that the party ahead was already over. It would not do to expose such a wonderful fantasy to harsh daylight. "Actually," I admitted, "I don't think I have the energy to go through with the real thing."

That, unfortunately, is the way a lot of people feel about their birthdays. Rather than risk being disappointed, they prefer to make it a day like any other day, a Sabbath not to celebrate. Yet there is a connection there. In church, or around the table, it is the many celebrating the one, and while it is all very well to pray in a closet, there is a place for formality, where we come together to show affection, acknowledge interdependence, and say to that one person, you make a tremendous difference.

Of course, it's far easier to say it than to hear it, just as it is not only better but easier to give than receive, unless you are a child. Yet let's not be too hard on children; for in the long run their approach to birthdays is right. They are occasions of hope.

1. Do you agree with the author's observation that the celebration of birthdays is still an important ritual?

2. Where and how does the author use narrative, analogy, comparison, contrast, classification, and analysis to help her discover why we celebrate birthdays?
3. What figures of speech do you find?

---

### 13-F   EPITAPH TO THE ELUSIVE ABOMINABLE SNOWMAN
#### *Sir Edmund Hillary*

This essay, here complete, first appeared in *Life* (1961). The writer, a mountaineer from New Zealand, led the first party to climb Mt. Everest.

Does the yeti, or "abominable snowman," really exist? Or is it just a myth without practical foundation? For the last four months our Himalayan scientific and mountaineering expedition has been trying to find out—and now we think we know the answer.

There has been a growing pile of evidence in favor of the creature's existence: the tracks seen by many explorers on Himalayan glaciers, the complete conviction of the local people that yetis roam the mountains, the yeti scalps and hands kept as relics in the high monasteries, the many stories about people who claim to have seen them.

But despite the firm belief of many Himalayan explorers and of some anthropologists, I began the search for the yeti with some skepticism. My own experience had been limited to two incidents. In 1951 a tough and experienced Sherpa (Sherpas are a mountain people of Tibetan stock) had told me with absolute conviction that he had seen a yeti and watched it for some time. In 1952 Explorer George Lowe and I had found a tuft of black hair at an altitude of 19,000 feet, a tuft that our Sherpas swore was yeti hair—and immediately threw away in obvious fear.

Last September we set off from Katmandu in Nepal and walked for a hundred miles through rain and leeches to the 12,000-foot-high Sherpa village of Beding. For eight days we were immobilized by weather, but we made profitable use of our time by interrogating the villagers and the lamas in the local monastery. One of our expedition members, Desmond Doig, speaks the language of Nepal with great fluency and has the ability, quite unprecedented in my experience, to gain the confidence and liking of the local peoples.

We confirmed much that we already knew and learned more besides. The Sherpas believe there are three types of yetis:

1. The chuteh: a vast, hairy, ginger-and-black creature, sometimes eight feet tall, generally vegetarian and not harmful to man unless disturbed or annoyed.
2. The miteh: usually four to five feet tall with a high, pointed skull. His feet are said to be placed back to front. He has a decidedly unpleasant temperament and delights in eating any humans who come his way.
3. The thelma: a small creature from 18 inches to two feet high who lives down

in the jungle, has human features and takes great pleasure in piling sticks
and stones into little mounds.                                                                    35

We couldn't find any Sherpa who had actually seen a yeti, but several had
heard them—usually when the winter snowfalls lay deep on the ground and
the villagers were confined to their houses. Then, one gathered, the sound of
the yeti was frequently heard at night, and next morning tracks were seen by
the frightened Sherpas.                                                                          40
One of our own Sherpas, Ang Temba, now proved to be a veritable Sherlock
Holmes. He scoured the villages for information and brought us the exciting
news that there was a yeti skin here, the prized possession of a lama and his
wife. The lama was away, and at first the wife refused to show us the skin. But
Ang Temba and Desmond Doig were a formidable combination, and after  45
much persuasion and chinking of rupees the skin became ours. In our opinion
it was a fine specimen of the very rare Tibetan blue bear, but all our Sherpas
disagreed emphatically. It wasn't a bear at all, they said, but undoubtedly the
chuteh, or biggest type of yeti. Nothing we said could sway this belief.
When the weather cleared, we moved up the Rolwaling valley and began  50
our search for signs of the yeti. Several weeks later our efforts were rewarded
by the discovery of many tracks on the Ripimu glacier between 18,000 and
19,000 feet. These tracks were positively identified by our Sherpas as those of
yetis, and they certainly fulfilled the required specifications: large broad feet
with clear toe marks.                                                                            55
We devoted much care to the examination of these tracks and made some
interesting discoveries. When we followed a line of tracks to a place where the
footprints were in the shade of rocks or on the cold north side of a snow slope,
the yeti tracks suddenly ceased to exist. In their place we found the small footprints of a fox or wild dog, bunched closely together as the animal bounded  60
over the snow. Again and again we saw precise evidence of the effect of the sun
on those bunches of small tracks. The warmth melted them out, ran them
together, completely altered their contours and made as fine a yeti track as one
could wish.
Probably the best known photographs of yeti tracks are those taken by  65
Explorer Eric Shipton and Dr. Michael Ward on the Menlung glacier in 1951.
The tracks that we discovered were less than two miles from the Shipton tracks
and at a similar height and time of the year. Dr. Ward, who came back to the
Himalayas as a member of my physiological team, said that among the yeti
tracks on the Menlung glacier he and Shipton had noticed a number of small
animal tracks, but at the time they had not thought them significant.
In November we continued our investigations in the Khumbu region at the
foot of Mt. Everest. In the villages of Namche Bazar and Khumjung we
obtained two more blue bear skins. Whenever we showed these skins to a
Sherpa, we got the confident reply, "Chuteh."
Doig and Marlin Perkins, our zoologist, carried out a thorough enquiry
among the Khumbu villages and monasteries. All the Sherpas believed in the
yeti, but it was practically impossible to find anyone who, under careful ques-

tioning, claimed to have seen one. Even in the Thyangboche monastery, traditionally the source of much yeti lore and many yeti sightings, we were unable to find anyone who had seen a yeti. In fact, the two oldest lamas, who had lived in the monastery since its founding over 40 years ago, said they had neither seen a yeti nor knew of anyone who had.

Relics of the yeti in the monasteries of Khumjung, Pangboche and Namche Bazar came in for special attention. The bones of a hand in the Pangboche monastery were thought by our medical men to be those of a man—possibly the delicate hand of a lama. The yeti scalps we were shown in these monasteries were more of a puzzle. They were in the shape of high, pointed caps covered with coarse reddish and black hair and seemed to be very old. If they were authentic scalps, their very form indicated that they belonged to no known animal. Although they had no seams or needle marks, there was the chance that they had been cleverly fabricated many years before out of the molded skin of some other creature.

Doig and Perkins worked hard on this second possibility. Ang Temba produced two skins which had hair similar in texture to the scalps. We made high, pointed molds out of blocks of wood. The skins were softened, then stretched over the molds and left to dry. The resultant scalps were similar enough to the yeti scalps we saw in the monastery to indicate that we might be on the right track.

We realized that unless we could get an authoritative answer on the scalps, they would remain a constant challenge to any theories about the yeti. But the village elders of Khumjung firmly believed that their community would suffer a plague, earthquake, flood or avalanche if their relic scalp ever was removed. They insisted that it was the remains of a famous yeti slaughter that took place 240 years ago, when there were so many man-eating yetis about that the Sherpas resorted to ruse to eliminate them. The Sherpas pretended to get drunk and to kill each other with wooden swords. At night the Sherpas substituted real swords, which they left lying about. The yetis, who had been watching them and were great imitators, proceeded to drink heavily also, slashed at each other with the real swords and killed each other off.

After much negotiation with the Khumjung elders, we persuaded them to lend us the scalp for exactly six weeks. In exchange I promised I would try to raise money for a school which they will share with nearby Sherpa villages. To guarantee that we would bring the scalp back, the elders said they would hold as hostages our expedition's three head Sherpas, as well as their property and possessions.

Our faithful Sherpas unhesitatingly agreed. Then the villagers chose Kunjo Chumbi, the keeper of the village documents, to accompany us and bring the scalp back. For his first trip to the West, he wondered if he should take Sherpas traveling rations with him—a dried sheep carcass, wheat flour and some of the local brew. After talking it over with Doig, he settled instead on some cakes of Tibetan brick tea and his silver teacup.

He, Doig, Perkins and I covered the 170 miles of steep country to Katmandu in $9\frac{1}{2}$ days. From there we flew to Chicago, Paris and London and showed the

scalp and the chuteh skins to zoologists, anthropologists and other scientists. 125
Their decision was unanimous: the yeti scalp was not a scalp at all. It had been
molded out of some other skin, and the scientists agreed that it was the skin and
hair of the serow, a rather uncommon Himalayan member of the large goat-
antelope family. Also our chuteh skins were confirmed to be Tibetan blue bear.

We now know that a yeti track can be made by the sun melting the footprints 130
of a small creature such as a fox or wild dog. The same effect could occur with
the prints of snow leopards, bears and even humans. We know that the large
furs so confidently described by our Sherpas as chutehs are in fact the Tibetan
blue bear. There is the strong possibility that some of these big, unfamiliar creatures strayed down from their only known habitations in eastern Tibet and 135
crossed the Himalayan range. The small thelma in its habits and description
sounds very much like the rhesus monkey. And the pointed scalps of the miteh
have proved to be made from the skin of the much less frightening serow.

There is still much to be explained. Our theory on the tracks does not cover
every case. We have not yet found a satisfactory explanation for the noise of 140
the yeti which many Sherpas claim to have heard. But all in all we feel we have
solved some of the major problems surrounding this elusive creature. Of course,
the yeti still remains a very real part of the mythology and tradition of the
Himalayan people—and it is undoubtedly in the field of mythology that the
yeti rightly belongs. 145

1. Does the title spoil Hillary's effort to create suspense?
2. What hypothesis did Hillary have when he began the search?
3. How much attention does he give to each piece of evidence? Which pieces seem
   most important to him? to you?
4. Proof that something exists is naturally easier to find than proof that something does
   not exist, and Hillary is understandably cautious in his final paragraph. Do you think
   that he is nevertheless convinced of the nonexistence of the yeti? Are you
   convinced?
5. What is a lama? a rupee?
6. Check the etymology, denotation, and connotation of *formidable, chinking, lore,
   ruse.*

---

**13-G**　　　　　YOUR GENERATION, MY GENERATION
　　　　　　　　　*Jonathan Steinberg*

These paragraphs form the final two-thirds of an essay in *New Society* (July 1980)
on the writer's twenty-fifth reunion at Harvard. "The Book" was a 980-page profile of
his former classmates, prepared for the reunion.

Deep into the night, before I left for Boston, I read our book. The stories of
success or failure engrossed me as if in some many-mirrored room I could see
other selves I might have become.

If "The Book" was a shock, the reunion itself was simply stunning. Imagine what it would be like, to be put back, almost by magic, among people you have not only not seen for a generation but not even thought about, and to be again in the same surroundings. As my brother's car turned into Quincy Street, and 70 I saw the sun glittering on the brown-red bricks of familiar buildings in Harvard Yard, I began to shake. I later discovered that every classmate had felt something similar.

The car stopped. There was the Freshman Union, teeming with elderly gentlemen wearing funny, floppy sun-hats with "Remember '55" on the brim. The union itself, which I had last entered 28 years before, looked the same, a neoclassical monster in the early American suburban bank style.

Inside was chaos, or so it seemed. We filed through rooms where we were 15 given T-shirts, soap, wastepaper baskets, frisbees, all inscribed with "Remember '55—once in your lifetime, Harvard Reunion June 1 to 5, 1980" on them. Hordes of children, wearing the hats and T-shirts and throwing the frisbees, charged round the place, followed by anxious mothers looking uneasily at the lapel identity badges they were forced to wear, and at the spectacle made by 20 other equally uncomfortable middle-aged ladies wearing funny sun-hats and carrying shopping bags with "Remember '55" on them.

Eyes met eyes, flickered down to the identity labels to seek confirmation that the aged fellow opposite really was George, Ed or Rusty, and then, guiltily flickered back to eye level. "Well, if it isn't Jonny Steinberg? How are you? What 25 have you been up to?"

If the men were bad, the women were worse: not the wives, for we had never known them, but the Radcliffe "girls" whose twenty-fifth reunion coincided with ours. For us, Radcliffe had been more than the women's college attached to Harvard: unless one had a car, Radcliffe was the only available source of 30 inexpensive romance. There they were, the beautiful girls turned into middle-aged ladies. I could cope with Tom, Dick or Harry, but Jane, Laura or Charlotte were unbearable.

One of the wonderfully calm members of the permanent staff, who get paid by Harvard to organize twenty-fifth reunions, told me that my very language 35 about Radcliffe dated me. Classes older than ours speak of "Radcliffe ladies," classes younger of "Radcliffe women." Our generation of "silent fifties" is the only one to say "Harvard men" but "Radcliffe girls."

After the shock of age began to wear off a little, I saw that a twenty-fifth reunion is the most extraordinary therapy group ever devised. When in 1853, 40 Thomas Bullfinch of the class of 1814 first proposed to President Walker of Harvard that the twenty-fifth anniversary of graduation, "this Indian summer of life, should be taken advantage of to give interest to the celebration of Commencement," he'd hit on an idea of genius. As he shrewdly observed, "The Class also at this era has its numbers very nearly undiminished; its members are 45 among the distinguished members of the community, and they have more money to spend than when younger and more heart to spend it than when older."

How right he was. The reunion costs some $500,000, of which the university contributes half out of its own funds and the reunion class half; but Harvard 50 expects to get its share back many times over. Our predecessors of 1954, a harder-drinking but more generous lot, contributed over $2 million. We only managed a paltry $1,250,000, so Harvard had its reunion investment in us returned fivefold.

Bullfinch saw more deeply when he pointed to the "Indian summer of life" 55 and to the fact that a reunion was a peculiar opportunity to accept it. What we had to face in those five days was the transience of life and the passing of self. Different people reacted differently. There was a lot of clinging to shreds of disintegrating identities. The important Washington bureaucrat, clutching his unread *New York Times*, hurried to make that important phone call. The 60 famous American writer, desperately trying to look the celebrity and graciously accepting greetings from awed classmates who were now dentists in Brookline or Dedham, was no more immune from the pulverizing effect of the reunion than the lesser among us. Not only were we all reduced by the funny hats and T-shirts but also by the plain fact that all of us, born in 1933 and 1934, are now 65 irretrievably middle-aged, however bright the eye, full the head of hair or flat the belly.

A deep psychological wisdom underlies the Harvard twenty-fifth reunion, which is why Bullfinch's formula has worked so remarkably for 127 years. The reunion is a rite of passage, and everything combined to enhance the impact: 70 the confusion of registration, the shock of discovery, the presence of wife and family, the hours and hours of talking over breakfast, lunch and dinner, or late at night over beer and sandwiches.

Reunion closed, as Bullfinch intended, with our giving "interest to the cele-bration of Commencement." It was a Thursday morning (it always is), as we 75 strolled through a Harvard Yard thick with people. ... The great, ungainly academic procession shuffled into place as it had that Thursday in 1955, but there was one difference. We were in another part of it. As we passed University Hall and the seated statue of John Harvard, we walked through the Class of 1980 in their black caps and gowns. We wore suits and our crimson 1955 class 80 ties.

The Class of 1980 applauded us as ... , earlier, we had applauded the Class of 1930. We looked into their eyes, which seemed to ask, "Will I ever be that old?" Our eyes answered: "You will." But we knew that they could not believe it.

85

1. Starting with the eighth paragraph, what conclusions do you find that the writer has reached inductively?
2. What does the writer mean by "the transience of life and the passing of self" in the tenth paragraph?
3. What specific, concrete details support and explain the writer's conclusions?
4. What abstract generalizations does he present in specific, concrete words and phrases?

**5.** Check the etymology, denotation, and connotation of *engrossed, teeming, neoclassical, paltry, Indian summer, transience, bureaucrat, irretrievably, rite of passage.*

## ASSIGNMENTS

1. Discuss the differing kinds of particulars that would be necessary in order to justify the following general statements:
   a. We have a football team.
   b. We have a good football team.
   c. We have the best football team we have had in ten years.
   d. We have the best football team in the state.
   e. We have the best football team in the United States.
2. From one of the biological or physical sciences that you have studied, choose an example of inductive reasoning, preferably one in which you yourself have performed experiments, and write it up, showing the particulars involved and the generalization that can be drawn from them.
3. The first paragraph of Mark Twain's essay (Unit 15-D) recounts particular experiences through which he finally arrived at an understanding of the general meaning of the word *lagniappe*. Write an account either of your own gradual acquaintance with some previously unfamiliar technical word or phrase encountered since you came to college, or of how you arrived, through inquiries and listening, at the meaning of some new slang phrase not yet in the dictionaries.
4. Write an essay in which you discuss what you have found to be the prevailing opinion on your campus or among your classmates on an issue, such as working one's way through college, engaging in extracurricular activities, cheating on examinations, supporting student protesters, joining fraternities or sororities, living in coeducational dormitories. Or if you prefer, write on student opinion on some state, national, or international issue. Be sure that your generalization fits the evidence that you are able to produce and that you make allowances for the size of your sample.
5. After reading "The Language of Uncertainty" (Unit 13-B), decide what percentages you yourself might reasonably imply by, or infer from, each of the following statements. Compare your figures with those of other members of the class.
   a. Everybody voted in the election.
   b. Nearly everybody voted in the election.
   c. Most people voted in the election.
   d. Many people voted in the election.
   e. Some people voted in the election.
   f. A few people voted in the election.
   g. Nobody voted in the election.

# UNIT 14

# *Deduction*

Deductive thinking is, in a sense, the reverse of inductive thinking, but they are interdependent. In induction we analyze particular instances to establish a general truth, but in deduction we begin with a general truth and from it "deduce," or derive, knowledge of a particular instance. Inductively, we progress from the parts to the whole; deductively, from the whole to the parts. The relationship between these two methods of reasoning can be visualized as two funnel-shaped containers placed with their wide openings together. The upper one, the inductive method, pours everything it has collected into the lower one, which then narrows this down to a specific deduction.

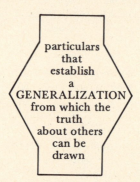

For example, doctors learned by inductively examining many patients that the combined evidence of a fever, a sore throat, and a particular kind of rash probably indicates a case of measles. Today, a doctor who finds all these symptoms in a patient will diagnose the case deductively in this way: All patients having a combination of certain symptoms have measles; this patient has such a combination of symptoms; therefore this patient has measles.

We use both induction and deduction constantly in our everyday thinking. In this unit, however, we shall concentrate on the deductive method as we did on induction in the preceding unit, to familiarize you with the uses and to warn you against the misuses peculiar to it.

Historically, the deductive process was established long before the inductive method as we now know it was developed. It proceeded from assumptions based on various sources: tradition, the works of Aristotle, the Bible. But in modern science, deduction logically follows induction, as Huxley has illustrated. Scientists take general truths, established inductively through testing, and draw conclusions based on them about particular instances. Induction, as we have noted, never arrives at more than strong probability. The law of gravitation, for example, assumes that all bodies will continue to fall only because all those observed in the past have done so. In contrast, deduction arrives at complete certainty within its own terms. If, to continue our example, we accept the statement that all bodies fall and that this is a body, the conclusion that this body will fall becomes inescapable.

The pattern of deductive reasoning is best seen through the **syllogism,** which logicians use in a variety of forms. This consists of three parts: two statements called premises, and a conclusion that derives from them by a process Stuart Chase has called "as automatic as a slot-machine." This is the classic example of a syllogism, with each part labeled:

> Major premise—All men are mortal.
> Minor premise—Socrates is a man.
> Conclusion—Therefore Socrates is mortal.

A syllogism should contain three terms (do not confuse these with premises). In this example the major term is "mortal," the middle term is "man," and the minor term is "Socrates." The middle term appears in both the major and the minor premise, and so it cancels out, leaving the minor term and the major term equated. This can be presented as a formula:

$$a = b$$
$$c = a$$
$$c = b$$

A diagram shows the relationship in another way. Because "Socrates" is included in "men" and "men" are included in "mortality," "Socrates" must of necessity be included in "mortality," too:

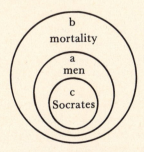

The conclusion arrived at through syllogistic reasoning is always logically *valid* if the terms are accurate and correctly arranged, but if they are not, it cannot be valid. Here are three examples of errors in using syllogistic reasoning:

**(1)**                    All fish can swim.
                          John can swim.
                          Therefore John is a fish.

The diagram shows where the error lies. "Swimming" includes "fish" and also "John," but fish are not the only creatures who swim, and so John's ability to swim does not make him a part of "fish," as a bass or a trout would be. Therefore the deduction is not valid.

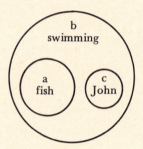

**(2)**                    All men drown in deep water.
                          John is a man.
                          .Therefore John will drown in deep water.

Here, the terms are properly arranged but the major premise is an inaccurate generalization. "Drowning" does not include all "men," only those who cannot swim, and John may belong to the group who can swim. Therefore the deduction is not *true*.

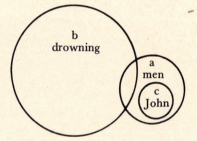

**(3)**                    All mammals nurse their young.
                          Turtles are mammals.
                          Therefore turtles nurse their young.

Here, the terms are again properly arranged, but the minor premise is inaccurate. "Nursing their young" includes all "mammals," but "mammals" do not include "turtles." Therefore the conclusion is false, and in the diagram "turtles" stand outside the concept of "nursing their young."

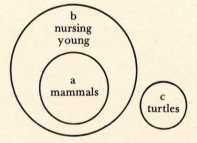

The important thing to note is that *the truth of a valid conclusion depends entirely on the reliability of the premises.*

Syllogistic reasoning may seem only a kind of game, but its importance becomes clear when we examine the actual logic behind some of our own hasty conclusions. "Bob shouldn't go to law school; he's one of the stupid Joneses." What is the reasoning here? Part of it looks like the following when we supply the implied but unexpressed major premise:

> Stupid people should not go to law school.
> Bob is a stupid person.
> Therefore he should not go to law school.

We are probably willing to accept the generalization, which is the major premise here; it seems a reasonable assumption. But what of the minor premise—what evidence have we that Bob is stupid? For this we have to go back to an earlier implied deduction, which reads:

> All the Joneses are stupid.
> Bob is a Jones.
> Therefore Bob is stupid.

Here the major premise is harder to accept. It may prove on closer examination to be based only on gossip, or at least to be an overstatement; perhaps some of the Joneses are stupid but Bob is one of the exceptions. Or if we are able to accept the generalization, the minor premise may not hold; perhaps Bob is adopted. In any event, this examination of our reasoning may lead us to be less satisfied with our first casual conclusion and to concede that we should let Bob's fitness for law school be determined by his performance on entrance examinations.

A football player once wrote in a theme that the trouble with his college was that "Writing is taught to too great an extent, thus causing players to be ineligible, games to be lost, and the college to lose its standing among institutions of higher learning." One suspects that even a devoted football fan, faced with the "general truth" to be found lurking behind this remark, would not attempt to defend it, for arranged syllogistically, the major deduction runs something like this:

Major premise:   All reputable colleges should have as their primary purpose the winning of football games.
Minor premise:   This is a reputable college.
Conclusion:       Therefore this college should have as its primary purpose the winning of football games.

Two students decided that they would not study a foreign language "because it wasn't practical." The unvoiced assumption behind their complaint, the suppressed major premise of their argument, was that only practical subjects (by which they presumably meant those that would help them earn money) are worth studying. Confronted with this generalization, they would have been logically compelled to revise their original statement.

Many of our conclusions rest, like the previous examples, on general assumptions—often unstated, sometimes not clear even to ourselves, and sometimes discovered only to be found false. There is no better way to learn how to read and write well—that is, to detect errors in the thinking of others and to think more accurately yourself—than to train yourself to discover these underlying assumptions and to examine their validity. But how can we determine the soundness of the generalization from which we wish to reason deductively? Let us examine its sources:

**a.** An unquestionable assumption like "All men are mortal," which has been reaffirmed by human experience from its beginning

**b.** Some less positively established inductive conclusion (see Unit 13), in which case we may need to examine the evidence on which it rests

**c.** A conclusion arrived at through a previous syllogistic deduction, as we have noted in the example of Bob Jones's stupidity, in which case we may need to examine the validity of the deductive reasoning that produced it

**d.** A statement by a person whose authority we shall need to establish adequately

**e.** An assumption that we fix arbitrarily by definition—for example, we could deduce whether or not to classify a certain type of music as good if we accept as an assumption, "Good music is music that elevates the soul."

As we have seen here and in the two preceding units, cause and effect, induction, and deduction are almost inseparable, and in much of our reasoning we use a combination of these logical processes. But in the assignments concluding this unit you should concentrate, for practice, on reasoning deductively. You are again warned, as in Unit 13, not to confuse the pattern of organization with the method of reasoning. Like its opposite, *inductive*, the term *deductive* is often used to describe a rhetorical pattern; in the deductive pattern a general statement is followed by particulars (see the section on organization in Unit 13). But here we are using the word to mean a kind of reasoning, not a kind of organization.

Some suggestions for good deductive reasoning follow:

**1. Recognize the general assumption behind your deduction.** Think back through your conclusions to their logical source, lest you find yourself making statements whose implications you cannot reasonably accept. If you conclude that social life on a campus is bad for academic work, you must be prepared to support a generalization about the purpose of a college that will not permit socializing.

**2. Consider stating your general assumption clearly.** It is not necessary to make it known, but there are advantages is doing so, even early in your paper. Then both you and your reader will be able not only to weigh its worth readily but to check against it the particular issue you discuss and the conclusion you draw. For example, if you reason that changes need to be made in the dormitory rules or in your curriculum, make clear the purpose that you feel the rules or the course of study should fulfill. The unexpressed or deliberately suppressed major premise can cause confused thinking in both you and your reader.

**3. Make certain the generalization you draw from is sound.** If it is one that may not be readily recognized as such by your reader, you should spend some time establishing it, perhaps inductively, before you proceed to reason from it. Have you experience or other evidence—witnesses, authorities—to support it? The greater your experience and knowledge of the subject on which you choose to reason deductively, the sounder will be your assumption (the major premise) and the more acceptable will be the conclusion you draw from it.

**4. Be sure your reasoning from your assumption is valid.** The particular you discuss (your minor premise) and your conclusion must be logically in line with the generalization from which you are working. If you start with the assumption that the primary purpose of a fraternity is to foster lasting friendships among its members, you will then show what present practices are antagonistic to this purpose and what changes would further it. If you feel that the chief object of a vacation is change, one set of deductions will logically follow; if rest, another set. Your reader will probably be willing to follow you in either line of thought, so long as your reasoning is consistent within itself.

**5. See that your particulars and your generalization are in accord.** Your conclusion about a particular is certain only if your major premise embraces *all* things in the class to which that particular belongs. But the deductive process may help you to arrive at useful conclusions even though the major premise is not all-embracing: the fact that most students enjoy watching football games does not prove that Frank does, but it indicates a strong likelihood. Just remember that if your assumption is qualified with a percentage or with words such as *most, usually,* or *sometimes,* your conclusion is only *probably, likely,* or *maybe.* (See item 6, page 204.)

## EXAMPLES

As with induction (Unit 13), the best example of deduction is to be found by returning to Huxley's essay at the end of Unit 12, where the two types of reasoning can be seen as they operate together.

**14-A**       AN OPEN LETTER TO BLACK PARENTS:
            SEND YOUR CHILDREN TO THE LIBRARIES
                       *Arthur Ashe*

This essay, here complete, is from the *New York Times* (February 1977). Ashe, an international tennis champion, retired from professional sports in 1980 because of heart trouble but continues to write sports commentary.

Since my sophomore year at University of California, Los Angeles, I have become convinced that we blacks spend too much time on the playing fields and too little time in the libraries.

Please don't think of this attitude as being pretentious just because I am a black, single, professional athlete. I don't have children, but I can make obser-  5
vations. I strongly believe the black culture expends too much time, energy and

effort raising, praising and teasing our black children as to the dubious glories of professional sport.

All children need models to emulate—parents, relatives or friends. But when the child starts school, the influence of the parent is shared by teachers and classmates, by the lure of books, movies, ministers and newspapers, but most of all by television. Which televised events have the greatest number of viewers?— Sports—the Olympics, Super Bowl, Masters, World Series, pro basketball play-offs, Forest Hills. ABC-TV even has sports on Monday night prime time from April to December. So your child gets a massive dose of O. J. Simpson, Kareem Abdul-Jabbar, Muhammad Ali, Reggie Jackson, Dr. J and Lee Elder and other pro athletes. And it is only natural that your child will dream of being a pro athlete himself.

But consider these facts: For the major professional sports of hockey, football, basketball, baseball, golf, tennis and boxing, there are roughly only 3,170 major league positions available (attributing 200 positions to golf, 200 to tennis and 100 to boxing). And the annual turnover is small. We blacks are a subculture of about 28 million. Of the 13½ million men, 5 to 6 million are under 20 years of age, so your son has less than one chance in 1,000 of becoming a pro. Less than one in a thousand. Would you bet your son's future on something with odds of 999 to 1 against you? I wouldn't.

Unless a child is exceptionally gifted, you should know by the time he enters high school whether he has a future as an athlete. But what is more important is what happens if he doesn't graduate or doesn't land a college scholarship and doesn't have a viable alternative job career. Our high school dropout rate is several times the national average, which contributes to our unemployment rate of roughly twice the national average.

And how do you fight the figures in the newspapers every day? Ali has earned more than $30 million boxing, O. J. just signed for $2½ million, Dr. J. for almost $3 million, Reggie Jackson for $2.8 million, Nate Archibald for $400,000 a year. All that money, recognition, attention, free cars, girls, jobs in the offseason—no wonder there is Pop Warner football, Little League baseball, National Junior Tennis League tennis, hockey practice at 5 A.M. and pickup basketball games in any center city at any hour.

There must be some way to assure that the 999 who try but don't make it to pro sports don't wind up on the street corners or in the unemployment lines. Unfortunately, our most widely recognized role models are athletes and entertainers—"runnin'" and "jumpin'" and "singin'" and "dancin.'" While we are 60 percent of the National Basketball Association, we are less than 4 percent of the doctors and lawyers. While we are about 35 percent of major league base-ball, we are less than 2 percent of the engineers. While we are about 40 percent of the National Football League, we are less than 11 percent of construction workers such as carpenters and bricklayers.

Our greatest heroes of the century have been athletes—Jack Johnson, Joe Louis and Muhammad Ali. Racial and economic discrimination forced us to channel our energies into athletics and entertainment. These were the ways out of the ghetto, the ways to get that Cadillac, those alligator shoes, that cashmere sport coat.

Somehow, parents must instill a desire for learning alongside the desire to be Walt Frazier. Why not start by sending black professional athletes into high schools to explain the facts of life? I have often addressed high school audiences, and my message is always the same. For every hour you spend on the athletic field, spend two in the library. Even if you make it as a pro athlete, your career will be over by the time you are thirty-five. So you will need that diploma.

Have these pro athletes explain what happens if you break a leg, get a sore arm, have one bad year or don't make the cut for five or six tournaments. Explain to them the star system, wherein for every O. J. earning millions there are six or seven others making $15,000 or $20,000 or $30,000 a year.

But don't just have Walt Frazier or O. J. or Abdul-Jabbar address your class. Invite a benchwarmer or a guy who didn't make it. Ask him if he sleeps every night. Ask him whether he was graduated. Ask him what he would do if he became disabled tomorrow. Ask him where his old high school athletic buddies are.

We have been on the same roads—sports and entertainment—too long. We need to pull over, fill up at the library and speed away to Congress and the Supreme Court, the unions and the business world. We need more Barbara Jordans, Andrew Youngs, union cardholders, Nikki Giovannis and Earl Graveses. Don't worry: we will still be able to sing and dance and run and jump better than anybody else.

I'll never forget how proud my grandmother was when I graduated from U.C.L.A. in 1966. Never mind the Davis Cup in 1968, 1969, and 1970. Never mind the Wimbledon title, Forest Hills, etc. To this day, she still doesn't know what those names mean. What matters to her was that of her more than thirty children and grandchildren, I was the first to be graduated from college, and a famous college at that. Somehow, that made up for all those floors she scrubbed all those years.

1. As the title indicates, Ashe has written a letter, not a formal argument, but his advice is based on the deduction that there are very few chances for success in professional athletics. What follows from this deduction?
2. What support does he give the deduction?
3. What use does he make of narrative, analogy, and analysis to support his argument?

---

*14-B*     ALEXANDER THE GREAT AND ALCOHOLISM
          *John Noble Wilford*

This report, here almost complete, is from the *New York Times* (September 1980). It describes recent research using current knowledge of alcoholism to reinterpret the behavior of Alexander the Great and ends with mention of other research interpreting Alexander's behavior as, instead, a response to his neurotic mother.

In 323 B.C., after years of conquering and a month-long debauch, Alexander the Great lay feverish in Babylon. He had a tremendous thirst and called for wine. He drank it, became delirious and died, four months short of his 33d birthday. Alexander had overrun most of the known world but, according to a new interpretation of his behavior, had lived and died an alcoholic.  5

Examining contemporary and historical accounts of Alexander in light of modern knowledge about the social, psychological and physiological aspects of heavy drinking, John Maxwell O'Brien of Queens College has concluded that the conqueror from Macedonia exhibited what modern clinicians consider "the classic symptoms of acute alcoholism" in the last seven years of his life.  10

For example, Alexander not only drank to excess but ordinarily continued drinking until he was incapacitated, a loss of control manifested by many problem drinkers. On these occasions, which became more and more frequent and extended, Alexander underwent drastic personality changes. He became unpredictably aggressive toward friends as well as enemies, suspicious of almost 15 everyone, incapable of tolerating criticism, remorseful over alcohol-related behavior and apparently convinced that new borders and horizons were the only remedies for his inner anguish.

Although he seemed to believe in his own divinity and indestructibility, Dr. O'Brien said, Alexander on a binge "became increasingly reckless, seemingly 20 inviting death in actions suggestive of the death-wish modern psychology associates with certain forms of alcoholism."

Dr. O'Brien has advanced this analysis of Alexander because it provides a textbook case of certain causes and effects of alcoholism and also a revised perspective on one of the world's greatest figures, whose short life and erratic 25 behavior has long fascinated and baffled historians.

Ancient accounts are replete with stories of Alexander's immoderate drinking, noting that he was "too fond of wine" or he "slept through the next day from drinking." But both ancient and modern chroniclers usually stopped short of labeling him an alcoholic or of ascribing his aberrant behavior to alcohol; 30 some even glossed over the excessive drinking as fabrications of Alexander's enemies.

Dr. O'Brien attributed this to the reluctance of scholars to believe that the conqueror of the ancient world could be a drunkard. "The alcoholic is viewed in our popular culture as seedy and ineffectual," Dr. O'Brien said, "and this 35 stereotype simply does not fit the undeniable greatness of the man."

According to Dr. O'Brien's study, it would have been surprising if Alexander had not been a heavy drinker. The Macedonians of his day were notorious for their drinking; the Greeks diluted their wine with water, but the Macedonians drank theirs straight—and often. Drinking prowess was a measure of manliness. 40

Alexander's father, King Philip, was renowned for his intemperance, and his mother, Olympias, was a devotee of the cult of Dionysus, the god of wine who was worshiped in orgies of intoxication. Moreover, Olympias continually urged Alexander to surpass his father, which he did with the drinking cup as well as the conquering sword.  45

The first clear-cut evidence that Alexander acted under the influence of alcohol, Dr. O'Brien said, was the burning of the royal palace at Persepolis in 330 B.C., seven years before his death. With torch in hand, a drunken Alexander led revelers in a procession in honor of Dionysus and threw the first firebrand, an act he bitterly regretted when sober. 50

Two years later, while in a drunken rage in Samarkand, Alexander seized a spear and killed Cleitus, the man who had once saved his life. Instantly appalled at what he had done, Alexander pulled the spear from the victim's body and tried to impale himself, but his bodyguards intervened. Later, in the manner of some alcoholics, Dr. O'Brien said, Alexander rationalized that it had not been 55 his fault, but Cleitus's, for starting the argument, or perhaps the act of a vengeful Dionysus.

Plutarch's biography of the conqueror described a mass orgy in 325 B.C. involving Alexander and his entire army: "Not a single helmet, shield or spear was to be seen, but along the whole line of march the soldiers kept dipping their 60 cups, drinking-horns or earthenware goblets into huge casks and mixing bowls and toasting one another, some drinking as they marched, others sprawled by the wayside."

Alexander's drinking grew more compulsive following the death of his most trusted commander, Hephaestion, in 324 B.C. They had been friends from youth 65 and, by most accounts, were lovers. Hephaestion also drank excessively. After successive drinking bouts, he came down with a fever and died after drinking a half-gallon of wine at breakfast. A distraught Alexander had the physician crucified for negligence.

The final year of Alexander's life was punctuated with massacres, bloody 70 purges and drunken binges. According to Dr. O'Brien's historical postmortem, Alexander died as a result of acute alcohol withdrawal, perhaps aggravated by malaria.

From what is known, therefore, Dr. O'Brien concluded that Alexander belongs in the category of cyclothymic drinkers. As described by two American 75 authorities on alcoholism, Drs. C. Peter Rosenbaum and John E. Beebe 3d, these drinkers are "a small but highly memorable group of people who seem extraordinarily dependent on the praise and esteem of others to feel good about themselves" and whose lives "seem to be muted forms of a manic-depressive cycle, hence the term 'cyclothymic.'" 80

Thomas W. Africa, professor of history at the State University of New York at Binghamton, is not sure that Alexander could be called "an alcoholic in the modern sense." His heavy drinking may have been more the symptom of deep psychological problems, rather than the cause, said Dr. Africa, who is writing a psychohistorical study of Alexander and his mother, Olympias. Alexander was 85 unstable, he said, because of his warped upbringing by the domineering, neurotic Olympias and became megalomaniacal and in the final years "openly distanced himself from reality."

"If he had lived today," Dr. Africa remarked, "Alexander would have spent a fortune on shrinks." 90

1. What pieces of Dr. O'Brien's evidence are cited by the reporter?
2. Into what different types can you classify them?
3. Why is Plutarch's biography important evidence?
4. Where is Macedonia and what was Alexander's connection with it?
5. Check the etymology, denotation, and connotation of *physiological, clinician, binge, chronicler, aberrant, glossed, fabrication, attributed, seedy, stereotype, notorious, prowess, intemperance, devotee, impale, intervene, orgy, aggravated, muted, megalomaniacal.*

---

*14-C*　　　　　　　　　LETTER FROM HOME
　　　　　　　　　　　　　*William Zinsser*

This essay, here complete, from the *New York Times* (May 1977), is by a member of the Yale faculty. What opinions does he share with the writer of the essay in Example D? with the writer of "The Fifth Freedom" (Unit 6-A)?

ANALYSIS

General problem

Now is the edgy time for Yale seniors. In three weeks they will graduate and join the rest of us out here in the real world. It is a place that they are inordinately afraid of.

Not all of them, of course, will take the icy plunge. Quite a few will stay on the academic assembly-line—in law 5 school or medical school or graduate school—to study for three or four years more.

Classification

This doesn't mean that they necessarily want to be lawyers or doctors or scholars. Some are continuing their education because their parents want them to. Some are 10 doing it just to postpone the day of decision. Some are doing it because lawyers and doctors make a good living. Some are doing it to acquire still another degree to impress a society in which they think credentials are the only currency. Some—the lucky ones—really do want to be law- 15 yers, doctors, scholars or specialists in a field that requires further skill.

Restatement of general problem

But they all are driven—those who are leaving Academia and those who are staying—by one message: Do Not Fail. It is a message that has been echoing in their heads 20 since they were admitted to the pre-kindergarten of their choice, beating less competitive toddlers. Score high, test well, play it safe. Next month's graduates have been so obsessively bent for four years on measurable achievement (grades) and a secure future (jobs) that they have hardly 25 had time to savor the present and to grow as well-rounded people. They know that the outside world is wary of experimenters, of late starters and temporary losers.

I'm talking about Yale students because I live in their midst and know them well. (I am Master of Branford College, one of Yale's twelve residential colleges. In our house I can lie awake and listen to some of the loudest stereo sets in the East. That, in fact, is why I lie awake.) And I'm talking about seniors because they are the ones who are most on my mind right now: panicky that they won't have enough A's to persuade an employer to hire them, though they are men and women I'd like to have working for me, if I were an employer, for qualities of intelligence and humor and humanity that don't show up on any chart.

But I could just as well be talking about Yale's juniors, sophomores and freshmen—or, I suspect, about the students at most colleges today. They are studying more and enjoying it less. At Yale, they play in fewer plays and musical groups, join fewer campus organizations, take part in fewer sports, carve out fewer moments just to linger and talk and put a margin around their lives. They are under pressure to do too much work in too little time.

If all their friends are studying in the library until it closes at midnight (and they are), they feel guilty if they want to go to a Woody Allen movie, though there is as much to be learned from a Woody Allen movie as from a book—much, in fact, that they will never learn from a book. Not surprisingly, their emotional health is often far from healthy. I see a lot of psychic disarray.

It is not that I don't wish them fame and fortune, especially the seniors as they lurch toward graduation, more stuffed with learning and shorn of money than they probably ever will be again. Obviously I do. But I also wish them a release from fear of the future. They should know that fame and fortune are not end products that they will automatically win if they follow a straight and safe route, but by-products that will accrue to them if they dare to poke down the unmarked side roads that lead to life's richest surprises.

Risk and change, art and music, joy and affection, the unexpected friendship of strangers—these are some of the essential tonics. "To affect the quality of the day, that is the highest of the arts," said Thoreau. I wish it could be chiseled over the door of every school, college, corporation and home.

Home is where the words "Do not fail" are first instilled and constantly repeated. One of next month's Yale gradu-

*Margin notes:*

Restatement of general problem

Minor premise

Restatement of minor premise

Example

*Line numbers:* 30, 35, 40, 45, 50, 55, 60, 65, 70

ates came to me on her first day as a freshman in 1973 and
said: "I want to be a great journalist—what courses should
I take for the next four years?" She wanted a blueprint at 75
seventeen. Many students come to me in the middle of
their sophomore year, afraid of changing the curriculum

**Example**

that they mapped but no longer think is the one that they
want to pursue. "If I don't make all the right choices now,"
one of them said, "it will be too late."                           80

Too late at eighteen? Sad words. They are growing up
old and set in their ways. They have been told to prepare
for one career—preferably one that will reflect well on
their parents—and to stick to it and succeed. They are not
told that they have a right to try many paths, to stumble 85

**Major premise**

and try something else, and to learn by stumbling. The
right to fail is one of the few freedoms not granted in our
Bill of Rights. Today it is more acceptable to change marriage partners than to change careers.

"Victory has very narrow meanings and can become a 90
destructive force," writes Bill Bradley in his book, "Life on
the Run." Bradley was an Ivy Leaguer himself and a
Rhodes Scholar—an earlier member of the same elite that

**Restatement of
major premise**

is now so preoccupied with success—before starting his
ten-year career of professional basketball, which has just 95
come to an end. "The taste of defeat," he writes, "has a
richness of experience all its own. To me, every day is a
struggle to stay in touch with life's subtleties. No one grows
without failing."

The fault is not with our children, but with the narrow- 100

**Conclusion**

ness of the flowerbed in which we expect them to germi-
nate. We are stunting their growth if we tell them that
there is only one "right" way to get through their education or to get through life. America has always been nour-
ished by mavericks and individualists—men and women 105
not afraid to go against the grain.

1. What, if anything, does Zinsser gain by delaying the statement of his major premise
   almost to the end?
2. The only analogy in the essay is at the very end, but many examples of figurative
   language are scattered throughout, beginning with "icy plunge" and "assembly-
   line" in the second paragraph. What others can you find and what do they contribute to the effectiveness of the essay?
3. Check the etymology, denotation, and connotation of *inordinately, credentials, currency, wary, lurch, accrue, tonics, elite, mavericks;* check the origin of *against the
   grain.*

*14-D*     AFTER GRADUATION, WHAT NEXT?
*Fred Hiatt*

This essay, three-quarters of which is given here, appeared first in the *Boston Globe* (May 1977). The writer, at that time a senior at Harvard, began by noting the changes on campus since the days of political activism and then quoted another student who claimed that many seniors were "genuinely concerned about the social, economic, and political problems of the world" and that after graduation they would "go out to work towards change."

Certainly, students can be "genuinely concerned" without occupying buildings. Concern, more than greed, motivates even many of the much-maligned pre-law and pre-med students in my class (though how long their concern will survive the conformist pressure of professional school is an open question). But for many of us . . . the concern is a complacent one.                                                5

One of my goals this year has been to teach the mechanics of typing to a cat I know, a cat who has always been fascinated by manual typewriters, pawing at the letter rods as they jumped out and watching with frustration when they lie quietly beyond his reach. I have spent hours pushing his paws on the keys and encouraging him to see the causal connection, to see that the letters have 10 no life of their own. But the cat, as fascinated as ever, still vainly hopes to catch one alive.

Similarly, many seniors are concerned, even fascinated, by their society and by its injustices, but baffled by the causal links, uncertain where the injustice comes from or what they could do about it. And so, though they are con- 15 cerned—"quiescent, but not acquiescent," as Harvard sociology professor David Riesman said—within a few years even many who are not yet pre-business will have lost interest in "working towards change."

Most of us, then, will pursue lucrative careers in business, law, or medicine. A survey of 1971 Harvard graduates showed more than 50 per cent choosing 20 one of the three within five years, and while the number of 1977 graduates going to law school may drop a bit, more will probably end up in business school.

Many will go not because they've wanted to be executives or attorneys, nor just to make money, but because they don't know what else to do. Part of the 25 appeal of the professional career is the desire, or need, for individual recognition. In school we learned to judge the quality of our work by the grade somebody else assigned it. At college we scrabbled for the prominent byline or the leading role on stage.

Now the reputation of the law school seems to matter more than what we 30 will do as lawyers, the prestige of the newspaper more than what we'd like to say in print. Only power and fame can bring "success" and happiness.

To opt for the cooperative, to work in legal aid without heading the office, to write without a byline, would be to reject everything we've been trained to be.

And that rejection would be doubly hard for women, who, instead of receiving 35
praise for spurning ego-gratification, would be blamed by many for regressing
to old passive roles.

Then, many seniors just don't see other options. Up to now, we've always
been most rewarded for performing the expected. To depart from the expected
now—to choose a career that doesn't guarantee power and $35,000 a year five 40
years from now—takes courage. Many Harvard graduates, though certainly not
all, can afford more easily than other college graduates to pass up the best-pay-
ing job; their family background and their degree render future starvation
unlikely.

Yet, most of us won't dare pass up that job. In a few years, we will persuade 45
ourselves that we "need" a car, a sunnier apartment, a winter vacation—and
that we "need" more money than we can imagine needing now. And as we
grow discouraged by the potential for real social change, working "within the
system" will seem more and more sensible—until one day we suddenly find
ourselves not infiltrators, but bulwarks, of that system. 50

Going to professional school is not the same as selling out, of course, and for
many women and minority graduates the struggle is just beginning. But many
of us seem to be headed past quiescence into acquiescence itself. Maybe the
only thing that can bring about a profound change is sex, the search for new
structures of romance. Senior year has affected different couples in different 55
ways. One man I know so feared a painful separation in June that he broke up
with his girlfriend in October.

Others, habitual commitment-phobics, relaxed during spring term, counting
on graduation day to disentangle them. Still others returned to the sad custom
of desperately searching for a mate to fill that yawning post-graduate loneliness. 60

For most seniors, however, the formulas are not so simple. At least some feminist values have seeped into the undergraduate consciousness and, together
with the seriousness with which most women face their careers, have prompted
new problems, new ground rules, new questionings of old assumptions. Whose
job should take priority—until now a problem for only a few, middle-class 65
career couples—is an issue, real or potential, for almost every graduate. If he
follows her, will the relationship suddenly seem more permanent than they
want it to be? If she follows him, is she giving in to sexist pressures?

Where political principles and the quest for adventure once stood in the way
of pure ambition, now only love interferes. He may work in a dead-end job to 70
help her through law school; she may settle for a second-rate medical school to
stay by his side.

It will be interesting to see, when we gather for our five-year reunion,
whether we have settled into our law firms with housewives and househusbands
at our sides, whether we have forsaken coupledom entirely—or whether the 75
compromises forced on us by relationships have derailed us from the straight,
ambitious track in a way that, for most of us, the search for adventure and the
commitment of political activism no longer can.

1. On what premises does Hiatt base his conclusions?
2. What specific, concrete details does he use?
3. What relationships can you see between Hiatt's opinions and those of Zinsser in the preceding example? of George F. Will in Unit 14-F?
4. How appropriate is the analogy of the inability of the cat to understand cause and effect?
5. Check the etymology, denotation, and connotation of *camaraderie, quiescent, acquiescent, bulwarks*.

---

*14-E*                          EDUCATION BY BOOKS
                                *Mark Van Doren*

This essay from the *Nation* (1933) is complete. The writer, a well-known poet, critic, and university professor, proposes a type of education that has since been put into practice in several colleges and many adult education programs.

Let us assume that an institution was founded for the sole purpose of requiring its members to read certain books. These members were called students, for the institution was something like a school or college; and there were a few exacting elders on hand who after announcing their authority began to teach.

The teaching in this institution, like the studying, was at the same time simple 5 and difficult. It consisted in the first place, as I have said, in requiring the students to read certain books. It consisted next in requiring that an intelligible account be rendered of the contents of each book. And it consisted last of all in requiring that the readers be able, in the course of discussing a given book, to prove that their memory of all previous books was accurate and complete.     10

It was as simple as that, and as difficult. The books were the acknowledged masterpieces of the past three thousand years—masterpieces of poetry, of history, of philosophy, of fiction, of theology, of natural science, of political and economic theory. There were two hundred or so of them, and none of them was read in an abridged edition. Neither was any of them approached through 15 a digest or a commentary, or through a biography of the author which told how many wives he had and what the biographer believed to be the modern significance of his mind. No, these books which the teachers selected for the students to read—Homer, the Bible, Herodotus, Thucydides, Aeschylus, Sophocles, Euripides, Aristophanes, Plato, Aristotle, Cicero, Lucretius, Vergil, Horace, 20 Ovid, Plutarch, Lucian, Marcus Aurelius, Plotinus, St. Augustine, the Volsunga Saga, the Song of Roland, Thomas Aquinas, Dante, Petrarch, Chaucer, Leonardo da Vinci, Machiavelli, Erasmus, More, Rabelais, Montaigne, Cervantes, Bacon, Shakespeare, Galileo, Grotius, Hobbes, Descartes, Leibnitz, Corneille, Racine, Molière, Milton, Spinoza, Locke, Newton, Swift, Voltaire, Fielding, 25 Hume, Rousseau, Adam Smith, Kant, Gibbon, Bentham, Goethe, Malthus, Hegel, Schopenhauer, Balzac, Mill, Darwin, Dickens, Thackeray, Marx, Tolstoy, Dostoevski, Pasteur, Ibsen, Nietzsche, Freud, Proust, Einstein—these authors,

or rather the principal works of these authors, were read naked and entire; and
understood.                                                                        30

A few students—some say a good many—had got into the institution by mistake. They complained about the lack of freedom to read what they pleased;
some of these books, they insisted, were not suited to their personalities, and
they had supposed that what one went to college for was to develop one's personality. Precisely, answered the head preceptor, closing the door behind them  35
with the most obvious and reckless relief. Others proved to be helpless once they
were face to face with an author's original sentences; they had been brought up
on outlines, introductions, histories of literature and thought, and collections of
excerpts, and so had long ago lost whatever ability to read they had been born
with. Still others had expected to learn a trade or a profession. Then there was  40
a final group of pedantic youngsters who snorted at the reading list because it
was not contemporary. They wanted as swift an introduction as possible to the
civilization about them. To the reply that this was that, they were very scornful
as they scurried off to become freshmen in some up-to-date college where field
trips to factories alternated in the weekly schedule with lectures on large and  45
immediate subjects.

These gone, the others settled down to the task that had been so arbitrarily
assigned them. At regular intervals they met in small groups with two or more
teachers who questioned them closely concerning the contents of the required,
the inevitable book. If they revealed by their answers that they had read it  50
badly, they were forced to read it again. There was no going forward until
Aristotle's conception of the individual, or Grotius's theory of natural law, or
the unity of "King Lear" was clearly stated. No excursions were made into the
culture of the Greeks or the domestic life of the Middle Ages; merely the books
themselves were read, discussed, and understood. And so on for four years.  55

At the end of which time a generation of students was set loose upon a world
with many of whose aspects they were not at the moment prepared to cope.
The only thing, indeed, to be said in their favor was that they were educated.
They were equipped, that is, with so much understanding of what the best
human brains had done in three thousand years that they realized without dif-  60
ficulty how few contemporary brains—naturally—were of the best. They were
so competent in the recognition of theory that they felt strangely at home in a
world most of whose citizens lived by theories without knowing it. They were
able to reduce a kind of order out of the childish chaos which they slowly recognized contemporary literature to be. They missed a great many ideas and  65
distinctions which they knew had been fruitful in past centuries, and some of
them set about considering the possibility of restoring these to an intellectually
impoverished world. Whether they succeeded is not yet known. But it can be
said of them that in their own minds they continued to be fairly secure. For
never would there be written a book which they could not understand simply  70
by reading it from the first word to the last. They might not save the world.
They might not change it. But they would comprehend it.

1. State the writer's argument in the form of a syllogism.
2. What general attitudes is the writer cricitizing by his description of the four kinds of dissatisfied students? What does he imply are the failings of secondary school education?
3. Classify the benefits he expects from the program he describes.
4. Check the etymology, denotation, and connotation of *preceptor, pedantic, scurried, arbitrarily, recognition.*

---

*14-F*                     THE HELL OF AFFLUENCE
                             *George F. Will*

This essay appeared in *Newsweek* (March 1977), for which the writer is a regular columnist. In the introduction, omitted here, Will quotes the economist John Kenneth Galbraith on the disappointments people in an affluent society may feel.

Galbraith's lament about the values of an affluent society may be valid, but it does not explain the disappointment many people feel about affluence. There is a vague feeling that economic growth has not fulfilled its promise. Affluence has not led to a decline in economic cares, to less preoccupation with money. Envy has increased while society has become more wealthy. This paradox is a 5 subject of an intriguing new book, *Social Limits to Growth*, by Fred Hirsch, a British economist.

Hirsch distinguishes between the "material economy" and the "positional economy." The latter is increasingly important and concerns goods, services and jobs that are *inherently* minority enjoyments. As affluence satisfies basic mate- 10 rial needs, more income and energy are devoted to "positional competition" for such things as a "choice" suburban home, an "exclusive" vacation spot, an "elite" education, a "superior" job. As affluence increases, competition moves more and more from the material sector to the "positional" sector, where one person's gain is a loss for many other persons. Unlike the demand for radial tires 15 and Right Guard, supplies of which can be expanded indefinitely, each demand for a positional good can be satisfied only by frustrating the similar demands of many other people.

Affluence sharply increases competition for positional goods. So society's economic success increases frustrations and tensions. The feeling that Affluent Man 20 is more harried than ever is sometimes explained in terms of consumption of material goods: the supply of such goods increases while the time to consume stays constant. But an additional explanation is the time and income needed for "positional competition."

Materially, growth has been a leveling force. Cars and air conditioners and 25 other luxuries of one generation have become the "necessities" of the next. But now affluent consumers face increasing frustration because the collective advance of the middle class is *inherently* impossible regarding "positional goods."

Tension, not satisfaction, results when the masses, observing the top strata of society, acquire an appetite for "elite" education, "superior" jobs, beachfront property. Positions of status and leadership, like beachfront, cannot be expanded to become majority enjoyments. The problem of the "positional economy" is social congestion: the desires of the middle class have expanded beyond middle-class opportunities.

The dominant political aspiration of the modern age is equality, but Hirsch's theory of the "positional economy" suggests that, in an important way, the affluent society will become steadily less egalitarian. Pursuit of positional goods will become steadily more important, and those goods are *inherently* restricted to a minority.

The complexity of positional striving is apparent in higher education. Economic growth has made possible the vast expansion of what is called "educational opportunity." But one reason there are so many bored or sullen students is that for many of them college is not an "opportunity." It is what Hirsch calls a "defensive necessity." The sullen student pursues a degree only because it will raise his income above what it would be if others got degrees and he did not.

This scramble for position is an aspect of modern society's mania for "credentials," like the current absurd pursuit of meaningless master's degrees. As Hirsch says, there is a sense in which "more education for all leaves everyone in the crowd standing on tiptoe and no one getting a better view." And the number of persons who are, or (as important) think they are, educationally equipped for "superior" jobs increases faster than the number of such jobs.

Well, maybe not. Today, even more than in 1935, there is much truth in what Bertrand Russell then said facetiously:

"Work is of two kinds: first, altering the position of matter at or near the earth's surface relatively to other such matters; second, telling other people to do so. The first is unpleasant and ill paid; the second is pleasant and highly paid. The second kind is capable of indefinite extension: there are not only those who give orders, but those who give advice as to what order should be given."

1. On what premises does Will base his claim that disappointment is inevitable for members of an affluent society?
2. Parts of Will's discussion can be stated as syllogisms:
   a. Affluence increases competition for "positional goods."
      American society is affluent.
      American society is increasingly competitive for "positional goods."
   b. Competition for "positional goods" causes tensions and frustrations.
      American society is competitive for "positional goods."
      American society has tensions and frustrations.
   Can you make other syllogisms based on other parts of the essay?
3. Check the etymology, denotation, and connotation of *affluence, paradox, inherently, elite, harried, collective, egalitarian, sullen, mania, facetiously.*

*14-G*               OUR GRASS IS NOT GREENER
                     *Ken Wank (student)*

There are many elements in today's society that may change people's attitudes from apathy toward life's difficulties to facing the fact that conflicts and
compromises are part of everyone's life. In the short story, "The Enormous
Radio," by John Cheever, the agonies of real life are broadcast directly into the
living room of the main character, Irene Westcott, through a large, malfunc- 5
tioning radio. Having always thought that she was in complete control of her
life, Irene expects to hear only the serious music she prefers, but finds herself
suddenly tuned in to the daily lives and traumas of her neighbors. She feels
compelled to keep listening, even though the discovery that she is surrounded
by people who are worried about money, health, and old age, chips away her 10
belief that she has achieved her goal of a sheltered life with no major problems.

There is a valuable lesson to be learned from this study of human nature.
Life's struggles are very much the same for each of us. Lack of money, old age,
and sickness may present problems to anyone. Although many people cannot
accept the fact that life is filled with hardship, we should recognize problems 15
as part of the human condition and learn to deal with them, to cope in a prob-
lem-filled world.

Some people find temporary solace by overlooking their problems in the hope
that things will work themselves out at a later date. These people try to fool
themselves into thinking that life is what they would like it to be, rather than 20
what it really is. In the story, Irene disposes of her problem of spending too
much money for clothes by telling herself that she is sure she will be able to pay
the bill next month. She cannot allow herself to be considered one of the ordinary mortals plagued with ordinary problems. She wants to believe that she has
arranged her life so that heartache won't exist. To accomplish this, she has 25
refused to become involved in problems. She did not attempt to comfort her
husband, Jim, when he realistically stated his disappointment about his business
and his own future. At this point in the story, there is no evidence to indicate
that Irene will acknowledge or deal with her problems.

History and common sense tell us that human problems have existed from 30
the beginning of the human race. The people who accept the view that a problem is a part of life rather than something which may vanish if ignored, will be
able to make strides in dealing with their problems. We cannot hide from problems indefinitely. Irene's problems surface when her husband reveals their
financial situation and his displeasure with her past actions. Whether or not 35
Irene copes with her problems in the future, she now knows that she is just as
vulnerable to the trials and tribulations as the masses.

It is a valuable experience to learn that we cannot arrange our lives so that
we will escape all chances of becoming ill, growing older, having an accident,
being lonely, or needing more money. Facing our problems involves acknowl- 40
edging that we may be responsble for them. If we are, we must analyze our
past actions and motives so that we can avoid repeating the same mistakes. It

also involves acknowledging the fact that some problems cannot be solved. A flat denial that problems exist indicates a lack of honesty, courage, and maturity. Facing our problems and admitting our responsibility may be painful, but we 45 cannot hope to solve any of them unless we first face them.

1. What are the premises that underlie this argument?
2. To what extent does this writer agree with the premises and discussion in Example D?

---

*14-H*                    LIGHT FROM AN APE'S JAW
                              *Robert Ardrey*

This essay is part of a chapter in *African Genesis* (1961), Ardrey's account of his efforts to discover traces in Africa of the earliest human beings.

Johannesburg brooded on its golden reef in the golden, southern autumn. A last rare storm of the rainy season darkened Dart's upper-floor office at the Medical School. My mood of discouragement returned. Fossil bones of extinct animals piled up before me. Unfamiliar Latin names assailed my eardrums. Despite all the best efforts of this sandy, smiling, persuasive, india rubber man, 5 I could gain no brainhold on concepts so fearfully specialized. Then I found in my hands what seemed a human jaw.

I mentioned in passing, in the introductory chapter of this account, the jaw of a twelve-year-old southern ape which Raymond Dart showed me on our first meeting. This was that jaw. And as I held it for the first time—staring into its 10 headless, disconnected history as into the darkness surrounding Cardinal Newman's aboriginal calamity—my discouragement fell away. My sense of incompetence vanished. One needed nothing but the lay common sense of a juryman to return a verdict that at some terrible moment in most ancient times, murder had been done.                                                                   15

The jaw was heavy. Three-quarters of a million years of residence on the floor of a dolomite cave had turned its bone and dentine to stone. The jaw seemed human. The cusped pattern of the teeth would have been familiar to any dentist. And the jaw seemed young. Several of the permanent molars were only partially erupted. One canine tooth had not yet come in at all, though I 20 could see its point hovering in the tooth canal. But the jaw while both young and heavy with antiquity was not human; for had the skull been attached, it would have revealed a braincase little larger than that of a chimpanzee.

What I held in my hand was the last remains of an adolescent australopithecine whose life had been brought short by a heavy blow. The four front teeth 25 were missing. Just below was a cracked, abraded area where the blow had fallen partially splitting the jawbone on the left side and breaking it quite through on the right. The injury could scarcely have occurred as some post-mortem indignity of nature afflicted on an old jaw lying about the cave, for in that case the

fragments would have been scattered about. Flesh must have held the frag- 30
ments together to be fossilized as a single whole. Nor could the blow—or other
simultaneous blows—have resulted in anything but death. There was no least
sign of knitting along the lines of the fracture.

My mind struggled to recapture the situation. Could the injury have been
acquired accidentally? By a fall, for instance? It seemed unlikely. When falling, 35
one inclines to land on almost any sector of one's anatomy other than the point
of the jaw. I thought of the cave in which the mandible had been found. Could
a rock jarred loose from the cave roof have been the instrument of accidental
injury? But to provide such a target for a falling fragment, one would have to
visualize the youthful man-ape as sleeping on the cave floor with his jaw 40
directed neatly to heaven, and even this unlikely situation brought difficulties.
The scar on the jawbone, rough and abraded, had an area of less than a square
inch. No falling rock so small as to leave a scar of this dimension could conceivably be heavy enough to produce the damage.

I dismissed accident as the mother of injury. The youthful creature had died 45
of purposeful assault.

I considered the means by which death might have been administered. Could
a fist have done it? Yes, a human fist to a human child. But the jawbone of the
southern ape, lacking a chin eminence, is more heavily constructed than ours.
This child's jaw had the thickness of bone that one would find in a man. The 50
aggressor, on the other hand, could have swung no such power as an adult
human male. *A. robustus* is not found at Makapan. And *A. africanus*,° we
recall, stood four feet tall and weighed, at the outside, ninety pounds. To visualize a fist causing such injury one would have to see a ninety-pound human
boy with a single swing knock out his father's front teeth and break the jaw in 55
two places.

A fist seemed unlikely. I inspected the point of impact where the blow had
landed. It was a rough place, very slightly flattened. Would a piece of stone,
grasped up impetuously from the cave floor and driven or thrown against the
jaw leave a scar of this order? It was possible, but it was not probable. A jagged, 60
sharp-cornered, uneroded rock fragment such as one finds in caves, to have
achieved fractures of the jaw on both sides, would almost surely at its point of
impact have left a more decisive mark. As compared with the likelihood of a
purposeful bludgeon of some sort—a bone or wooden club which would have
left a flattened, roughened mark precisely like that beneath my thumb—the 65
use of an expedient stone shrank into moderate improbability.

The afternoon darkened with a fleeting thunderstorm. A window rattled with
the earth movement of a collapsing tunnel in the gold reef a mile below us. I
had put the jaw on Dart's desk, just before me, and it jiggled. Dart stood at the
window looking out at the storm while I contemplated the remnant of antique 70
assassination. Evidence for murder lay clearly before me, but the mere question
of murder shrank rapidly in significance. A specter far and away more grisly

---

° *A. robustus* and *A. africanus* are the scientific names of two types of ape.

entered the dark periphery of my consciousness. Long before the time of man, had this creature surrendered his life to a weapon?

1. Would Ardrey agree with Huxley that much scientific reasoning is simply "lay common sense" (Unit 12-I, opening paragraphs)?
2. What steps of reasoning does he take to reach each of these conclusions: (a) the ape died young; (b) it died from a blow; (c) it was killed by another creature; (d) it was struck by a weapon?
3. Which steps or parts of steps require only "lay common sense" and which require some special knowledge?
4. Check the etymology, denotation, and connotation of *brooded, assailed, india rubber, aboriginal, calamity, dolomite, dentine, cusped, molars, erupted, canine tooth, canal, australopithecine, abraded, mandible, assault, bludgeon, expedient, assassination, periphery.*

## ASSIGNMENTS

1. To test the validity of the following statements, supply the general assumptions that underlie them and arrange them in syllogistic form. Then point out any flaws revealed in the facts or the logic.
   a. I'm glad to find that both my new chemistry professors are fat, because they're sure to be good-natured and easygoing.
   b. Jack must be twenty-one because he just got married.
   c. American automobiles are getting better every year: they have more equipment and more different styles and are more expensive.
   d. Maggie must be Irish because she comes from Boston, which has a large Irish population, and her name sounds Irish.
   e. Tom and Jane will never be honor students; they're both Phys Ed majors.
2. Note the interdependence of the forms of reasoning discussed in Units 12–14.
   a. Go back to Unit 12, "Cause and Effect," and reread Huxley's "The Method of Scientific Investigation" (Example I), examining his illustrations of the deductive reasoning that accompanies the inductive method.
   b. Go to Unit 16, and read Krutch's "Killing for Sport" (Example G). Notice the implied generalization in paragraph 2 that "all activity that lessens the amount of vitality in the world is evil." Complete the syllogism and discuss it, as fact and as logic. Do the same with the assumption in paragraphs 5 and 6 that "all pleasure resulting from cruelty is wrong." What evidence does he offer in support of this generalization?
3. Look through a copy of a popular magazine, examining the advertisements in search of examples of deductive reasoning. Do not be discouraged by the absence of an expressed major premise in such appeals as "Use ——, the choice of thousands." Supply the underlying generalization, decide on its source (see page 224), and determine its soundness and the truth and validity of the deductions made from it. (You may have to draw up more than one syllogism in order to express all the implications of the implied reasoning.)
4. In a famous short story entitled "The Other Side of the Hedge," E. M. Forster pictures the confusion of a man from a highly competitive society upon entering a

world where athletes run and swim for the joy of running and swimming, with no one to race against, and singers sing for the joy of singing, although there is no one to listen. Being as objective as possible, examine the assumptions underlying some of our ordinary activities, such as brushing our teeth, smoking, watching a football game, playing on a team, fishing, going to religious services, enrolling in college, cutting classes, watching popular TV shows, having a hobby, joining a club devoted to that hobby, getting a suntan, participating in student government, joining a fraternity or sorority, playing a guitar in private, playing a guitar in public, or refusing (for reasons of time? health? morality? religion?) to enter into some activity that others indulge in and urge on you. Do not be satisfied with the first explanation that comes to mind. Push your thinking as far back into your basic assumptions as you can. When you have found a subject among these possibilities (or among others suggested by them), write an essay that makes clear the deductive logic, or lack of logic, involved.

5. Examine carefully one of your own strongly held and perhaps frequently voiced opinions, or an opinion held by a friend, a relative, a teacher, or a political leader, to see on what assumption or assumptions it is based. Then write an essay on the subject, using deductive reasoning.

# UNIT 15

# *Definition*

The further you go with your education, the more you must enlarge your vocabulary, both general and specialized. Biology, grammar, music, chemistry, economics, drafting, literature—each has its own terminology which beginners must learn before they can understand the field. Changing world conditions produce new terms to meet new needs, and we constantly encounter new words and phrases or old ones that have taken on new meanings. Semantics, the study of meaning, emphasizes the need for a more accurate use of words. Notice how much attention textbooks give to definition and how often on examinations you are asked to define, and you will see what an important role definition plays in expository writing.

## *The Formal Definition*

A formal definition is based on a concise, logical pattern that permits a maximum of information in a minimum of space. It has three parts: the **term** (word or phrase) to be defined; the **class** of object or concept to which the term belongs; the **differentiating characteristics** that distinguish what the term defines from all others of that class.

| *term* | | *class* | *differentiating characteristics* |
|---|---|---|---|
| Water | is | a liquid | made up of molecules of hydrogen and oxygen in the ratio of 2 to 1. |
| An owl | is | a bird | with large head, strong talons, and nocturnal habits. |

Practice in writing such formal definitions is good mental discipline and an excellent training in conciseness and care in the use of words. You may find it surprisingly difficult to make accurate, generally acceptable definitions, in your own words, of the most familiar terms; but you will seldom get credit for knowing what something is unless you can define it.

**1. Do not define a word with *is* or *are when* or *is* or *are where*.** In "Vacations are when people don't work" and "A grocery is where food is sold," the "when" and "where" clauses modify the verbs "are" and "is" because they follow them, instead of modifying "vacations" and "grocery." In a definition, *is, are, was,* and *were* function like equal marks; the word or group of words forming the definition should match the grammatical structure of the word or words it defines. "Vacations are times when people don't work" ("Vacations = times"); "A grocery is a store where food is sold"; "To run is to move quickly"; "*Lambent* means *softly bright.*"

**2. Do not define a word by mere repetition.** "A baked potato is a potato that has been baked" adds nothing to what the term "baked potato" has already told us.

**3. Do define a word in simpler and more familiar terms.** The purpose of definition is to clarify, not to confuse. In his eighteenth-century dictionary, Samuel Johnson humorously defined "network" as "anything reticulated or decussated at equal distances with interstices between the intersections"—a well-known example of how *not* to define. Compare it with the definition of the same word in your own college dictionary.

**4. Keep your class small but adequate.** It should be large enough to include everything covered by the term you are defining but no larger. To define the term *lieutenant,* the class *soldier* is too small, because there are lieutenants in the Navy and police as well as in the Army and Marines. On the other hand, the class *officer* is too large because it includes the noncommissioned and commissioned. *Commissioned officer* is a happy compromise.

**5. State the differentiating characteristics precisely.** "A flute is a musical instrument played by blowing" is too general because it covers far too many musical instruments that are not flutes.

> In your own words, without help from a dictionary, write formal one-sentence definitions of the following familiar terms:(1) apple; (2) cow; (3) dictionary; (4) eye; (5)typewriter; (6) vinegar; (7) microscope; (8) foul ball; (9) professor; (10) democracy. Then check the five "warnings" and make any necessary revisions and corrections before handing in your definitions.

## The Essay of Definition

The difficulties you encountered with summaries in Unit 7 when you packed all your information into a few words have probably shown you the limitations of a brief definition. Dictionaries must be similarly brief, but for most purposes additional information is desirable. In the essay of definition you may write as much as you find necessary to make your definitions accurate, clear, and useful for your readers.

Catch and hold your **reader's interest.** A formal one-sentence definition usually has as much interest for a reader as a mathematical equation. The essay of definition, however, can be personal, amusing, vigorous, stimulating, memorable. But always remember that *your first duty is to define.* It is not essential to include a formal definition; but your paper must be an expansion of the basic material that would make one, never an evasion of it. Without this fact in mind, you may find that you have written a charming informal assay on a given subject but not a definition of it.

Choose a **generic subject,** not a specific one. We define a dog, for instance, rather than our Rover; a cathedral, rather than Notre Dame of Paris; supersonic aircraft, rather than the Concorde. (Note the kinds of topics suggested at the end of this unit.) Describe particular persons and things to illustrate your definition but not as your main subject.

To develop your basic data in an essay of definition and make it interesting, you may use singly or in combination any of the expository methods we have examined. Note how many are in the suggestions that follow.

**1. Descriptive details** are often valuable in the essay of definition. For example, the bare definition of a dog as a "carnivorous domesticated mammal of the family Canidae" will be clearer with descriptive details as to size, build, color, use, and so on.

> The *masonquo* is a six-stringed lyre having a hollow leather-covered sound-chamber much like that of a banjo. It has a bridge and, since it lacks a neck or fingerboard, the strings are stretched to a framework of sticks. The keys are primitive but ingenious and effective. All six strings are struck simultaneously with a small piece of leather or a feather. (Harold Courlander, *Musical Quarterly*.)

**2. Examples and incidents** (narration) can make the definition of a general subject more specific. Protestantism might be clarified by reference to the Lutheran or other denomination. Or incidents may be used to make abstract terms concrete: the old story of Abe Lincoln's walking miles to return a few cents was popular because, by illustrating honesty in action, it made the idea of that virtue much more vivid than could any discussion of honesty in the abstract.

> Drop a cricket ball from your hand and it falls to the ground. We say that the cause of its fall is the gravitational pull of the earth. In the same way, a cricket ball thrown into the air does not move on forever in the direction in which it is thrown; if it did, it would leave the earth for good and voyage off into space. It is saved from this fate by the earth's gravitational pull, which drags it gradually down, so that it falls back to earth. The faster we throw it, the farther it travels before this occurs; a similar ball projected from a gun would travel for many miles before being pulled back to earth. (Sir James Jeans, *The Universe Around Us*.)

**3. Comparisons** may define the unfamiliar by showing how it resembles the familiar or differs from it.

> Like gliding, ballooning depends for movement on luck with thermals, which are air currents rising off sun-warmed fields and hills; unlike gliding, ballooning gives a pilot no control of direction—except up and down. *(The New Yorker.)*

A strange object may be described through likeness as having "the shape of a hen's egg" or "the color of a tomato."

To the wanderer from temperate zones, the papaya might be a dwarfed Tom Watson or an unripe cantaloupe. This interesting native of the torrid zone assumes a variety of shapes and sizes. It may be elongated like a watermelon, or almost spherical, or even slightly compressed on one end, like our crook-neck squash. Within, it is much like a muskmelon, with a multitude of seeds which cling tenaciously to a firm, thick, salmon-colored lining which is its edible part. (G. W. James, student, the *Green Caldron*.)

On the other hand, a thing may be described through difference as "larger than a tennis ball" or "not so sour as a lemon." The following example is from a definition of the word *tact*.

A great many would-be socialites entertain the illusion that politeness and tact are the same thing. That is why they are only would-be's. Politeness is a negative, and tact a positive, virtue. Politeness is merely avoiding trampling on another person's toes, while tact is placing a Persian carpet under his feet. (Margaret Van Horne, student, the *Green Caldron*.)

**4. Negative comparisons** may be helpful. Explaining what a thing is *not*, can clear the ground for explaining what it *is*. This method is particularly useful in eliminating things that might otherwise be confused with the thing to be defined: "Botanically speaking, a tomato is not a vegetable." "A leprechaun is not to be confused with a ghost."

Research is a word that is often used narrowly, but I am using it not in any mean and cramped sense. It is not, for instance, restricted to the uncovering of specific new facts, or the development of new scientific processes, although it is partly this. It is not encompassed by learned papers in scholarly journals, although it is certainly this among other things. By research I mean, as well as all this, the publication of a biography, or a volume of poetry, or the delivery of a lecture that sets off a mental chain reaction among students. (Claude T. Bissell, *What the Colleges Are Doing*.)

**5. Classification** can extend the definition of a term that denotes a group by indicating the classes of which it is composed; a definition of service organizations might include the major kinds of clubs—Rotary, Kiwanis, and so on.

I found the Negro community the victim of a threefold malady—factionalism among the leaders, indifference in the educated group, and passivity in the uneducated. All of these conditions had almost persuaded me that no lasting social reform could ever be achieved in Montgomery. (Martin Luther King, Jr., *Stride Toward Freedom*.)

**6. Analysis** is another logical means of expanding a basic definition. You may break down the object to be defined into the parts composing it: "A good composition has a beginning, a middle, and an end."

A power mower, so popular with householders today, consists of a source of power, usually a small gasoline engine; a cutting blade, usually rotary; a transmissior system by which the power is applied to the blade; and a frame to support the mechanism, a set of wheels to make it movable and a handle by which the operator can guide it.

**7.** The **origins and causes** are essential for definitions of some subjects. The meaning of a word like *radar* is implicit in its origin (it is composed of "ra" for *radio*, "d" for *detection*, "a" for *and*, and "r" for *ranging*); and a phenomenon like a geyser or a volcano can best be explained through its cause.

> The meter was originally intended to be one ten-millionth of the distance from the equator to the pole of the earth, measured on the surface. The measurements by means of which the first meter was prepared were inaccurate, however, and the real meter is the distance, measured at the freezing point of water, between two marks on a bar of platinum-iridium kept at the International Bureau of Weights and Measures at Sèvres, France. (W. A. Noyes, *Textbook of Chemistry.*)

**8.** The **results, effects, and uses** are also essential for some subjects. *Christianity* and *Communism,* for example, should be explained in terms of their results as well as of their origins, and *war* and *depression* in terms of their effects. Definitions of mechanisms and processes (radar is again an example) are equally likely to involve a discussion of the uses to which they are put.

> In adjusting to his new way of life the hunting ape developed a powerful *pair-bond,* tying the male and female parents together during the breeding season. In this way, the females were sure of their males' support and were able to devote themselves to their maternal duties. The males were sure of their females' loyalty, were prepared to leave them for hunting, and avoided fighting over them. And the offspring were provided with the maximum of care and attention. (Desmond Morris, *The Naked Ape.*)

## Organization

As you note how many of the expository patterns and aids previously studied are included in this list of the methods of definition, you will realize that no one simple pattern or plan can be laid out for writing the essay of definition because any or all of these patterns may be successfully combined in it. Your plan will depend entirely on the demands of your subject and on your taste as a writer. A definition of Americanism, for instance, might involve a detailed breakdown of the term into the qualities that you believe it covers; it might include examples of true Americanism in action, a comparison of real Americanism with false varieties or with other "isms," and a discussion of how it came to be and of its effects on a people and the world. But how best to arrange and mingle this ample and varied material is a problem for which there is no ready-made answer.

### EXAMPLES

The selections that follow vary in subject matter from the tangible to the abstract; in style from expanded formal definitions to informal essays; in length from a single paragraph to a couple of pages. Determine for each, as has been done for Example A, what methods have been used in development.

*15-A*                        CYCLONES
                           *Walter Sullivan*

This report from the *New York Times* (November 1977), here complete, is by a
writer whose special field is science. It was published shortly after a cyclone caused
severe damage in Bangladesh and parts of India.

ANALYSIS          November is the month dreaded by coastal residents in
Introduction    India and Bangladesh, for it is then that the most devastat-
                ing cyclones occur.

Comparison        These storms are essentially the same in the way they
                form and behave as the hurricanes of the western Atlantic  5
                and western Mexico and the typhoons of the western
                Pacific.

                  In the Indian Ocean they are known as cyclones,
                although they have no relationship to the "cyclone" that
                transported Dorothy to the Land of Oz. That was a Middle-  10
                Western usage referring to a tornado—a localized, funnel-
                shaped cloud.

Details           Indian Ocean cyclones have caused some of the greatest
  historical example  disasters in history. In November 1970, such a storm swept
                across the Ganges delta in what was then East Pakistan,  15
                and is now Bangladesh. It drove the sea far inland over the
                flat landscape, flooding countless villages. The death toll
                may have reached a half million.

  historical example  At the start of November 1971, a similar storm struck
                the east coast of India and many more thousands died.  20
                When a cyclone hit Darwin, on the north coast of Australia,
                in 1974 two-thirds of the city's homes were destroyed, but
                only 49 people were killed.

Causes and effect   The explanation for the disparity in the death tolls
  in example     appears to be that because of flimsy construction, dense  25
                population and flat landscape in the deltas of India and
                Bangladesh, those living there are highly vulnerable. Air
  in general    pressure drops so radically during such storms that high
                tides rise far above normal. The 1970 disaster occurred at
  in example    a time in the lunar cycle when tides would have been very  30
                high in any case.

Details           Torrential rains add further to the flooding and high
                waves are driven inland by the violent winds.

Cause and effect    Such storms are typically born in the intertropical con-
  in general    vergence zone. This is the region where converging trade  35
                winds of the Northern and Southern Hemispheres meet
                and form an updraft. When that zone is far enough north
                or south of the Equator for the earth's rotation to impart
                circular motion to the converging winds a storm may be

born. The motion is counterclockwise when the process  40
occurs north of the equator and clockwise when it occurs
in the Southern Hemisphere.

Cause and effect
in general

Small at first, the storm feeds on the hot, moist air that
it sucks in from surrounding areas. As the air rises inside
the storm, the moisture condenses into heavy rains. The  45
latent heat that evaporated that moisture in the first place
is released to drive the rotating winds even faster, and
more air is drawn in.

Effect

Thus the storm swells to cover an area several hundred
miles in diameter. Like an upside-down whirlpool, it  50
rotates about an open funnel in the center—the "eye"—in
which skies are clear and winds minimal. Once over land
the storm loses energy for lack of moist oceanic air and
fades away.

Details

The ideal time for Indian Ocean cyclones is November.  55
In the Atlantic, the Caribbean Sea and Gulf of Mexico the
hurricane season extends from June to October.

Cause and effect

Modest efforts have been made to tame such storms by
seeding clouds in front of them, thus dumping their rain
before the clouds are drawn into the storm and feed it  60
energy. Until the effects of such action can be more accurately predicted than at present, it is feared that, following
such treatment, a storm might change its path and head
for a populated center instead of remaining harmlessly at
sea.                                                     65

1. To define cyclones in the region of Bangladesh and India for American readers,
   what information must Sullivan give besides that directly describing the cyclones
   themselves?
2. What use does he make of comparison, both literal and figurative?
3. Check the etymology, denotation, and connotation of *typhoons, tornado, disparity,
   latent, seeding.*

---

*15-B*                     PARENTAGE AND PARENTHOOD
                              *Ashley Montagu*

This paragraph is from *The American Way* (1967), an anthropological and sociological study. Note how Montagu defines the two terms by drawing distinctions
between them.

It is apparently very necessary to distinguish between parenthood and parentage. Parenthood is an art; parentage is the consequence of a mere biological
act. The biological ability to produce conception and to give birth to a child has
nothing whatever to do with the ability to care for that child as it requires to
be cared for. That ability, like every other, must be learned. It is highly desir-  5

able that parentage be not undertaken until the art of parenthood has been learned. Is this a counsel of perfection? As things stand now, perhaps it is, but it need not always be so. Parentage is often irresponsible. Parenthood is responsible. Parentage at best is irresponsibly responsible for the *birth* of a child. Parenthood is reponsible for the development of a human being—not simply a 10 child, but a human being. I do not think it is an overstatement to say that parenthood is the most important occupation in the world.

1. How are parentage and parenthood defined in an unabridged dictionary?
2. To what extent do the dictionary definitions show—or fail to show—the distinctions Montagu draws?

---

*15-C*                          THE MUSICIAN'S FILIBUSTER
                              *Karen Thompson (student)*

The term *vamp*, when applied to music, has a meaning all its own. It is not short for *vampire;* nor has it anything to do with the construction of a shoe. The vamp is a musical device used primarily in operetta and musical comedy when the composer or musicians are pressed for a time-waster or a link between the recognizable tunes. It can be a cover-up when a singer is desperately trying to 5 remember the first line of his song.

A vamp is nearly always short—hardly ever more than four measures long. The repeat signs before and after, however, can extend the little ditty indefinitely. A vamp embodies the musical intricacies of the oom-pah-pah variety. The nuances of this complicated rhythmical structure and the technique 10 required to execute it—a most appropriate term—are hardly worth discussing. The orchestration, however, is vitally important. If the violins are playing a descending passage, the flutes will most assuredly have an ascending one. A little counterpoint never hurts a healthy vamp. The violas and double basses play or plunk on the offbeats, and the celli, more than likely, sustain a low note 15 for the duration of the interlude. The winds, brass, and percussion also perform these same three basic functions: doubling the melody, supplementing the rhythm, or sustaining a basic chord.

Orchestra members have their own devices to counteract the monotony of a vamp. If the vamp is adequately extended, one may light up a Lucky (or a 20 Winston, or a Salem—if the prompter has fallen asleep, the whole state of North Carolina could go up in smoke). Other orchestra members tell jokes to pass the time. Some block out the sound, if only for an instant, by getting in one good yawn. Generally, however, a mood of relaxation overtakes the entire orchestra, and a subdued snicker circulates among the members.                          25

The unsuspecting audience has little, if any, warning of an approaching vamp. If it is too dark to leaf through the program, the best thing for a member of the audience to do is to grit his teeth and endure the awful noise. After all, it can't last forever.

A vamp may be used for any number of reasons. Costume changes and set 30 changes are frequently done to the tune of a vamp. Usually it is only when a singer has forgotten his first phrase that the vamp is extended to an unreasonable length. Sooner or later someone, perhaps the piccolo player, will think of the line and shout it to the singer.

The vamp is definitely an integral part of musical comedy. Its use has, on 35 occasion, been exaggerated far beyond the point of absurdity, yet its deletion would set musical comedy back several decades.

1. What specific examples does the writer give to illustrate her definition?
2. What colloquial words do you find and what may be the writer's reason for using them?
3. Why is "filibuster" an appropriate part of the title?

---

**15-D**            LAGNIAPPE
                 *Mark Twain*

These paragraphs are from Twain's *Life on the Mississippi* (1875). Note how the student writer of Example E makes use of Twain's definition.

We picked up one excellent word—a word worth traveling to New Orleans to get; a nice, limber, expressive, handy word—"Lagniappe." They pronounce it *lanny-yap*. It is Spanish—so they said. We discovered it at the head of a column of odds and ends in the *Picayune* the first day; heard twenty people use it the second; inquired what it meant the third; adopted it and got facility in 5 swinging it the fourth. It has a restricted meaning, but I think the people spread it out a little when they choose. It is the equivalent of the thirteenth roll in a "baker's dozen." It is something thrown in, gratis, for good measure. The custom originated in the Spanish quarter of the city. When a child or a servant buys something in a shop—or even the mayor or the governor, for aught I 10 know—he finishes the operation by saying:

"Give me something for lagniappe."

The shopman always responds; gives the child a bit of licorice root, gives the servant a cheap cigar or a spool of thread, gives the governor—I don't know what he gives the governor; support, likely.    15

When you are invited to drink—and this does occur now and then in New Orleans—and you say, "What, again?—no, I've had enough," the other party says, "But just this one time more—this is for lagniappe." When the beau perceives that he is stacking his compliments a trifle too high, and sees by the young lady's countenance that the edifice would have been better with the top com- 20 pliment left off, he puts his "I beg pardon, no harm intended," into the briefer form of "Oh, that's for lagniappe." If the waiter in the restaurant stumbles and spills a gill of coffee down the back of your neck, he says, "F'r lagniappe, sah," and gets you another cup without extra charge.

1. What words and phrases indicate Twain's humorous intention?

2. Classify the different kinds of situations in which Twain says *lagniappe* could be useful.
3. Which of the kinds of writing listed on pages 246–48 does Twain use here to enliven his definition?

---

**15-E**  "NO SWEAT"
*John D. Myers (student)*

"No sweat" is one of the most descriptive slang terms that I have ever encountered. I first heard the term used in Korea, where it appeared in almost every conversation among the American soldiers stationed there. It is admittedly a somewhat vulgar expression for formal use, but for saying much in a few words, it is hard to beat. ⁵

Strangely enough, "no sweat" does not refer to the amount of work involved in doing something, nor yet to the temperature. It refers to the absence of worry and apprehension involved in a certain action. Used properly, it carries a note of reassurance; it is a short way of saying, "Don't work yourself up over this matter, as it is all taken care of." ¹⁰

For example, let us suppose that a lovely young lady, in backing her car out of a parking lot, accidentally scrapes a young man's fender. The young man gallantly releases her from all responsibility by saying cheerfully, "No sweat," and the situation probably terminates in a date instead of a lawsuit.

But the expression means more than a release from obligation, as can be seen ¹⁵ from the following example: a production engineer calls in his foreman and explains that he will need four thousand brake units by the end of the week. The foreman replies, "No sweat," and the production engineer knows he is safe in telling the company's sales representative to confirm delivery.

If "no sweat" had been current in New Orleans at the time Mark Twain ²⁰ wrote "Lagniappe," the restaurant scene in which the waiter spilled coffee down the customer's neck would have had a different outcome. Before the careless fellow had had time to make any kind of apology, the injured patron would have looked up with a smile and said, "No sweat," and the incident would have been closed. ²⁵

Which of the kinds of writing listed on pages 246–48 does the writer use here to enliven his definition?

---

**15-F**  ON MATURITY
*Carlos Moras (student)*

This essay and the one following it were written for the same assignment—a definition of maturity.

Maturation involves two processes: internalizing the constraints society puts on us and shifting away from self-centeredness toward an awareness that we are not the only ones on the face of the earth.

When we're children we have to be told what to do. Our parents, teachers, and other authority figures act as mediators between us and that complicated 5 world where "right" and "wrong" don't exist as easily discernible extremes. In our world there are too many shades of "right" and "wrong." Our childish minds are incapable of making a choice from among so many alternatives, and so we have rules. We spend a large part of our childhood obeying or disobeying these rules. As we grow older we begin to see the reasons behind some of them, 10 and we start doubting the validity of others. At this point the internalizing process begins. Our adolescence is a period of rebellion against constraints imposed by others. We want to rule ourselves. But soon many of us come to realize that rules are important in a society as complicated as ours. We then become our own arbitrators btween "right" and "wrong," our own rule-makers and 15 enforcers.

Maturity is also a shift away from self-centeredness toward a more realistic image of ourselves. A baby's actions are all directed toward itself. The self-centered infant can't be blamed for its selfish attitude, because its world doesn't extend beyond itself. As the baby grows older, its world's boundaries extend, 20 and it then notes that others exist as well. First the baby notes that it has a mother on whom it depends for food. The selfish baby exploits this relationship. It cries until it is fed. It also cries until it receives attention. Quite early in life, the baby learns to see the rewards it can get from this relationship. Later on, the child learns from interactions with the family what a "give and take" rela- 25 tionship is and then starts to shift away from self-centeredness.

As we mature we should become aware of our position in relation to others in our world, a position no greater and no less than that of any other person. Not everyone succeeds in developing a realistic concept of self, and not everyone is able to internalize the constraints society puts on each of us. Thus, mental 30 maturity, unlike physical maturity, does not come automatically to all.

1. Are there any specific details to enliven this generalized definition?
2. How has the writer used classification as an organizing principle?

---

**15-G**                 **LEARNING HAS NO END**
*Irma Cruz (student)*

This essay was written for the same assignment as the preceding essay. The writer, a middle-aged student who had just begun her college career, draws on personal experience to enliven her remarks.

Mature people have a growing understanding of themselves, of others, and of social, moral, and ethical problems. They have the ability to translate words into meanings, to grasp the ideas presented, and to sense the mood suggested.

They have curiosity and enthusiasm for a wide variety of experiences, directly and also indirectly through reading, and they relate new ideas to previous experiences. Thus, they acquire new and deeper understandings, broadened interests, rational attitudes, and richer and more stable personalities.

I have few memories of my early childhood. My parents were poor and so involved in the struggle to survive that they could offer me little or no personal enrichment. No books were given or read to me, there were no trips to museums, zoos, theaters, or movies, there was no money to buy the kinds of toys that would have stimulated my imagination. My early days in kindergarten were bright days. I remember looking forward to the mornings that I would spend in school, but another memory like a rainfall, bitter in taste, is of being labeled by the system as a remedial child. I was made to feel that I was not going far in life. A year later when my younger sister joined me in school, my parents and teachers gave me the message that she was bright and I wasn't. From that moment on I imprisoned my soul with the ridiculous challenge of proving that I too had abilities.

In my early twenties I fell in love and married. I can truly say, as I look back many years later, that on the day of my marriage I was born again; I wish that I could change my entire name to suit my second birth. I entered marriage with no identity, no sense of myself, no experience of life whatever. Through my husband's patience, through my struggles with everyday life, through bearing children, caring for them and trying to meet their needs in a more conscious way than mine were met, through reading more and reading with a more critical view, and through developing my love for art, I began to grow and continue to grow.

I have chosen a career in education and have worked as a paraprofessional teaching "target" children, children who need to catch up. I am in college, an activity which my relatives and I had thought I would never be capable of but which I had always wanted. I look forward with great hope to continuing to experience and to grow more mature in life, for learning has no end.

---

**15-H**          THE MEANING OF "NEGRO"
                  *Negro History Bulletin*

This essay was published as an editorial in an issue of the *Bulletin* in 1971.

The word "Negro" has a long history. The Spanish and Portuguese with their Latin background began the African slave trade. They called black Africans "Negroes" because *negro* meant black in their languages. During most of the 19th century, black Americans preferred the terms African or Colored or African-American. Those who favor the latter point out that many Americans are called by the name of their ancestors' land, Italian-American, Polish-American, Jewish-American; and others prefer the word "black" and are using it widely, so that books and magazine articles carry it, as the opposite to "white." However, black is a misnomer, just as white is, for neither white nor black convey adequately the color or race of the people described; and certainly, there is genetically neither a white race nor a black race.

The word "Negro" is mainly a sociological word and has little relation to biology. Persons who by appearance are "white" have been designated as Negroes because there were some ancestors who were Africans. Accordingly, the study of "the Negro" in the United States has to face first of all the difficulty of definition. It is difficult to give a fixed and definite meaning to this word. It has been used in its narrow sense, to include the primitive group of darker African peoples, characterized by darker skins, curly hair, broad facial features and dolichocephalic [long] heads; their colors varied from nearly black to light brown and yellow. Their original habitation was Africa, south of the Sahara and north of the line running southeast from the Gulf of Biafra to the Tana River, and they have never numbered more than a million persons. In its widest sense, it has been used in the United States, especially, to embrace all of the peoples— not only those of dark skin, but also any person whose ancestors have been Negroes. In few cases of racial designations is the term more loosely used and in no case is it more difficult to fix an established meaning. The term "white" and "black" are equally indefinite and are used as loosely without scientific exactness.

In the United States, one may be called a Negro and be white in appearance. In Africa one may be called a Negro only if he is one of the definite Negroid types, who perhaps have never been in relatively large numbers as the continent goes. The brown, the yellow and some of the black peoples of Africa are excluded in the African use of the term. If we use the term "Negro" in its American use—for if one is a Negro for all negative purposes, certainly the positive purposes do not make one any less a Negro—we then find that the Negroes of Africa and the United States have been the creators of a valuable civilization, and have no need to hide themselves under the umbrella of a new name.

There has not been and there is not one unvarying Negro type. Persons of various colors and features have been found in Africa. Many of the Bantus, for instance, have been known to have "Caucasian-like features." The pygmies have been described by some observers as coffee-brown, and at times, by others as red and light yellow. The Fellatahs and Nigritians vary in color from light brown to dark brown. The Fellatah girls were described by one traveller as having beautiful forms which with their complexions "of freshest bronze" gave him the impression that they could not be "excelled in symmetry by the women of any other country." Another seventeenth century contemporary wrote, "The women of Nekans (in north) are handsome body'd and fair, with black and shining hair, which makes them take pride to frequent the Bathes." The Bahima people were a "tall and finely formed race of nutty brown color with almost European features." This variation of color has been so typical over the African continent that one student of the problem has been led to conclude that the mulatto is as typically African as the black man.

The Negroes in America are essentially Americans and not Africans. There is little except color which shows their relationships to Africa and there are 55 Negroes whose color does not show it, but who are proud of their African background. They have learned the language and social techniques of the United States, the country in which they lived. But they came to this country from a culture which had been developing in Africa through many centuries. There are few traces of African culture in Negro life in America, and the Negro- 60 American seems not to be essentially different in this respect from the Irish-American, the German-American, the Jewish-American, the Scotch-American, or any other American types so far as the cultures of the lands of their ancestors are concerned. Millions of Europeans have come to America and millions of Africans have been brought from Africa to America. They have all become a 65 part of the American population.

These Africans, designated as Negroes, have been marching forward in all lines of endeavors and achievement. They are proving that civilization and contributions to it are not based on race or color but upon the individual men or women of ability who seek to advance themselves, be they white or black. In 70 these respects God is no respecter of persons, whatever their names and colors.

1. Where does the writer use classification in developing the definition?
2. What specific examples does the writer use to illustrate or explain generalizations?
3. How is the essay organized?

## ASSIGNMENTS

1. There are many types of terms from which you may draw subjects for essays of definition:
   a. Words like *ruana, sukiyaki, goober, pedicab,* which may be in common use in some areas but which are so limited in locale that they are unfamiliar to many readers.
   b. Technical terms like *azimuth, ombudsman, recidivism, onomatopoeia,* which are so specialized as to be either unknown to most readers or not well understood by them.
   c. Slang terms like *gam, smokey, pad, spiv, skedaddle,* which are either too dated or too limited in use to be generally understood in all their implications.
   d. Abstract terms like *culture, sportsmanship, education, freedom,* which continually require specific definition because of the variety of interpretations possible.
   e. Familiar terms like *freshman, spring fever, conscience, homesickness,* which are known to all but which may have a special personal meaning for you that you would like to express.
2. Many words may be usefully defined in pairs to overcome frequent confusion of the two: courtesy and etiquette, job and profession, art and science, knowledge and

intelligence, house and home, infer and imply, naturalist and biologist, religion and theology, possibility and probability.

3. When you have chosen a subject,

   a. Write a formal one-sentence definition.

   b. Expand that definition into a paragraph by increasing the differentiating details, but keep it formally informative.

   c. Expand it into a longer essay of definition by using devices and adding information that will make it enjoyable as well.

4. The importance of definition can be seen by the number of times that it is used in the examples of other units. See Unit 2-D; Unit 6-A; Unit 9-G; Unit 10-A and C; 11F and G. In which is it needed more? In Unit 3-A the failure to accept each other's choice of words brings a waitress and customer into conflict.

# PART FOUR

# *Special Types of Writing*

The first three parts of this book have emphasized the chief ways to use illustration, organization, and reasoning in expository writing, and we have seen how much they overlap and support each other. Now we turn to applying all those skills to several types of writing that you will probably use often.

The first two types, argumentative and critical writing, appear frequently in newspapers, magazines, and books that form important parts of much research writing. You will use them for most of your writing assignments in college and later.

Unit 18 discusses the research paper, the product of a scholarly investigation of material that you have gathered from books and other sources. It will give you the opportunity to use all of your writing skills and also to learn the standard scholarly techniques for handling material and acknowledging sources.

Unit 19 discusses the essay examination, a common writing assignment in academic work, and Unit 20 discusses the business letter, a type of writing we are likely to use all our lives. Courses in business letter writing examine this subject much more thoroughly, but the essentials of form and content provided here will show you how to handle ordinary business correspondence competently.

# UNIT 16

# Argument and Persuasion

In everything you write, an essential part of the purpose is convincing your readers that the information you present is accurate and important and that your opinions are right or that, at the very least, what you are saying deserves your readers' serious consideration. There are as many degrees of intensity in writing as there are in human relationships—from the gentle suggestion of the signs saying "Please try not to smoke" in a London department store to the open threat of "Smoking forbidden: offenders will be prosecuted," in a chemical factory.

In all the examples of writing included in this book, the authors try to catch and hold our attention, to interest us in their subject matter, and to convince us that their observations, interpretations, analyses, inductions, deductions, and so on, are logical and enlightening. The more their subject matter is open to different opinions, the more strongly they try to persuade us to accept their views. Notice, for instance, how the general tone of the examples in Unit 8, "Process," differs from that of the examples in Unit 14, "Deduction." The writers quoted in Unit 8 can safely assume that their readers already want to learn how to do something or that the advantages of using the methods they describe will be self-evident. In Unit 14, however, the writers assume that their readers may have opposing views or that the deductions they present may not be self-explanatory. As a result, most of the writers quoted in Unit 14 use the techniques of argument and persuasion.

In composing a persuasive argument, you will find that all the aids to writing that we have examined in earlier units may be helpful and that definition, analysis, induction, and deduction are essential.

**1. Define the problem that forms your subject or underlies it.** You may define it by means of description, narration, classification, analogy, analysis, or cause and effect. Most probably, you will need a combination of some of these, perhaps of all.

**2. Analyze the nature of the problem fully.** Be sure to include specific examples. Choose only the best, of course. A few good ones thoroughly explained will be more effective than a superficial description of a large number. For the analysis you will probably need to summarize, compare, contrast, and classify parts of your material. To make your presentation vivid you may need description, narration, and characterization. To make it logical you will need induction and deduction.

**3. Include a full recognition of the opposing points of view and analyze them to show their strengths and weaknesses.** A one-sided argument convinces no one for long. Moreover, recognizing your opposition will show your fair-mindedness and the thoroughness of your research.

**4. Resist the temptation to oversimplify the problem** or the opinions of the opposition. An oversimplification may make your position seem stronger for the moment, but as soon as your readers have had time to think about it, they will realize that you are slanting the evidence. Do not, for instance, blame voter apathy alone as the cause of a low turnout in a particular election if you know that the candidates ignored local problems or that the weather was stormy on election day.

**5. Give your solution to the problem, if you have a solution, but admit it frankly if you have none.** If your solution is relatively simple and straightforward, you may be able to present it in a single section of your essay. If, however, it is complex or requires making several steps, your reader will probably follow it more easily in a presentation that takes it up point by point and relates each to the appropriate points of the problem. The advice in Unit 9 for organizing comparisons and contrasts will help you here.

**6. End with your most convincing material,** such as a brief restatement of your solution that your readers can remember easily, or a clinching example or analogy, or a quotation from an eminent authority.

**7. Support your argument throughout the main body of your essay.** Remember that your readers may know little or nothing about your subject or that they may hold views very different from yours. A mere assertion of your opinion, with no support, will tell them only that you hold that opinion and will not change their minds. Give as much factual evidence as you can, such as statistics, historical background, newspaper reports, your own experience, your direct observation of the experience of others, and references to books and articles that present such observations. When you can, support your opinions by briefly quoting or summarizing the views of the experts.

**8. Strengthen your argument by giving your qualifications.** The less your readers are likely to know about you or the more specialized your subject is, the more fully you should describe your qualifications to write on the problem. For example, in writing to your college newspaper to support a candidate in a student election, you would need to say only how long you have been at the college and in what situations you had observed the candidate; but in writing to the editor of a newspaper with a large circulation to give your views on energy conservation, you would need to show that you have special knowledge from your academic training or practical experience. In presenting yourself, be honest about your limitations. If your readers suspect that you are exaggerating your experience or abilities, they will distrust everything you say.

**9. Appeal to your readers' interests and sympathies.** An argument based entirely on logic may convince your readers that your opinion is correct, but it may not move them to action. The most effective argument is also a persuasion. It makes readers want to do or believe what you say by appealing to their emotions. This does not mean that you should rely on a sprinkling of emotionally "loaded" words such as "foul" and "heroic." These may add drama to your essay and will show the strength of your convictions, but you must go further. Whenever possible, appeal to your readers' own needs and beliefs. Elderly people in a retirement community may not see why their tax dollars should be spent on improving the playground in a local park, but if you can demonstrate that the rest of the park will be quieter and neater as a result of the playground and that outdoor activity improves children's health and social development, and if you remind them of their own childhood pleasures, you will appeal to their concern for their own comforts, to their sense of duty toward the development of good citizens, and to their sentiments. If you know that other retirement communities elsewhere have supported similar projects, you can also use the "bandwagon" effect—suggesting that your readers join the general trend.

## EXAMPLES

These examples differ considerably in emotional intensity because they differ in purpose and subject matter and therefore in word choice and the degree to which they emphasize logic. To judge the success of any one of them as a persuasive argument, be sure to take all those features into account.

### 16-A               AMERICA, THE REVOLUTIONARY
#### *Andrew J. Young*

This is the complete commencement address given in 1977 at Michigan State University by Mr. Young, who was then U.S. Ambassador to the United Nations.

It was inconceivable to me at the time of my graduation that I would ever be an ambassador. And yet I found myself very rapidly swept up in a movement of history.

I remember the end of the Second World War. I remember the disillusionment and the idealism that combined in that period as veterans came back from 5 the wars to face problems at home. There was a threat of continued communist expansion and Europe looked to the United States of America to stem that tide and give the nations of Europe an opportunity to redevelop and reemerge as a strong and free people.

The American people rose to that challenge. 10

Now, in the year 1977, we face a similar challenge. We face a challenge of a world having just come through a series of wars and rumors of wars—Vietnam, Angola, Southern Africa, tensions in Cyprus and in the Middle East. We are yet engaged in an arms race which involves more money than two-thirds of the world has for all its purposes. In fact, on a world scale, $1 out of $6 each 15 year goes into armaments at a time when there are people who are very, very hungry, at a time when unemployment and inflation tend to rampage all across the earth.

We find regimes that are our friends becoming more and more repressive because the rising tide of aspirations around the earth demand more and more to feed the hungry, to clothe the naked. But it would be a mistake to think of those rising aspirations as being inspired by communism. Those rising aspirations around the world are due more to American technology, spreading the gospel of a good life, coming after a gospel that was spread by many of your missionary dollars when you went around the world through your churches and told everybody that they were God's children. It was American missionary education, Protestant and Catholic, that trained most of the leaders in the world today that are now demanding freedom and liberation. And it was the lessons they learned in a western Judeo-Christian tradition added to the technological revolution that has created the revolutionary ferment in the world today.

Some years ago, I was down in Latin America and I remember little children the age of my children, six and seven years old at the time, sleeping in doorways covered by newspapers on a very cold night. In front of the Sears-Roebuck store there was a television set in the window showing old American movies, and these hungry children, who were walking the streets with tin cans begging for food all day long, were huddled in front of a Sears-Roebuck store looking at movies of a middle-class American family. I could see in their little heads the wheels going around saying, why can't we live this way?

Those are the seeds of revolution in the world. And it's a revolution that this free enterprise system which we are a part of has been responsible for.

Yet when we create those aspirations and expectations and have no mechanism to deliver, we find that the governments get more and more repressive.

The world looks to us for leadership in the problems of world development. The challenge of the world today may be even greater than the challenge in the '40s. When we open economies as we did open our economy to Europe and take them in, we make an investment because we are expanding our markets with consumers and trading partners.

As our economy has expanded, through free competition, we find, not only do our partners live better, but that we share a better life ourselves. I'm not talking just about government resources. The American banking community, the transnational corporations that are much maligned, have done a great deal to share their experience. We read about the records of exploitation, we read about the corruption that comes when transnational corporations go astray, and we should read about it and we should condemn it, but we should also realize that of the thousands of corporations that are doing business all over the world today, very, very few of them are involved in the kind of corruption and exploitation and attempts to overthrow governments that we have become ashamed of. There are corporations, also, that are providing tractors for people to grow food. There are corporations that are providing the technology to get the natural resources out of the ground.

As we look to our futures, we should realize that we have a system of which we have no need to be ashamed. While we have made mistakes and will continue to make mistakes, more than any nation on the face of the earth we admit our mistakes, we correct our mistakes, and we go on to continue finding ways to do a better job. There is also no need for us to be ashamed of the profit 65 motive, for there is, if you look at it, a certain morality in profit. The morality comes because you cannot force anybody to buy what you make. If you make a good product and they want it, their purchasing attaches the value and insures you the profit. If you make something that nobody in the world wants, there is no way in the world you can force it on them. Neither should we be ashamed 70 of the virtue of free competition. The American way of life seeks out competition for we know that in honest competition we ourselves improve and arrive at new heights and levels of our own development.

I was recently in Sudan and in Kenya and one of the things I saw there was young men and women, though mostly men, I must confess, who were educated 75 in American institutions in the '60s, and they were now running their countries in the '70s. One young man in Kenya, a district officer, had three pictures over his mantlepiece. He had Jomo Kenyatta on the left, he had Jesus Christ in the middle and he had Mark Hatfield, former governor of Oregon, on the right. I didn't expect to see a Republican senator's picture up on a mantlepiece in 80 Kenya, so I asked him, why these three? He said, "When I was a student in Oregon, I cut this picture out of a Sunday magazine supplement because I saw a commitment to serving mankind in Governor Hatfield's administration that I wanted to bring back to my people in Kenya."

1. How does the author use narration to present his argument?
2. What use does the author make of cause and effect? of deduction? of supporting examples?
3. Check the etymology, denotation, and connotation of *rampage, aspirations, inspired, gospel, ferment, maligned, exploitation*.

---

### *16-B*  DEFENDING FREE SPEECH FOR THOSE WE DESPISE
### MOST
#### *Aryeh Neier*

This editorial, published in *Civil Liberties* (November 1977), states the position of the ACLU (the American Civil Liberties Union) in agreeing to defend an American Nazi group that had been refused permission to march through a Jewish neighborhood in Skokie, Illinois. The ACLU is ordinarily considered politically liberal. Following this editorial, a letter to the *New York Times* (16-C) presents an opposing view.

ANALYSIS
Definition of
problem by
description

A letter I received from a woman in Ohio gave a different twist to a criticism of the ACLU's defense of free speech for Nazis. Many critics say that, while they recognize that interference with the Nazis' right to march in

Skokie violates the First Amendment, the ACLU should 5
use its limited resources elsewhere. My usual response is
that we could have ducked the issue by talking about limited resources—but it would have been false.

Analysis of problem

The ACLU takes all free speech cases. We have always
viewed free speech as our prime responsibility. Other 10
cases—prison, mental commitment, juvenile rights, political surveillance, abortion, race and sex discrimination, privacy—require major commitments of resources. Not so
with free speech cases. They usually don't require the construction of complete evidentiary records. They are gen- 15
erally simple and straightforward and it would be untrue
to say we don't have the resources to handle them.

Cause and effect

The woman in Ohio made a point, however, which
could not be so readily answered. ACLU is losing a lot of
members and a lot of money because we defend free 20
speech for Nazis. This means, she rightly pointed out, that
we will have less resources to handle other cases. Is it really

Redefinition of
problem

so important to defend the rights of Nazis that we are willing to make ourselves less able to defend the rights of
others? 25

Further analysis

The same thought crossed the minds of many of us who
make day to day decisions for the ACLU. Do a few con-
temptible Nazis deserve to wreck some important ACLU
programs? Some of my colleagues have even wondered out
loud whether the real purpose of the Nazis and the KKK 30
is to harm the ACLU by presenting themselves as clients in
free speech cases.

Specific, immediate
problem defined

Regardless of such dark speculations, however, we have
to recognize what is at stake in Skokie. Skokie tests whether
we really believe that free speech must be defended for 35
all—even for those we despise most.

Author's
qualifications

As a Jew, and as a refugee from Nazi Germany, I have
strong personal reasons for finding the Nazis repugnant.
Freedom of speech protects my right to denounce Nazis
with all the vehemence I think proper. Free speech also 40
protected the right of Al Wirin, the ACLU of Southern
California's long-time general counsel, to picket a high
school where a rightwing rally was being held—after
Wirin had won in court a decision allowing the rally to be
held. 45

Deduction

If the ACLU does not maintain fidelity to the principle
that free speech must be defended for all, we do not
deserve to exist or to call ourselves a civil liberties organization. Caving in to a hostile reaction—some of it from

ACLU members—would only advance the notion that speakers may be silenced if listeners are offended. That is the issue in Skokie, as it has been in a very large number of the free speech cases ACLU has taken on over the years. 50

Comparisons with similar examples

Did the wobblies have a right to speak in company towns? Did Jehovah's Witnesses or birth control advocates have a right to pass out leaflets in Catholic neighborhoods? Did Norman Thomas have a right to speak in Frank Hague's Jersey City? Did Paul Robeson have a right to sing at a concert in Peekskill, New York? Did Martin Luther King, Jr., have a right to march in Selma, Alabama or in Cicero, Illinois? 55 60

Further comparisons

Did the Jewish Defense League have a right to picket the Soviet embassy or the home of someone they say was a Nazi war criminal? Did anti-war demonstrators have a right to demonstrate at a military base? Did opponents of Richard Nixon have a right to picket the White House? Do Nazis have a right to hold a demonstration in Skokie? 65

Cause and effect

A lot of examples I have cited resulted in violence. Wobblies were murdered in many Western cities. Jehovah's Witnesses were stoned. Norman Thomas narrowly escaped a lynch mob in Jersey City. There was a riot in Peekskill and scores of people were injured. Civil rights marchers were attacked all over the South, in Chicago and its suburbs, and in many other places. 70

Analogy
Analysis of problem

Is any of these instances analogous to shouting fire falsely in a crowded theater? Of course not, although with the hindsight we know that violence took place. Free speech— as Justice Holmes said and as the great majority of the thousands of letters about Skokie I have received point out—does not protect the shouter of fire. On the contrary, shouting fire falsely in a crowded theater is the antithesis of speech. No other point of view can be heard. A panic takes place too quickly. 75 80

Comparison and contrast

Deduction

By contrast free speech could operate in Skokie. Opponents of the Nazis are free to speak and to condemn the Nazis. There is no need for opponents of the Nazis to respond violently, but if they do, their violent response is no reason to silence the Nazis. Speakers must not be silenced because their listeners do not like what they say. 85

Cause and effect

It is disheartening to get letters from members quitting the ACLU over defense of free speech for the Nazis and the KKK. These letters ask the ACLU to betray its very reason for existence. I take pride in saying that I detect no weakening of resolve in the ACLU's leadership. 90

Solution          We will continue to defend free speech for everyone. It 95
is costing us a great deal and it is forcing us to cut back on
some of the things we should be doing. But if we cannot
ourselves hold to the principle that the right to express

Deduction      views must be defended even when the views offend listeners, including ACLU members, we can hardly call on 100
governments to follow that principle.

**1.** Who were the "wobblies" (line 54)? Who are the other persons and organizations
mentioned in this paragraph?
**2.** What is the origin of the word *lynch?*

---

*16-C*                 THE ACLU'S GRIEVOUS MISTAKE
                            *Abba P. Lerner*

This letter to the editor of the *New York Times* (March 1978) is representative of
the reasoned arguments against the ACLU's position given in the preceding example
(Unit 16-B). The writer is a professor of economics at Florida State University.

The American Civil Liberties Union has been sticking to its principles in
defending the right of the American Nazi Party to march in a demonstration
through a Jewish-populated area where it will outrage victims and relatives of
victims of the German Nazi bestialities. The officers of the ACLU feel it is their
duty, although a very unpleasant one, to defend the Nazis' right to such dem- 5
onstrations in the course of defending the general right of freedom of speech
for everyone. They fear that if freedom of speech is denied to some this opens
the way to denial of freedom of speech to others.

Their intention is noble, but their understanding of their duty is faulty. The
overriding purpose of the ACLU is to promote and defend a democratic social 10
order in which freedom of speech is secure. If this purpose comes into conflict
with freedom of speech directed at destroying such a democratic social order,
their obligation is surely to protect the social order of free speech rather than
the free speech of its destroyers.

It is true that unpopular as well as popular speech must be kept free—pop- 15
ular speech does not need to be defended—but it is not the *unpopularity* of
Nazism that deprives Nazis of free speech rights. It is their opposition to that
right for all, and their intention to destroy it, that make it monstrously imper-
tinent for them to claim it. It is a grievous mistake for the ACLU to accept
Nazism as merely another unpopular point of view to be defended against prej- 20
udice and intolerance.

There is a similar confusion in the nature of the complaints about the use of
a Berkeley city park by a Nazi group. The police are perfectly right in claiming
that they cannot refuse the park to the Nazis just because they limit participation in their meetings. Other groups also limit participation. But surely this is 25

not the true objection to the Nazis. All would not be remedied if they invited everybody to attend their hate indoctrination sessions. The true objection is that they would not permit Jews or free-speakers to survive, beginning with barring Jews from public parks; and nobody has a valid claim to a right he would deny to others. 30

Protecting democratic rights of Nazis is often defended by the plea that to deprive them of these rights would make us as intolerant as the Nazis themselves. But, as in mathematics, negatives cancel each other. Intolerance of intolerance is not intolerance, just as the negative of a negative is not negative. It is the *toleration* of intolerance that allows it to grow and to threaten our freedoms. 35

1. Which of the "aids" to writing an argument listed earlier does the writer use here? (His qualifications were indicated by his title as a university professor, given beneath his signature.)
2. Where has the writer used balanced sentences for emphasis?

---

**16-D**        THIS LAND IS WHOSE LAND?
*Meg Greenfield*

This essay from *Newsweek* (June 1977) is here complete. As a regular contributor to *Newsweek*, the writer had no need to state her qualifications.

Which came first—the Passamaquoddy Indians or the settlers of Maine? The Basque people or the Spanish state? The Palestinian Arabs or the Palestinian Jews? From Molucca to Rhodesia to Quebec to Northern Ireland and back again, it sometimes seems as if all of humankind were suddenly engaged in a great global title search. To whom did the land originally belong? On which 5 group does ancient history confer modern rights—or at least modern grievances because those rights are being denied? The trend is there. It is growing. And it is, in my view, treacherous.

I got to thinking about all this courtesy of Menahem Begin, the Israeli election victor who has been citing Scripture as the basis of both the Israeli national state 10 and his own conception of its proper boundaries. "I understand he knows the Bible by heart," Begin said of Jimmy Carter, "so he knows to whom this country by rights belongs." Begin was correct in assuming that Carter himself has dallied with this fundamentalist view of Israel ("I think it was a fulfillment of Bible prophecy to have Israel established as a nation"). But that does not make either 15 man's vision any less feeble or risky as a rationale for the existence of a modern state.

If you want to know why this is so, only ask yourself whether Israel would be better off if (1) its existence were acceptable only to those who believe in the Old Testament, (2) its continuance as a nation could be called into question by 20 the unexpected and revolutionary finding of some archeological dig, or (3) the international community, weak as its support for Israel has become, were made

to feel free of any responsibility at all, on the theory that it was God, not the
U.N. or the West, with whom the modern state of Israel had negotiated its
charter. 25

The Israeli case may be the most dramatic and the most poignant. But others
run it a close second, and I would argue that none of the ethnic confrontations
we are now witnessing over borders, cultural sovereignty, self-determination
and the rest can be conclusively or fairly resolved by recourse to the dustier
archives. For like that stereotypical white man of the movies, history speaks 30
with forked tongue. The Mongols, the Seljuk and Ottoman Turks, the Romans,
the Greeks, the Persians, the Crusaders, the Arabs, the Jews, the British, the
French (including Napoleon himself)—I am just naming a few of those who
have exercised sovereign rights in the region we call the Middle East at some
point in recorded history. Something comparable can be done with North 35
Africa, the Iberian peninsula, the Indian subcontinent, the Balkans and innumerable other land masses where we today see the vestiges of departed cultures—both their artistic achievements and their racial and religious
animosities.

Who is to sit on the court of claims that will sort out the real-estate implica- 40
tions of all this? Pope Paul, Fidel Castro, Kurt Waldheim, Margaret Mead and
a panel of anthropologists? In fact, not even colonial history lends itself to quick,
clean judgments as to who is entitled to what. Surely 400- and 500-year-old
settlements, shifting population movements and centuries' worth of racial and
ethnic intermingling in some places, and implicit social bargains in others, argue 45
against summary expulsions of people by color, heritage or class. This is not just
a North-South, black-white problem. In Yugoslavia and in eastern Canada large
portions of the population regard themselves as victims of oppressive and historically unjustified colonial rule. My point is that the enduring intensity of feeling these conflicts generate demonstrates the futility of trying to base modern 50
policy on making sense of them, on figuring out some theory of ethnic
entitlement.

At this point we trip over the notion of restitution, reparation and—in some
instances—sheer, ugly revenge. I have in my possession a treasured news clip
from a year or so back, datelined Vatican City and headlined: ATHEISTS ASK $100 55
MILLION FROM CATHOLICS. A group called the United World Atheists, it says, had
demanded this handsome sum in "retribution" for "atrocities" committed
against their kind by the church "over the past twenty centuries."

All right—that may not be the most serious claim you ever heard of, unless
of course you are a member of the group. But its very absurdity does illustrate 60
the flaw in seeing oneself as the remote-control victim or legatee of other peoples' fights and bestialities and triumphs. Is Madalyn Murray O'Hair's quarrel
really with Savonarola? In what sense are you or I or Tip O'Neill or Andy Young
part of that venerable "Anglo-Saxon" conspiracy General de Gaulle saw coming
to full flower in our country's foreign policy a few years back? These identities 65
dug out of history are frequently fake or secondhand—and vicious in effect. I
understand the concept of a "homeland" in the Middle East for both Jews and
Arabs, for instance. But I prefer the idea of "haven" to that of "homeland."

That is because "homeland" suggests some historical property right sufficient to justify all manner of repression and attack. When people start talking about the "homeland," history tells us we'd better look out.

It needs to be admitted right here that the alternatives to this mining of the distant past for a present role are neither particularly reassuring nor wholly satisfactory. When you ask international lawyers how borders and historical ethnic claims are meant to be resolved, they will tell you that anything on the other side of the U.N. Charter is more or less regarded as fixed and that anything occurring since then is meant to be legitimate unless it is the product of force or coercion. Well, we all know how strictly these general precepts have been abided by. And we also know how much oppression and unfairness has occurred where they actually *have* been honored.

Even so, I would argue for the preferability of the messy modern secular and somewhat mongrelized political state to the ethnically pure and historically consistent enclave. A heritage can be appreciated, even cultivated, and, at the same time, transcended in a modern nation. But when it becomes the touchstone of all things, it breeds pain and ugliness. I can draw a line from the Treaty of Versailles to the outrages of the Palestinian terrorists now. For if we know anything, it is that racial, religious and national exclusion as policy creates violent reaction in the form of virulent chauvinism on the part of the excluded—and that the thing simply works itself out in a series of chain reactions. In fact, in very nearly every one of the ethnic disputes going on around the world now, you are simply seeing the predictable and inevitable payoff for someone else's overbearing and over-refined sense of identity. We aren't historically pure—any of us. To know that is the beginning of wisdom.

1. Notice the writer's use of questions to catch her readers' attention and direct it to the problem she presents. Where does she state the problem explicitly? How is the problem implied in the opening paragraph?
2. What recognition does the writer give to opposing theories and opinions?
3. What is the effect of the use of "we," "us," and "our"?
4. Check the etymology, denotation, and connotation of *title search, stereotypical, forked tongue, sovereign rights, vestiges, animosities, implicit, restitution, reparation, legatee, venerable, vicious, mongrelized, enclave, transcended, touchstone, virulent, chauvinism.*

---

*16-E*                   WHERE IS MY CHILD?
                           *Dorothy Collier*

This essay appeared in the *London Sunday Times* (November 1977) and is here complete. For reasons that the essay makes clear, the writer has used an assumed name.

Franklin D. Roosevelt once announced, in a voice choked with emotion, that December 7, 1941 was "a date that would go down in the annals of infamy." I feel much the same about November 26, 1976.

On that date the Children Act came into operation. This permits adopted

people to gain access to their own birth records and thus to find out who they 5
are. Many of them, though by no means all, want to go further than that and
find out if their natural parents, and in particular their mothers, are "all right."
The implicit question here is: Did my mother recover from the shock of parting
with me, did she pick up the pieces of her life?

I have no quarrel with that Act. It was wise, it was humane, and, in light of 10
recent evidence from America, it puts Britain in the forefront of the caring
Nations. My point is that the Act is infamously incomplete.

Two principles underlie the Act. The first is that everybody, whether adopted
or not, has a need to know about his lineage, his background, his family. Cut
out that knowledge, and, whether the child be adopted, fostered or placed in a 15
Home, he will feel a basic sense of insecurity, a feeling of incompleteness. There
is plenty of clinical evidence to support that view, and I myself have been in
such close contact with so many adopted people that I know it to be true. I also
know how "finding out" brings peace of mind.

The second principle is that, in the majority of orthodox adoptions, the child 20
was too young to understand what was happening. Something was done to him
without his knowledge or consent, and justice demands that when he reaches a
more mature age he should reach his own conclusions. When you come to think
of it, there is an analogy here with Christian practice, whereby a child is bap-
tised soon after birth and later confirms—or doesn't confirm—his attitude to 25
life.

What is now emerging, ever more clearly, is that just as the baby does not
know what is happening when the Adoption Order is made, neither does the
mother.

In 1943 I was a young married woman. I had fallen out of love with my 30
husband and into love with another man. The situation was such that when I
became pregnant—or rather when I could no longer conceal my pregnancy—
the expected baby could not possibly have been my husband's.

He turned me out. I had nowhere to go, and he took me back again. I was
permitted the full term of pregnancy. I was permitted to go into hospital and 35
have my baby delivered. I was permitted to take my little son home and to
suckle him. One evening I was informed that he would be taken from me that
following morning and placed for adoption. From the moment of that
announcement I was frozen; I remained frozen for many years.

I would like to make it clear that the baby was not snatched from me, I didn't 40
struggle. I handed over my son as a robot might have handed him over. A few
weeks later I signed papers, presumably consents to his adoption, and I was
literally unconscious at the time. The enormity of what was happening was too
great for my mind to handle, either in intellectual or in emotional terms, and
it shut itself off. It was many years later, after acutely disruptive emotional 45
disorder, that my mind reopened itself to the shock. By that time my husband
was dead. Whatever arrangements he made for my child, whatever knowledge
he had of my son, died with him. I am prohibited now from finding out if my
boy is "all right."

My purpose in writing is not to seek sympathy for myself. Over and over and 50 over again I have spoken with mothers whose stories are similar to my own. My conviction is that the female psyche cannot cope with carrying a child full term—feeling him quicken, feeling him kick—with the delivery of him, with hearing his first cry, with learning that he is safe and well, even, as in my case, with feeding him at the breast and *then* with severance. Emotional paralysis is, I am sure, inevitable; when she signs her consent to adoption, the mother cannot "know" what she is doing.

But of course the lawmakers are mostly male, aren't they?

The child cannot know what is happening, the mother cannot know. If the child needs to know about lineage retrospectively, the mother needs to know prospectively—that her line continues. If the child needs to know about grandparents, the mother needs to know about grandchildren. If the child needs to know that Mum's "all right," the mother needs to know—oh, how desperately!—that her son flourishes and is well.

Yet the law only applies to the child. He has all the rights and all the initiatives. If my son, the child that I bore, is dead, I am denied even the right to know where his body lies. I cannot believe that that right should be abrogated by the stroke of the pen at a time when the mind has ceased to function. I believe firmly that, with the same safeguards as now apply to the children, the right to know, the right to acquire basic information, should be granted to the natural parents of adopted persons.

1. In the fourth and fifth paragraphs the writer clearly labels two principles that form the basis of her argument. What principles are implied in other parts of her essay?
2. Why does the writer wait until the sixth paragraph to state the problem explicitly?
3. Check the etymology, denotation, and connotation of *infamy, implicit, lineage, orthodox, enormity, psyche, severance, abrogated.*

---

**16-F**          CAMPUS VANDALISM
                  *James Brown (student)*

This essay was an in-class exercise. The writer had a choice of three topics and took "How serious is vandalism on our campus and what can be done to reduce it?"

*"Hey, grab that cat!" screamed one student, and a friend jumped to block the cat's escape.*

*"I got him!" shouted a third as he lunged for the animal.*

*The three students proceeded to spray-paint the entire cat green. They dissolved into hysterical laughter as the terrified creature fled into the bushes.*

This is a fictional episode, but, who knows, spraying cats green may be next year's favorite campus stunt.

Major contributors to vandalism are students who don't know what to do with their spare time. Many children go through stages of petty larceny and destructiveness and get a thrill from stealing a stick of gum from the local candy stores or smashing pop bottles in vacant lots. The students who destroy their own campus have never outgrown that stage. They have never found a way to be noticed except to brag to their friends that they have performed such great deeds as pouring glue over the box of spoons in the campus cafeteria. One of my room- mates goes around stealing anything he can get his hands on. To date, in our room we have a "University Dining Room" sign, two extra chairs, a McDonald's flag, several road signs from nearby streets, and a blinking light used to warn cars of a road block. If this is what just one person can collect in a semester, imagine what the entire student body may have stowed away. 15

Many of these stunts are amusing and may seem harmless. But even the most seemingly harmless practical jokes can be destructive in the end, and most cause expenses for repairs. This contributes to our ever-increasing tuition charges. Why must mature, innocent students pay for the silly behavior of the childish, guilty ones? 20

The main reason vandals are not apprehended is that they are protected by their peers. No student wants to come forth and "rat" or "snitch" on another. For the university to eliminate some of the vandalism, there must be a system for students to identify a vandal without having to do so face to face. In the outside world many people are intimidated by criminals when they are asked to testify, and that is exactly what these campus vandals are—criminals, young students who are finally free of family rule and who want to explore all the things they could not do at home. 25 30

Also, fraternities and sororities have a duty to try to stop the ritual of destruc- tion, instead of encouraging it. In hazing, they must not force pledges to destroy a car to qualify for membership. Think how good the results would be if instead they required pledges to police the campus every day for a month. 35

Vandals must be dismissed from the university. After one or two are found guilty and expelled, vandalism will decrease dramatically. Every student must understand that he is not helping a friend by protecting him; he is only allowing the friend to continue hurting everyone, including himself. If everyone works together, maybe we'll never have to see a green cat. 40

**1.** Is the narrative beginning effective? Would a less dramatic but true example have been better?
**2.** Which of the other "aids" to argument does the writer use?

---

*16-G*                          KILLING FOR SPORT
                            *Joseph Wood Krutch*

These paragraphs form about one-quarter of an essay that first appeared in *The American Scholar* (1956).

It wouldn't be quite true to say that "some of my best friends are hunters." Still, I do number among my respected acquaintances some who not only kill for the sake of killing but count it among their keenest pleasures. And I can think of no better illustration of the fact that men may be separated at some

point by a fathomless abyss yet share elsewhere much common ground. To me, 5
it is inconceivable that anyone can think an animal more interesting dead than
alive. I can also easily prove, to my own satisfaction, that killing "for sport" is
the perfect type of pure evil for which metaphysicians have sometimes sought.

Most wicked deeds are done because the doer proposes some good for himself. The liar lies to gain some end; the swindler and the thief want things which, 10
if honestly got, might be good in themselves. Even the murderer is usually
removing some impediment to normal desires. Though all of these are selfish or
unscrupulous, their deeds are not gratuitously evil. But the killer for sport seems
to have no such excusable motive. He seems merely to prefer death to life,
darkness to light. "Something which wanted to live is dead. Because I can bring 15
terror and agony, I assure myself that I have power. Because of me there is that
much less vitality, consciousness and perhaps joy in the universe. I am the spirit
that denies." When a man wantonly destroys one of the works of man, we call
him "Vandal." When he wantonly destroys one of the works of God, we call
him "Sportsman." 20

The hunter-for-food may be as wicked and as misguided as vegetarians sometimes say, but he does not kill for the sake of killing. The ranchers and the
farmers who exterminate all living things not immediately profitable to them
may sometimes be working against their own best interests; but whether they
are or are not, they hope to achieve some supposed good by the exterminations. 25
If to do evil, not in the hope of gain but for evil's sake, involves the deepest
guilt by which man can be stained, then killing for killing's sake is a terrifying
phenomenon and as strong a proof as we could have of that "reality of evil"
with which present-day theologians are again concerned.

Despite all this, I know that sportsmen are not necessarily monsters. Even if 30
the logic of my position is unassailable, the fact remains that men are not logical
creatures, that most, if not all, are blind to much they might be expected to see,
and that the blind spots vary from person to person. To say, as we all do, "Any
man who would do *A* would do *B*" is to state a proposition mercifully proved
false almost as often as it is stated. The murderer is not necessarily a liar, any 35
more than the liar is necessarily a murderer. Many have been known to say that
they considered adultery worse than homicide, but not all adulterers are potential murderers and there are even murderers to whom incontinence would be
unthinkable. The sportsman may exhibit any of the virtues—including compassion and respect for life—everywhere except in connection with his "sport- 40
ing" activities. It may even be too often true that, as "antisentimentalists" are
fond of pointing out, those who are tenderest toward animals are not necessarily
the most philanthropic. They, no less than sportsmen, are not always consistent.

Yet, if the Puritans really did forbid bearbaiting, not because it gave pain to
the bears but because it gave pleasure to the spectators, they were not neces- 45
sarily so absurd as Macaulay has made us believe. That particular pleasure *was*
evil in itself, and to this day the Puritan logic is also that of the Roman Catholic
position (based on St. Thomas): namely, that cruelty to animals is wrong, not
because animals have any rights, but because cruelty corrupts men. And I am
so sure this is true that I was offended when President Eisenhower told reporters 50

that on his vacation he hoped to find time "to shoot a few crows." I have no doubt that crows have to be kept down. But I have strong doubt that killing them ought to be a pleasure.

If anyone asks me why we shouldn't get a little fun out of a necessary activity, I will reply: "For the same reason that legal hangings are no longer made a public spectacle. The fallacy is precisely that of the Mikado, whose sublime object it was to 'make each prisoner pent / Unwillingly represent / A source of innocent merriment / Of innocent merriment.'"° 55

1. Krutch states in ¶1 that he can establish to his own satisfaction the generalization that "killing 'for sport' is the perfect type of pure evil." Does he establish it to your satisfaction as well?
2. List the examples he gives of other killings whose evil he finds less "pure." What is the basis for his claim?
3. Does his admission later that sportsmen may have some virtues in other areas weaken his case?
4. Why does he uphold the Puritans' objection to bearbaiting and the Roman Catholic position on cruelty to animals? Why does he object to Eisenhower's shooting crows and to the Mikado's making prisoners "a source of innocent merriment"?
5. Check the etymology, denotation, and connotation of *fathomless, abyss, gratuitously, wantonly, phenomenon, theologians, incontinence, compassion, bearbaiting,* the *Mikado, pent.*

## ASSIGNMENTS

1. Reread the examples in this unit. Is there an author with whom you disagree, wholly or in part? If so, write an argumentative essay of about 500 words replying to the author.
2. Choose a recent editorial from your local newspaper or your college paper and write a 500-word argumentative essay explaining why you agree or disagree with it. If you agree, be sure to support your argument in ways and with material not used in the original.
3. What improvement do you think is most needed in the neighborhood in which you live? Write an argumentative essay urging the residents and the appropriate officials to make the improvement. Be sure to choose something specific such as a traffic light at a dangerous intersection, better parking facilities in a particular area, a summer recreation program for children, a stricter enforcement of regulations about unleashed dogs, or a bigger selection of books and magazines in the public library.
4. What change do you think is most needed at the college or university you are attending? Choose something specific and write an argumentative essay urging the other students or the appropriate members of the faculty or administration to make the change.
5. What annoying or dangerous habit does one of your friends or a member of your family have that you think can be corrected? Write a tactful argument persuading him or her to break the habit.

°The quotation is from a song in the operetta, *The Mikado,* by Gilbert and Sullivan.

# UNIT 17

# *Critical Writing*

The word "criticism" is often used to mean finding fault. In this unit we shall use it in the larger sense of analyzing the strengths and the weaknesses of something in order to reach a carefully considered judgment. Professional critics develop objective standards of judgment through reading, observation, and analysis, and most devote their lives to their fields. Critical analysis can be applied to subjects as far apart as livestock and personal conduct, machinery and government policies.

You will have many opportunities in college to develop your critical judgment. Most of your instructors will ask you to write critically about assigned readings, such as scholarly articles, chapters of a book, whole books, and works of literature. You should go beyond what you may have written for high school "book reports," which were probably only summaries of your reading. Your instructors will expect you to compare, contrast, evaluate, and reach conclusions on what the authors say.

In choosing a subject, you may, depending on the assignment, criticize a complete work, covering all its main points and the methods of presentation, or concentrate on a particular aspect or section. Professional book reviewers, drama and music critics, and so on, cover a whole work or performance because they are writing about new ones and therefore must give their readers an overall view. But critics writing on an established work usually concentrate on a section or an aspect of it that they think has been neglected by the critics or inaccurately evaluated or interpreted.

You are unlikely, for example, to have anything new to say about the whole of Shakespeare's *Hamlet*, at least until you have become an authority on Shakespeare, but you may have some interesting thoughts on a small element of the play, such as one of the minor characters, or two or three lines in an important speech. You may also find that a comparison and contrast between a minor character in *Hamlet* and one in another of Shakespeare's plays sheds light on one or both characters.

A specific critical approach may help you to form a new interpretation. In writing about a minor character in *Hamlet*, for example, you might consider primarily that character's psychology as revealed in words and actions, explaining to your readers the exact psychological theory you are applying and why you chose it. You might examine the same character from a historical point of view to determine Shakespeare's degree of accuracy in portraying the attitudes and customs of a historical period, his own or an earlier one. You might apply linguistic analysis to the words in several lines, determining both their etymology and use by Shakespeare's contemporaries, to arrive at a fuller understanding of his use of language.

When writing on something that others have already criticized, you should take their criticism into account and tell your readers why there is room for another view—yours. The professional criticism can itself be a subject for a critical paper. Instead of giving a new interpretation of a minor character in *Hamlet,* you could show why the interpretation by critic X is better than the interpretations by critics, W, Y, and Z—assuming, of course, that X made little or no reference to W, Y, and Z, because if X attacked them effectively you will probably have nothing significant to add.

To find a subject for a critical paper, apply the same principles you used to find subjects for the other kinds of writing discussed in this book. The broader your topic and the more familiar it is to others, the less likely you are to have something new and forceful to say. Just as you were advised in Unit 1, you should narrow your topic so that you can handle it thoroughly and have something fresh to say.

In writing any criticism, you will find helpful all the skills discussed earlier, particularly analysis, classification, comparison, and definition. Whatever methods you use, be sure to do four things: Define the type and scope of the work or works you are criticizing, indicate the scope and nature of your critical approach, summarize the content of the work briefly to give your readers a firm basis for understanding your opinions, and interpret or evaluate the work.

**1. Classify the work with which you are dealing.** For example, if it is a written work, you must tell your readers whether it is a biography, a novel, a report on an economic survey, a political analysis, and so on. You must also tell them what areas it covers and to which readers it seems directed. A dictionary, as Mark Twain remarked humorously, can scarcely be blamed for having little plot. Similarly, we apply one set of critical standards to an article on a particular problem in foreign policy if the article appears in a scholarly journal and a rather different set of standards to another article on the same problem that appears in a general-circulation magazine.

**2. Indicate the scope and nature of your critical approach.** If you are going to limit your discussion to a minor character in "Hamlet," tell your readers exactly that and explain your interest in that character. If you are going to base your criticism on a psychological theory, define that theory and say why you are using it.

**3. Summarize the content of the work.** An adequate summary gives your criticism a firm foundation; however, be brief—include only the essential features of the work, and remember that your main purpose is to criticize it, not to save your readers the effort of reading it for themselves. It is customary to use the present tense to summarize the main actions of any narrative, whatever the literary form, because you then have the past and future tenses to refer to events before and after the part of the narrative under immediate consideration. With paintings, musical compositions, and other works in nonverbal media, give a brief description. If the work is very well known, *Hamlet*, for example, or Beethoven's Fifth Symphony, a summary or description is not necessary, but be sure to let your readers know which section you are discussing so that they can recognize it quickly and easily. (**Note:** for a discussion of summary writing, read the introductory section of Unit 7.)

**4. Interpret and evaluate the work by using as many of the skills discussed earlier as are appropriate.** Make your remarks convincing by using the argumentative methods discussed in Unit 16. Have the courage of your convictions and do not feel intimidated by the fame of the writer or artist whose work you are criticizing or of the critics with whom you disagree. As in argumentative writing, use objective analysis and logic as the basis of your criticism and rely on emotional words and phrases only to add vitality and color to it. Be sure to explain how your interpretation and evaluation resembles or differs from those of major critics. Support your remarks with specific illustrations from the work and with any relevant information, such as the historical background, and explain how the illustrations and information support them.

## Satire

Satire is a special kind of criticism. Writers use it to attack something they think is wrong. Instead of stating their beliefs and objections directly, they take the risk of being indirect. They try to make their readers think for themselves and look through the literal meaning on the surface to the deeper meaning. By doing this, successful satire can often be more effective than straightforward critical writing. Only a few specialists are now familiar with Jonathan Swift's direct attack on the causes of poverty in eighteenth-century Ireland but his satiric attack, "A Modest Proposal," has become such a classic that any piece now using that title immediately announces to every educated reader that it is satiric.

To be made fun of is always more painful than simply to be scolded, and satire makes what it attacks ridiculous. It may grossly **exaggerate,** as Orwell does in his novel *1984* by taking totalitarian control far beyond what it had reached when the book was published in 1949. It may **reverse** the facts, as Swift does in the fourth book of *Gulliver's Travels,* with human beings (the Yahoos) as savage beasts and with horses (the Houyhnhnms) as intelligent, virtuous creatures. Or it may **transfer** the situation to a different area where its ridiculousness will be apparent, as a writer annoyed by the excesses of time-and-motion studies in a government bureau once did when he applied the efficiency experts' principles to conducting a symphony orchestra.

When you write satire, whatever your method, make sure that your readers will know that it is satire. If you choose exaggeration, you must exaggerate grossly; if you choose to reverse or transfer the facts, you must give clues to your satiric purpose early in your essay.

## EXAMPLES

These methods for writing criticism apply to any subject, but since most of your critical writing in college will be on what you read, six of the eleven examples that follow criticize written works. The first six give some indication of the variety of approaches to criticizing something that has been criticized many times before—Shakespeare's *Romeo and Juliet*. The sixth is a review of several scientific books; the seventh, of an album by a popular singer; and the final three are satires.

**17-A**              MISADVENTURES IN VERONA
                          *Brendan Gill*

These paragraphs begin a review of a 1977 production of *Romeo and Juliet*. The writer, the chief drama critic for the *New Yorker*, first states his general opinion of the production—it was "an honorable failure"—and then, to show the basis for his judgment, gives his interpretation of the play. In the rest of the review, omitted here, he explains how the production failed to fulfill his expectations.

The new production of *Romeo and Juliet* at the Circle in the Square is an honorable failure. The director of the play, Theodore Mann, has evidently worked hard with a large and motley cast, but he is not known for having a light touch, and, oddly enough, it is a light touch that the play requires. For *Romeo and Juliet* is a tragedy that must be played as if it were a comedy, or 5 it won't succeed; tether it to solemnity and it becomes an earthbound recounting of a series of preposterous misadventures. Because its tone is continually at odds with its content, it is a play far more difficult to perform than one would expect from a mere reading acquaintance with it. From first to last, bodies pile up on the stage at a fearful rate, and the emotions aroused in us by a carnage almost 10 as ample as that in *Hamlet* ought surely to be pity and terror, but no such thing: the language of the play is so lyrical, so springlike, so charged with the energetic hopefulness of first love that we scarcely take in the grim evidence of our senses. After an ideal performance, we leave the theatre elated rather than deeply moved, remembering Romeo and Juliet not as corpses in a tomb but as dear, 15 harmless, amorous children. Though Romeo takes two men's lives and is a suicide, these formidable offenses against God and the state strike us, in their romantic context, as only mildly reprehensible. Moreover, if *Romeo and Juliet* were an authentic tragedy instead of a nominal one, the protagonists would be,

of course, Capulet and Montague, who by their senile pride and other flaws of 20
character bring ruin to those presumably dearest to them.

That Shakespeare himself intended the play to be taken lightly is hinted at
in its last words, spoken by Escalus, Prince of Verona: "For never was a story
of more woe/Than this of Juliet and her Romeo." The couplet reduces the play
to a pretty toy, which one may be grateful for but need not take too seriously; 25
the effect is startlingly like that evoked by the ending of *A Midsummer Night's
Dream*, which Shakespeare is thought to have written a year or so earlier. Both
plays are washed in the same blue moonlight, and the celebrated "aria" describing Queen Mab could have been given as readily to Theseus as to Mercutio.
The passage has, at the very least, the look of being a delectable leftover, too 30
precious to discard.

1. To support his claim that the play "is a tragedy that must be played as if it were a
   comedy," what use does the writer make of specific examples? of quotation? of
   comparison with other plays?
2. Check the etymology, denotation, and connotation of *motley, tether, preposterous,
   formidable, reprehensible, nominal, protagonists, senile, aria, delectable.*

---

*17-B*                          CLUES TO MEANING
                                 *John Hankins*

These paragraphs are from a 3000-word essay introducing a widely used paperback
edition of *Romeo and Juliet*. The essay is intended to give the general reader an overall
view of the play and the chief critical interpretations.

ANALYSIS                In recent years numerous attempts have been made to
                        state a central theme for the play. One critic views it as a
Classification #1       tragedy of unawareness. Capulet and Montague are una-
analysis                ware of the fateful issues which may hang upon their quar-
                        rel. Romeo and Juliet fall in love while unaware that they 5
                        are hereditary enemies. Mercutio and Tybalt are both
                        unaware of the true state of affairs when they fight their
                        duel. In the chain of events leading to the final tragedy,
                        even the servants play a part and are unaware of the results
                        of their actions. The final scene, with Friar Laurence's long 10
                        explanation, is dramatically justified because it brings
                        Montague, Capulet, Lady Capulet, and the Prince to at
                        least a partial awareness of their responsibility for what has
                        happened. Supplementing this view of the play is one
Classification #2       which finds it to be a study of the wholeness and complex- 15
analysis                ity of things in human affairs. The issues of the feud may
                        appear to be simple and clear, but in reality they are highly
                        complex, giving rise to results which are completely

unforeseen. The goodness or badness of human actions is relative, not absolute, an idea symbolically set forth in 20 Friar Laurence's opening speech on herbs which are medicinal or poisonous according to the manner of their use.

Other clues to the meaning of the play may be found in the repetitive imagery employed by Shakespeare. The 25 images of haste, of events rushing to a conclusion, are found throughout. When Romeo says, "I stand on sudden haste," Friar Laurence answers, "They stumble that run fast," and thus expresses one moral to be drawn from the play. Romeo and Mercutio symbolize their wit-combat by 30 the wild-goose chase, a reckless cross-country horse race. "Swits and spurs," cries Romeo, using the imagery of speed. Numerous other instances may be found.

Closely allied to the imagery of haste is the violence expressed in the gunpowder image. The Friar warns that 35 too impetuous love is like fire and powder, "which, as they kiss, consume." Romeo desires a poison that will expel life from his body like powder fired from a cannon. This may identify the Apothecary's poison as aconite, since elsewhere Shakespeare compares the action of aconite with that of 40 "rash gunpowder" (*2 Henry IV*, IV, iv, 48). Violence is also expressed in the image of shipwreck which may end the voyage of life. Capulet compares Juliet weeping to a bark in danger from tempests. Romeo describes his death as the shipwreck of his "seasick weary bark." Earlier, after 45 expressing a premonition that attendance at Capulet's party will cause his death, he resigns himself to Him "that hath the steerage of my course," anticipating his later images of the ship and the voyage of life.

Also repeated in the play is the image of Death as the 50 lover of Juliet. She herself uses it, her father uses it beside her bier, and Romeo uses it most effectively in the final scene. The effect of this repeated image is to suggest that Juliet is foredoomed to die, that Death, personified, has claimed her for his own. It thus strengthens the ominous 55 note of fate which is felt throughout the play.

That *Romeo and Juliet* is a tragedy of fate can hardly be doubted. Shakespeare says as much in the Prologue. The lovers are marked for death; their fortunes are "crossed" by the stars. The reason for their doom is likewise given: 60 only the shock of their deaths can force their parents to end the senseless feud. At the end of the play Capulet calls the lovers "poor sacrifices of our enmity," and the Prince

Classification #3
analysis

Classification #4
analysis

Classification #5
analysis

evaluation

Classification #6
analysis

describes their deaths as Heaven's punishment of their parents' hate. Romeo's premonition of death before going to the party attributes it to "some consequence yet hanging in the stars." The note of fate is struck repeatedly during the play. "A greater power than we can contradict / Hath thwarted our intents," says Friar Laurence to Juliet in the tomb. The numerous mischances experienced by the lovers are not fortuitous bad luck but represent the working out of some hidden design. Critics who attack the play for lacking inevitability have misunderstood Shakespeare's dramatic technique. Like Hamlet's adventure with the pirates, the sequence of mishaps here is deliberately made so improbable that chance alone cannot explain it. Only fate, or the will of Heaven, affords a sufficient explanation.

General conclusion

1. What transitional devices does the writer use to lead the reader from one "central theme" to another?
2. What kinds of support does the writer give for the various interpretations of the central theme?
3. Check the etymology, denotation, and connotation of *hereditary, supplementing, imagery, apothecary, bark* (as used here), *steerage, bier, thwarted, fortuitous.*

---

### 17-C  PUNS AND OTHER WORDPLAY IN *ROMEO AND JULIET*
#### *M. M. Mahood*

These paragraphs conclude the chapter on *Romeo and Juliet* in *Shakespeare's Wordplay* (1957), a scholarly book devoted to a close analysis of a specific aspect of Shakespeare's writing to determine what light it may shed on interpreting the plays.

Some of the most notorious puns in Shakespeare occur in this scene between Juliet and her Nurse, when the Nurse's confusion misleads Juliet into thinking Romeo has killed himself:

> Hath Romeo slaine himselfe? say thou but *I*,
> And that bare vowell *I* shall poyson more
> Then the death darting *eye* of Cockatrice,
> *I* am not *I*, if there be such an *I*.
> Or those *eyes* shut, that makes thee answere *I*:
> If he be slaine say *I*, or if not, no.
>
> (III.ii.45–50)

Excuses might be made for this. It does achieve a remarkable sound-effect by setting Juliet's high-pitched keening of "I" against the Nurse's moans of "O Romeo, Romeo." It also sustains the eye imagery of Juliet's great speech at the opening of this scene: the runaways' eyes, the blindness of love, Juliet hooded like a hawk, Romeo as the eye of heaven. But excuses are scarcely needed since 15 this is one of Shakespeare's first attempts to reveal a profound disturbance of mind by the use of quibbles. Romeo's puns in the next scene at Friar Laurence's cell are of the same kind: flies may kiss Juliet, but he must fly from her; the Friar, though a friend *professed*, will offer him no sudden means of death, though ne'er so mean; he longs to know what his concealed lady says to their 20 cancelled love. This is technically crude, and perhaps we do well to omit it in modern productions; but it represents a psychological discovery that Shakespeare was to put to masterly use in later plays. Against this feverish language of Romeo's, Shakespeare sets the Friar's sober knowledge that lovers have suffered and survived these calamities since the beginning of time. For the Friar, 25 "the world is broad and wide," for Romeo, "there is no world without Verona wall." When the Friar tries to dispute with him of his "estate," the generalised, prayer-bookish word suggests that Romeo's distress is the common human lot, and we believe as much even while we join with Romeo in his protest: "Thou canst not speak of that thou dost not feele." Tragedy continually restates the 30 paradox that "all cases are unique and very similar to others."

The lovers' parting at dawn sustains this contradiction. Lovers' hours may be full eternity, but the sun must still rise. Their happiness has placed them out of the reach of fate; but from now on, an accelerating series of misfortunes is to confound their triumph in disaster without making it any less of a triumph. 35 With Lady Capulet's arrival to announce the match with Paris, love's enemies begin to close in. Juliet meets her mother with equivocations which suggest that Romeo's "snowie Dove" has grown wise as serpents since the story began, and which prepare us for her resolution in feigning death to remain loyal to Romeo:

> Indeed I neuer shall be satisfied 40
> With Romeo, till I behold him. Dead
> Is my poore heart so for a kinsman vext.
> (III. v. 94–96)

This is a triple ambiguity, with one meaning for Juliet, another for her mother and a third for us, the audience: Juliet will never in fact see Romeo 45 again until she wakes and finds him dead beside her.

A pun which has escaped most editors is made by Paris at the beginning of Act IV. He tells the Friar he has talked little of love with Juliet because "Venus smiles not in a house of teares." Here *house of tears* means, beside the bereaved Capulet household, an inauspicious section of the heavens—perhaps the eighth 50 house or "house of death." Spenser's line "When oblique Saturne sate in the house of agonyes" shows that the image was familiar to the Elizabethans, and here it adds its weight to the lovers' yoke of inauspicious stars. But this is one of very few quibbles in the last two acts. The wordplay which, in the first part of the play, served to point up the meaning of the action is no longer required. 55 What quibbles there are in the final scenes have, however, extraordinary force. Those spoken by Romeo after he has drunk the poison reaffirm the paradox of the play's experience at its most dramatic moment:

> O *true* Appothecary:
> Thy drugs are *quicke*. Thus with a kisse I die.                60
>                 (V.iii.119–20)

Like the Friar's herbs, the apothecary's poison both heals and destroys. He is *true* not only because he has spoken the truth to Romeo in describing the poison's potency, but because he has been true to his calling in finding the salve for Romeo's ills. His drugs are not only speedy, but also *quick* in the sense of 65 "life-giving." Romeo and Juliet "cease to die, by dying."

It is the prerogative of poetry to give effect and value to incompatible meanings. In *Romeo and Juliet*, several poetic means contribute to this end: the paradox the recurrent image, the juxtaposition of old and young in such a way that we are both absorbed by and aloof from the lovers' feelings, and the sparkling 70 wordplay. By such means Shakespeare ensures that our final emotion is neither the satisfaction we should feel in the lovers' death if the play were a simple expression of the *Liebestod* theme, nor the dismay of seeing two lives thwarted and destroyed by vicious fates, but a tragic equilibrium which includes and transcends both these feelings.                 75

1. What generalizations does the writer give to guide us among the many specific examples he cites?
2. Check the etymology, denotation, and connotation of *notorious, keening, sustains, imagery, quibbles, confound, equivocations, feigning, inauspicious, yoke, paradox, apothecary, potency, salve, prerogative, juxtaposition, Liebestod, equilibrium, transcend.*

---

**17-D**                 JULIET'S NURSE
                    *Susan Ross (student)*

This essay was written for an open-book essay test. The assignment was to show how one of the minor characters in the play helps us to understand one or more of the major characters. Countless critics have written on Shakespeare's use of minor characters, and students are unlikely to find anything fresh to say. This student, by concentrating firmly on the nurse, makes a vigorous statement that avoids clichés and sweeping generalizations and that shows a close reading of the play.

The most important minor character in *Romeo and Juliet* is the nurse. Her enthusiasm for sex and her lack of inhibitions are shown in her constant joking references to sexual intercourse. She makes it easy for us to understand Juliet's capacity for love and making love even though she is so young—only fourteen. In one sense, Juliet has led a sheltered life, but because she has been brought 5 up by the nurse she is not an ignorant little girl who knows nothing of the facts of life. When she falls in love with Romeo she acts like a passionate woman, not a teenager with a crush.

The nurse also shows us how young Juliet is in many ways in most of the

play. She gives Juliet advice on all sorts of things, and Juliet turns to her con- 10
stantly. She even trusts the nurse to keep the secret of her marriage to Romeo.

All of this makes us realize how much Juliet grows up in the few days covered
by the action of the play. In her last scene with the nurse Juliet is desperate
because her father is insisting that she marry Paris or be thrown out of the
house. Juliet again turns to the nurse for advice. The nurse knows all about 15
Juliet's secret marriage to Romeo and up to this point has been full of praise for
Romeo's good looks and charm, but now she tells Juliet to go ahead and marry
Paris because Paris is rich and handsome, Romeo is in exile, and a bird in the
hand is worth two in the bush. The fact that this would be bigamy doesn't
bother the nurse at all. Horrified by this treacherous immorality and insensitiv- 20
ity, Juliet calls the nurse "Ancient damnation! O most wicked fiend!" and swears
never to trust her again. From there on, Juliet realizes that she must solve her
problems alone.

By using contrasting characters Shakespeare helps us to understand Romeo
and Juliet and the picture of a beautiful young love. An essential contrast is the 25
nurse. Her crude earthiness and materialism make her a perfect foil for Juliet's
passionate idealism.

---

*17-E*                          FOR LOVE OR MONEY
                            *John Porter (student)*

This essay was written as homework on the assigned question: How important is
money in *Romeo and Juliet?* Note how the writer examines carefully all the relevant
lines to find their significance to the larger elements of the play.

When most poeple think of *Romeo and Juliet* they think of the beauty of
the balcony scene or the tragedy of the lovers' deaths in the tomb, but in the
background there is a busy city where money talks. We notice this particularly
with Juliet's father, Capulet.

In the first act one of his servants describes him as "the great rich Capulet," 5
and Juliet's nurse tells Romeo that the man who marries Juliet "shall have the
chinks" meaning that he will get a wife with a big dowry. In the third act
Capulet tells Juliet that she must marry Paris. When she refuses, he is furious
and threatens her. He tells her to "beg, starve, die in the streets" if she won't
obey him and says he will cut her off without a penny: "What is mine shall 10
never do thee good." In the next act Juliet takes the potion and goes into a
coma. Capulet thinks she is dead and is overcome with grief, but even in his
grief he thinks about his money:

> Death is my heir;
> My daughter he hath wedded. I will die                      15
> And leave him all. Life, living, all is Death's.

At the end of the play he is still thinking of money. He meets Romeo's father when the dead bodies of Romeo and Juliet are discovered in the tomb and asks to shake hands with him, saying

> This is my daughter's jointure, for no more          20
> Can I demand.

When Romeo's father answers that he will have a pure gold statue of Juliet made in her honor, Capulet meets the bid and says that he will have a statue that is just "as rich" made of Romeo. In Capulet, Shakespeare shows us a very realistic picture of a rich businessman who is used to bossing people around. All 25 these references to money, particularly to Juliet's dowry and inheritance, help us to understand the pressures on Juliet to obey her father and make us appreciate all the more her courage in defying him.

There are other examples of the importance of money to some of the characters. For instance, the nurse is pleased to take a tip from Romeo when she 30 gives him a message from Juliet, and at the beginning of the last act Romeo gets some illegal poison by giving forty ducats to an apothecary who says he is too poor to refuse the bribe.

Throughout the play, Shakespeare combines realism and idealism, and all these mentions of money make an ironic contrast to the attitudes of the lovers. 35 It is very appropriate that when Romeo first sees Juliet he says that she

> hangs upon the cheek of night
> Like a rich jewel in an Ethiop's ear—
> Beauty too rich for use, for earth too dear!

The lovers' feelings are far above the world of money and business, and that is 40 why they are such perfect symbols of young love.

---

**17-F**                     THE TRAGIC SENSE IN LOVE
                            *Rollo May*

These paragraphs from a chapter in *Love and Will* (1969) form a subdivision, which is here complete except for one parenthesized sentence. The writer, a well-known psychologist, takes a critical approach that is the reverse of that in Examples C, D, and E. Instead of focusing on a small, specific area in a single work, he touches on many works. By relating them all to a single point, the concept of love, he helps us to see new relationships among the works and to gain insight into modern attitudes and the nature of tragedy.

I recall a discussion with a highly-respected psychotherapist colleague and friend on the significance of the tragedy of Romeo and Juliet. My friend stated that the trouble with Romeo and Juliet was that they hadn't had adequate counseling. If they had had, they would not have committed suicide. Taken aback, I protested that I didn't think that was Shakespeare's point at all, and that 5 Shakespeare, as well as the other classical writers who have created and molded the literature which speaks to us age after age, is in this drama picturing how sexual love can grasp a man and woman and hurl them into heights and depths—the simultaneous presence of which we call tragic.

But my friend insisted that tragedy was a negative state and we, with our scientific enlightenment, had superseded it—or at least ought to at the earliest possible moment. I argued with him, as I do here, that to see the tragic in merely negative terms is a profound misunderstanding. Far from being a negation of life and love, the tragic is an ennobling and deepening aspect of our experience of sexuality and love. An appreciation of the tragic not only can help us avoid some egregious oversimplifications in life, but it can specifically protect us against the danger that sex and love will be banalized also in psychotherapy.

I am, of course, not using tragedy in its popular sense of "catastrophe," but as the self-conscious, personal realization that love brings both joy and destruction. I mean in this context a fact which has been known all through man's history but which our own age has accomplished the remarkable feat of forgetting, namely, that sexual love has the power to propel human beings into situations which can destroy not only themselves but many other people at the same time. We have only to call to mind Helen and Paris, or Tristan and Iseult, which are mythic presentations, whether based on historical personages or not, of the power of sexual love to seize man and woman and lift them up into a whirlwind which defies and destroys rational control. It is not by accident that these myths are presented over and over again in Western classic literature and passed down from generation to generation. For the stories come from a mythic depth of human experience in sexual love that is to be neglected only at the price of the impoverishment of our talk and writing about sex and love.

The tragic is an expression of a dimension of consciousness which gives richness, value, and dignity to human life. Thus the tragic not only makes possible the most humane emotions—like pity in the ancient Greek sense, sympathy for one's fellow man, and understanding—but without it, love becomes saccharine and insipid and eros sickens into the child who never grows up.

But the reader may raise an objection. Whatever the classical meaning of tragedy may be, are not the so-called tragic presentations in today's art, on the stage or in the pages of the novel, a portrayal of meaninglessness? Is not what we see in O'Neill's *The Iceman Cometh* the lack of the greatness and dignity in man, and is not *Waiting for Godot* a presentation of emptiness?

To this, I would make a double response. First, in presenting the *ostensible* lack of the greatness in man and his actions, or the lack of meaning, these works are doing infinitely more. They are confronting exactly what *is* tragic in our day, namely the complete confusion, banality, ambiguity, and vacuum of ethical standards and the consequent inability to act or, in *Who's Afraid of Virginia Woolf?*, the paralyzing fear of one's own tenderness. True, what we see in *The Iceman Cometh* is that greatness has fled from man, but this already presupposes a greatness, a dignity, a meaning. No one would ever think of reminding a Greek audience that it means something when Orestes kills his mother. But Willy Loman's wife in *Death of a Salesman* pleads, "Attention must be paid," and she was entirely right. It *does* mean something if a man is destroyed even if he is only a traveling salesman. . . . In my judgment, the best of the novels and dramas and paintings in our day are those which present to us the tremendous meaning in the fact of meaninglessness. The most tragic 55 thing of all, in the long run, is the ultimate attitude, "It doesn't matter." The ultimately tragic condition in a negative sense is the apathy, the adamant, rigid "cool," which refuses to admit the genuinely tragic.

But I would also ask, in rebuttal, do not these works we are citing profoundly reveal what is wrong with love and will in our day? Take the contradiction in 60 acting so vividly portrayed in *Waiting for Godot*. Didi says, "Let us go," and the stage direction in the play states, "They do not move." There could be no more telling vignette of modern man's problem with will, his inability to make significant acts. They wait for Godot: but in this waiting there is *expectation:* the waiting itself implies hope and belief. And they wait together. Or take the 65 rabid denial of love in the savage in-fighting of the married couples in *Who's Afraid of Virginia Woolf?*. This presentation of the inability to come to terms with whatever love and tenderness they do have shows more vividly and convincingly than reams of research what modern man's problem in love is.

1. What kinds of specific support does the writer give for his claim in the second paragraph that the tragic can be ennobling and can protect us from the danger of devaluing sex and love?
2. What transitional devices does he use?
3. Check the etymology, denotation, and connotation of *superseded, ennobling, egregious, banalized, catastrophe, mythic, personages, rational, insipid, eros, ostensible, adamant, rebuttal, citing, vignette, rabid, reams.*

---

*17-G*                 THE HOLES IN BLACK HOLES
                        *Martin Gardner*

These paragraphs are from a review of several books published in 1977 on astrophysics. A reviewer of new books has a special duty to evaluate their merits for his readers as well as to describe them. The comments on two of the books and some of those on a third are omitted here.

Black holes are hot. Although this is literally true (according to the latest theories) of some black holes, I mean they are hot as a topic. The books [below] are only fragments of this year's crop that deal entirely or in part with black holes. Why such obsessive interest in astronomical objects that may not even exist, and that in any case cannot be fully understood without knowing general relativity 5 theory and quantum mechanics?

Let the first paragraph of Isaac Asimov's book [*The Collapsing Universe: The Story of Black Holes*] set the tone for what I believe is the answer.

> Since 1960 the universe has taken on a wholly new face. It has become more exciting, more mysterious, more violent, and more extreme as our knowledge concerning it has suddenly expanded. And the most exciting, most mysterious, most violent, and most extreme phenomenon of all has the simplest, plainest, calmest, and mildest name—nothing more than a "black hole."

Black. Black is beautiful, black is ominous, black is awesome, black is apocalyptic, black is blank. "A hole is nothing," Asimov continues, "and if it is black, we can't even see it. Ought we to get excited over an invisible nothing?"

Nothing. Why does anything exist? Why not just nothing? This is the superultimate metaphysical question. Obviously no one can answer it, yet there are times (for some people) when the question can overwhelm the soul with such power and anguish as to induce nausea. Indeed, that is what Sartre's great novel, *Nausea*, is all about.

Suddenly we are being told that if a star is sufficiently massive it eventually will undergo a runaway collapse that ends with the star's matter crushed completely out of existence. Not only that, but our entire universe may slowly stop expanding, go into a contracting phase, and finally disappear into a black hole, like an acrobatic elephant jumping into its anus. There is speculation (not taken seriously by the experts) that every black hole is joined to a "white hole"—a hole that gushes energy instead of absorbing it. The two holes are supposedly connected by an "Einstein-Rosen bridge" or "wormhole." When a huge sun collapses into a black hole, so goes the conjecture, a companion white hole instantly appears at some other spot in spacetime. This could explain the incredible outpouring of energy from the quasars, those mysterious objects, apparently far beyond our galaxy, that nobody yet understands. Was the big bang which created our universe the white hole that exploded into existence after a previous universe collapsed into its black hole?

It is easy to understand why the religiously inclined are excited by such wild, speculative cosmology. The heavens declare the glory of God and the firmament showeth his handiwork. Nor is it hard to understand why those who are into Eastern philosophy, pseudoeastern cults, parapsychology, and unorthodox science are also fascinated. If the universe can be *that* crazy, so goes the argument, then why be disturbed when the Maharishi announces, as he recently did, that transcendental meditation can enable one to levitate and become invisible? Black holes are the latest symbols of unfathomable mystery. Public interest in them is, I am persuaded, no indication of interest in science, but rather a peculiar by-product of the specter of the supernatural that is now haunting North America.

For the reader with no understanding of relativity and quantum theory—that is, the average reader—Asimov's book is the best of the lot. The old maestro writes with his unfailing clarity, humor, informality, and enthusiasm. Like all top science-fiction writers, he knows exactly where to draw the line between serious science and fantasy. Periodically he reminds his readers that there is as yet no clear observational evidence that black holes exist, and that "almost anything some astronomers suggest about a black hole is denied by other astronomers."

• • •

[Omitted here are several paragraphs summarizing Asimov's presentation of the chief theories on black holes.] Readers who want to go more deeply into the structure of black holes will find Robert Wald's book [*The Theory of the Big Bang and Black Holes*] a worthy purchase. He is a physicist at the University of Chicago's Fermi Institute, and his book is based on a series of lectures he gave at the university in 1976. It covers the same ground as Asimov's book, but with more technical information. The last chapter is particularly good in summarizing the recent discoveries of the young Cambridge mathematical physicist, Stephen Hawking. . . . 60

Hawking's major discovery is that black holes are not black. Quantum theory, it turns out, implies that in the powerful gravitational field surrounding a black hole there is constant creation of particles (of every kind) and their antiparticles. Some of these particles fall into the hole, others escape as radiation. There is thus a constant leakage of energy, and a flux around the hole that could be observed. 65

If black holes are large, this loss of energy is slow and negligible. Hawking believes, however, that the big bang may have been chaotic enough to have fabricated billions upon billions of micro black holes, each smaller than a proton, but containing a mass of a few hundred million tons. These "primeval" miniholes would now be in their final stages of evaporation. They would get hotter and hotter, smaller and smaller, and finally explode in a tremendous burst of particles and gamma rays. 70 75

Nigel Calder's big, handsome volume [*The Key to the Universe: A Report on the New Physics*] devotes only two chapters to black holes, but they are excellent nontechnical summaries, and the other chapters are a splendid introduction to the latest theories of matter. Calder is one of the most reliable of British science writers. His book, based on a popular BBC television show which he wrote and presented last January, is abundantly illustrated with diagrams and photographs, including pictures of famous physicists whose faces the public seldom sees. 80

Calder is unusually skillful in explaining quark theory and why it is rapidly outrunning its nearest rival, the "bootstrap" theory. The bootstrap hypothesis is the "democratic" view that none of the particles that make up matter is more fundamental than any other. Each is simply an interaction of a set of other particles. The entire family thus supports itself in midair like a man tugging on his bootstraps, or a transcendental mediator in the lotus position, suspended a few feet above the floor. 85 90

Quark theory is the aristocratic view that particles are combinations of more elementary units which Murray Gell-Mann named quarks after the line in *Finnegans Wake*, "Three quarks for Muster Mark!" At first only three kinds of quarks were believed necessary; up, down, and strange, together with their antiparticles. The three kinds are called "flavors." There are now reasons for thinking there is a fourth flavor, "charm." Each flavor comes in three "colors." In the U.S. the colors naturally are red, white and blue. (Calder's plates use red, blue, and green, with turquoise, mauve, and yellow for the anticolors.) This makes twelve quarks in all, with their twelve antiquarks. 95 100

Color and charm are, of course, whimsical terms unrelated to their usual meaning, although the mixing of quark colors does obligingly correspond (as Calder shows) to the mixing of actual colors. Some theorists think there are still other quark properties such as truth, beauty, and goodness. Abdus Salam, the noted Pakistani physicist, is now promoting a "quark liberation movement" that 105 regards quarks as made of "prequarks" or "preons." In Peking a group of young physicists have a similar view involving "stratons" that form an infinite nest like a set of Chinese boxes.

The essences of these debates are skillfully outlined in Calder's book. He even leads you to the brink of the new, exciting "gauge theories" that may someday 110 unify the strong, weak, and electromagnetic forces—perhaps even gravity—in one fundamental theory.

• • •

Our two remaining books, entirely about black holes and related matters, plunge into unrestrained fantasy. Adrian Berry, science writer of a London newspaper, makes only a feeble attempt to separate fact from reasonable con- 115 jecture, or reasonable conjecture from eccentric conjecture. His book [*The Iron Sun: Crossing the Universe Through Black Holes*] is best read as you would an Asimov science-fiction novel. Indeed, some of Asimov's novels anticipate much of what Berry has to say.

Berry is concerned mostly with the conjecture that every black hole is joined 120 by a wormhole to a white hole in some other part of the cosmos, or to a white hole in a completely different cosmos. Perhaps the "other" world is made of antimatter, like the Antiterra of Nabokov's novel *Ada*. Matter pours into our black holes to emerge as antimatter in the other world's white holes, while its antimatter pours into its black holes to emerge from our white holes. 125

Some recent calculations have suggested that a spaceship just might be able to rocket into a black hole and avoid hitting the dreadful singularity. Berry imagines a future in which spaceships use black and white holes as entrances and exits for instantaneous travel across vast distances. When this becomes pos- sible, he writes, mankind will be able to roam and colonize the entire universe. 130 Science fiction heroes have been doing this for decades, but Berry dresses it up in the latest jargon, and his book is fun to read if you don't take it seriously.

John Gribbin's book [*White Holes: Cosmic Gushers of the Universe*] on white holes carries this kind of fantasy to still greater heights. Indeed, his book is almost as funny as John G. Taylor's *Black Holes*, published in 1973. Taylor 135 is the mathematical physicist at the University of London whose latest book, *Superminds*, is about British children whom Taylor is convinced can bend spoons by paranormal powers better than Uri Geller's. The psi force is probably electromagnetic, Taylor argues. His black hole book is less preposterous, but it does use the black hole as a jump-into point for occult speculations. 140

Gribbin, who has a doctorate in astrophysics, is the co-author of an earlier book of quasi-science, *The Jupiter Effect*. This great work explains why "there can be little doubt" that in 1982 Los Angeles will be the site of "the most mas- sive earthquake experienced during this century." In 1982 all nine planets will be on the same side of the sun. Jupiter's pull will thus be augmented by the other planets. This will cause unusual sunspot activity which will agitate the earth's atmosphere. This in turn will agitate the San Andreas fault. "There can be little doubt" is the phrase that should have forewarned the good Dr. Asimov before he wrote his introduction to this book.

The most absurd passage in Gribbin's new book, the one on white holes, speculates on how tachyons may explain psychic spoon bending. Tachyons are conjectured particles that go faster than light. There is not the slightest evidence they exist, but if they do they would, for certain observers, move backward in time. "Perhaps," writes Gribbin,

> the spectacular production of the bent spoons produces the wave of astonishment from the audience, releasing a flood of tachyons which travel backward in time to cause the spoons to bend just before they are produced to cause the surprise. If such a process could be triggered deliberately, it would explain telepathic phenomena as the direct tachyonic communication between minds, but something as physical as spoon bending seems to require the pooled effort of many minds— except, according to John Taylor, in the case of children. This should be no surprise in the light of the above; children have more vivid imaginations than most adults, with more powerful emotions presumably releasing stronger tachyonic vibrations. Perhaps this tachyonic link even provides a clue to such mysteries as poltergeists!

Black holes and bent spoons. The healthy side of the black-hole craze is that it reminds us of how little science knows, and how vast is the realm about which science knows nothing. The sick side of the black-hole boom is the appropriation of astrophysical mysteries to shore up the doctrines of pseudoscientific cults, or the shabby performances of psychic rip-off artists.

Penrose [Roger Penrose, a theoretical physicist at Oxford University, whose work on black holes was cited in an omitted section of the review] is now doing research and publishing papers on a bizarre mathematical entity he has invented, called a "twistor.". . . I wouldn't be surprised to learn that even now some hack journalist is working on an article for *Reader's Digest* titled "Twistors: Cosmic Carriers of Psychic Energy?" With a little help from the media, twistors could become hotter than black holes.

1. What seem to be the author's reasons for taking up the books in this sequence?
2. What examples do you find of analogy, classification, induction, deduction, and definition?
3. How do the last paragraphs form a conclusion to the opening paragraph of the essay?
4. Where and how does the writer combine a summary of the contents of a book with his evaluation of it?
5. Where and how does the author use satire? colloquial words and phrases?
6. Check the etymology, denotation, and connotation of *apocalyptic, levitate, unfathomable, specter, fabricated, bootstrap, conjecture, instantaneous, preposterous, appropriation, shore up.*

*17-H*  DAVID BOWIE LOOKS BACK IN HORROR
*Tom Carson*

This review from the *Village Voice* (October 1980) of Bowie's 1980 album is almost complete. Notice how the writer tries to describe music—a nonverbal medium—through words.

If any one figure summed up the '70s—as music, *Zeitgeist*, pose, whatever—it was David Bowie. From the start he parodied every rock and roll ideal of the relation between performer and community, performance and feeling. . . . His abandonment, in the late '70s, of the role of new-age spokesman, and subsequent retreat into the avant-garde, had the earmarks of his usual canny timing; 5 but it was also, I think, a case of utopianism gone sour.

RCA, can't blame them for trying, are doing their best to treat *Scary Monsters* as Bowie's return to the commercial fold, and the album does address itself to the world outside with a concreteness the *Low* trilogy determinedly shied away from. . . . The images Bowie advanced then as gambits, analogues, imag- 10 inative strategies, have been turned into lifestyles—it's one thing to feel disengaged and dehumanized, and another to love it—and that seems to haunt him: on *Scary Monsters*, he looks back in horror. Only an idiot could dance to this nightmare.

The album doesn't have the arctic grace of *Low* and *"Heroes,"* or *Lodger's* 15 airborne sweep and watercolor washes of sound—instead, it's the musical equivalent of brutalist in architecture: dissonant, abrasive, deliberately unpretty, all the raw materials left sticking bluntly out. On the opening cut, "It's No Game," the music comes swaying and shuddering into a leaden caricature of a funk beat; Bowie's vocal is one wrenching, off-key howl, intercut with bursts of Jap- 20 anese that sound like an interrogation scene from a war movie. At the end, the song falls apart, chunk by chunk, until all that's left are the maddening pushbutton tones of a Frippertronics tape loop, before Bowie's shouts of "Shut up!" abruptly abort the track. (Fripp's presence, and other evidence—lockstep bass-and-drum dynamics that recall similar motifs on *"Heroes,"* the fact that some 25 of the topical references are slightly dated—suggest that some of this material was cut before *Lodger.*)

*Scary Monsters* takes the dread that's been in all Bowie's work and makes it, for the first time, the only theme. The characters that drift through these songs are numb inside, bewildered and lost everywhere else—blankly estranged from 30 cause and effect. . . . and most of them don't know it or are too far gone to care. On the title cut, the drums come in at a panicky gallop, the guitar oscillates like a police siren outside the window, and the telegraphic cut-up lyrics sound like they could be about half the girls at Max's Kansas City—"She had a horror of rooms she was tired you can't hide beat/When I looked in her eyes they were 35 blue but nobody home."

Bowie has created a cold, dense, jagged, sound of half-heard textures and freeze-frame discontinuity—as visceral and dankly frightening as anything since *Second Edition*. Fripp's guitar evokes a formalized hysteria, while the synthesizer struggles to hold the tunes on course; for all their rhythmic top-heav- 40 iness, these songs have no real anchor, and Bowie's use of dissociated repeti-tion—recycling one instrumental part while completely altering its context—mirrors the shellshocked disorientation at the album's center. And there are his-torical references that throw the songs into sudden relief, like the disjointed Bo Diddley riff that lurches "Up the Hill Backwards" into gear, or the startling 45 juxtaposition at the end of "Teenage Wildlife," when Bowie's voice goes soaring off into a letter-perfect Four Seasons falsetto.

This record is just as self-referential as the trilogy, but now the references are to Bowie-the-star. . . . most spectacularly on "Ashes to Ashes," an answer to "Space Oddity." With its disembodied echoing keyboard notes dropping like a 50 drunken rain, it's a condemnation of the anywhere-out-of-this-world escapism Bowie once made so attractive. The shifting sensations of strung-out decay—abasement, pride, the attempts to impose the illusion of order on quicksand—are brilliantly detailed and there's an epic finality in the song's last, deathly verdict on the age: "Ashes to ashes, funk to funky/We know Major Tom's a 55 junky. . . ." The sleep of reason does bring forth monsters. . . .

Significantly, the LP's one hint of redemption is in someone else's words, in Bowie's cover of Tom Verlaine's "Kingdom Come." Even here, the hope is muted, choked back. The original gets its force from a dynamic rhythm and the amazing fluidity of Verlaine's guitar; Bowie reduces Verlaine's kinetic swirls 60 to a static synthesizer riff, rigidifies the beat, and staves off the title line until the coda. This way, salvation seems even more distant, and it's no conclusion. After "Because You're Young," a recap of "It's No Game"—not harrowing this time, just exhausted—fades the album to an unresolved end.

*Scary Monsters* has its failings: occasional cleverness, a few lapses into 65 Bowie's old hypercharged imagist kitsch. But its larger problem, I'd guess, is that he's been so distanced and knowing in the past that people may not trust his claims on horror now. I think I do, but then I always suspected him of being more of a romantic—which is to say, a moralist—than he ever let on. Is it really any wonder that when he finally lets his romanticism out of the bag, it comes 70 out as a shriek of outrage?

1. Where and how does the writer use comparison and contrast, background infor-mation, specific examples, and generalizations to present his opinions?
2. To describe the album, where does the writer use concrete, specific words? figura-tive language? specialized terminology?
3. Check the etymology, denotation, and connotation of *Zeitgeist, canny, utopianism, gambits, analogues, watercolor washes, dissonant, abrasive, tape loop, lockstep, estranged, oscillates, freeze-frame, visceral, dankly, riff, falsetto, referential, disembodied, abasement, quicksand, kinetic, staves off, coda, imagist, kitsch, romanticism.*

*17-1*       THE TELEPHONE . . . BOON OR BANE?
                    *Anthony Rush (student)*

In this essay the writer uses exaggeration to satirize the tyranny of telephones.

Of all the marvels of technology that our wizards have conjured out of their Busy-Box brains through the past hundred years, the most traumatizing is the telephone.

It did not start out that way. No. At its inception, people rejoiced. Through the years they no doubt saw their initial exuberance justified many times over. 5 Who can deny that its capacity for early warning has saved untold numbers from perils of countless kinds and all degrees of severity? Disasters, major and minor, have been averted and human life preserved. A street or home accident, the smell of smoke, or any other apparent danger immediately and automatically triggers in us the need to communicate farther than we can be heard by 10 shouting and faster than we can run. So we seek a telephone. We augment our powers and, in the instances cited, we apply them to the social good. This is a most happy state of affairs.

But this obedient servant can turn into a diabolical master. Like death itself, from nowhere and unannounced, it charges into the very center of our brains 15 and destroys any precious moment of reflection we may have been successful in snatching for our private selves in this harried world. It commands. It demands! Worse than a toothache or a baby's crying, the causes of which are known, it persists and insists that we drop everything else and pay it heed, but it never offers the tiniest clue why we should. This is wrong. Wrong! Wrong! 20 Wrong! (and ring! ring! ring!)

If I barge into your solitude and indicate that I am about to rob you of any measure of your human dignity, then I am like a filthy fly on your lip as you doze on the beach; I am a mosquito on the tip of your little toe; I am an ant in your picnic sandwich; I am a pernicious pest! If A. G. Bell, in his hot pursuit to 25 make "big mouths" of us, had been constantly interrupted by phone calls, his invention would have been stillborn, a Rube Goldberg contraption fit only for a cartoon. So, weep over all the music, poetry, painting, and sculpture that we have been cheated of just because a telephone rang.

Remove it! Tell all your friends to write you letters. You can read them at 30 your leisure, and you will save lots of money. In fact, you will save so much money that you will easily afford frequent mini vacations at a remote mountain lodge where there are no phones and where friends' letters will carry more meaning—even when they come postage due.

Remember: there is no known physical, moral, or spiritual law anywhere in 35 this glorious universe that enjoins you to answer a ringing phone.
Don't.

1. What clues does the writer give that his essay is a satire? How early in it would a reader be sure to see the writer's intention? Is his exaggeration too much even for satire?

**2.** What devices does he use to catch the reader's attention in his first paragraph? in his second paragraph?

**3.** How and where does he use figurative language?

**4.** Check the etymology, denotation, and connotation of *traumatizing, inception, exuberance, pernicious, stillborn, contraption.*

---

*17-J*      HOW TO WRITE LIKE A SOCIAL SCIENTIST
             *Samuel T. Williamson*

These paragraphs form half of an essay from the *Saturday Review* (1947). To satirize long-winded writing, the author reverses his real meaning.

There once was a time when everyday folk spoke one language, and learned men wrote another. It was called the Dark Ages. The world is in such a state that we may return to the Dark Ages if we do not acquire wisdom. If social scientists have answers to our problems yet feel under no obligation to make themselves understood, then we laymen must learn their language. This may 5 take some practice, but practice should become perfect by following six simple rules of the guild of social science writers. Examples which I give are sound and well tested; they come from manuscripts I edited.

*Rule 1. Never use a short word when you can think of a long one.* Never say "now," but "currently." It is not "soon" but "presently." You did not have 10 "enough" but a "sufficiency." Never do you come to the "end" but to the "termination." This rule is basic.

*Rule 2. Never use one word when you can use two or more.* Eschew "probably." Write, "it is probable," and raise this to "it is not improbable." Then you'll be able to parlay "probably" into "available evidence would tend to 15 indicate that it is not unreasonable to suppose."

*Rule 3. Put one-syllable thoughts into polysyllabic terms.* Instead of observing that a work force might be bigger and better, write, "In addition to quantitative enlargment, it is not improbable that there is need also for qualitative improvement in the personnel of the service." If you have discovered that 20 musicians out of practice can't hold jobs, report that "the fact of rapid deterioration of musical skill when not in use soon converts the unemployed into the unemployable." Resist the impulse to say that much men's clothing is machine made. Put it thus: "Nearly all operations in the industry lend themselves to performance by machine, and all grades of men's clothing sold in significant 25 quantity involve a very substantial amount of machine work."

*Rule 4. Put the obvious in terms of the unintelligible.* When you write that "the product of the activity of janitors is expended in the identical locality in which that activity takes place," your lay reader is in for a time of it. After an hour's puzzlement, he may conclude that janitors' sweepings are thrown on the 30 town dump. See what you can do with this: "Each article sent to the cleaner is handled separately." You become a member of the guild in good standing if you put it like this: "Within the cleaning plant proper the business of the industry involves several well-defined processes, which, from the economic point of view, may be characterized simply by saying that most of them require separate 35 handling of each individual garment or piece of material to be cleaned."

*Rule 5. Announce what you are going to say before you say it.* This pitcher's wind-up technique before hurling towards—not at—home plate has two varieties. First is the quick windup: "In the following section the policies of the administration will be considered." Then you become strong enough for the 40 contortionist wind-up: "Perhaps more important, therefore, than the question of what standards are in a particular case, there are the questions of the extent of observance of these standards and the methods of their enforcement." Also you can play with reversing Rule 5 and *say what you have said after you have said it.* 45

*Rule 6. Defend your style as "scientific."* Look down on—not up to—clear simple English. Sneer at it as "popular." Scorn it as "journalistic." Explain your failure to put more mental sweat into your writing on the ground that "the social scientists who want to be scientific believe that we can have scientific description of human behavior and trustworthy predictions in the scientific 50 sense only as we build adequate taxonomic systems for observable phenomena and symbolic systems for the manipulation of ideal and abstract entities."

1. Briefly rewrite the six rules under the heading "How *Not* to Write like a Social Scientist." What is lost in the probable effect on the reader?
2. Williamson's main points are much the same as Zinsser's in "Clutter" (Unit 6-D). Which presentation is more likely to influence a reader?
3. Check the etymology, denotation, and connotation of *eschew, taxonomic, phenomena, entities.* When and what were the Dark Ages in European history?

---

**17-K**                     VIRTUOUS SIN
                           *The New York Times*

This short satire, given here complete, makes its point by a transfer of the real object of the criticism—the use of gambling and pornography—to other areas.

By sponsoring weekly bingo games, churches and synagogues across the land have long enjoyed the tribute that vice can be made to pay to virtue. Their example has led to "Las Vegas Nights," on which such pastimes as blackjack, roulette and even craps are turned to worthy purposes. And now we learn from *Variety* of senior citizens in Bemidji, Minn., who arranged for showings of an 5 X-rated film, "Erotic Adventures of Zorro," to raise money for a new senior citizens center. It brought $825. Clearly, the vistas of vice are vast: pot parties for the benefit of the American Cancer Society perhaps; after-hours clubs run by Alcoholics Anonymous; massage parlors to finance Planned Parenthood.

Since the goods would no doubt be exemplary, the prices fair and the advertis- 10
ing honest, the cause of moral uplift would be well served.

1. How appropriate are the other areas to which the satire is transferred?
2. Check the full dictionary entry for *exemplary*.

## ASSIGNMENTS

In each of these assignments, try to persuade your readers to accept your point of
view. Remember to support your criticism with specific details about your subject and
to make use of the aids to exposition, organizing, and reasoning discussed in earlier
units.

1. Write a critical review of a movie, TV drama, book, or play that you saw or read
   recently.
2. Which one of the essays you have read so far in this book has interested you most?
   Write a critical analysis of its good points—and of its bad points, if you find any—
   and explain why you think other readers might like it.
3. Which TV commercials do you think are the best? the worst? Write a critical analysis, contrasting one or two commercials that you like with one or two you dislike.
4. Who is your favorite singer, composer, music group? Write a critical analysis of the
   qualities you admire. Include discussion of any weaknesses.
5. What recent record album do you think shows decided talent or lack of talent?
   Write a critical analysis explaining exactly what you think is right or wrong in it.
6. Write a critical analysis of the performance of the best and poorest players on the
   athletic team you watch most often.
7. Rewrite one or more of these essays as a satire.

# The Research Paper

The label "research paper" is applied to a considerable range of writing and is frequently used interchangeably with "report," but the further you go in scholarly work the more you will see the difference between a report and a true research paper. Both the writer of a report and the writer of a true research paper base their work on information they have gathered from various sources, and for both this process of gathering information by discovering facts and opinions is "research." There the similarity ends.

The writer of a report does not try to find facts unknown before or to make new interpretations of known facts. Although the writer of a report may include many of his or her own opinions, there is no suggestion in the report that these opinions have never been made by others. Many magazine and newspaper articles use "research" in this way. The information presented may be new to their readers but it has been available in books or other publications and was not discovered for the first time by the writers. Writing such a paper can be a very rewarding activity: you learn something that is new to you, and your paper will inform others. However, you are not adding anything to the body of facts and opinions that already exist on the subject.

The primary purpose of the writer of a true research paper is to reach a new understanding of a subject either by analyzing new facts and opinions or by reevaluating known facts and opinions, or by both methods. The writer of a true research paper not only gives a clear orderly report on information gathered from various sources but also uses that information to say something not said in the sources. As you go on in scholarly work, you will be increasingly expected to perform original research of this kind.

While you are an undergraduate it is unlikely that you will have a chance to discover something that is both new and important, such as a cure for cancer or a rock carving proving absolutely that Egyptians visited Mexico four thousand years ago. But this does not mean that you cannot do original research that will be interesting and valuable. Two general approaches are open to you:

**1. You can gather information on a relatively small subject that no one has examined before or that no one has examined thoroughly.** For example, you can collect all the available facts on a local political situation or environmental problem, or use newspaper files to put together the story of an unsolved crime and work out your own suggestions for the solution, or interview an elderly person and, with the help of background reading in appropriate historical material, write a chapter in a projected biography of that person. There are thousands of such subjects, full of facts that have not yet been sorted out and interpreted.

**2. You can examine a well-known subject in a new light.** For example, new theories continue to appear on the assassination of President Kennedy, and a good researcher will examine each new theory, comparing and contrasting it with earlier ones and also reexamining the earlier ones in the light of the new one, so that with each new theory a revision must be made of all previous ones, if only to conclude, with supporting evidence, that the new one does not change anything.

Whichever general approach you choose, you may gather information from printed sources of all kinds, from laboratory experiments, from opinion surveys, or from a combination of all of these. The more information you have, the more authoritative you will be on your subject and the better able to say something significant.

Writing a research paper is hard and exacting work, and most of that work takes place before the actual writing of the paper. You will spend many hours searching for, selecting, and using source materials. You will go down blind alleys and will have to try to reconcile conflicting opinions or contradictory evidence. The process is often like detective work, and sometimes an answer you are hunting down will escape you, but the hunt itself can be exciting, and each new piece of evidence that you discover will make you feel triumphant.

In writing every research paper, you must take five major consecutive steps: (1) choose a subject; (2) build a bibliography; (3) gather information from reading and whatever other sources are appropriate, such as surveys and laboratory experiments; (4) sort out and organize the information; and (5) write and document the paper. Each of these steps is explained in the pages that follow.

## Choosing a Subject

Choose a subject that you enjoy. A research paper, compared to the other assignments in this book, is a long-drawn-out affair, and you will have to live with your subject for several weeks. What are you interested in? What would you like to know more about? If you are a business major, you might examine the economic forecasts published in newspapers and business journals in a particular month in the recent past and then determine their accuracy by finding out about the present state of the economy. If you are a science major, you might examine the published opinions on the value of a new drug or on a new cancer threat, find out its history and that of others similar to it, ask physicians for their opinions, and arrive at your own conclusions. If you are a sports fan, you might analyze your favorite team's successes and failures in the last year, the opinions of sports writers and of the coach and players themselves. If you are interested in history, you have an irreplaceable resource in any elderly person you know, and you can write a biography by setting the facts of his or her life in the appropriate historical context. If you are interested in human behavior you can devise a questionnaire on a controversial topic, make an opinion survey of the students on your campus, and use the results along with your reading on the subject as the basis for an analysis of the psychological and social significance of the students' answers.

Whatever subject you choose, be sure to *limit* it so that you can cover it thoroughly. The broader the subject, the less likely you will be to find anything new to say. If you are writing a biography of one of your grandparents, concentrate on a few years or even on a few months or weeks and give those in full detail, with at most only a summary of the rest of his or her life as a frame for the most interesting part of it.

Narrowing your subject to a specific, manageable topic and then forming an opinion—or main point—on that topic, is a continuing process. The more you learn about your subject in general and your topic in particular, the more precisely you will define what you want to cover.

Whatever your subject, the resources of your college and local libraries will almost certainly be of major importance to your research. An important step in defining your topic should be a survey of library resources on your general subject. What you find will help you decide on a particular topic.

Begin with a bird's-eye view of what is known on your subject by looking it up in several sources of general information. Encyclopedias are most likely to be helpful. These include not only the *Britannica, Americana,* and *New International,* but others specializing in a single field, such as religion, education, or sociology; collections or brief biographies, such as the international *Who's Who,* the *Dictionary of National Biography* for the British, and *Who's Who in America* for Americans; and collections of facts and statistics, such as the *World Almanac* and other yearbooks. *Winchell's Guide to Reference Books,* kept up to date by occasional supplements, classifies by type and subject matter all kinds of reference works besides the famous ones just mentioned.

As you look through all these, make notes on 3″ × 5″ or 4″ × 6″ ruled index cards of the names and facts they emphasize. Write only one note on each card so that you will be able to arrange and rearrange them later in many relationships. Record with each the title and page number of the work from which you took it. These notes will help you to keep the main outlines of your subject straight so that you will see the significance and relationships of the parts. If an encyclopedia article mentions important books on your subject, make notes of these by author and title on separate cards so that you can check later on their availability in your library.

Next, consult your two big sources of information on the material printed on your subject—the library catalog and the appropriate periodical indexes. The catalog, whether it is in card or book form or computerized, lists every book in the library alphabetically by both author and title and usually also under several headings for the subjects with which the book deals. For example, you will probably find *The Uses of Enchantment* by Bruno Bettelheim listed not only under *B* by the author's name and under *U* by its title, but also in several subject categories, such as "Fairy Tales—History and Criticism," "Psychoanalysis," "Folk-lore and Children," and "Child Psychology."

**Note:** Remember that besides the main college library there may be special departmental collections, such as chemistry or agriculture, in the buildings that house those departments. If these are not indexed in the main catalog and if any are likely to have material relevant to your subject, you must consult their catalogs as well.

The periodical indexes, probably shelved in the reference room of the library, will help you find articles in periodicals—newspapers, magazines, and journals of all kinds.

The *Reader's Guide to Periodical Literature* is issued monthly in magazine form and at intervals cumulated into volumes covering several years. It indexes, under both author and subject headings, the contents of the better-known American (and a few British) periodicals on general subjects since 1900.

*Poole's Index* covers British and American periodicals from 1802 to 1906.

*The International Index* covers a selected list of American and European periodicals in the humanities, social sciences, and sciences, from 1916 to 1965. The *Social Science and Humanities Index* covers about 175 American and British periodicals from 1965 to 1974. Two separate publications continue the listing, the *Social Sciences Index* and the *Humanities Index*.

There are many specialized indexes for particular fields, such as agriculture, engineering, psychology, industrial art, literature, dentistry, medicine, and law. Some of these list books and bulletins as well as articles and periodicals.

The *New York Times Index,* published annually, covers all that newspaper's stories and articles. Since most major news is handled on the same or the following day by all the principal newspapers, this index can help you locate material in other papers as well.

Check the catalog to find out which periodicals related to your subject are in your library; ask a reference librarian what others are available at nearby libraries and how to arrange for photocopies of articles in periodicals held by libraries you cannot visit.

The reference collection in any library is your chief means of finding where to look for material on any subject. Familiarize yourself with what the one in your library contains. Walk beside the shelves, reading titles and leafing through any work that seems promising. Knowing how to take full advantage of the reference collection is as necessary for a researcher as knowing how to use the telephone is for most Americans.

Probably the most valuable of all sources of information in any library are the reference librarians, who are specially trained in information retrieval. Turn to them when you find yourself in a blind alley, but always first try to solve problems yourself—the more practice you have, the more efficient a researcher you will be.

In your preliminary survey of resources, do not try to make a thorough search or you will be overwhelmed by the quantity available. Instead, just make sure that there is plenty of material on your general subject and that it includes up-to-date items—check publication dates. Also, all the time you are looking over the catalog and the indexes, be alert for clues that will help you to narrow your subject to a manageable topic. The titles of books and articles will give you an overall impression of what others have said and may suggest a topic appropriate for your purposes. Keep your mind open for such possibilities and jot them down as they occur to you.

When you have made a quick survey of the available material, think over what you now know of your subject, keeping in mind the constraints of the length and deadline for the paper and of the need to give your readers something on your subject—facts, opinions, or both—that they will not find elsewhere. Now choose a specific topic, but remember that further research may make you revise it more than once. This topic will be the basis for your next step, building a bibliography.

## Building a Bibliography

In surveying your subject and the availability of material, you have already begun to build what will eventually become your final bibliography—a list of all the printed material you used for the paper. At this stage you should build your working bibliography—a much longer list with everything you find mentioned that seems worth at least a glance.

With a supply of 3″ × 5″ index cards in hand, go back to the library catalog and the periodical indexes. For every work listed that looks at all promising, take down the information you need to find it in the library, one card for each book or article. The general information that you have already gathered from reading the encyclopedias and surveying the library resources will help you to recognize what may prove useful, as may the titles of the works. If in doubt about the value of something, fill out a card on it anyway. It is better to have to discard items later than to miss a good one.

For each book you will need the full name of the author (last name first, for convenience in alphabetizing), the title (underlined to indicate a book), and the library call number for your later convenience in locating the book in the stacks. You should also take down the place of publication, the name of the publisher, the date of publication and any special information that the library catalog gives as to an editor, translator, or edition other than the first. All this will be required for your final bibliography. A typical example of a completed card looks like this:

> Tindall, Gillian
>
> <u>Dances of Death</u>
> New York: Walker, 1973
> PR 6070
> .I45
> D3

The information needed for articles is slightly different. For each, give the author, with last name first, as before (if the article is anonymous, leave blank the line where the author's name would regularly go and alphabetize the card by the article title instead); the title (in quotation marks to indicate that it is only part of something); the title of the periodical (underlined); the volume number (only if it is not a weekly or monthly periodical) and full date of the copy that contains the article; and the inclusive page numbers within which it appears. A typical example of a completed card looks like this:

> Brower, Kenneth
>
> "Environmental Vigilante"
> <u>The Atlantic Monthly</u>
> (November 1980),
> pp. 65-68

## Primary and Secondary Sources

There are two kinds of source material: primary and secondary. If your topic is a particular company's chance for future success, then any information issued by the company and any statements made by its officials, either oral or written, are primary sources. Information and opinions of writers discussing the company in books and periodical articles are secondary. But if your topic is an evaluation of the accuracy of the forecasts about the company made by financial analysts, then their opinions become primary sources, and secondary sources for such a study would be other analysts' opinions of their opinions.

In research, base your opinions on primary sources whenever possible—information "straight from the horse's mouth." Use secondary sources to show the extent to which you agree or disagree with others who have written on the subject and to give general background information. If your topic is a biographical study of your grandfather and his struggles as a farmer in the Depression of the 1930s, your chief source of information will be what he and any of his contemporaries can tell you (primary) and economic reports published at that time (primary). For background material you should rely on facts and opinions about the period given in books and articles by respected authorities (secondary), especially the more recent ones, since those writers will have the benefit of greater perspective.

When you begin your project you may not know which writers are respected, well-known authorities, which are respectable though little known, and which are questionable. Your ability to judge will grow as your familiarity with the subject grows. But even at the start, watch out in your secondary sources for any signs of biased opinions, illogical deductions, unsupported claims, and sweeping generalizations. What sources do they use? What other writers on the subject do they refer to as authoritative? If you are in doubt about a book, see if it is mentioned in the *Book Review Digest* or reviews in appropriate scholarly journals and, of course, ask your instructor's advice.

Remember that articles in newspapers and popular magazines are intended as introductions to a subject. They are very useful for up-to-the-minute information, but for a more thorough analysis you must go to specialized magazines, scholarly journals, and books. Always check the most recent publications as well as the famous and basic ones.

## Reading and Note-Taking

When you have listed on your index cards all the promising materials on your subject available in the library, you are ready to proceed to the actual reading and note-taking.

Much of your reading in school and college has been the word-by-word digestion of the content of textbooks, but now you must move rapidly through masses of material to select what you will look at carefully later. Remember that the preface of a book may often indicate whether it is likely to include anything for your purpose. The table of contents is even more useful; a glance at chapter headings may save you from going further or direct you quickly to the one section that may be all that will be useful. Learn to "skim"—to glance rapidly through material in search of the significant. By these means, eliminate items that now seem unsuitable. Then you can settle down to a thorough reading of what seems really worthwhile.

As you read, you must, of course, take accurate notes of any facts and opinions that you may later wish to quote or refer to in your paper. Good notes will not only form the basis of your paper but will also help you to organize it. As you form a general picture of your subject, decide on its main divisions and subdivisions and use these as headings for the note cards, always remembering that you can at any time make further subdivisions or change a note from one subdivision to another as your knowledge of the subject grows. For example, for a biographical study of your grandfather you may want to subdivide a preliminary heading "education" into "education—elementary school" and "education—high school" or into "education—formal" and "education—practical."

Write your reading notes, like your bibliographical notes, on cards. Convenient sizes are 4″ × 6″ and 5″ × 8″; be sure to stick to one size for convenience in handling and filing. Limit each card to a single note on a single topic taken from a single source. Then, instead of a hodgepodge, you will eventually have a mass of material that you can arrange easily under common headings, and you will be able to rearrange and discard items without disturbing the rest. The flexibility of such notes makes selecting and organizing the material relatively simple.

**Note:** Make your work easier for yourself by writing on only *one* side of each card so that you can see all of it at a glance. If a note is too long to fit, continue on a second card, marking it at the top with the source and "cont.—p. 2" so that if it is ever separated from the first you will instantly recognize where it belongs.

Most of your notes will be summaries; they will give in your words the gist of the material you read. But in your paper you may often wish to support important points with the exact words of your source. Be sure to copy these precisely as they appear in the original, with all the grammar and punctuation intact and even with any errors in facts or writing that they may contain. Set each one off with a pair of double quotation marks so that later you will be able to see at a glance that they are quotations. You may eventually use only a few of these, but remember that although you can easily summarize a direct quotation when writing your paper, you cannot turn your summary back into a quotation unless you have the exact words before you.

In addition to a heading classifying the topic, a note card must show clearly the exact source of the borrowed material. Your finished work must show not only the book or article from which the idea came but also the page number (and with newspaper articles, the column number as well). After every note you take, jot down the page number or numbers on which the information originally appeared. In the upper right-hand corner identify the source by giving the author's last name or a short form of the title of the work or both—as briefly as possible but with enough information to avoid any chance of confusion with another author or work with a similar name. A completed note will resemble the following card written by the student whose research paper appears later in this chapter and used as part of the basis for her paragraph beginning "If we lose the sense of play":

morals             Huizinga

Spectators want traditional moral virtues upheld by players – part of being civilized –

"The cheat or spoil-sport shatters civilization itself."

p. 19

The best way to combine reading and note-taking must be learned from experience. Taking notes at frequent intervals may result in repetitions. But to read a long article or most of a book without jotting down notes is certain to result in many rereadings. How much material you can cover before taking notes on it will depend on the nature of the material and the strength of your memory. Through practice you will soon learn your own capacities. *Important:* Be prepared to add to your bibliography as you go along. You may discover some of your best material through references to sources mentioned in your reading and through the bibliographies that most scholarly works include.

## Organizing and Writing the Paper

When you have gathered most of what you think will be your important material—by reading, interviewing, conducting a survey, performing an experiment, and doing whatever else is necessary for your project—you are ready to follow the advice given in Unit 1 for composing a paper (pages 6–22). But remember that at this point your insights and plans for organization are still tentative. In any research project there is always the possibility of turning up some fact or having some new insight that will make you recast part of your work, perhaps all of it. Keep your mind open for new thoughts and for reseeing your earlier thoughts.

Glance over all your material, jotting down any new ideas that occur to you and considering the possibility of other divisions and subdivisions that may show new relationships in it. Then draft a tentative statement of your main point and make a rough outline for your own use. These steps will help you to know how much more research you should do and in exactly what areas. If your instructor requires a formal outline of your paper, these steps will be the basis for it.

When you have finished whatever additional research you find necessary, you can make your rough outline definite and begin writing. Imagining that your readers will have some knowledge of the subject but opinions different from yours, compose a rough draft for your tentative ending of the paper— what you want those readers to have in mind when they finish reading. Then look rapidly over your outline together with your ending, changing them if you see ways to make them stronger and clearer. Next, with the same imagined readers in mind, compose a rough draft of your beginning—what your readers will need so that they can easily follow what you say in the main body of the paper.

You are now ready to write a rough draft—perhaps the first of several—of the whole paper. Remember that the basic principles of clear, logical writing discussed in the earlier units all apply to writing a research paper. Review particularly the advice in Units 11 to 14 on the chief ways to develop and support the main point and to present evidence coherently and logically. In a research paper the chief support for your opinions will, of course, be the facts that you have gathered and the opinions of others that you cite.

Remember that revision is a continuing process throughout the composition of any paper, particularly longer ones. Each new fact and opinion gathered may make you resee and therefore revise your ideas. Each time you review your work you may see new relationships among the parts. Certainly, when your first rough draft is complete and you can see the paper as a whole, you will want to make changes to unify and strengthen it. You may even want to make drastic changes in the organization and content. Professional writers often find that their final draft bears little resemblance to their first draft.

In making the final copy and proofreading it, follow the directions in Unit 1, pages 22–23, and the directions that follow on quoting and documenting material from other sources.

## Documenting Your Sources: Footnotes and Endnotes

Whenever you quote words written or spoken by someone else or use facts or opinions that can in any way be considered the special property of another, you must document them, giving full credit to your sources. In a research paper, as in all scholarly writing, there are conventional procedures for doing this.

Two styles of documentation are in general use. The MLA system, formalized by the Modern Language Association and most recently presented in the *MLA Handbook* (1977), is used in scholarly writing on literature, history, and biography, and has been traditionally used in any works, regardless of subject matter, directed to the general reader. The APA system, formalized by the American Psychological Association and used in psychology and most of the other social sciences, is increasingly popular. It is most recently presented in the second edition of the *Publication Manual of the American Psychological Association* (1974). The laboratory sciences—chemistry, biology, and so on—have not agreed on a single style, but some scholarly publications in those fields follow the APA system.

In the **MLA system,** you may use either **footnotes** or **endnotes** to document sources. Footnotes are placed at the bottom of the page on which the sources they document appear; endnotes are placed together in a separate section at the end of the paper. Footnotes are more convenient for the reader who wants to know a source immediately, but endnotes are more convenient for the writer who then does not have to save space at the bottom of each page. Most authorities recommend that students use endnotes in research papers unless the papers are to be microfilmed.

Number your notes and the material they document with Arabic numerals consecutively throughout the paper. Always place the number in the text at the *end* of the material it documents, after any punctuation marking the end of the material, or, if there is no punctuation, immediately after the last letter of the last word. The number itself should not have any punctuation, such as a period or parentheses. Raise it half a space above the line in which it appears so that your readers will recognize it easily as indicating a note. The corresponding number always precedes the note itself and is also raised and not punctuated. In typing, skip one space between the note number and the first letter of the first word of the note.

Write or type each note as if it were a one-sentence paragraph, with normal paragraph indentation for the first line and with any subsequent lines beginning at the left margin, exactly like the paragraphs in the text of your paper. If you are typing, double-space your notes, as you do the main body of the paper, so that they will be easy to read.

Examples follow of the kinds of printed sources you are most likely to use. Notice that four basic types of information are required: the author's name, in the form used by the author and in normal order since notes are not alphabetized; the title of the work and, if it is published in a larger work, that title as well; the publication data; the specific page reference. To find the publication data required for a book, look at both sides of the title page. If more than one city is listed, name only the largest, and give the name of the state or country for all except very large cities. If no date of publication appears, place *no date* or *n. d.* in the space usually occupied by the date.

Italicize the titles of all books and periodicals (underline a title to indicate italics), and set off the titles of short works published in larger works with a pair of double quotation marks. Capitalize the first letter of the first and last word and of the first word after a colon or semicolon, no matter what the words are, and of all important words in the titles of all written and dramatic works. ("Important" words are all those except *the, a, an, and, but, or, nor, yet,* and the prepositions; some authorities recommend capitalizing prepositions of five or more letters.)

Abbreviate the word "page" as *p.* and "pages" as *pp.* If the documented material extends to more than a page in the original, give the second page number in full when it is below 100; for larger numbers, give only the last two figures of the second if it is within the same hundred as the first.

Throughout the examples, notice the use of punctuation (commas, colons, parentheses) to set off the parts of the notes.

**1.** The first edition of a book by one author has the simplest form of note:

[1]Lewis Thomas, *The Medusa and the Snail* (New York: Viking Press, 1979), p. 35.

**2.** If a work is published in more than one volume, the volume number—in Roman numerals—precedes the page number; the distinction of the Roman and Arabic numerals makes "vol." and "p." unnecessary:

[2]Frank Dalby Davison, *The White Thorntree* (Sydney: Ure Smith, 1970), II, 567.

**3.** If you are using a later or revised edition, give that information before the publication data (always try to use the latest edition of any book unless the author's earlier version and changes are in some way significant to your paper):

[3]René Wellek and Austin Warren, *Theory of Literature,* 2nd ed. (New York: Harcourt Brace Jovanovich, Inc. 1956), p. 74.

**4.** If you use a reprint of any edition, be sure to include the date of the edition from which the reprint was made as well as full information on the book you actually used:

[4]Philip Roth, *Goodbye, Columbus* (1959; rpt. New York: Bantam Books, 1968), p. 31.

**5.** The name of an editor or translator is preceded by *ed.* or *trans.*:

[5]Omar Khayyam, *The Rubaiyat,* trans. Edward Fitzgerald (New York: Crowell, 1923), p. 17.

**6.** An article in an anthology is listed by its own author, with the article title set off in quotation marks:

[6]Margaret Mead, "Alternative to War," *War,* ed. Morton Fried, Marvin Harris, and Robert Murphy (Garden City, N.Y.: Natural History Press, 1968), p. 225.

**7.** If you use prefaces, appendixes, or anything written by editors or translators, name them as authors, but include "ed." or "trans." after their names; give page numbers of prefaces in small Roman numerals.

[7]Morton Fried, Marvin Harris, and Robert Murphy, eds., "Foreword," *War* (Garden City, N.Y.: Natural History Press, 1968), p. xiv.

**8.** Articles in encyclopedias are usually signed with initials, which are identified elsewhere in the set. (For an unsigned article, begin the note with the title.) The article in the example was signed "A. MacD. A.," but the list of contributors in the introductory pages of the first volume gave the author's full name. With well-known encyclopedias, you need not give the place of publication, the name of the publisher or the volume number since the articles are arranged alphabetically, but you must give the number of the edition used or the date.

[8]Rev. Arthur MacDonald Allchin, "Women's Religious Orders," *Encyclopaedia Britannica*, 1970 ed., p. 631.

**9.** Notes for articles in periodicals follow much the same pattern. The simplest kind of note refers to a periodical that numbers its pages consecutively throughout a year's issues, as some quarterlies and monthlies do; only the year is needed, between the volume and page numbers:

[9]Richard Gilman, "Reflections on Decadence," *Partisan Review*, 46 (1979), 183.

**10.** For articles in periodicals that start numbering anew with each issue, give the month; for articles in biweekly and weekly publications, give the full date (the military style, with the day preceding the month, simplifies punctuation; abbreviate the names of months more than four letters long):

[10]Pete Axthelm, "A Toast to Polo," *Newsweek*, 30 Apr. 1979, pp. 66–67.

**11.** References to articles in newspapers follow the same pattern, with the headline treated as the title. A reference to a big city newspaper may also require the name of the edition and the section name or number; column numbers are a convenience for the reader who may want to look up the article:

[11]John H. Allan, "Bond Prices Take a Sharp Drop," *New York Times*, 6 March 1980, Late City Ed., sec. D, p. 7, cols. 4–6.

**12.** Begin a note on any unsigned piece of writing with the title:

[12]"The Net Effect of Takeovers Is Positive," *Forbes*, 11 June 1979, p. 66.

Only the first reference documenting each source must have all the information given in the examples. In later references you need give only the surname of the author and the page number of the new reference. For unsigned works, a short form of the title is enough. Later references to the works cited in notes 6, 9, and 12 could be

[14]Mead, p. 223.
[15]Gilman, p. 179.
[16]"The Net Effect," p. 65.

If you use two authors with the same surname or two works by the same author, you must give enough information in later references to avoid confusion. Later references to a work by three or more authors can be shortened by using "et al.," an abbreviation of the Latin *et alii*, meaning "and others." It is not italicized. A second reference to the source cited in note 7 would be only

[17]Fried et al., p. iv.

Your **final bibliography,** following the **MLA system,** should be on a separate page at the end of your paper after the text and, if you are using endnotes, after the notes. (If you are typing, double-space all entries.) It should list alphabetically all the printed sources from which you have used material or to which you feel particularly indebted for background information, whether or not you mentioned them in the paper. The information in the bibliography entries is similar to that in the source notes, with a few differences in arrangement and punctuation.

Since the bibliography is alphabetized, the author's last name appears first, followed by a comma and whatever form of first name and initials the author uses. Unsigned works are alphabetized by title, always omitting *a, an,* and *the* from consideration. Unlike notes, which are punctuated as if they were one-sentence paragraphs, bibliography entries are punctuated as if each were a paragraph composed of several sentences. Use a period after each of the three main divisions of an entry—the author's name, the title of the work, and the publication data, and also after any additional information, such as the edition or the number of volumes, that comes between the title and the publication data. Use parentheses only around a year that is preceded by a volume number in an entry for a periodical article.

For articles or any short works contained in larger works, give the inclusive page numbers, all those occupied by the work (if the short work begins on one page and is continued in the back pages of a periodical, give its beginning page number followed by *f.* for "following page" or *ff.* for "following pages.")

To make alphabetized words stand out clearly, use reverse paragraph indentation. Begin the first word of each entry at the left margin; if the entry runs to two or more lines, begin the second line and each one after that about five spaces to the right of the left margin. If you have two or more works by the same author, alphabetize them with each other by title, and in each entry after the first use a bar in place of the author's name, followed by a period (in typing, use ten unspaced hyphens for the bar).

If your bibliography contains more than twenty or thirty items, you may make it more readable by dividing it into categories such as books and periodical articles or primary and secondary sources.

Study the arrangement and punctuation of the following. Explanations for some special features are in brackets.

Davison, Frank Dalby. *The White Thorntree.* 2 vols. Sydney: Ure Smith, 1970. [No page numbers are given because the whole book was used.]

Fried, Morton, Marvin Harris, and Robert Murphy, eds. *War.* Garden City, N.Y.: Natural History Press, 1968. [Only the first author's name is reversed, for alphabetizing.]

Gilman, Richard. "Reflections on Decadence." *Partisan Review,* 46 (1979), 175–187. [The inclusive page numbers, those occupied by the entire article, are given; the year is parenthesized to set it off from the volume and page numbers.]

"Return of the Golden Ones," *Forbes,* 16 Apr. 1979, p. 122. [An unsigned work is alphabetized by title; for weekly and biweekly magazines and for newspapers give the full date; *p.* or *pp.* is necessary to distinguish the number for the page reference; this article occupies only one page.]

Thomas, Lewis. *The Lives of a Cell.* New York: Viking Press, 1974.

———. *The Medusa and the Snail.* New York: Viking Press, 1979. [Another work by the author of the preceding work.]

The **APA system** for notes documenting printed sources is much simpler. Each note usually gives only the author's surname, the year the work was published, and, if the reference is to a specific page, the page number. Place these in parentheses immediately after the words you wish to document. If the author's name or the date appears nearby in the same sentence, you need not repeat them in the note. The reader wishing more information is expected to consult the list of references at the end of your paper.

If you used works by two or more authors with the same surname, give their first initials to avoid confusion. If a source has three or more authors, give all the surnames in the first note, but in any subsequent notes give only the name of the first author followed by "et al." to represent the rest. Document material for unsigned articles with a short form of the title followed by the date or, if you give the title in your own sentence, by the date alone.

In the APA system, documentation on the work cited in note 1 in the examples of the MLA system would appear in one of these ways in a sentence in the text of the paper:

> The behavior of some tiny creatures can provide interesting parallels with human behavior (Thomas, 1979).

> Thomas (1979) compares the behavior of some tiny creatures with human behavior.

To document a quotation or a reference to a specific point, include the page number:

> We find that "it is only this species of medusa and only this kind of nudibranch that can come together and live this way" (Thomas, 1979, p. 5).

> Two tiny sea creatures in the Bay of Naples collaborate to stay alive (Thomas, 1979, p. 5).

> In 1979 Thomas described two tiny sea creatures in the Bay of Naples who collaborate to stay alive (p. 5).

In the **APA system,** the final bibliography is called the **reference list** and includes only sources referred to in the paper, not those read for general background information. The information given on each source and the method of presentation is almost exactly the same as that recommended by the MLA, and the differences are all minor.

**1.** Give only the initials of authors' first names.

**2.** Capitalize only the first letter of the first word in titles of articles, books, and chapters of books (the first letters of all proper names including those of periodicals, are, however, capitalized in conventional fashion). Italicize (underline) not only book and periodical titles but also volume numbers of periodicals, but do not set off article titles in quotation marks.

**3.** If you use two or more works by the same author, repeat the author's surname and initials for each and arrange the works chronologically, starting with the earliest. If an author published two or more works in one year, alphabetize the works within that year by title (always omitting *a, an* and *the* from consideration) and differentiate among them with a small letter in parenthesis—(a), (b), and so on—at the end of each entry.

With both systems, to document **sources not in print**—ones that you heard or saw rather than read, such as lectures, concerts, theatrical performances, or paintings—follow the same general methods. Begin with the name of the lecturer, conductor, director, or whoever was most responsible for the content and style of the performance. Then give the title and author of the work and the place and date of the performance. In capitalizing letters in titles, each system follows its practices for referring to printed sources.

With unpublished written material of any kind, such as honors papers, M.A. theses, letters, and answers to surveys, identify the persons concerned, give the dates and whatever other information your readers will need if they wish to try to see the material.

Since all these sources are not printed, they do not belong in the final bibliography (MLA) or the reference list (APA). If you are using the MLA system, make a separate list of the information following the final bibliography and head it "Other Sources Consulted." Arrange the material in appropriate categories, alphabetizing the entries within each category. If you refer to such a source in the text of your paper, follow the full MLA procedure for a note, presenting the same information to identify the source at the appropriate spot in your footnotes or endnotes.

If you are using the APA system, make a separate list, following the text of your paper but preceding your reference list and headed "Reference Notes." Number and arrange the notes in sequence according to the order of the material they document; the result will be almost identical with MLA notes for similar material. In the text of the paper, immediately after the documented material, insert "(Note 1)," "(Note 2)," and so on. A sentence would look like this:

> James Bridges' film, *The China Syndrome* (Note 1), dramatizes the risks of nuclear fuel.

For help in documenting any sources that create special problems, consult the *MLA Handbook* or the APA *Publications Manual*.

## Information Notes

You may also wish to use notes for a somewhat different purpose—to tell your readers something that would not fit smoothly into the general style of your paper, such as a critical comment, an explanation, a definition, or an illustrative anecdote.

There is no set form for such a note. If you are presenting your documentation in footnotes, place this kind of note at the bottom of the page along with the rest, numbered in sequence with them, and place a number after the material to which it refers, just as you do with the ordinary notes.

If you are presenting your documentation in endnotes, you may list such a note with them, numbering it along with the rest, or place it at the bottom of the page on which the material it refers to appears. (If you want to make sure that your reader connects it with its reference, this position will be better.) Since it is then not part of the regular sequence of your notes, you should not number it. Instead, place an asterisk (°) where you would ordinarily place a note number—immediately after the material in the text of your paper to which the note refers and immediately before the note itself. If such a note requires documentation of its own, give it in parentheses at the end of the note, in whatever form you use for your bibliography or reference list.

## Summarizing, Paraphrasing, and Quoting

In most research papers, the opinions and facts presented by other writers are a large and essential part of the support for the main point, and you will often summarize, paraphrase, or quote them.

A summary is a condensed version of the original, giving its main point accurately but in fewer words. For example, in the sample research paper that follows, the long quotation set in a block (lines 117–23) could have been summarized as

> Through games, society can have a respite from customary patterns, talk to itself, and thus gain self-confidence. Play goes with a true awareness of the huge disproportion between the apparent and the real in life.

A paraphrase translates all of the original into simpler language and is therefore usually somewhat longer than the original. A paraphrase of the first sentence of the quotation might be

> Games are situations that are artificially constructed and controlled; they grow out of the awareness that a group has of itself and allow short periods of relief from the usual patterns of the group's behavior.

When you quote, be sure to follow the words and internal punctuation of the original and set them off in quotation marks. You may change the terminal punctuation—a capital letter at the beginning and a punctuation mark at the end—to make the quoted words fit smoothly into your own sentence or paragraph, but you may change nothing else. If part of a quotation is not relevant to your point, you may omit it. Indicate the ellipsis, as it is called, with three spaced periods ( . . . ) called ellipsis or suspension points. If the omission includes the last words of a sentence, add a period as well. If you wish to make a comment of your own within a quotation, enclose it in square brackets, never parentheses; anything enclosed in parentheses is read as part of the original. "At the same season, during the following year (albeit a month later), the King [Henry VIII] was again married." If you type your paper, add the brackets in ink. If a quotation contains any kind of error or questionable information, show that you recognize it but are following the original; place "sic" in brackets after the error.

This is Latin for "thus" or "just so": "Colombos [sic] discovered America in 1493 [sic]."

Short quotations, ones of roughly three lines or less in print, may be incorporated in your own sentences and paragraphs. Use transitional words or phrases to make them fit smoothly and set them off with quotation marks. With a longer quotation, readers may forget initial quotation marks and think that they are reading your words. To avoid this confusion, place longer quotations in a block, double spaced and conspicuously indented on the left. Since this method sets them off sharply from your sentences, no quotation marks are used. (See the example on pages 320–21.)

Failure to acknowledge the source of ideas or words of someone else is **plagiarism.** It is a crime because it is a form of theft, and it is legally punishable. Always acknowledge your sources in notes or in the text of your paper. You do not need to give sources for widely known facts or opinions, but if you use another writer's words to present them you should acknowledge that writer as your source, no matter how widely known the facts or opinions may be. Conversely, if you present a fact or opinion that is available in only a few sources, even though you are presenting it entirely in your own words, you should acknowledge your sources.

Do not fear that acknowledging your sources will make you seem unable to produce an original idea. Your particular combination of facts and opinions from others will be your own and is a form of original work. Also, the more you show that you have read widely in respectable sources, the more convincing your research will seem to your readers.

## *EXAMPLE*

The research paper that follows shows how the writer used what she read to try to reach opinions of her own. Although, as she confesses somewhat sadly at the end, she has not arrived at many firm answers, her research has helped her to define her questions on her topic more precisely so that eventually she may reach the answers she seeks.

Notice her punctuation and different ways of fitting material from other writers into her sentences and paragraphs:

(1) quotations incorporated completely into her sentences—see those with material documented by notes 3, 7, 9, 12, and 17;

(2) paraphrases and summaries—see the material documented by notes 4, 5, 6, 10, 11, and 15;

(3) omissions of unnecessary parts of quotations—see those documented by notes 3, 12, and 13;

(4) a long quotation—see the one documented by note 13 and set as a block on the page;

(5) introductory remarks and insertions within quotations, paraphrases, and summaries to identify the authors—see those for material documented by notes 1, 2, 8, 14, and 16.

Notice, also, how she handles two rather common problems in documentation. In note 3 she identifies the source of the quotation as an article by another writer. When you cannot determine where a quoted remark was first published, give the full information for the work in which you found it, as done here. Notes 2 and 14 document two articles from the same anthology, but each gives full bibliographical information. This repetition saves readers the trouble of looking back at note 1 if they want the source only of the second article. The same principle applies in the entries in the bibliography.

### SOCIOLOGY AND THE SPORTS SPECTATOR: SOME QUESTIONS
*Jill Taylor (student)*

Although sports have always formed an important part of popular culture, "spectatorism," the watching of sporting events directly or on TV, has not received much attention as a subject for serious social research. As Harry Edwards remarked in 1973 in *The Sociology of Sport,* "Perhaps the least studied and understood role in the institution of sport is that of the 'fan.'"[1] A. S.  5
Daniels raised the question a few years earlier when he noted that "We can offer no scientific explanation why football in some American universities will draw 85,000 spectators into the stadium six times in the span of ten weeks, while no university program in music, art, or even education and science can approach this."[2]  10

I have chosen to try to investigate this subject because I have had a long familiarity with fanatic (from which word, incidentally, we derive the word "fan") TV and live-sports spectators. The chief example for me has been my father. For years, I have been amazed at the behavior he exhibits while spending innumerable hours in front of sports programs on TV. From my earliest  15
childhood on, I have never dared to interrupt him at any point from the time the "Star Spangled Banner" has ended and a game is about to start until the time when the last whistle has been blown and the winners have been announced. I am quite overwhelmed by the extensive sports knowledge displayed by this man who has never actually participated in any athletic  20
endeavor. The vicarious identification with certain teams and players, the emotional outbursts emitted into the late hours of the night, even including wild screams by a man who at all other times is the personification of quiet gentleness, make me feel that sports-watching as a leisure activity and as a mass entertainment is truly a fascinating behavioral phenomenon.  25

The history of sports-watching is long. In ancient Greece the various games began as a means of celebrating individual competition, honoring the gods, and entertaining the "fans." Organizing athletes into groups to represent their home towns began at the most famous of the ancient games, the ones held at Olympia, and athletic achievement was celebrated by the greatest sculptors and poets of  30
the day. The Romans continued the idea of individual competition, and during the Middle Ages in Europe the aristocracy enjoyed knightly jousting in tour-

naments and ordinary people organized village and parish teams to compete in various athletic contests. The custom spread to America and by the nineteenth century town-versus-town baseball games were common, and spectatorism flourished as a shared experience among enthusiastic supporters. Tristram P. Coffin, the folklore scholar, has remarked that "most of the games . . . ended up in brawls" but that the games represented "some semi-civilized replacement for village-to-village wars. And this is an aspect of the game that has never left it."[3]

In a sociological analysis it can be seen that today, as in the past, spectatorism as a form of mass enjoyment is based on a unifying association of people. Individual "fans" are united by their identification with a team or athlete who represents some kind of community to which they themselves belong, such as a school, city, nation, race, or religion. There are countless examples of this. Coffin cites the American League pennant race in 1967 which brought work to a virtual standstill in four large American cities, while everyone listened to the games.[4]

The spread of spectatorism as a leisure activity is probably the result of the increase in the accessibility of all sports. Before World War II, newspapers disseminated facts about sports to a wide audience. After World War II, television programs on sports, with close-up shots, instant replays, slow motion, and explanatory commentaries, helped to bring sports into practically every home in America and made them much more understandable to the audience. Television has been the chief cause of the increase in the number of "passive fans," the spectators who find enjoyment within the privacy of their own homes. However, the great response of "active fans," who attend sports events by the thousands, is also a noticeable part of spectatorism, and there is some evidence that this response is growing more intense. The Burns Security Institute points to increasing destructiveness by fans of both the winning and losing teams after a big game.[5]

Because spectatorism has not received widespread attention from scholars in social research, there have not been many empirical studies to give verifiable conclusions about it. But various sociologists have discussed the spectator role in terms of its functions and purposes. Although I cannot make generalizations on the subject, I can provide some analysis of these views on spectatorism within a sociological perspective. The reader must remember, however, that these statements are hypotheses, not generalizations based on empirical studies.

Arnold Beisser, a psychiatrist, offers the psychosocial view that spectatorism serves a social function. In a mass society it satisfies the alienated individual's need for identity and a feeling of belonging to a group.[6] This concept brings to mind the faithful college alumni who support their teams long after graduation. At almost any college game, and certainly at all the big ones, middle-aged and elderly fans can be seen—and heard—rooting with all their might for their old alma mater. Another social function of spectatorism, according to Beisser, is social communication. Viewing live sports and even sports programs on TV gives fans a way to share their feelings and opinions with a large number of others who are participating in the same experience. Nothing else gives such a chance to be "at one with a sympathetic crowd," knowing that we do not stand alone in our intense feelings but "that such feelings are shared by a host of others."[7] Total strangers will exchange remarks with no signs of inhibition, and in moments of great enthusiasm over a touchdown or a home run they may slap each other on the back or even hug each other and dance up and down.

A psychological function of spectatorism is giving socially acceptable outlets to forms of behavior that are not otherwise acceptable or approved by society. It releases suppressed tensions. Watching any baseball or football game makes this clear. The screaming, yelling, cheering, and booing which are a characteristic part of these games are wholly acceptable and even expected. Some social scientists see this psychological function as related to the social function of identification mentioned above. "The public seems to need a permissible outlet for certain barbaric impulses," Michael Roberts remarks. "Behavior such as assault and battery and indecent exposure are considered quite correct under the etiquette prevailing at, say, the Texas–Oklahoma football game."[8] Beisser, making the same point, mentions the standard cry "Kill the bums!"[9] Sociologists suggest that the violent and emotional outbursts are the result of a fanatical level of identification with the athletes. In recent years there have been many news stories from Latin America and European countries describing murders and suicides that have resulted from soccer scores.

Perhaps these emotional outbursts, acts of violence, and verbal assaults on players, coaches and judges are the result of the frustrations felt by the fans in their everyday lives. Violent fans, Harry Edwards suggests, may be unconsciously directing against the players and coaches the anger they cannot express against their employers, their families, and whatever other persons they may see as obstacles in their efforts to achieve the goals and the social and psychological security they want.[10]

In a related hypothesis, Gregory Stone suggests that spectators have destroyed the "play" aspect of sports and turned them into a spectacle or "display," played for the spectators, not for the players. He thinks that sports have lost many of their original qualities and are being turned into a type of ritual, a predetermined and therefore predictable activity.[11] If Stone is right, then perhaps the violence will gradually decrease as the activity becomes more ritualized. Walter E. Schafer sees the identification of the fans with the players as the result of feeling that "it is the *thing* to support your school's football, basketball, and . . . track team,"[12] and that fans are merely conforming to what they see as "normal" behavior.

If we lose the sense of play, of enjoying games for their own sake, we may suffer as a society. Marshall McLuhan says:

> Games . . . are contrived and controlled situations, extensions of group awareness that permit a respite from customary patterns. They are a kind of talking to itself on the part of society as a whole. And talking to oneself is a recognizable form of play that is indispensable to any growth of self-confidence. . . . To take

mere worldly things in dead earnest betokens a defect of awareness that is pitiable. . . . Play goes with an awareness of huge disproportion between the ostensible
situation and the real stakes.[13]

Johan Huizinga makes the same point when he says that "real civilization cannot exist in the absence of a certain play-element, for civilization presupposes 125
limitation and mastery of the self."[14] This is in agreement with Harry Edwards'
claim that the most important function of sports is the reaffirmation of established values and beliefs and through them of the spectators' sense of their own
worth.[15] To Huizinga, "the cheat or spoil-sport shatters civilization itself."[16]

All these views are hypotheses, calling for a great deal of further research. 130
Many of these views fit with what I have observed as a spectator. The identification with a team, the reinforcement of membership in a larger social unit,
the release of pent-up emotions and frustrations, all match my own experiences
as a spectator and as an observer of other spectators. I also see the role of the
fan as a means of reinforcing the values of "the American Way," our belief that 135
competition, hard work, ambition, and determination are the qualities needed
for individual success and for a strong America, qualities that are embodied in
the "Horatio Alger" myth.

As I look back on what I have written, my training in social science makes
me recognize that I have not provided many answers, but I think I have raised 140
questions worth examining. Statistical reports and research studies on spectatorism are definitely needed to answer them. This is good, because new research
in social science depends on proposing new questions.

The questions I would like to see answered include the following: Among TV
spectators, are feelings shared with others and is a sense of unification evident? 145
If they are, then what differences, if any, exist between the feelings and behavior of TV spectators and spectators actually present at an event? Why do spectators choose to follow a particular sport? What are the characteristics and
causes of "fanatical behavior"? What differences, if any, are there between the
behavior and feelings of spectators at an amateur event and ones at a profes- 150
sional event? Although I do not agree with Gregory Stone's claim that all sports
are spectacles put on by the players for the benefit of the audience, I think that
his idea is provocative, especially in the light of the growing commercialism of
our product-consumption oriented society. This brings up the question of the
role of economics in the "sports industry," the attitudes of spectator toward the 155
high cost of some tickets, the high salaries of some players, the "scholarships"
for college athletes, and the heavy betting on some games.

Other questions that should be explored empirically include the class inequal-
ities in spectator sports. Many sociologists have remarked on the fact that members of the lower economic class tend to identify with baseball, perhaps because, 160
as George Vecsey suggests, during the Depression it was a sport for "hooky
players, unemployed, or anybody else with a clear mind and lots of time," while
football, "packaged like white bread and Detroit cars, has been accepted by

many upper class people" as "our game."[17] A particularly important and complex question deserving research is why the great majority of spectators for all   165
sports are male.

After raising so many questions, I feel somewhat discouraged that I have not
made any conclusive findings. Yet I also feel that an important part of sociological thinking is to go on critically examining and raising questions. Many of the
questions I have raised will, I hope, be answered in the future by the continued   170
development of organized research in the sociology of sport. The books and
articles that I read show that the research is beginning.

*Endnotes*

[1]Harry Edwards, *The Sociology of Sport* (Homewood, Illinois: Dorsey Press, 1973),
p. 238.

[2]A. S. Daniels, "The Study of Sport as an Element of Culture," in *Sport, Culture,
and Society*, ed. John W. Loy and Gerald S. Kenyon (London: Collier-Macmillan, Ltd.,
1969), p. 21.

[3]Tristram P. Coffin, as quoted by Michael Roberts, "The Vicarious Heroism of the
Sports Spectator," *The New Republic*, 23 Nov. 1974, p. 18, col. 2.

[4]Roberts, p. 19, col. 1.

[5]Roberts, p. 19, col. 2.

[6]Arnold Beisser, *The Madness in Sports* (New York: Meredith Publishing Company,
1967), p. 129.

[7]Beisser, p. 130.

[8]Roberts, p. 19, col. 2.

[9]Beisser, p. 130.

[10]Edwards, p. 243.

[11]Gregory Stone, "American Sports: Play and Display," in *The Sociology of Sport:
A Selection of Readings*, ed. Eric Dunning (London: Cass, 1971), p. 46.

[12]Walter E. Schafer, "Some Social Sources and Consequences of Interscholastic Athletics," in *Proceedings of the C. I. C. Symposium on the Sociology of Sport*, ed. Gerald
Kenyon (Chicago: The Atlantic Institute, 1969), p. 33.

[13]Marshall McLuhan, "Games: The Extensions of Man," *Understanding Media*
(1964; rpt. New York, New American Library, n.d.), p. 215.

[14]Johan Huizinga, "The Play Element in Contemporary Civilization," in *Sport, Culture, and Society*, ed. John W. Loy and Gerald S. Kenyon (London: Collier-Macmillan,
Ltd., 1969), p. 19.

[15]Edwards, p. 243.

[16]Huizinga, p. 19.

[17]George Vecsey, "Fans," *Esquire*, Oct. 1974, p. 155.

*Bibliography*

Beisser, Arnold. *The Madness in Sports*. New York: Meredith Publishing Company,
1967.

Daniels, A. S. "The Study of Sport as an Element of Culture," in *Sport, Culture and
Society*. Ed. John W. Loy and Gerald S. Kenyon. London: Collier-Macmillan, Ltd.,
1969, pp. 21–32.

Edwards, Harry. *The Sociology of Sport*. Homewood, Illinois: Dorsey Press, 1973.

Huizinga, Johan. "The Play Element in Contemporary Civilization." *Homo Ludens: A Study of the Play Element in Culture*. Boston: The Beacon Press, 1950. Rpt. in *Sport, Culture, and Society*. Ed. John W. Loy and Gerald S. Kenyon, London: Collier-Macmillan, Ltd., 1969, pp. 5–20.
McLuhan, Marshall. "Games: The Extensions of Man," *Understanding Media* (1964; rpt. New York, New American Library, n.d.), pp. 207–216.
Roberts, Michael. "The Vicarious Heroism of the Sports Spectator." *The New Republic*, 23 Nov. 1974, pp. 17–19.
Schafer, Walter E. "Some Social Sources and Consequences of Interscholastic Athletics." *Proceedings of the C. I. C. Symposium on the Sociology of Sport*. Ed. Gerald Kenyon. Chicago: The Athletic Institute, 1969, pp. 33–34.
Stone, Gregory. "American Sports: Play and Display." *The Sociology of Sports: A Selection of Readings*. Ed. Eric Dunning. London: Cass, 1971, pp. 42–49.
Vecsey, George. "Fans." *Esquire*, Oct. 1974, pp. 151–155.

## ASSIGNMENTS

Besides the suggestions made earlier in "Choosing a Subject," here are others that may appeal to you:

1. A critical history of a particular music group set in the context of trends in contemporary music.
2. What was happening in the world on the day you or one of your parents was born and what has been the outcome of some of the problems and events described in newspapers for that day.
3. A critical analysis of the coverage of a particular event by a variety of periodicals.
4. An analysis of changes in advertising for women's fashions—has the women's liberation movement had an effect on what the advertisements say and on the pictures used?
5. The history of your hometown in the context of the history of the country, the region, or the state.
6. An examination of the special words and phrases used by any particular group or in any specialized activity with which you are familiar, such as slang used by children and teenagers, the combinations of slang and professional terminology of plumbers, jazz musicians, or the fans of any particular sport, or an analysis, comparison and contrast of the slang used by U.S. soldiers in World War I, World War II, and the Vietnam War.

# UNIT 19

## The Essay Examination

Some of your most important writing in college (in terms of immediate results) is what you produce on examinations. Yet many good students, who have been conscientious in preparing assignments, attending classes, taking lecture and reading notes, and reviewing thoroughly, do not get the term grade they deserve because they give too little thought to the importance of the actual writing of the examination. Examinations are of two main types: the objective, which requires answers of a word or a symbol; and the essay, which requires answers to be written out at some length.

### The Objective Examination

You are familiar with the objective examination in various forms—true-false, filling-in-blanks, multiple-choice, matching; these reduce the problem of writing to a minimum. The material covered by the examination is either supplied in full for you to manipulate, or is given so completely that you have to add only a missing term or figure. Faced with such an examination, you have two concerns—to understand the material and *to follow directions exactly*. If you read hastily through true-false statements and jump to conclusions, if you use plus and minus signs when "T" and "F" are asked for, if you write your answers at the sentence ends instead of in the designated places, or if you use ink when a #2 pencil is required, you may fail an examination for which you are perfectly prepared. Objective correction keys and computers make no allowances for personal idiosyncracies and give no credit for good intentions.

The objective examination is frequently a time test as well as an information test, designed to check your speed as well as your knowledge. Consequently, you should first read through it rapidly, answering only those questions whose answers occur to you immediately. Then you can return and spend the necessary time on the troublesome ones, without worrying that you will be caught at the end of the period with some obvious ones unanswered.

Objective examinations are generally popular with students and instructors because of the speed with which they can be taken and corrected and because the answers are definitely right or wrong. They are best suited to subjects that require you to memorize numerous facts, since they test what you know, not what you can do with your knowledge. You may write a perfect paper of the objective kind, but only on the essay examination can you write an extraordinary one.

## The Essay Examination

On an essay examination you must write out your answers at some length, but as in taking an objective examination, you must follow directions carefully. The student who handed in an unfinished paper late and complained that there was not enough time to answer ten questions got little sympathy from the instructor who pointed out that the directions called for answering only seven of the ten. Whenever you have a choice of questions, do not try to prove your superiority by writing on all of them. Since your instructor will probably read and grade you only on the required number, you should spend your time on a fuller treatment of that number.

When you receive a set of questions, you may feel a great urgency to start writing at once. Don't. First, you should take the time to read all the questions and directions carefully. Every set of questions represents an instructor's estimate of what most of the students in the class should be able to do in the time allowed. If you spend too much time on the first question, you will be rushed on the last ones.

Moreover, by reading through all the questions before you start to write you can discover the ones you are best prepared to answer. An exceptionally good and complete discussion of some of the questions may compensate, in your instructor's judgment, for a relatively brief treatment of others about which you know less. (Here is an advantage of the essay examination over the objective type, in which you can never be better than correct.) Also, some questions may overlap, and with careful preliminary reading you will save time by deciding in advance just what to include in each answer. Altogether, the few moments necessary to go over the entire examination will save you many minutes in the actual writing.

Pay particular attention to directions on the manner in which certain questions are to be answered. For example, among the questions that call for true essays there are often factual ones that are more nearly objective in nature. If you are asked to "list six reasons" or "enumerate eight causes," do not write a long discussion of reasons and causes. You cannot expect your instructor to take the time to dig the vital points out of your discussion. If you are asked to state something in a single sentence, use no more and no less; but when you are told "discuss at length" or "explain fully," you should write at least a paragraph.

In answering such discussion questions, you will find a use for the types of writing discussed in this book. You may be asked to describe a battle (Unit 2), or to narrate the chief events in the life of a literary or historical figure (Unit 3). You may be asked to characterize someone important in history, literature, or government (Unit 4), to tell how to make a piece of laboratory equipment or how an industrial process is carried on (Unit 8), to compare two characters in a book of fiction or the circumstances leading up to two events (Unit 9), or to classify people, poetry, or natural phenomena (Unit 10).

Examination questions not only call for the use of the various aids to exposition and the common expository patterns treated in Parts One and Two of this book but also present you with many of the reasoning and writing problems discussed in Parts Three and Four as well. You will be required on occasion to name and explain the parts of a flower or a piece of machinery, or to analyze a social problem (Unit 11). You will frequently be asked to discuss causes and effects—the reasons for the Depression, the results of Prohibition (Unit 12); to report the results of an experiment or to draw conclusions from evidence (Unit 13); and to apply general laws of science or principles of economics to specific cases (Unit 14). Most frequently of all, perhaps, you will be called on to define terms from the new vocabulary that practically every course forces you to learn (Unit 15).

You may be asked to defend an opinion or theory (Unit 16) or to make a critical analysis of your outside reading (Unit 17). Examinations being necessarily brief, you will often be asked to outline the main points of an argument or lecture (Unit 6) or to summarize a book, a theory, or an event (Unit 7). You may even be asked to correlate various reading materials as in a brief form of the research paper itself (Unit 18). In fact, the fields in which you are studying are so varied and the possibilities for kinds of essay-type examination questions so numerous that there is scarcely a method of thinking or writing that you will not be called upon to use on examinations at one time or another.

The length of your answers should be determined by three factors: the number of questions, the time allowed, and your knowledge of your own speed of thinking and writing. Instructors who give a single question as a three-hour final will naturally demand a wealth of detail that they will by no means expect if they give twenty questions to be answered in an hour. The more comprehensive your answer is supposed to be, the more pains you should take in planning it. (The habit of jotting down a rough outline of the main points you mean to discuss, on the back of your paper or in a margin, is essential.)

There is no special premium to be placed on length alone. Your instructor, who must read dozens of examination papers every time you write one, is likely to be more favorably impressed by a concise answer that drives straight to the point than by a long and flowery piece of rhetoric. A brief generalization supported by a few well-chosen examples, in the examination as well as in other writing, is worth pages of vague abstractions.

It goes without saying, of course, that just as you should take a little time at the beginning of the period to acquaint yourself with all the questions, so you should reserve a few moments at the end to reread your work, to catch possible inaccuracies of expression as well as content. Even though your writing time is thus further shortened, the time is again well spent. Whether or not instructors consciously lower grades for inaccuracies of composition, they cannot avoid being at least subconsciously impressed by careful as well as by careless writing.

In other ways, too, you should consider the instructors who will be reading your papers. Since your success in essay examinations depends on subjective evaluations of your work rather than on an objective score, your neatness, or lack of it, may affect your grade. No one will object to careful deletions or to additions between the lines on the examination paper; but the more easily your instructors can read your papers, the better. Write legibly in ink, with reasonable margins and with spaces setting off neatly numbered answers. This is not to imply that on the college level there is a "grade school" premium on neatness, but your instructors will be better able to appreciate the contents of papers that they can read easily.

Another mechanical but important aspect of examination writing is the numbering of your answers. Your replies should not only appear in the order of the questions but should be carefully labeled to match them. Questions labeled with Roman numerals may be subdivided into parts labeled with capital letters, and ones with Arabic numerals may have parts marked "a," "b," and so on. Be sure to label your corresponding answers with both designations, clearly and in order, and place them at or in the margin where they can be seen immediately, not buried within a paragraph. If there is a question that you cannot answer, include its number and leave a space so that you can return to it later if something suitable occurs to you. This method will also prevent your instructor from suspecting that you left out the number deliberately.

## Preparing for the Examination

You have probably been told many times that cramming is a vicious habit—and every word you were told is true. Students who have the good sense and willpower to make reviewing a simple everyday matter instead of cramming all night before an examination will have their reward not only in superior grades, which, after all, are only of immediate, temporary concern, but in their far better knowledge of the subject. Those who do their final reviewing the day before, get a night's sleep, and come to the examination without further study will gain more from their resulting clear-headed perspective of the whole subject than those who frantically cram their minds with details up to the last minute.

This may sound like an ideal—but it can be done.

## ASSIGNMENTS

This is a unit for which you can best supply your own examples.

1. If you have access to files of old examination questions, look through them to discover the type of writing that is required in the answers. If among them are ques-

tions covering the work of courses you are now taking, try writing answers to any with which you are already familiar.

2. Save your own examination questions and compare them with your answers after your paper has been returned. If your grade was lower than you expected, try to discover whether you were penalized for lack of preparation or poor presentation. (If in doubt, ask the instructor to go over the paper with you.) Practice rewriting some of your answers, after referring to the suggestions given in the preceding units for the types of writing they require.

One of the most important results of your college training in composition should be that through leisurely and painstaking writing, like that in the themes you prepare outside of class, you gradually learn to write papers of comparable quality while working rapidly and under pressure, as you are obliged to do in writing examinations and themes in class.

# UNIT 20

# The Business Letter

Any firm doing business with the public by mail can testify to the confusion and delay caused by the carelessness or ignorance of its customers. You can avoid most difficulties by becoming familiar with the accepted forms and practices of business correspondence.

Should you decide to make business a career, you will find books and courses devoted entirely to the subject of Business English, which covers all kinds of commercial problems. Here we shall disregard communications between businesses and from firm to customer, and take up only those kinds of business letters that you as an individual are most likely to write, along with the basic letter forms and business practices you will need in writing.

Such forms and practices have become highly conventionalized. Liberties may, of course, be taken to obtain special effects; for instance, a sales letter may begin with an attention-getting "Good Morning!" instead of the customary "Dear Sir" or "Dear Madam." But the following procedures have become standard business practice, and you can use them with confidence, knowing that they are correct.

## Business English

"Business English" is not a new or different kind of expression. It requires as much clearness and correctness as does all your other writing. But, because it has the very practical purpose of getting something done rather than of merely informing or entertaining, business writing tends to be simpler and more direct. Your business letter should say what it has to say as clearly and as briefly as is consistent with presenting all the necessary facts effectively.

The modern trend is a sharp turn away from the great formality of the past, a formality that once reduced the business letter to little more than a series of elaborate set expressions. As a publisher devoted to better business letters puts it:

> Most correspondents simply mimic the style of the person who preceded them. And their predecessors mimicked the style of the fellow before them.

If we're not careful, the standard terminology of business letters can be pretty silly. Used thoughtlessly, it can be downright insulting. Here are some common expressions—with the possible reactions of a modern reader:

I have before me your letter . . . . . . . . . . Okay, answer it!
In due course of time   . . . . . . . .After the usual boondoggling.
I wish to state . . . . . . . . . . . . . . Why wish? Just say it!
We are this day in receipt of . . . . . . . . . By George, they got it!
Kindly advise the undersigned   . . . . Who's writing the letter, anyhow?
Please accept our order . . . . . . . . . . . . . . . Any time!
Thank you for your patronage.   . .   Patrons went out of style a century ago.

And so did these expressions. (The Economics Press, Inc., Fairfield, NJ)

Such time-wasting patterns are being dropped in favor of a direct and simple reply, worded to suit the particular circumstances that called it forth. Beginnings such as "Replying to your letter of March 6" and endings that glide into the complimentary close ("Hoping to hear from you soon, we remain") now sound old-fashioned because they recall the day of stereotyped formality.

The modern demand for simplicity sometimes goes to an extreme known as the telegraphic style, however, in which the writer lops off words as though they were costing a dollar each.

> Received your letter. Adjustment suggested is satisfactory. Will return goods at once and await immediate refund.

Make your business English the language of natural speech, but remember that the complete sentence is usually desirable for clarity even in speaking.

## Business Letter Form: Five Essential Parts

The conventional form for a business letter has five essential parts, besides the message itself. Preceding the message are the heading, the inside address, and the salutation, and following the message are the complimentary close and the signature, which end it. As you study the requirements for each part, refer to the model letters on pages 335–36 for illustrations of their use.

**1.** The **heading** includes your address and the date on which you are writing. It usually occupies three lines as far up in the upper right corner as is required for a good arrangement of your letter length, and far enough to the left to ensure that the longest line will end at whatever margin you intend to maintain on the right. Business firms, generally, use prepared letterheads with their names and addresses. If you have stationery on which your address already appears, probably at top center, you need write only the date, either in the customary upper right corner position or centered on the page but always below the address.

(Include the correct zip code numbers in all addresses—heading, inside address, envelope—always following the state, with no punctuation.)

**2.** The **inside address** contains the name and address of the person or firm to whom you are writing, just as it will appear on the envelope. Although its use is essentially a matter of office procedure for convenience in filing, it has become conventional for all business letters. Begin it at the left margin at least two spaces below the date. (More space is allowable here, if you are arranging a short letter on a large page.)

If your letter is addressed to a firm but you wish it to come to the attention of a particular person or officer, you may include an "attention note" (see page 336) beginning at the margin between the inside address and the salutation, with a space above and below.

**3.** The **salutation** appears at the left margin, two spaces below the inside address, and consists of the words with which you greet the person to whom you are writing. They have been conventionalized into a few set phrases, among which these are most frequently used.

When you do not know whether you are addressing men or women, or when you know that you are addressing both, use a salutation that includes both sexes:

*To more than one recipient:*
Dear Sirs and Mesdames:
Ladies and Gentlemen:
Dear Committee Members:
Dear Classmates:

*To one recipient:*
Dear Sir or Madam:
Dear Committee Member:
Dear Classmate:

If you know the sex but nothing else, use "Gentlemen" or "Sirs" or "Mesdames" followed by a colon.

When you are writing to a recipient whose name and sex you know, you will find these set phrases convenient:

*To a male recipient:*
Dear Sir:
My dear Mr. Blank:
Dear Mr. Blank:

*To a female recipient:*
Dear Madam:
My dear Miss (*or* Ms. *or* Mrs., as appropriate) Blank:
Dear Miss (*or* Ms. *or* Mrs., as appropriate) Blank:

**Plurals:** For "Mr." use "Messrs."; for "Mrs." and "Madam" use "Mmes."; for "Miss" use "Misses"; "Ms." may be either singular or plural.

**Note:** "My dear Mr. Blank," "My dear Miss Blank," and so on, are generally regarded as slightly more formal than "Dear Mr. Blank," "Dear Miss Blank," and so on. (This is the reverse of British usage.) "Dear Sir" and "Dear Madam" remain the most formal salutations of all. *Never* write "Dear Gentlemen" or "Dear Ladies."

For a less formal salutation that avoids the problem of a title for the recipient, you may simply use his or her full name: "Dear John Blank" or "Dear Jane Blank."

**a.** Choose a salutation that matches the inside address in number and gender, disregarding any intervening attention note.

**b.** Choose one expressing the degree of formality suited to the occasion.

   c. Capitalize the first word and all nouns.

   d. Punctuate with a colon always—nothing more.

   **4.** The **complimentary close,** the words by which you take your leave, should begin far enough from the right margin for your name and title, if any, to end before the right margin. Place them at least two spaces below the last line of your letter. (This space, like that between the heading and the inside address, can be increased for arrangement's sake.) Like the salutation, the complimentary close has become conventionalized into a few acceptable phrases, of which the following are most popular:

   a. Very truly yours, Yours very truly, Yours truly,

   b. Sincerely yours, Yours sincerely, Yours very sincerely, Sincerely,

   c. Cordially yours, Yours cordially, Cordially,

The first group is very impersonal, the second friendlier, the third the warmest. Words like "faithfully" and "respectfully" have gone out of general business use in America.

   a. Choose a close that will match the degree of formality expressed in your salutation.

   b. Capitalize the first word only.

   c. Punctuate with a comma.

   **5.** Directly under the complimentary close, **sign your name** as you are in the habit of writing it. Be sure that it can be easily read; do not pride yourself on one of those highly distinctive signatures that look more like a careless drawing than a row of letters (experts say they are more easily forged than are decipherable ones). If you type your letter, type your name also, to make certain of its legibility, but leave room (four lines will do it) between the complimentary close and the typed name for your handwritten signature, to certify the letter as your own. If you are writing in any official capacity, your title should appear below your name:

> Jane Blank
> President
> Pre-Med Society

   As for social titles, a man never signs himself "Mr.," since that title is taken for granted. But a woman may wish to indicate her marital status with "Miss," "Ms." or "Mrs." for the convenience of the person replying. Those titles are not part of her legal signature, however, just as "Mr." is not part of a man's, and should therefore be enclosed in parentheses:

> *An unmarried or independent woman:*
> (Miss) Jane Blank
> (Ms.) Jane Blank
>
> *A married woman:*
> Jane Blank
> (Mrs. John R. Blank)

Two pairs of initials that usually appear at the left margin of a business letter opposite or slightly below the signature are those of the person sending the letter and of the secretary who typed it, for purposes of record. As an individual writing your own business letters, you do not need to add initials in this spot.

**Note: Abbreviations.** You must use the abbreviations "Mr." and "Mrs.," since these forms are never written out. "Ms." is used increasingly for women, to replace "Miss" or "Mrs.," especially if the addressee's marital status is unknown. Other abbreviations in common use include "Dr." and (after names) "Jr.," "D.D.S.," "M.D.," and so on. You may abbreviate first names to initials (especially if the owners do so themselves), terms describing businesses if the business itself does (Sears, Roebuck and Co., Mumford & Jones), and directions (1014 E. Morton Street, 444 Vermont Street N.W.—designating a section of a city). Names of countries are not abbreviated except "U.S.A." and "U.S.S.R.," but those of states usually are when they are part of a written address. A complete set of two-letter abbreviations of the states has been authorized by the U.S. Postal Department for use with zip code numbers.

Other abbreviations (of months, street names, etc.) are generally frowned on in business letters; the slight saving of time is not enough to offset the appearance of haste or lack of effort.

## General Format

**1. Type your letter,** if you can; if not, write neatly and legibly in blue or black ink—never use pencil or ink of any other color. Make a carbon copy for your own records; it may prevent many problems later.

**2. For stationery,** use a good grade of white paper of standard "typewriter size" ($8\frac{1}{2} \times 11$ inches). It should always be unruled (use a ruled guide under a handwritten letter to keep lines reasonably straight). For very brief letters you may use the half-sheet size of paper ($8\frac{1}{2} \times 5\frac{1}{2}$). On this size you may write either the long way, producing a short letter of standard width (this is generally preferred, for convenience in handling and filing), or the short way, producing a miniature letter of standard proportions (this is chosen by some for its appearance).

**3. Arrange your whole letter** carefully on the page. Whatever size paper you use, the letter should look like a well-framed picture.

**a.** Make the spacing of the parts and the width of the margins appropriate to the length of the letter as a whole.

**b.** All four margins should be approximately equal, with the bottom somewhat wider than the others.

**c.** Use single-spacing, with double-spacing between paragraphs for typed letters of three or more lines. With a very brief letter, use double-spacing and a half-sheet of paper to avoid the lonely look of a single line or two of message.

**d.** Hyphenate very long words at the ends of the lines to keep the right-hand margin roughly in line. (Check the dictionary to determine where to divide words.)

**e.** Be concise; try to keep to one page. If your letter must be longer, keep the margins at least $1\frac{1}{2}$ inches wide and make sure that you have at least three lines of the message on the last page. Number each page after the first.

**f.** *Never* write on the back of a sheet.

**4. Arrange the parts** of the letter in **semiblock** or **full-block** style.

**a.** In semi-block (see the example on page 335), all the lines of the inside address begin at the left margin, as does the salutation; all the lines of the heading begin at one inside margin, and the complimentary close and signature begin at another. In typed letters, the paragraphs may begin at the left margin because double-spacing between them will be enough to show paragraph divisions. In handwritten letters, indented paragraphs are advisable.

**b.** In full-block (see page 336), all the lines of the heading, salutation, complimentary close, and signature begin at the left margin.

**c.** The only punctuation *ending* these parts is a colon after the salutation (a comma is conventional in a social letter) and a comma after the complimentary close.

**d.** The only punctuation *within* these parts is a comma in the traditional style of date, separating the day and year, and in the address, separating the name of the town or city from that of the state.

**5.** Use a **white envelope** of the same quality and finish as your paper. The standard small size ($3\frac{3}{4} \times 6\frac{1}{2}$) will take a half-sheet letter or a full-sheet one of one page. For a longer letter or one with bulky enclosures, use the official size ($4\frac{1}{4} \times 9\frac{1}{2}$).

**a.** Make the outside address identical with the inside, beginning it at the approximate center of the envelope so that it will occupy roughly the lower right quarter of the envelope face.

**b.** Put your name and complete address in the extreme upper left corner.

**c.** Place any special directions such as an attention note, "Personal," or "Please Forward" in the lower left corner.

**d.** Attach the stamp—right side up—well inside the upper right corner of the envelope. It will look better and be protected from accidental tearing.

**6. Fold the letter** so that the recipient can withdraw it easily.

**a.** Fold a half-sheet letter in three parts. The two wings should be slightly narrower than the center section, with the right folded in first and the left over it.

**b.** Fold a one-sheet letter into six parts. Bring the bottom up to within half an inch of the top, and crease; then fold it as you would a half-sheet letter.

**c.** Fold a longer letter into three parts, bringing the bottom up about two-thirds of the way to the top and the top down to about half an inch from the resulting crease.

425 Merton Road
Danville, OH 43014
December 2, 1981

Dr. William Macauley
25 Manistee Boulevard
Cleveland, OH 44107

Dear Dr. Macauley:

I regret that I cannot keep my appointment with you
on Tuesday, December 15, at 4 p.m.  A change in my
examination schedule will keep me in Danville on
that date.

May I see you at 4 p.m. on Monday, December 21?
Please write confirming this time, or suggesting a
later one at your convenience.

Sincerely yours,

*Robert G. Weston*

Robert G. Weston

This letter is in semi-block style.  Note the spacing
between the parts:

2 — 4 spaces

2 spaces

2 — 4 spaces

```
        Route 3, Box 61
        Naylorton, TN 37836
        January 19, 1982

        The Acme Photo Company
        1018 East Moore Street
        Detroit, MI 48200

        Attention: Mr. H. A. Green, Framing Department

        Gentlemen:

        The price you quote in your letter of January 11 for
        enlarging and framing the photograph of my two sons,
        about which I wrote you in December, is entirely
        satisfactory.

        I am therefore enclosing the negative and the folder
        with mat samples on which I have marked my preference.
        I look forward to receiving the completed picture in
        about ten days, as you have indicated.

        Very truly yours,

        Linda Williams

        Linda Williams
        (Mrs. Arthur Williams)
```

This letter is in full-block style. Notice that the spacing between the parts is the same as that in semi-block. Notice, also, the use of an "attention" note and of the writer's married name to indicate how she wishes to be addressed.

## ASSIGNMENTS ON GENERAL FORMAT

1. Identify the conventional letter parts before and after the messages in the two model letters.

2. Name the arrangement used in each.
3. In what respects is the form of the two letters identical? in what different?
4. Which form is the more commonly used? What are the advantages and disadvantages of each? Which do you prefer?
5. Do the choices of salutation and complimentary close correctly indicate in each letter the degree of formality that seems to be intended?
6. Address an envelope (an appropriately sized rectangle will serve for practice) for the letter in semi-block style, including your return address.
7. Practice folding an $8\frac{1}{2}$-$\times$-11-inch sheet and inserting it properly into a commercial-size envelope; into an official-size envelope. Repeat with a half sheet and a commercial-size envelope. Practice until you can perform the required operations smoothly and correctly, without pausing to think.
8. How many errors can you discover in this letter form?

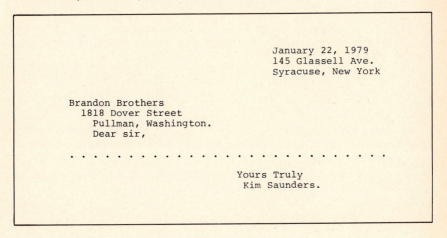

## Types of Business Letters: The Inquiry

You will frequently need to write a business firm to ask for information, prices, catalogs, types of accommodations. Beyond following the matters of form already discussed, your letter should observe three requirements.

**1. Be explicit.** Be sure that your request is clear and that you have included enough details to make a definite reply possible. A letter to a hotel asking if it has rooms available is pointless if you omit the date for which you need them; one inquiring about rates is equally time-wasting unless you mention the number of people concerned and the type of accommodations preferred. Make your inquiry so clear that the reply may be an answer instead of a request for more specific information, with consequent additional correspondence and delay.

**2. Be brief.** Include all necessary details but nothing that is beside the point. A request for information about a company's product may appropriately include the use to which you plan to put it, but an inquiry about tickets for the theater need not include your reasons for wishing to see the play.

**3. Be courteous.** Even though your inquiry will probably lead to a business transaction that the firm will be glad to have, you should remember that, at the moment, you are asking a favor. "Send me your catalog" will doubtless get results, but a more gracious wording is to be preferred; although servility in business correspondence is a thing of the past, "please" and "thank you" are still welcome oil in the gears. Avoid, however, the hackneyed "Thanking you in advance." Should your inquiry ask for information or material that is only for your benefit (except for the good will the company may win by supplying it), the need for courtesy is of course sharply increased.

Notice how the two letters that follow meet these requirements.

> Will you please send me a copy of your current "Gardener's Guide" as advertised in the May issue of *Flower and Garden*.

**1.** A question like this which is not really a question but merely a politely worded command, is usually punctuated with a period instead of a question mark.

**2.** A mention of the source through which you learned of the literature requested is an added courtesy. It helps the company not only to know exactly what you wish but also to check on the efficacy of its advertising media.

> I own a four-quart pressure cooker, model 2TK64B, that my parents bought about thirty years ago. The gasket on the cover has begun to leak steam, reducing the pressure inside.
>
> Except for this difficulty, the cooker works well, and I would like to be able to use it, but my local hardware store has no gaskets of the right size.
>
> Do you still have gaskets for this model in stock? If you do, please let me know the types and prices. If you do not, can you suggest a substitute?

**1.** This gives all the details that the company will need to make a reply.

**2.** Because the letter is brief and all on one subject, it could have been treated as one paragraph. The short paragraphs make the writer's problem and hope for a solution clearer.

**3.** The first and last sentences of the third paragraphs are real questions, unlike the polite command in the preceding letter, and therefore have question marks.

## Types of Business Letters: The Order

Many firms selling goods by mail supply order blanks in their advertisements and catalogs. Lacking a blank, you must write a letter. Be sure to include three kinds of information:

**1. The exact description of the article desired:** quantity, catalog number (if known), size, color, and price.

**2. The method of shipment:** air, parcel post, express, freight; the "fastest" or the "cheapest" way; special delivery; prepaid or collect.

**3. The arrangement for payment:** C.O.D.; cash, stamps, check, draft, or money order, which you have enclosed; a charge to your account or credit card, with the name and number.

> Please send me one (1) pair of your new line of stereo headphones with the SM-700 "Studio Master," using $2\frac{3}{4}$-inch Mylar-diaphragm drivers.
>
> I enclose my check for $65.00, the advertised price, and understand that you will send it postage paid.

**1.** This letter is both brief and explicit—qualities the order should share with the inquiry.

**2.** It further satisfies the particular requirements of the order letter by making clear the item desired, the method of shipment, and the arrangement for paying.

If you are ordering a number of items, you can help the person who fills your order by arranging them one per line, in columns such as an order blank would provide.

The words "immediately," "promptly," and "at once" in shipping directions are so commonplace as to be almost useless. However, if you must have the goods by a certain date, or if for any reasons you want shipment postponed until a specified time, an explanation of the circumstances accompanied by the exact date will usually secure for your order the special attention it requires.

> I wish to order 50 yards of your #614 red, white and blue bunting, at $2.00 a yard, provided it can be shipped so as to reach me by July 4 without fail. If you can supply it, please send it by parcel post, special delivery, and charge the goods and the shipping costs to my account.
>
> If you cannot, please wire me collect upon receipt of this order, so that I can make other arrangements.

## Types of Business Letters: The Complaint

Business transactions sometimes produce difficulties that require correction. Goods fail to arrive, they are damaged in transit, the wrong item is sent or the right one proves unsatisfactory—such situations call for the letter of complaint. In this type of correspondence not only is courtesy a pleasing grace but it pays; for, as the old saying goes, more flies are caught with honey than with vinegar. To the business firm the "customer is always right"—particularly if he or she is also reasonable.

**1. Be sure that your cause for complaint really exists.** Better to wait a day or two, for instance, than to send a complaint of nonarrival that crosses the shipment in the mail. You may find yourself too close for comfort to the situation of the old farmer in the anecdote who sent a thundering letter complaining of a delay, to which he had added: "P.S. The mailman just now brought the stuff."

**2. Be equally sure that your complaint is just.** Check your order to make sure that you wrote the size correctly, before you blame the store because your new boots do not fit.

**3. Write reasonably and courteously.** Be exact and clear in recounting the cause for your dissatisfaction, and suggest what you regard as a suitable adjustment.

Psychologists say that the wise person will handle every unpleasant situation in terms of the desired results rather than of the immediate emotion that he or she is tempted to express. This observation certainly applies to the writer of a letter of complaint. Consider the probable effect of each of these:

> Last week I spent good money to go clear in to Memphis to buy a sweater at your Sports Bar. I got one, but your salesclerk was careful not to tell me that it was soiled from lying around too long on your shelves waiting for a sucker like me, and I didn't find it out till I got home. I think any store that does that kind of business ought to be ashamed of itself, and I can promise you that you won't get any more trade from me or any of my friends.

**1.** The writer now probably feels much better—for the time being.

**2.** The store has been given not only no suggestion as to a suitable adjustment but no opening for making any.

**3.** If the writer is wise, he or she will follow Mark Twain's practice by tearing this caustic masterpiece into shreds and sending the following in its place.

> When I was in Memphis last weekend I bought a beige wool slipover sweater at your Sports Bar for $25.98. Not until I got home did I discover that there were two badly soiled streaks down the center of the back where it had lain folded on the shelf.
>
> Do you wish me to return it in exchange for another, or would you prefer to pay me for having it cleaned locally? (The cost would be $3.50.) I should prefer to have it cleaned, because I did not see another one in your stock of just this style and shade.

**1.** The lack of recrimination is not only courteous but just, since it appears that no one is particularly at fault. (Customers can scarcely blame the salesclerk for not noticing what they themselves overlooked.)

**2.** The psychology of taking for granted that an adjustment will be made is particularly sound and far superior to merely asking if the firm will make one.

**3.** The suggestion of specific adjustment possibilities, with a statement of the customer's preference, will be a boon to the adjustment office.

## Types of Business Letters: The Job Application

Unless you are one of those fortunate individuals who have jobs waiting for them the minute they graduate, you will probably start writing application letters very seriously in your senior year. You may write them much sooner for summer and part-time work, and you may have occasion to write them again, later in your career. Since such a letter is likely to mean your very bread and butter, it may be the most important business letter that you will ever write.

**1. Appeal.** The letter of application must have appeal. Courtesy and clearness are sufficient graces for the letter of inquiry, the order, and the complaint, but it is wise to think of the job application letter for what it is—a sales letter. Remember that individuals, like businesses, do not get very far in the face of modern competition without some knowledge of the psychology of salesmanship.

    **a. Do not be too modest.** The door-to-door salesman who used to go up to housewives saying, "You don't want to buy some magazines, do you?" may have gotten a few orders out of pity, but he didn't get fat on commissions. Never begin with such expressions as "I don't know whether I would succeed in this position or not," or "I have never had any experience in your type of work." When you apply for a job, it is not enough to put your best foot foremost; keep the other safely out of sight.

    **b. Do not be boastful.** A statement like "I have always been a super salesman ever since I was a child," or "I have always outranked every other student in my class" may be perfectly true, but it is likely to antagonize. Leave such information for others to supply in the letters of recommendation they write for you.

    **c. Do not sound superior to the work you are applying for.** No employer was ever won by such remarks as "I am willing to work for you until I can find a place that suits me better," "My previous experience has been with bigger firms than yours," or "I should not be looking for a job except for recent financial reverses in my family."

    **d. State honestly the achievements that may fit you for the job.** But do not include irrelevant items from your past. Remarks that may be entirely appropriate in one application may be mere boasting in another. "All through high school I spent my spare time caring for the neighbors' children" would be relevant information in an application for work in a nursery school, but hardly for a bookkeeper's position. "In college I was elected the most popular member of my class" might be useful information if you are asking for work in a sales organization, but inappropriate boasting if you are applying for work as a laboratory technician.

    **e. Think first of the viewpoint of your prospective employers.** They are more interested in what you can do for them than in what they can do for you, even in this age of social conscience. "Because of my long interest in popular music and because I have been taking piano lessons for the past three years, I believe I can make myself useful in your record store" is more likely to appeal to the store owners than "I want to work for you because I would like a discount on buying records," or "because my best friend works in the coffee shop across the street from your store."

    **f. Try to make your letter stand out favorably from others.** Your prospective employers may receive dozens or even hundreds of letters from qualified persons, and you must try to make them notice yours. But do not mistake mere freakishness for individuality. Your letter of application should be serious and dignified, without any of the extra devices often used in other types of sales letters.

2. **Content.** The material included in your letter of application will normally fall into five main sections: **introduction, personal data, qualifications, list of references, and conclusion.**

a. **Introduction.** How you begin your letter will depend on the kind of circumstances that call for it.

(1) If you are answering an advertisement, you will of course begin with a reference to that fact.

(2) If you have learned indirectly of an opening, you should mention the name of the agency or friend who informed you.

(3) If you have no knowledge of a particular opening but are sending out a number of letters to employers for whom you think you would like to work, you may begin with some mention of your reasons for applying to this one in particular.

b. **Personal Data.** Include a list of objective facts about yourself as an individual, such as your age, height, weight, sex, marital status, and any other items, such as nationality or religion, that may be pertinent to a particular job.

c. **Qualifications.** Most important is a statement of the qualifications that fit you for the job applied for: your education, experience, interest, aptitude.

d. **References.** List the names, official positions, and addresses of the people whom you have chosen as best qualified to recommend you, as to both character and ability, for the kind of position in which you are interested. (You will of course already have gotten their permission to name them as references, and later you will thank them for recommending you.)

e. **Conclusion.** Like every good sales letter, the application should end with some effort to induce action: a request for an interview; a reminder that you have enclosed a stamped, self-addressed envelope for convenience in replying; an indication of your hope for an early and favorable reply.

Which of these many items to stress and which to omit will depend, of course, on the nature of the work that you seek. Religious belief, for instance, may be important in getting a teaching position in a church-supported summer camp, but not a cashier's job in a supermarket. Experience and references from previous employers are always important, especially so when they are related to the kind of job you are seeking; since you are a student, your education (with specific reference to relevant courses) and recommendations from faculty members who know you well will probably be your chief assets.

3. **Resumé (Data Sheet).** If the material that you wish to include covers half a typed page or more, you should shift the objective, or factual, information

(personal data, qualifications, references) to a separate unit called the resumé or data sheet. Here the information can be neatly and clearly arranged under suitable headings and subheadings that will be easy for prospective employers to consult and file if they are interested, or to disregard if they are not.

One advantage of the resumé or data sheet is that you can reproduce it in quantity, thereby saving time in writing the actual letters of application. These must, of course, be personal, not mass-produced. Another advantage is that this method makes the letter itself shorter and more readable and frees you to concentrate on the more important task of making the letter your personal appeal. Here you will present your subjective material in what will amount to a short essay: an account of your interest in the job, your general aptitude and inclination for it, and the hopes you have for accomplishment in the field. Remembering that the letter of application is essentially a sales letter, you will recognize the importance of these remaining items and of the impression they will make on employers, who may read between the lines and be more impressed—favorably or unfavorably—by what they guess about you as an individual than by all the facts in the resumé.

The following letters are specific examples of the general kinds of letters you as a student are most likely to have occasion to write. In the first, the student answers a newspaper advertisement that gave only a box number to which to reply:

> (Wanted: college student to read to invalid afternoons or evenings. Box 41, Sheldon *Post.*)

Dear Sir or Madam:

I have just seen your request in today's *Post* for a college student to read to an invalid, and I am writing to ask that I be considered for the position.

I have already had some experience as a reader because my grandmother, who had lost her eyesight, lived in our home while I was in high school. Now I am a junior in the university, where I am majoring in speech, and my chief interest is in interpretive reading.

Professor John Secord of the Speech Department has kindly agreed to write a recommendation about my ability to read aloud, and Mrs. Elizabeth Davis, director of volunteer services at Northside Hospital where I worked as a candy-striper last summer, may be consulted about my personality and character.

My present schedule leaves me free every afternoon except Tuesday and Thursday, and I am available most evenings. I would very much like to have several hours a week of such congenial part-time work. May I have an interview? My phone number is 586-6774.

In the second letter, a student has been told of an opening by someone who will act as a reference:

Dear Professor Baker:

Dr. M. R. Hamilton, head of the Biology Department here at Blesser College, has told me that your university offers a few graduate assistantships to B.A. holders who wish to continue toward advanced degrees. I would like to apply for an assistantship in your department for the coming academic year.

I expect to complete my work for the B.A. with a major in biology at Blesser in June and hope to begin work on an M.A. at your university next fall. My goals are a Ph.D. and a position in a research laboratory.

On graduation I shall have 42 semester hours of credit in biology courses here at Blesser, 15 of them in courses open to graduate as well as undergraduate students. My grade average for all my undergraduate work to date has been B, and in my biology courses it has been A—. My major interest has been bacteria, on which I took a senior seminar and on a particular aspect of which I am now writing my honors thesis.

For the past year and a half I have worked as an undergraduate assistant for Dr. Hamilton, helping to supervise some of the laboratory work and grading papers in one of his freshman courses here. He has offered to write to you about me, at your request, as has Dr. Susan Smith, director of my honors thesis, and Dean Robert Snow of the Liberal Arts College. If there is any chance that I may be eligible for consideration for one of your assistantships, I shall be glad to send my complete transcript for your evaluation and to supply any other information you wish to have about me, my work, or my plans.

The third letter is written in the hope of an opening in a company for which the student particularly wants to work, as her letter indicates. She addresses it to the chief personnel officer, whose name she learned by telephoning the company's head office.

Dear Mr. Robinson:

My chief ambition has always been to become a flight attendant, and because I also have a special interest in South America, I would particularly like to work for Panagra. Since your main flights are to South American cities, and since I speak fairly good Spanish and some Portuguese, I think I can be particularly useful to your company.

At present I am a senior at Flanham College, where I am majoring in psychology with special emphasis on personnel work. I am also active in a number of campus organizations and so am gaining experience in working with people. My college minor is in Spanish and Portuguese. Also, I have always been much interested in all phases of aviation and am learning to fly at Hoadley Airport nearby. I now have twelve hours of flying time to my credit.

The accompanying resumé will give you more details on my preparation and experience and includes a list of persons to whom you may write for further information about me. I do not know whether you accept beginners for your special training course, but if you do I shall be happy to come to Chicago for an interview any time this spring (preferably on Saturday, when I have no classes). If you have no openings at present but anticipate some in the near future, I hope that you will keep my application on file.

```
                         Resumé
Personal
   Name: Mary Louise Donham
   College address: Sarah Black Residence Hall, Flanham College,
                    Danvers, Iowa 51091
   Home address: 286 N. Oak Street, Moulton, Illinois 62987

   Age: 22              Nationality: American
   Height: 5'5"         Marital status: single
   Weight: 120 lbs.     Health: excellent

Education
   Moulton High School graduate, February, 1978
   6 months in Wahl Business College, Moulton, 1978
   B.S., Flanham College (expected in June, 1982)
   Major in psychology
   Minor in languages
   General courses: English, history, mathematics, physics,
                    chemistry, psychology, sociology
   Special courses: Meteorology, navigation, engineering, drawing,
                    service and operation of aircraft

Activities
   Airways Club (founding member)
   Dramatic Society (parts in three major productions)
   Science Club (program chairman, 1 year)

Experience
   Secretary to director of personnel, Ames Aircraft Corporation,
      Benzie, Illinois (1 year)
   Student assistant to head of Sarah Black Residence Hall, Flanham
      College (2 years, part-time)

References
   Dr. Ernest Beers, Head of Psychology Department, Flanham College
   Ms. Edna Markham, Director of Personnel, Ames Aircraft
      Corporation, Benzie, Illinois 61572
   Mr. Ted Houston, Manager, Hoadley Airport, Danvers, Iowa 51092
```

## ASSIGNMENTS

The following requirements are stated generally, instead of being given in the form of specific problems, so that you can choose subjects that interest you, real-life situations for which you can write actual letters instead of merely going through the motions of a classroom exercise.

1. Write an inquiry about vacation tours, resort accommodations, services offered, goods for sale, to any actual business firm from whom you would really be interested

in getting information. (Look through the current issue of a popular magazine for suggestions.)

2. Write a letter ordering merchandise, repairs, tickets—anything that you would really like to have from a real firm with a real address.

3. Write a letter complaining about any unsatisfactory goods or services (repairs, transportation, and the like) that you have recently had the misfortune to encounter.

4. Write a letter replying to a classified ad in your local paper, in which you apply for a position that you are qualified to fill.

5. Write a letter applying for summer work at some place where you know there is an opening in some line of work for which you are qualified.

6. Write a letter of application, accompanied by a data sheet, applying for the position that you think you would like when you graduate. Direct it to an actual firm, institution, or person by whom you would like to be employed.

# Author and Title Index

Asterisk indicates an example with marginal notes.

# Subject Index